DRIFTING DRAGONS

Taku Kuwabara

2

DRIFTING DRAGONS

Table
of
Contents

This is a work of fiction.
Any resemblance to real people, groups,
and events is purely coincidental.

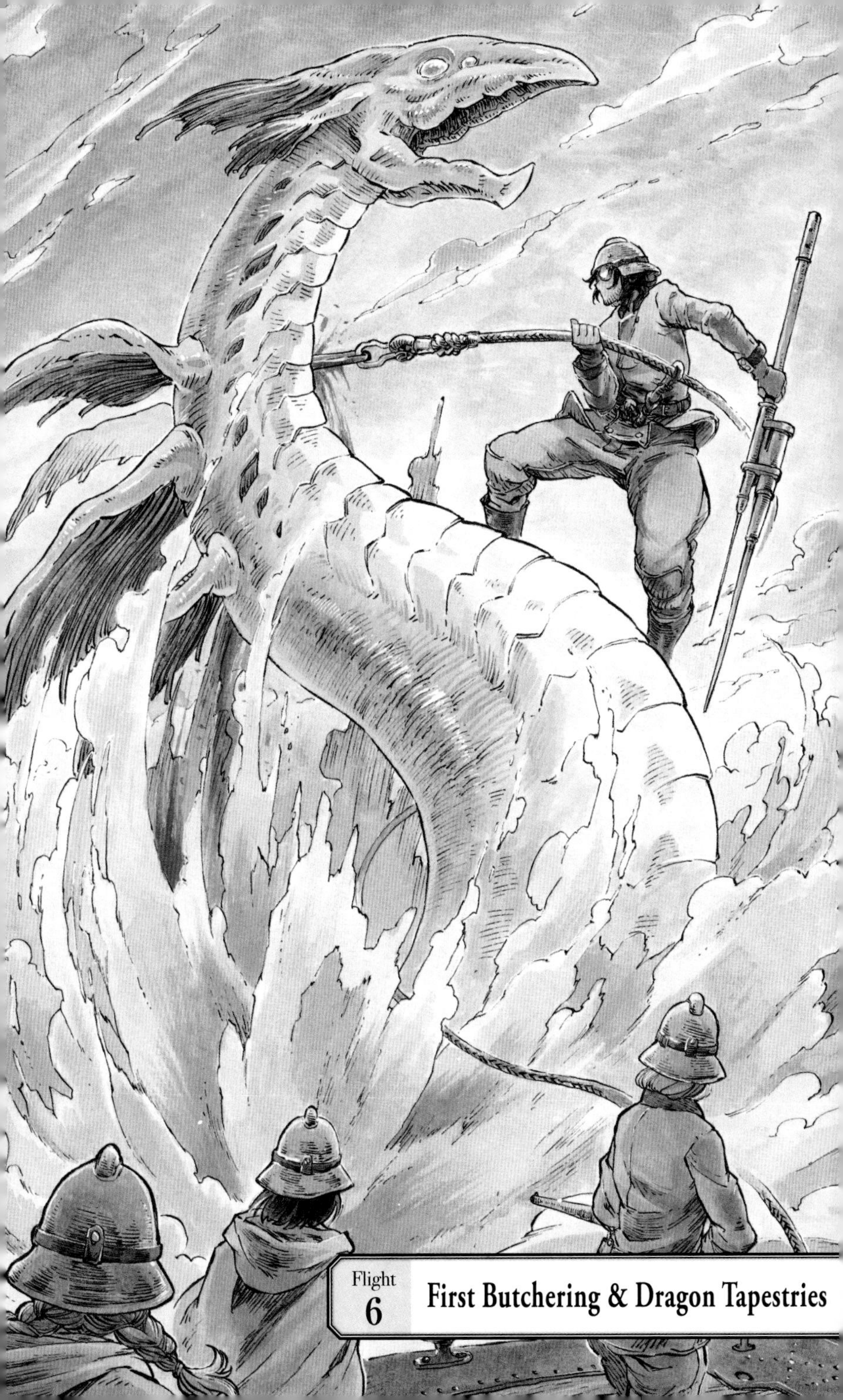

Flight 6 First Butchering & Dragon Tapestries

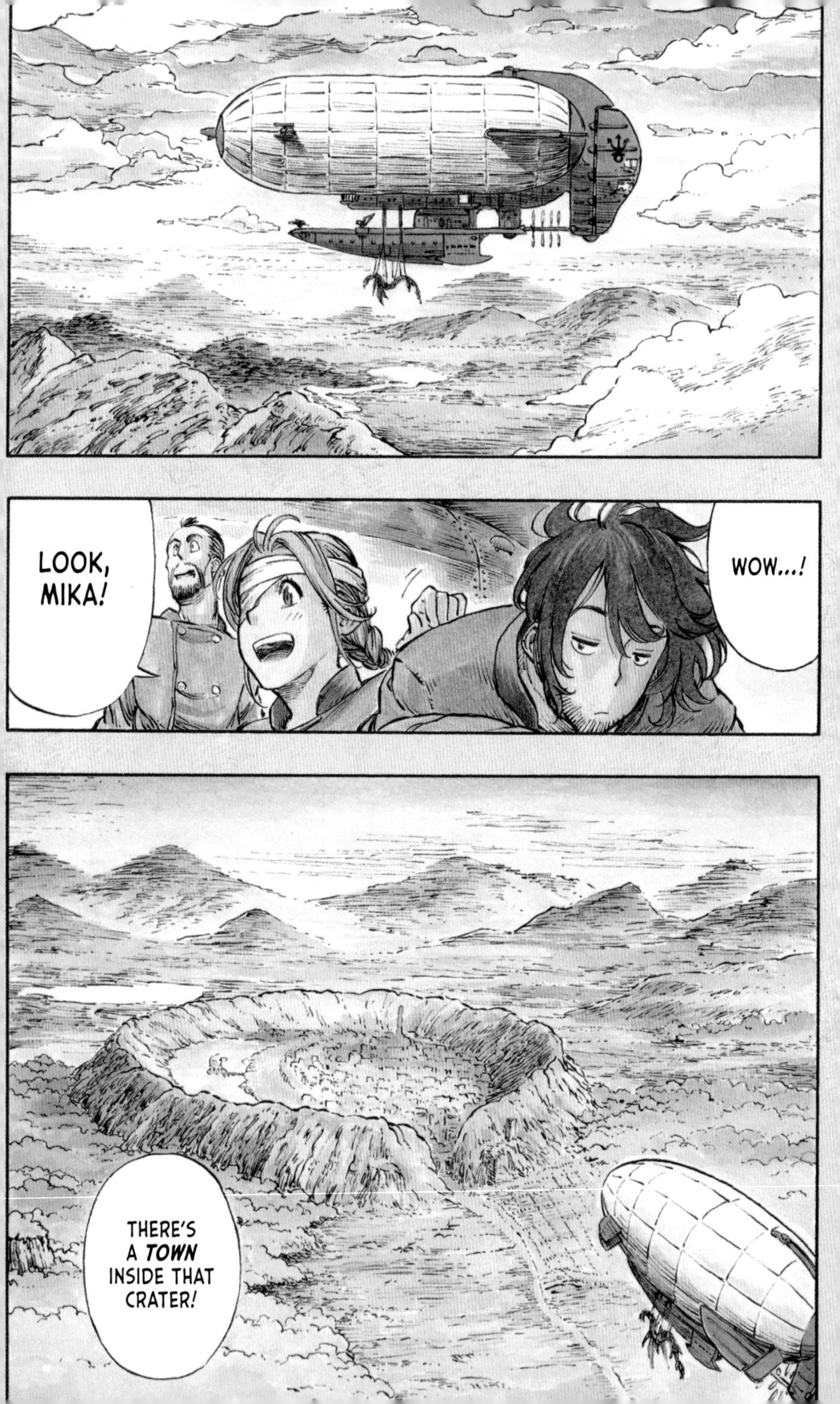
WOW...!
LOOK, MIKA!
THERE'S A *TOWN* INSIDE THAT CRATER!

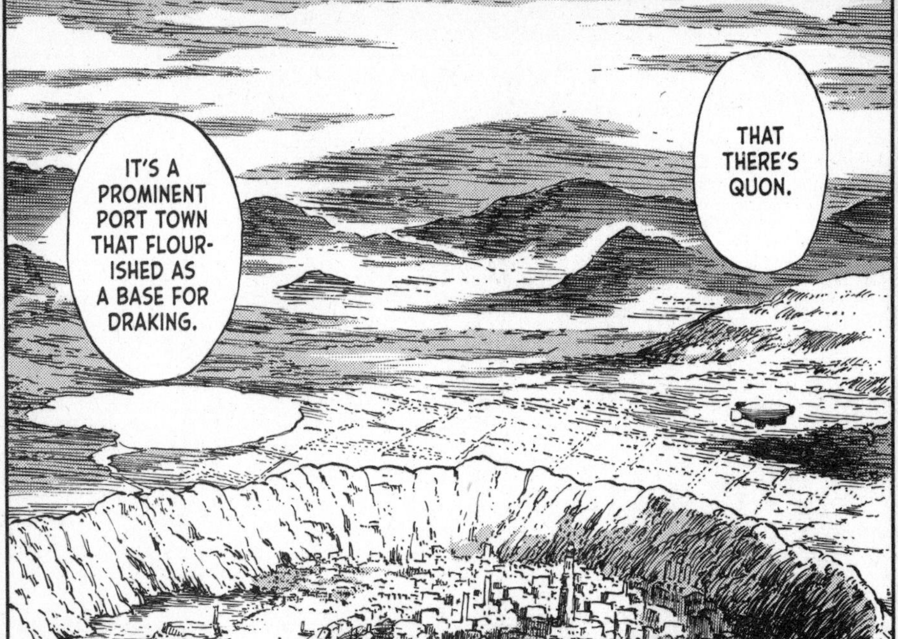
THAT THERE'S QUON.
IT'S A PROMINENT PORT TOWN THAT FLOUR-ISHED AS A BASE FOR DRAKING.

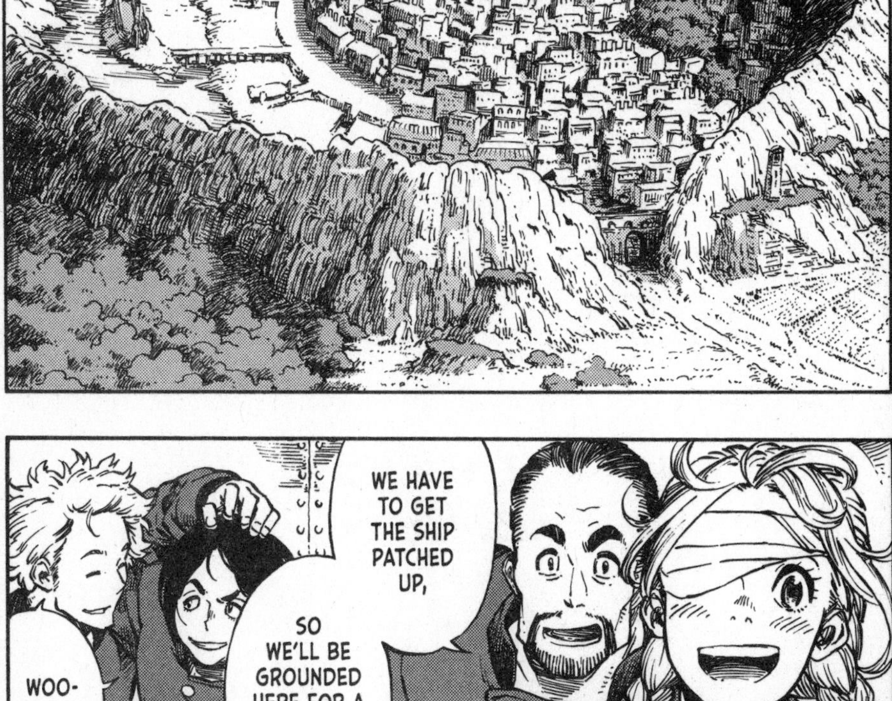
WE HAVE TO GET THE SHIP PATCHED UP,
SO WE'LL BE GROUNDED HERE FOR A WHILE.
WOO-HOO!

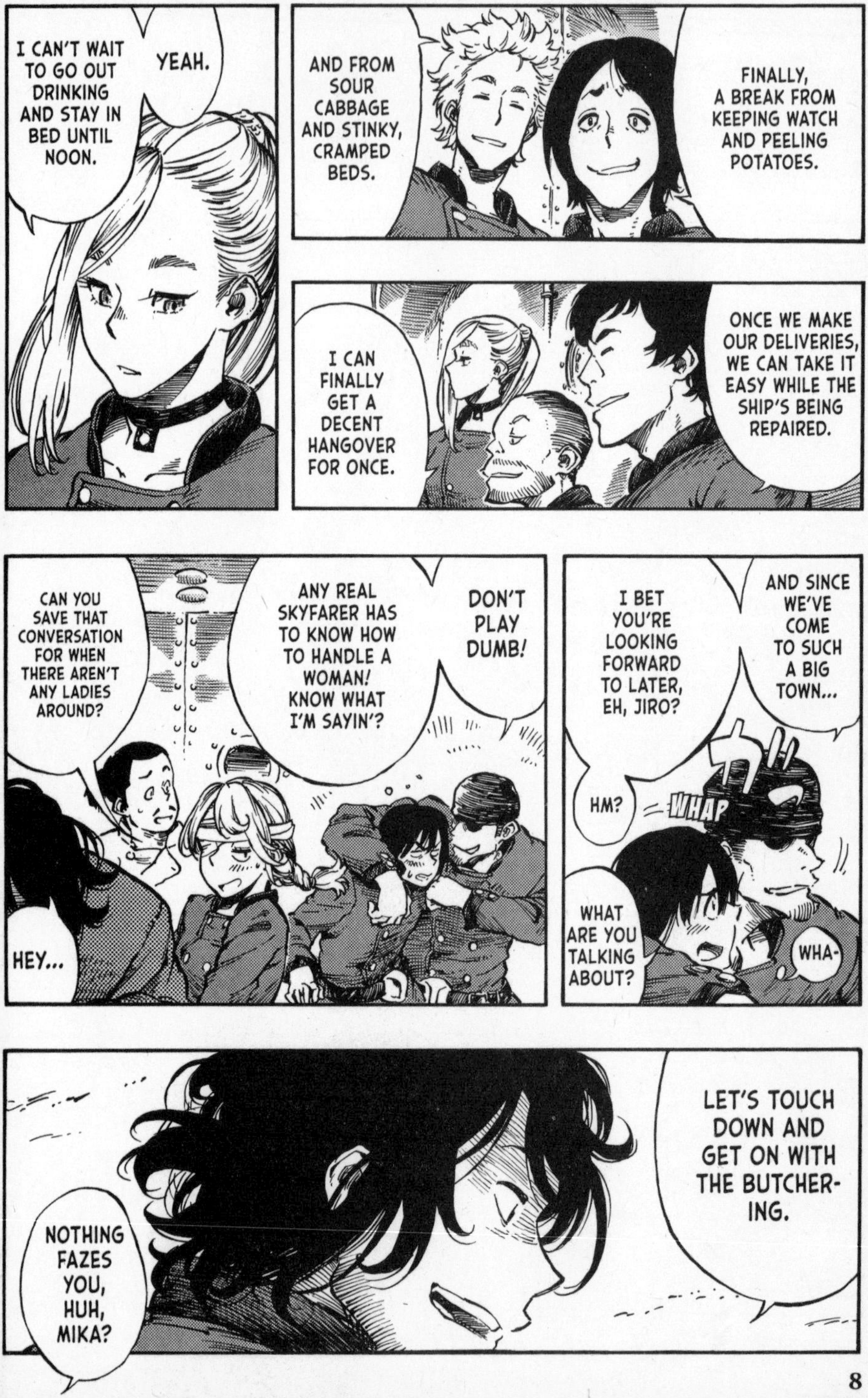
FINALLY, A BREAK FROM KEEPING WATCH AND PEELING POTATOES.
AND FROM SOUR CABBAGE AND STINKY, CRAMPED BEDS.
ONCE WE MAKE OUR DELIVERIES, WE CAN TAKE IT EASY WHILE THE SHIP'S BEING REPAIRED.
I CAN FINALLY GET A DECENT HANGOVER FOR ONCE.
YEAH.
I CAN'T WAIT TO GO OUT DRINKING AND STAY IN BED UNTIL NOON.
AND SINCE WE'VE COME TO SUCH A BIG TOWN...
I BET YOU'RE LOOKING FORWARD TO LATER, EH, JIRO?
HM?
WHAP
WHA-
WHAT ARE YOU TALKING ABOUT?
DON'T PLAY DUMB!
ANY REAL SKYFARER HAS TO KNOW HOW TO HANDLE A WOMAN! KNOW WHAT I'M SAYIN'?
CAN YOU SAVE THAT CONVERSATION FOR WHEN THERE AREN'T ANY LADIES AROUND?
HEY...
LET'S TOUCH DOWN AND GET ON WITH THE BUTCHER-ING.
NOTHING FAZES YOU, HUH, MIKA?

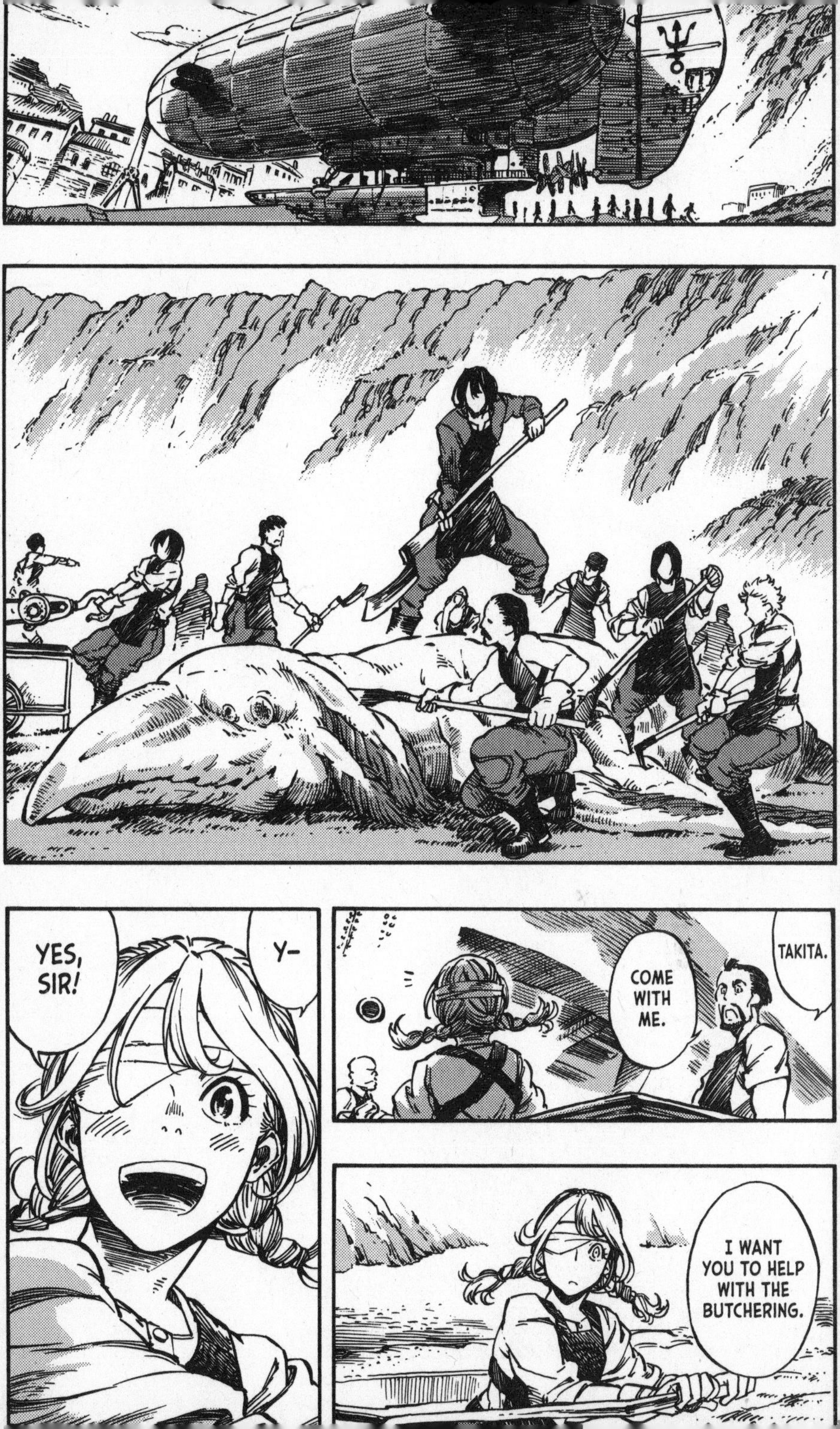
TAKITA.
COME WITH ME.
I WANT YOU TO HELP WITH THE BUTCHERING.
Y-
YES, SIR!

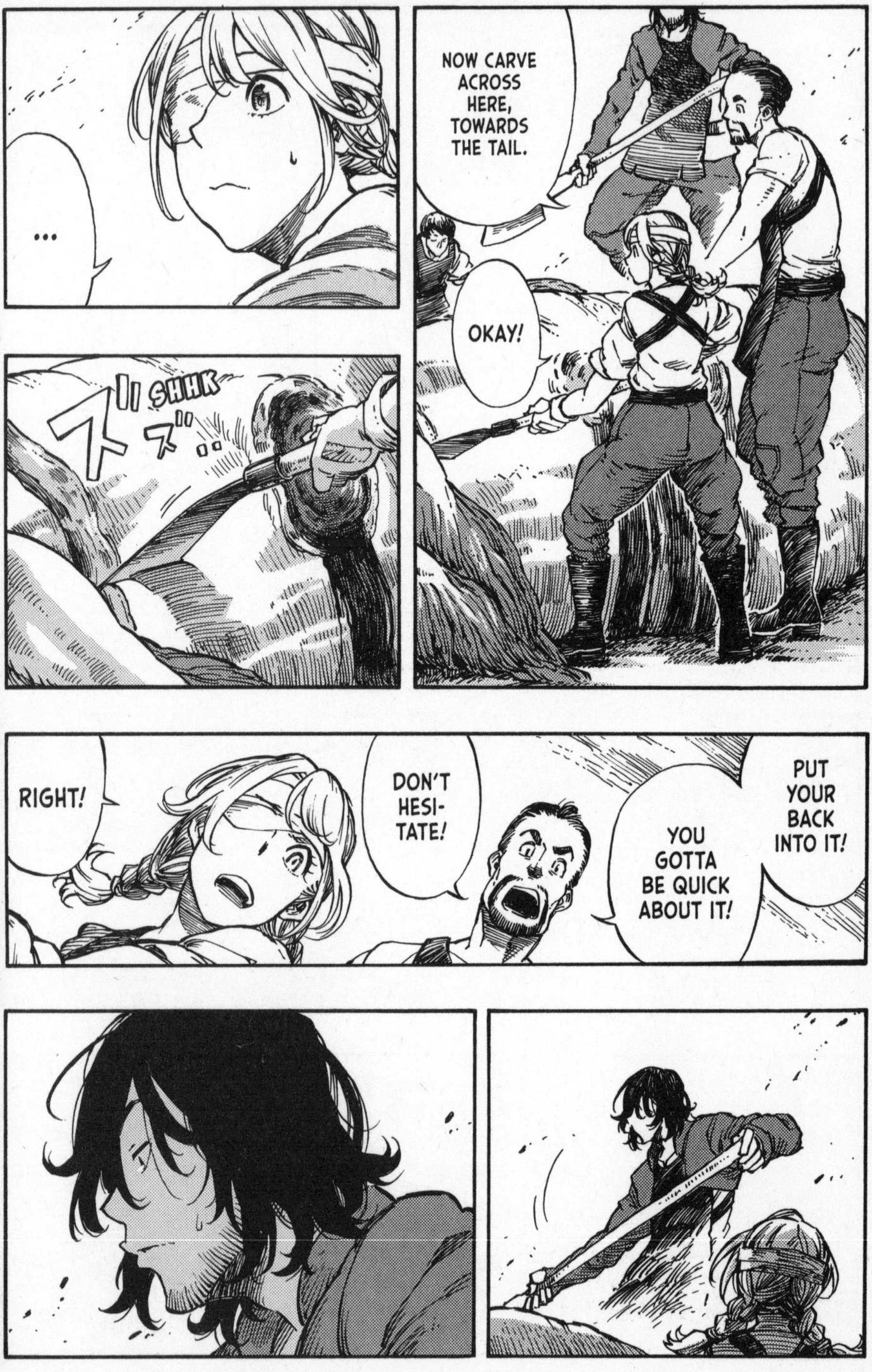
NOW CARVE ACROSS HERE, TOWARDS THE TAIL.
OKAY!
...
SHHK
PUT YOUR BACK INTO IT!
YOU GOTTA BE QUICK ABOUT IT!
DON'T HESI-TATE!
RIGHT!

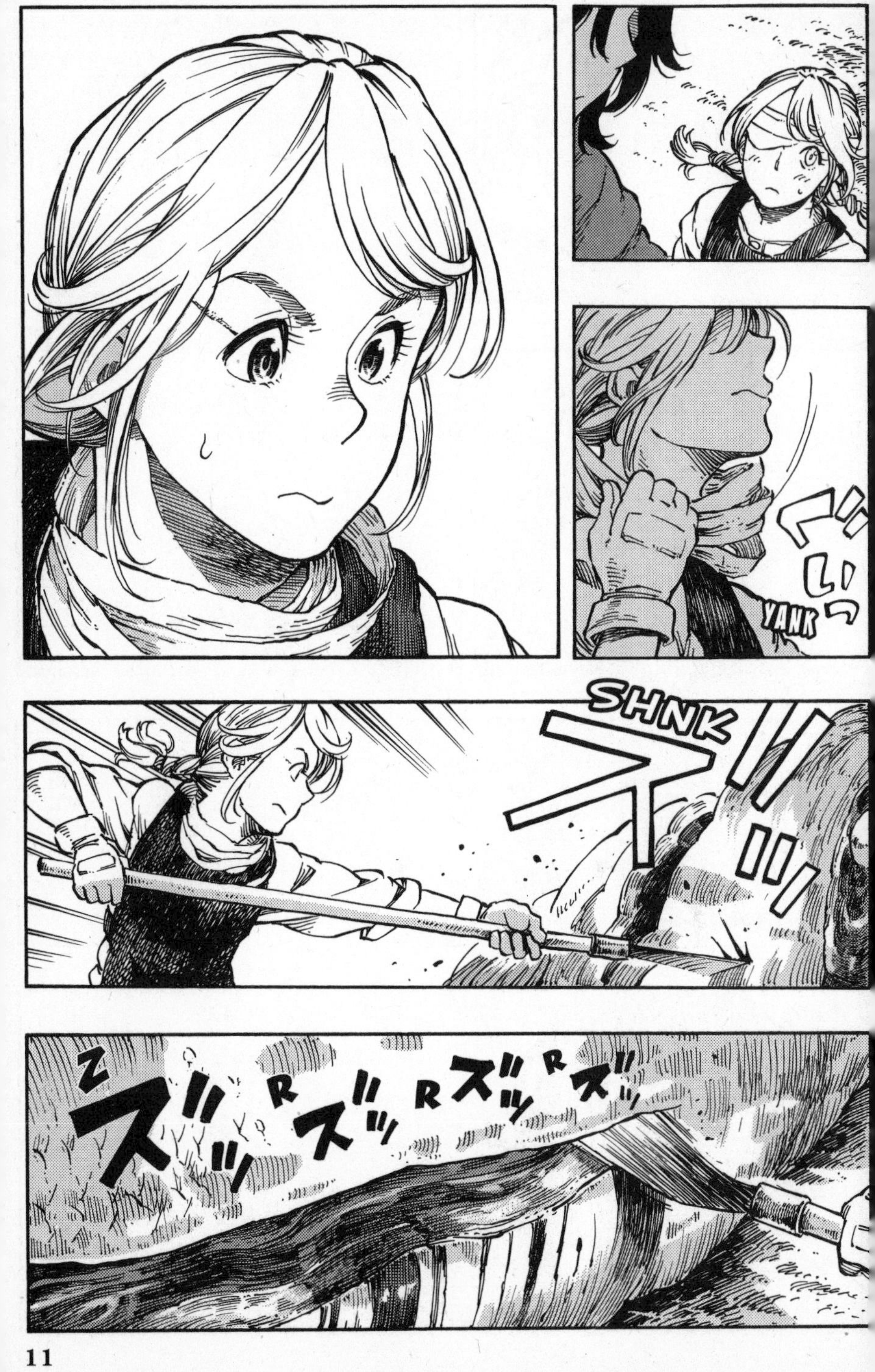
ぐいっ
YANK
SHNK
ズ
Z ズッ
R ズッ
R ズッ
R ズッ

SHIK

SHIK

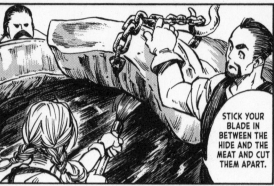

STICK YOUR BLADE IN BETWEEN THE HIDE AND THE MEAT AND CUT THEM APART.

PHEW...

YES, SIR!

NICE WORK, TAKITA! NOT TOO BAD FOR YOUR FIRST TIME.

LET'S DO THE RED MEAT NEXT.

12

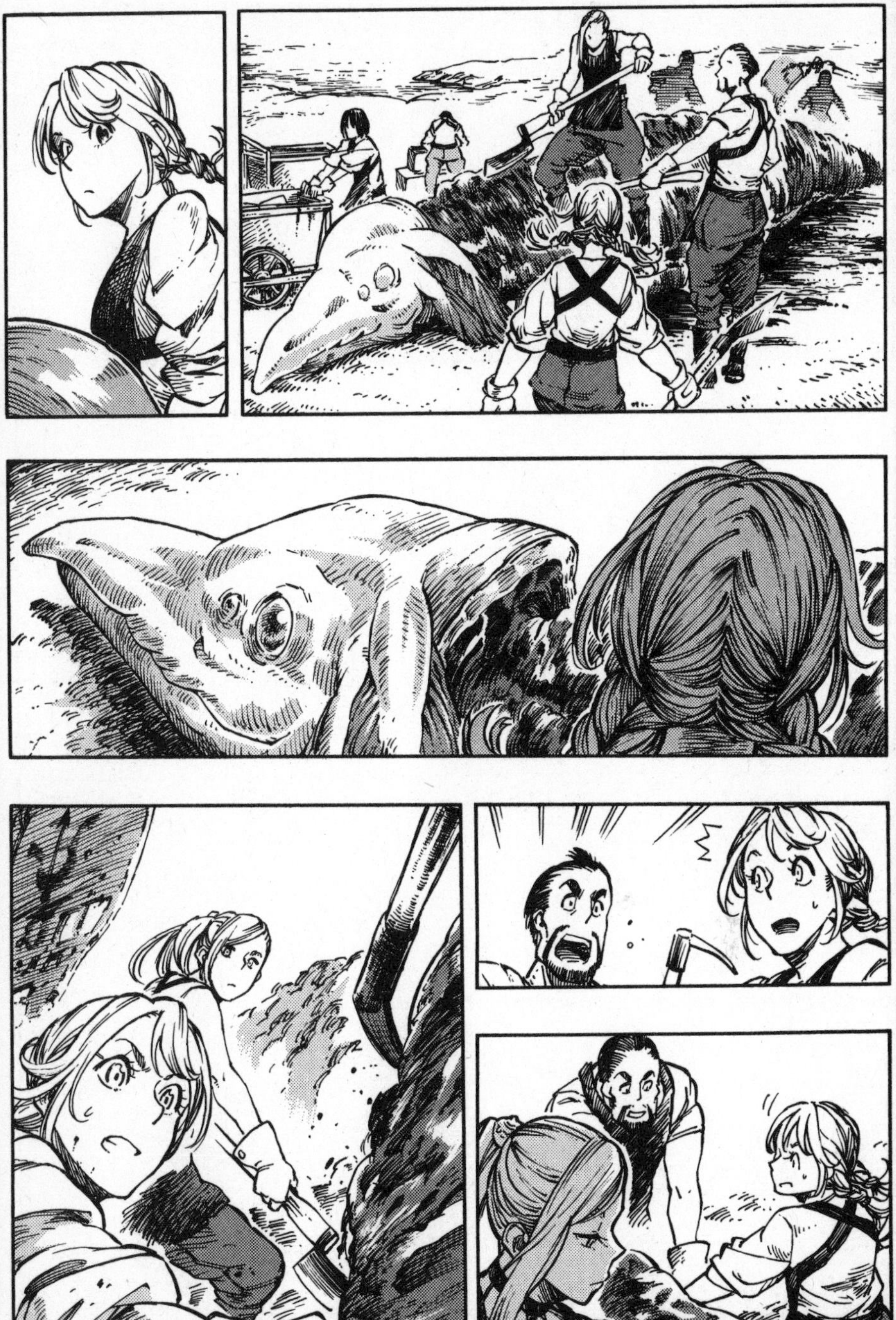

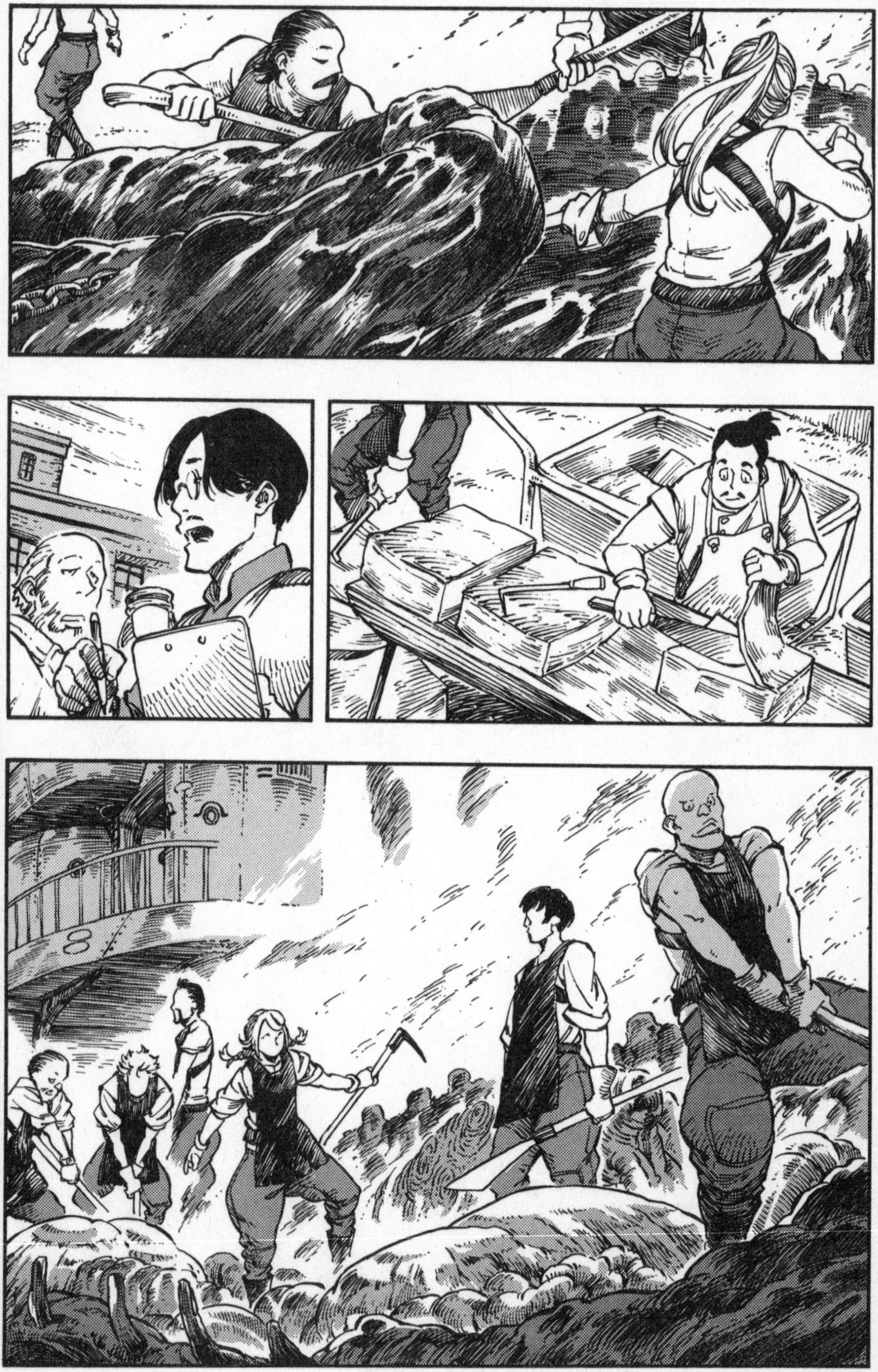

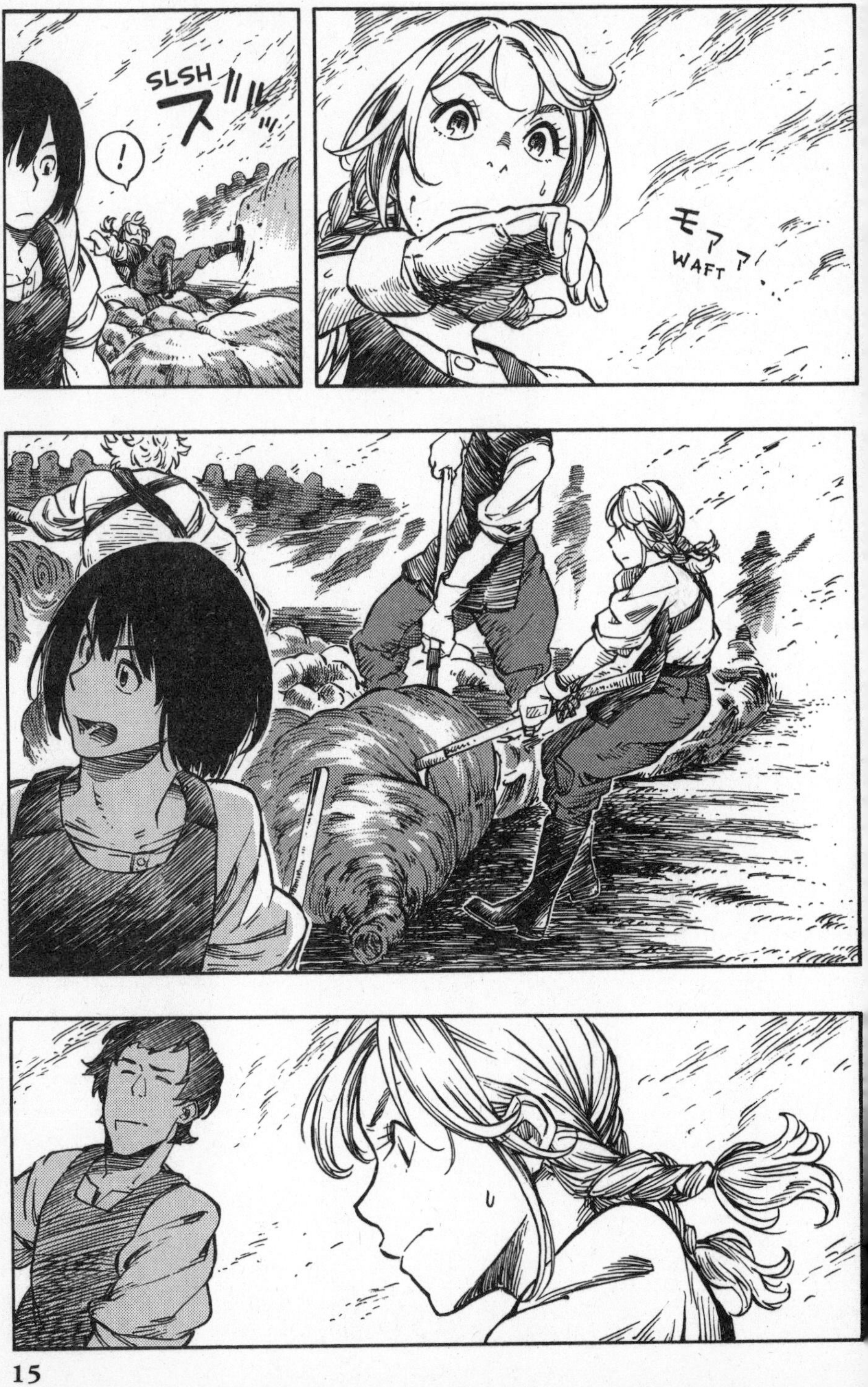
モアア
WAFT
SLSH
ズル
!

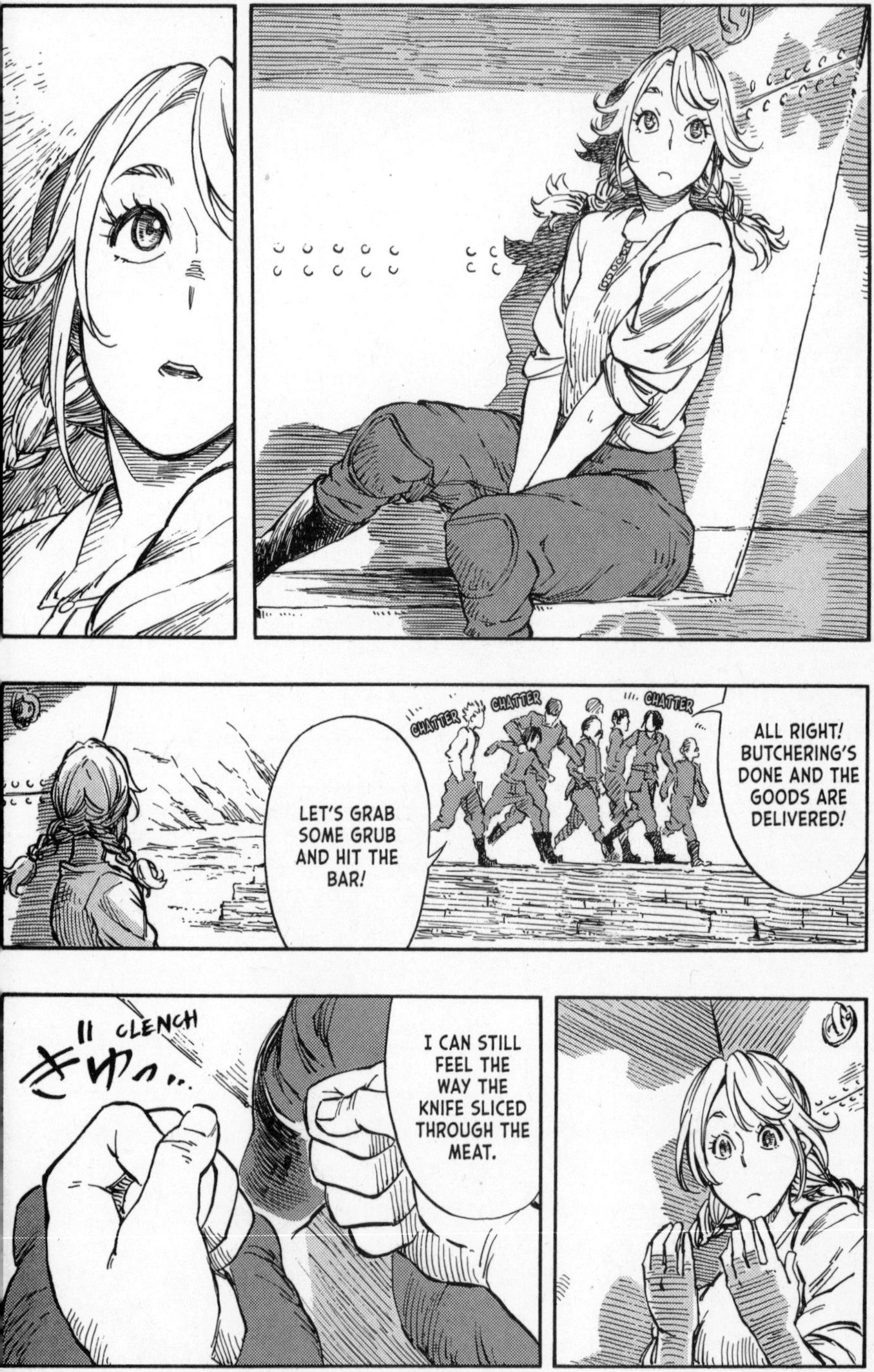
CHATTER
CHATTER
CHATTER
ALL RIGHT! BUTCHERING'S DONE AND THE GOODS ARE DELIVERED!
LET'S GRAB SOME GRUB AND HIT THE BAR!
I CAN STILL FEEL THE WAY THE KNIFE SLICED THROUGH THE MEAT.
ぎゅっ…
CLENCH

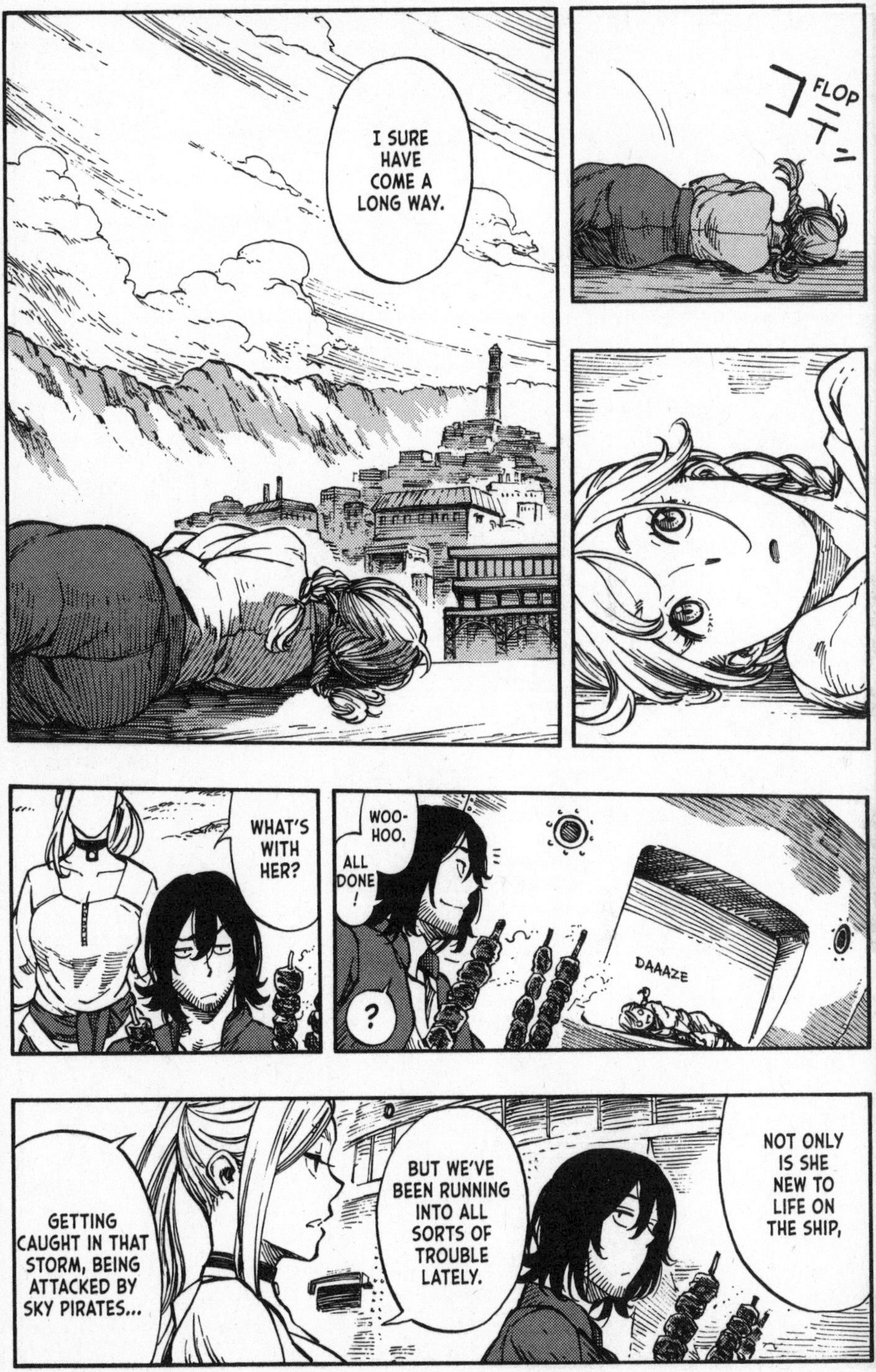
FLOP
コテン
WOO-HOO.
ALL DONE!
?
DAAAZE
WHAT'S WITH HER?
I SURE HAVE COME A LONG WAY.
NOT ONLY IS SHE NEW TO LIFE ON THE SHIP,
BUT WE'VE BEEN RUNNING INTO ALL SORTS OF TROUBLE LATELY.
GETTING CAUGHT IN THAT STORM, BEING ATTACKED BY SKY PIRATES...

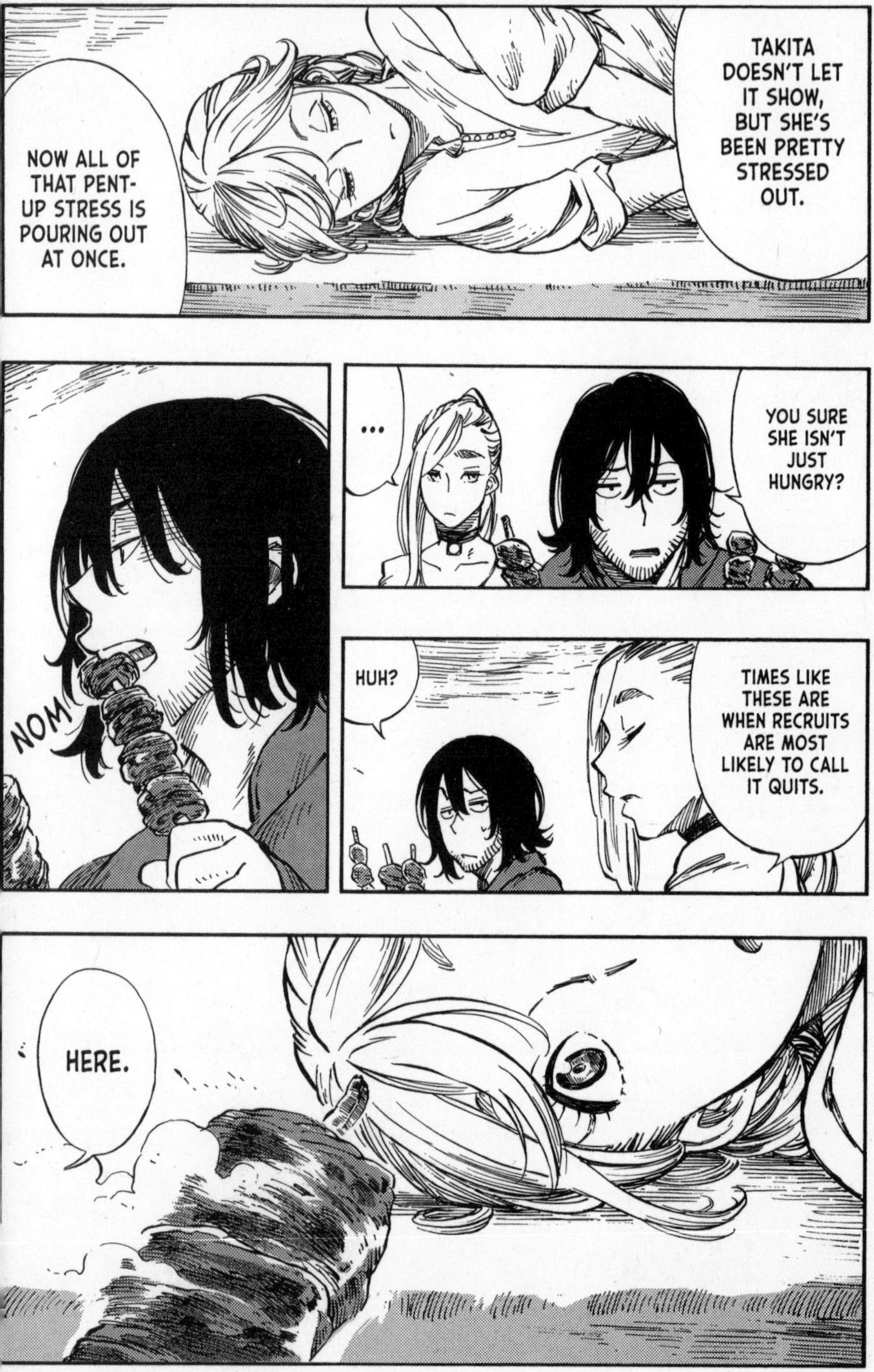
TAKITA DOESN'T LET IT SHOW, BUT SHE'S BEEN PRETTY STRESSED OUT.
NOW ALL OF THAT PENT-UP STRESS IS POURING OUT AT ONCE.
YOU SURE SHE ISN'T JUST HUNGRY?
...
TIMES LIKE THESE ARE WHEN RECRUITS ARE MOST LIKELY TO CALL IT QUITS.
HUH?
NOM
HERE.

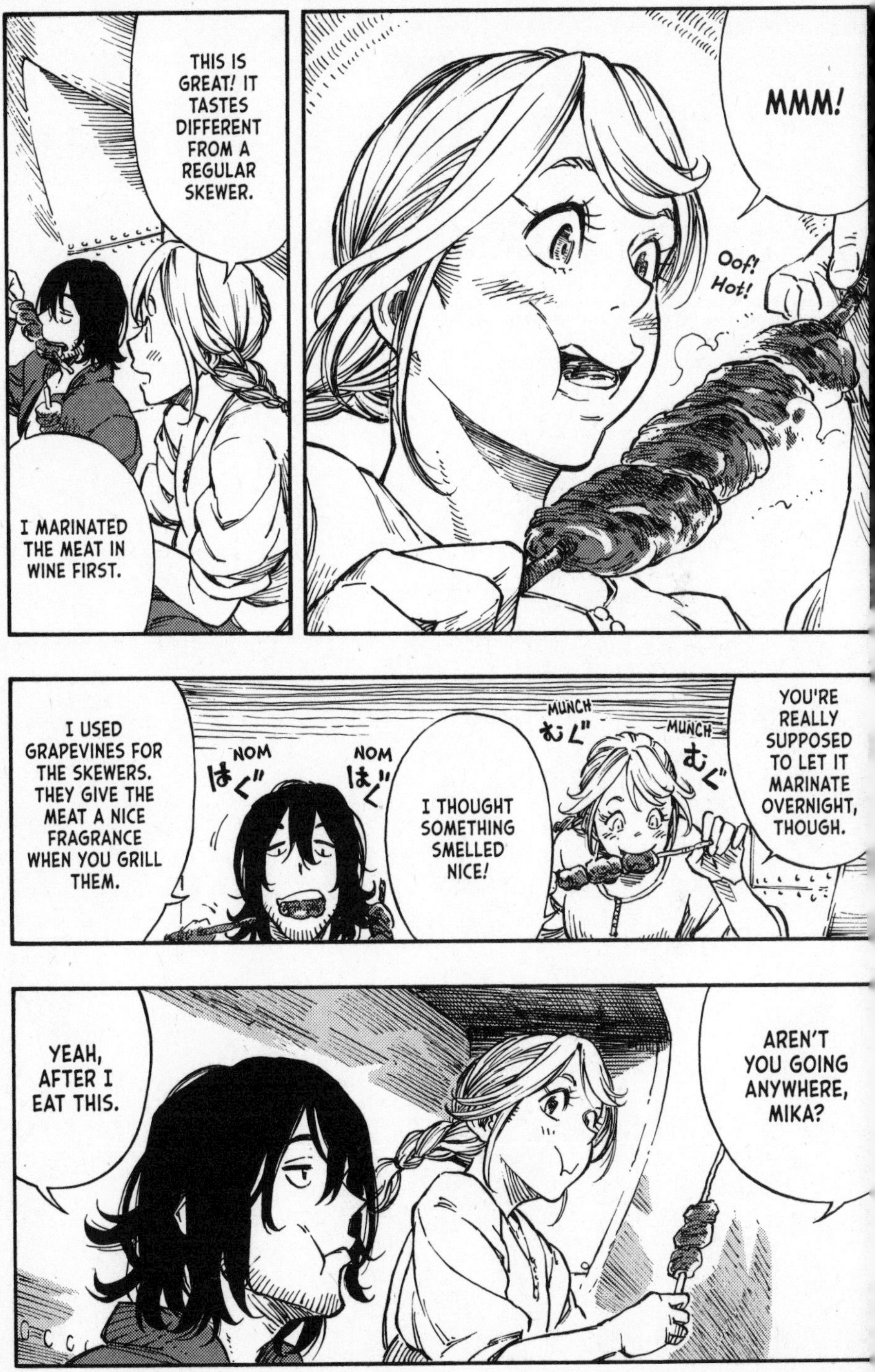
MMM!
Oof! Hot!
THIS IS GREAT! IT TASTES DIFFERENT FROM A REGULAR SKEWER.
I MARINATED THE MEAT IN WINE FIRST.
YOU'RE REALLY SUPPOSED TO LET IT MARINATE OVERNIGHT, THOUGH.
MUNCH むぐ
MUNCH むぐ
I THOUGHT SOMETHING SMELLED NICE!
NOM はぐ
NOM はぐ
I USED GRAPEVINES FOR THE SKEWERS. THEY GIVE THE MEAT A NICE FRAGRANCE WHEN YOU GRILL THEM.
AREN'T YOU GOING ANYWHERE, MIKA?
YEAH, AFTER I EAT THIS.

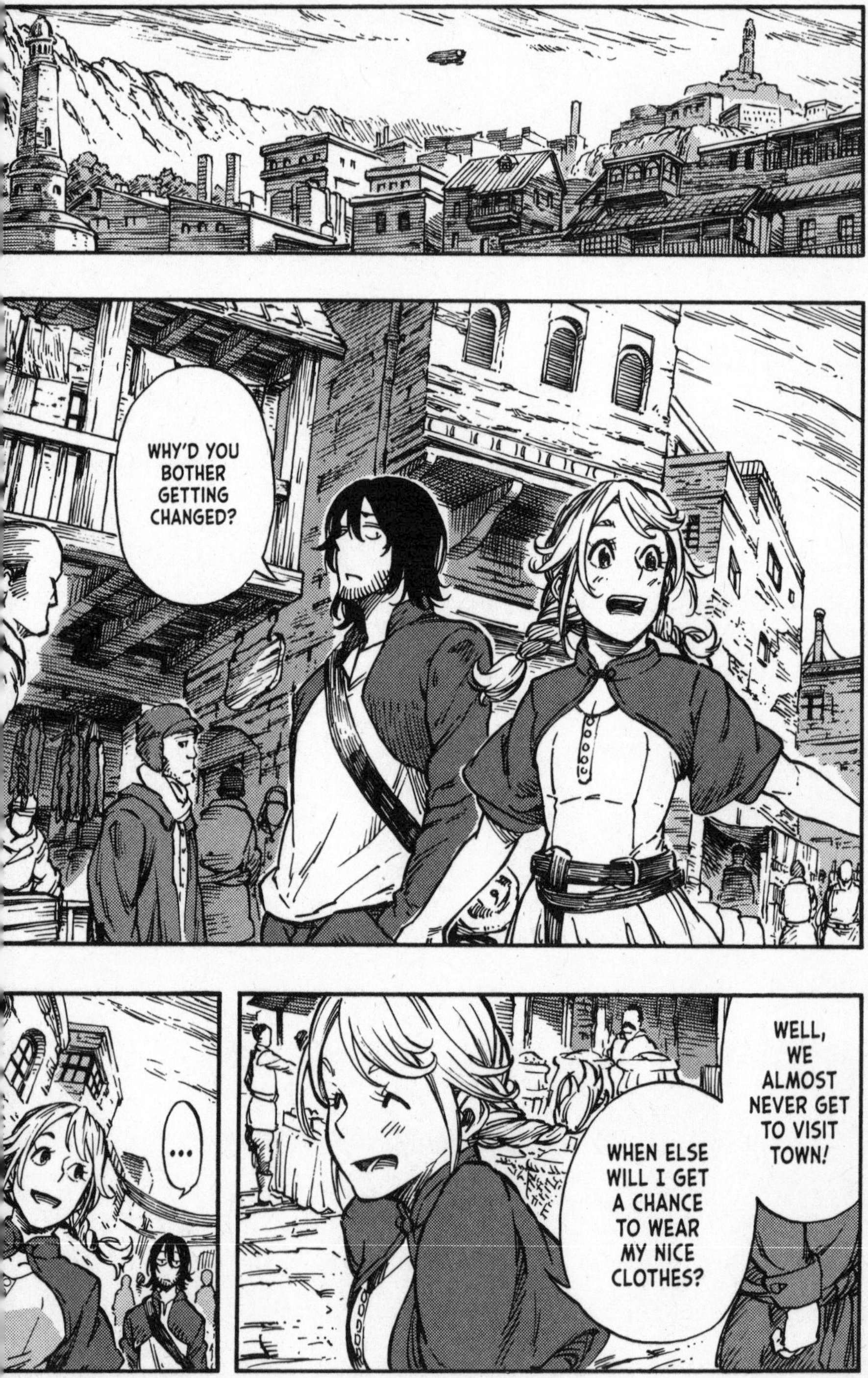
WHY'D YOU BOTHER GETTING CHANGED?
WELL, WE ALMOST NEVER GET TO VISIT TOWN!
WHEN ELSE WILL I GET A CHANCE TO WEAR MY NICE CLOTHES?
...

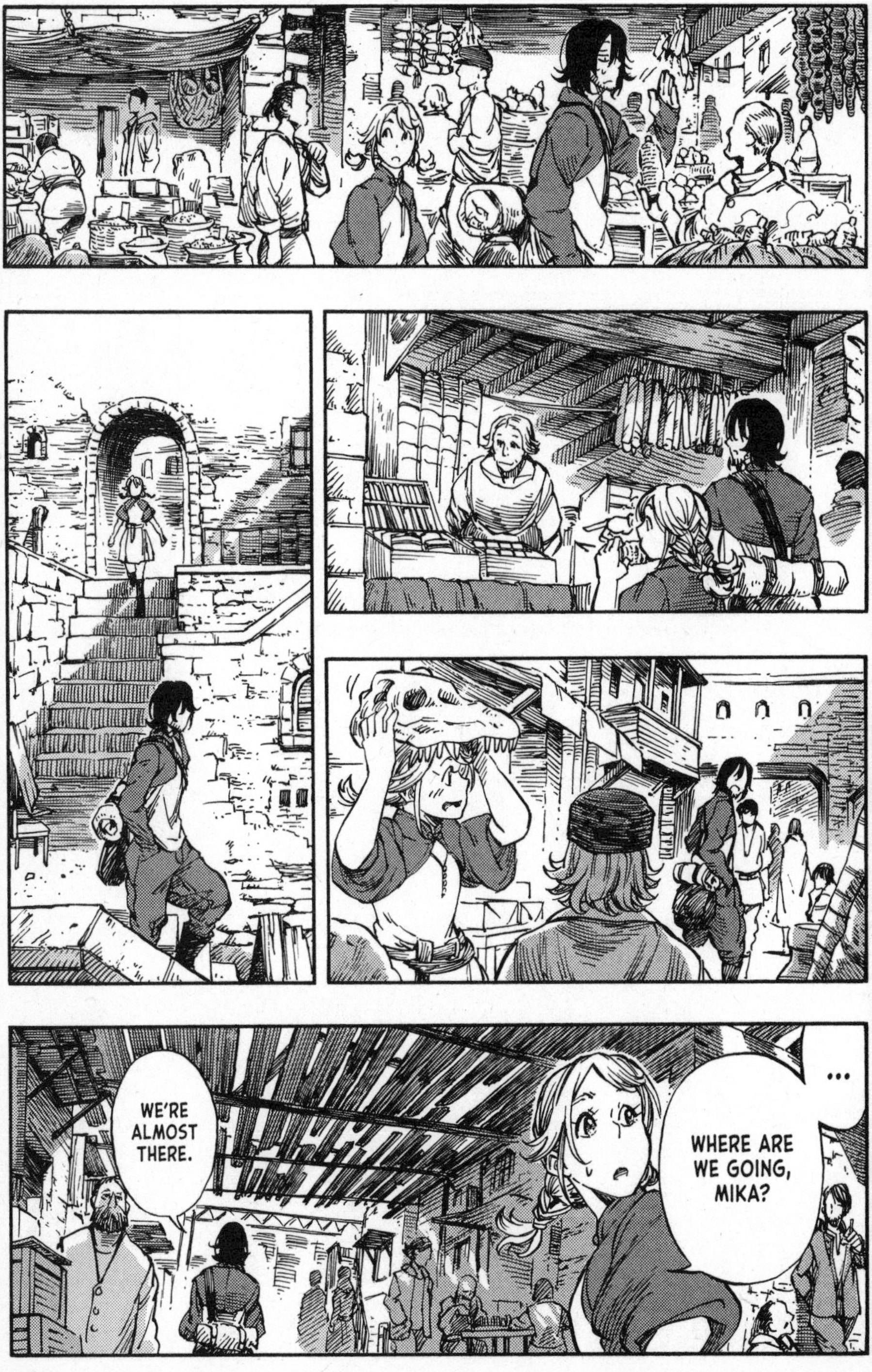
...
WHERE ARE WE GOING, MIKA?
WE'RE ALMOST THERE.

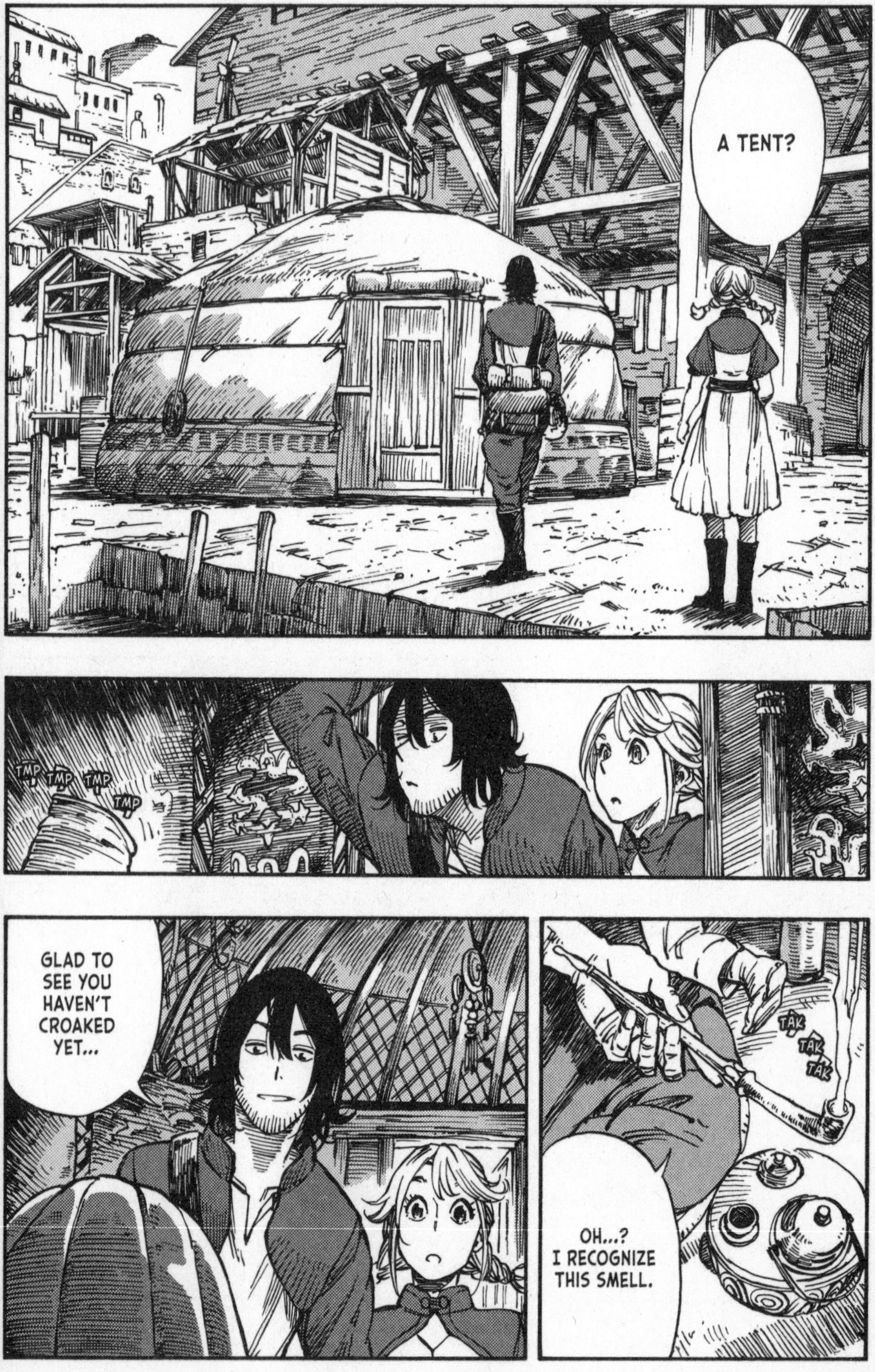
A TENT?
TMP TMP TMP TMP
TAK TAK TAK
OH...? I RECOGNIZE THIS SMELL.
GLAD TO SEE YOU HAVEN'T CROAKED YET...

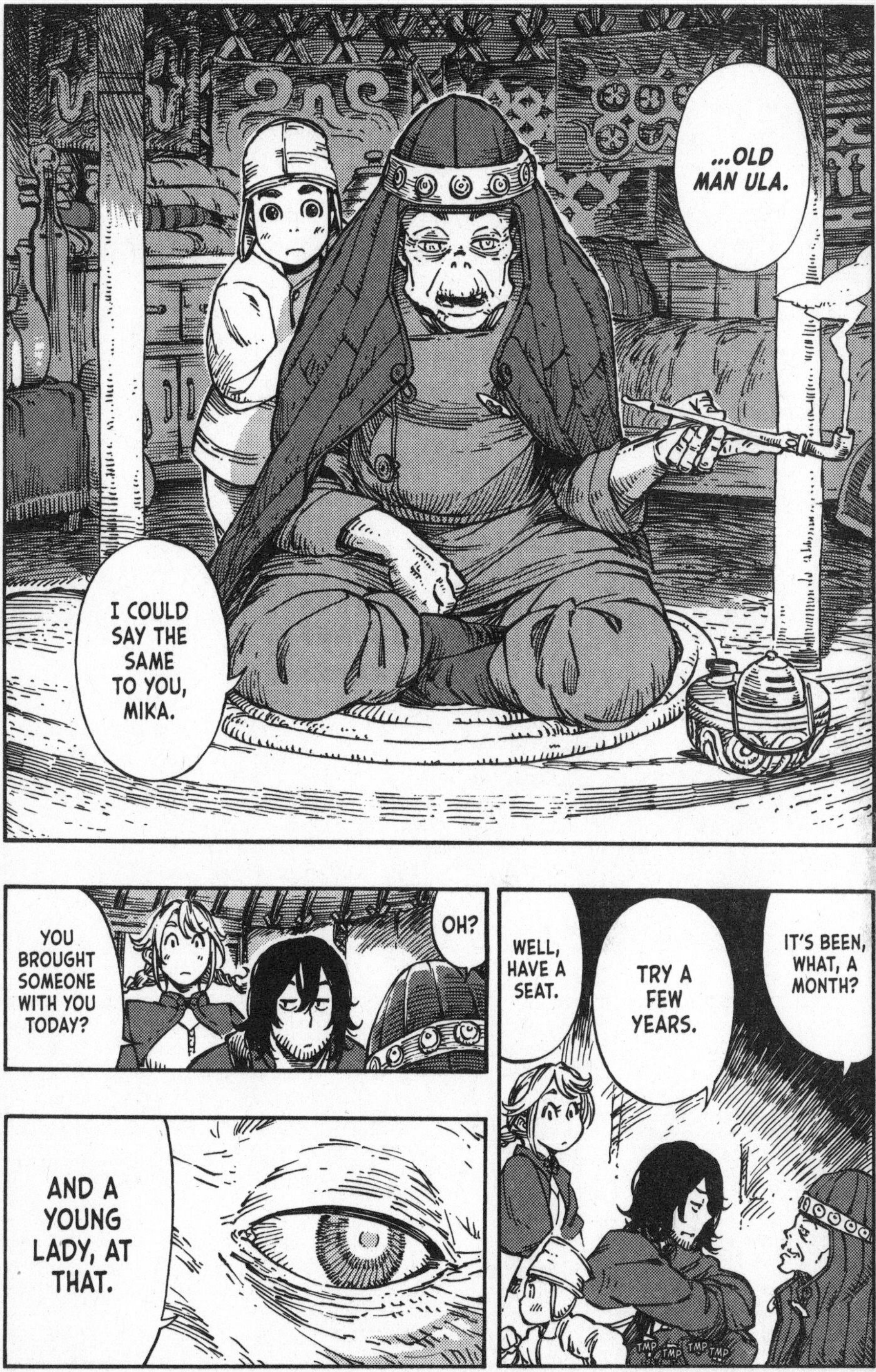
...OLD MAN ULA.
I COULD SAY THE SAME TO YOU, MIKA.
IT'S BEEN, WHAT, A MONTH?
TRY A FEW YEARS.
WELL, HAVE A SEAT.
TMP TMP TMP TMP TMP
OH?
YOU BROUGHT SOMEONE WITH YOU TODAY?
AND A YOUNG LADY, AT THAT.

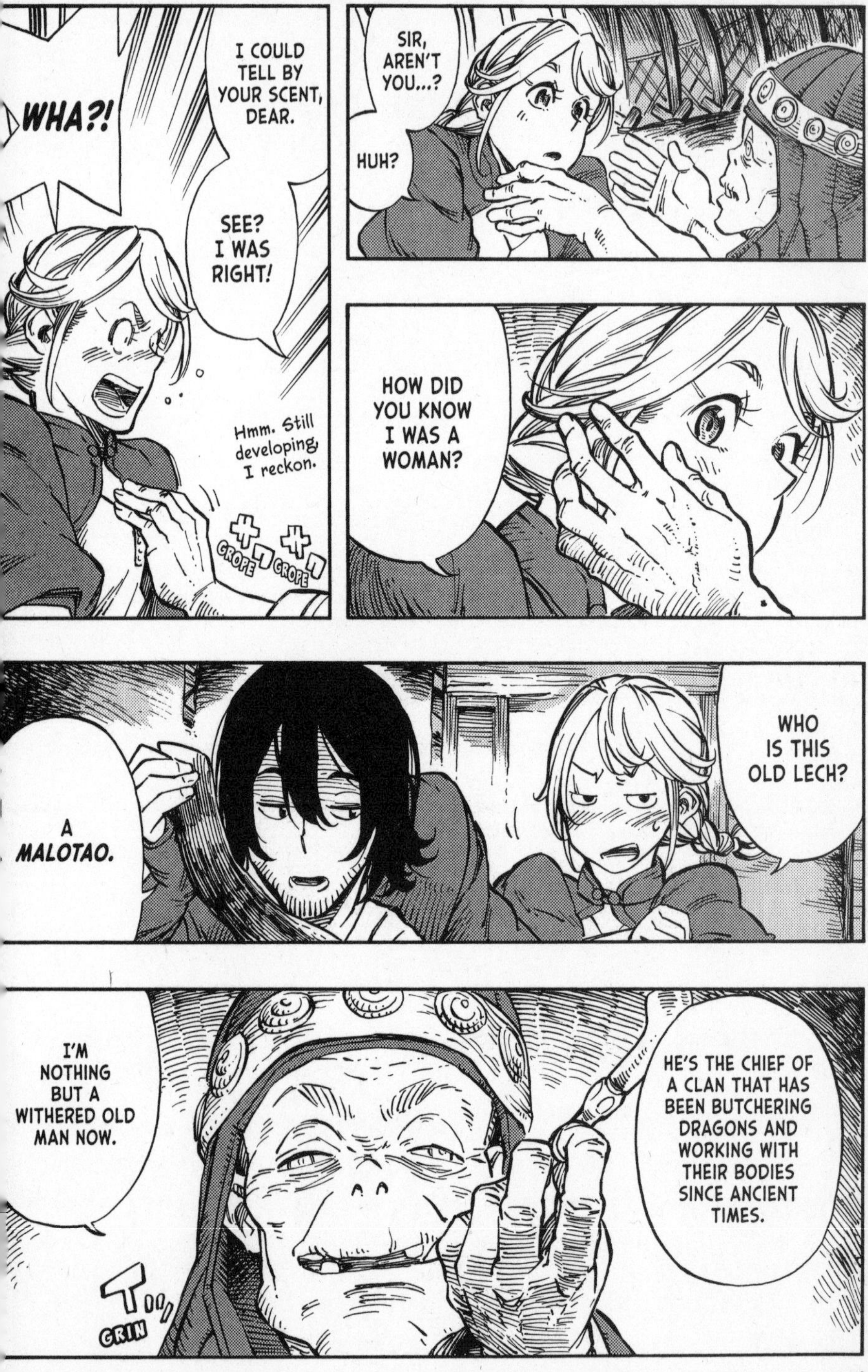
SIR, AREN'T YOU...?
HUH?
HOW DID YOU KNOW I WAS A WOMAN?
I COULD TELL BY YOUR SCENT, DEAR.
SEE? I WAS RIGHT!
WHA?!
Hmm. Still developing, I reckon.
GROPE GROPE
WHO IS THIS OLD LECH?
A MALOTAO.
HE'S THE CHIEF OF A CLAN THAT HAS BEEN BUTCHERING DRAGONS AND WORKING WITH THEIR BODIES SINCE ANCIENT TIMES.
I'M NOTHING BUT A WITHERED OLD MAN NOW.
GRIN

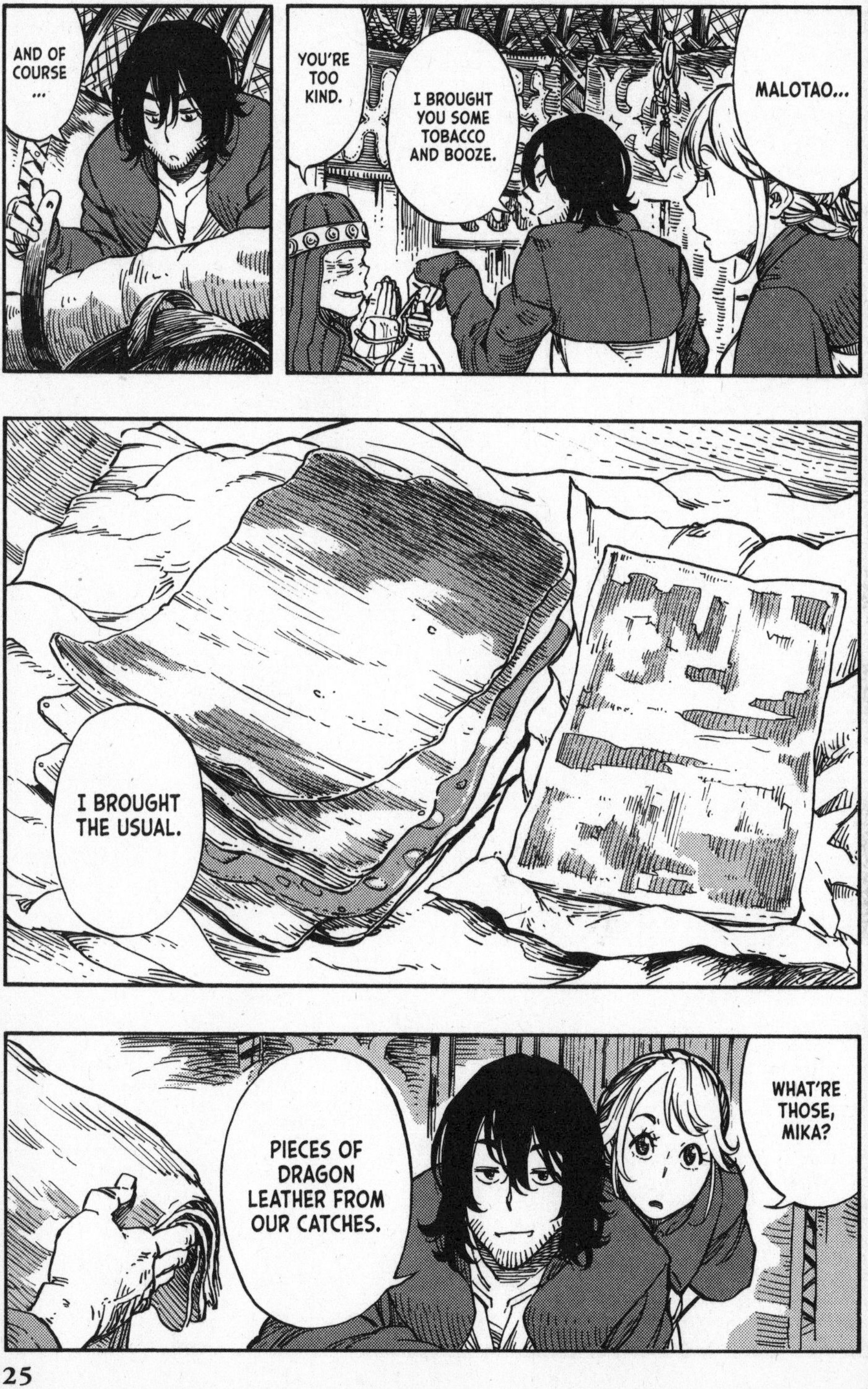
MALOTAO...
I BROUGHT YOU SOME TOBACCO AND BOOZE.
YOU'RE TOO KIND.
AND OF COURSE ...
I BROUGHT THE USUAL.
WHAT'RE THOSE, MIKA?
PIECES OF DRAGON LEATHER FROM OUR CATCHES.

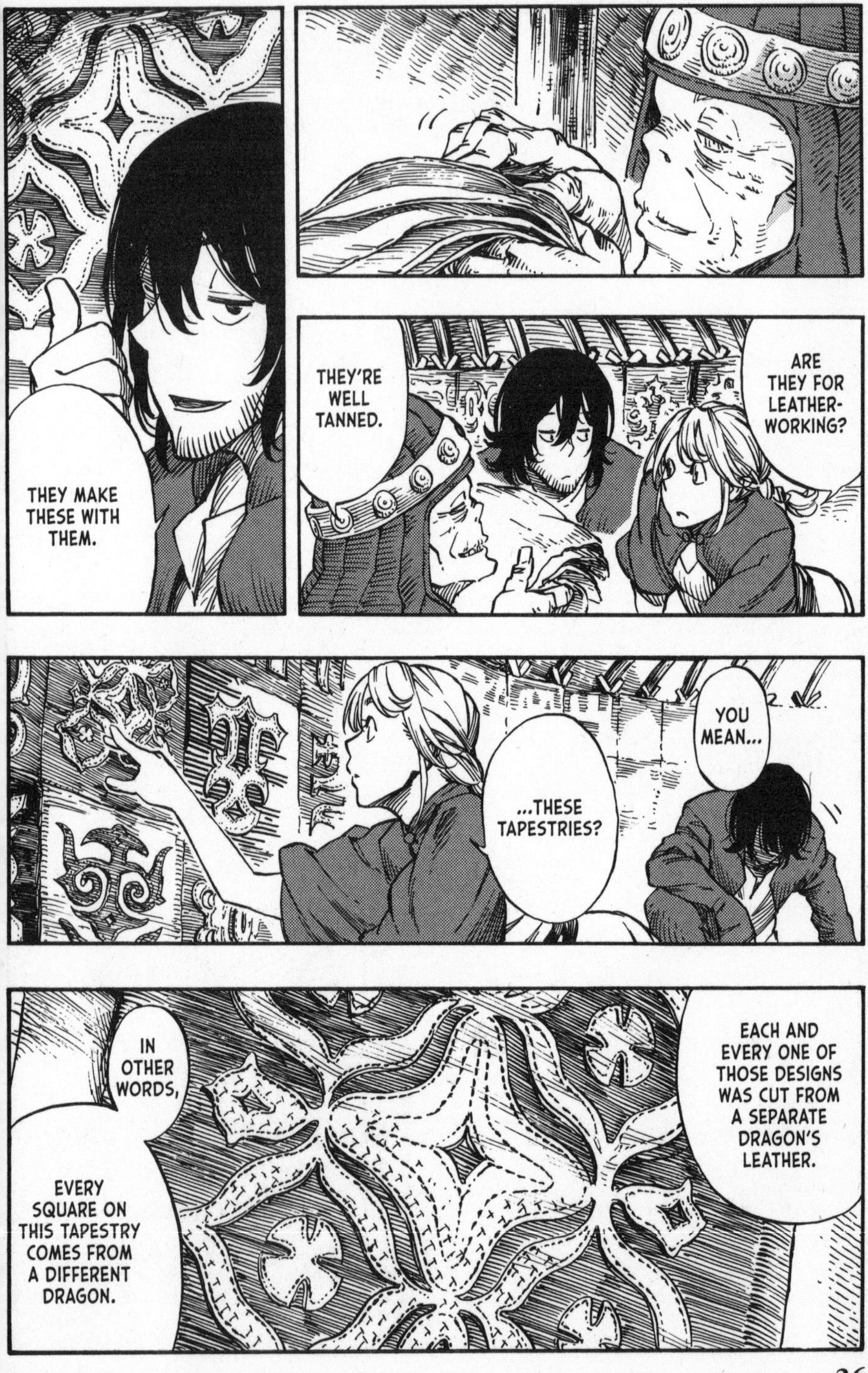
ARE THEY FOR LEATHER-WORKING?
THEY'RE WELL TANNED.
THEY MAKE THESE WITH THEM.
YOU MEAN...
...THESE TAPESTRIES?
EACH AND EVERY ONE OF THOSE DESIGNS WAS CUT FROM A SEPARATE DRAGON'S LEATHER.
IN OTHER WORDS,
EVERY SQUARE ON THIS TAPESTRY COMES FROM A DIFFERENT DRAGON.

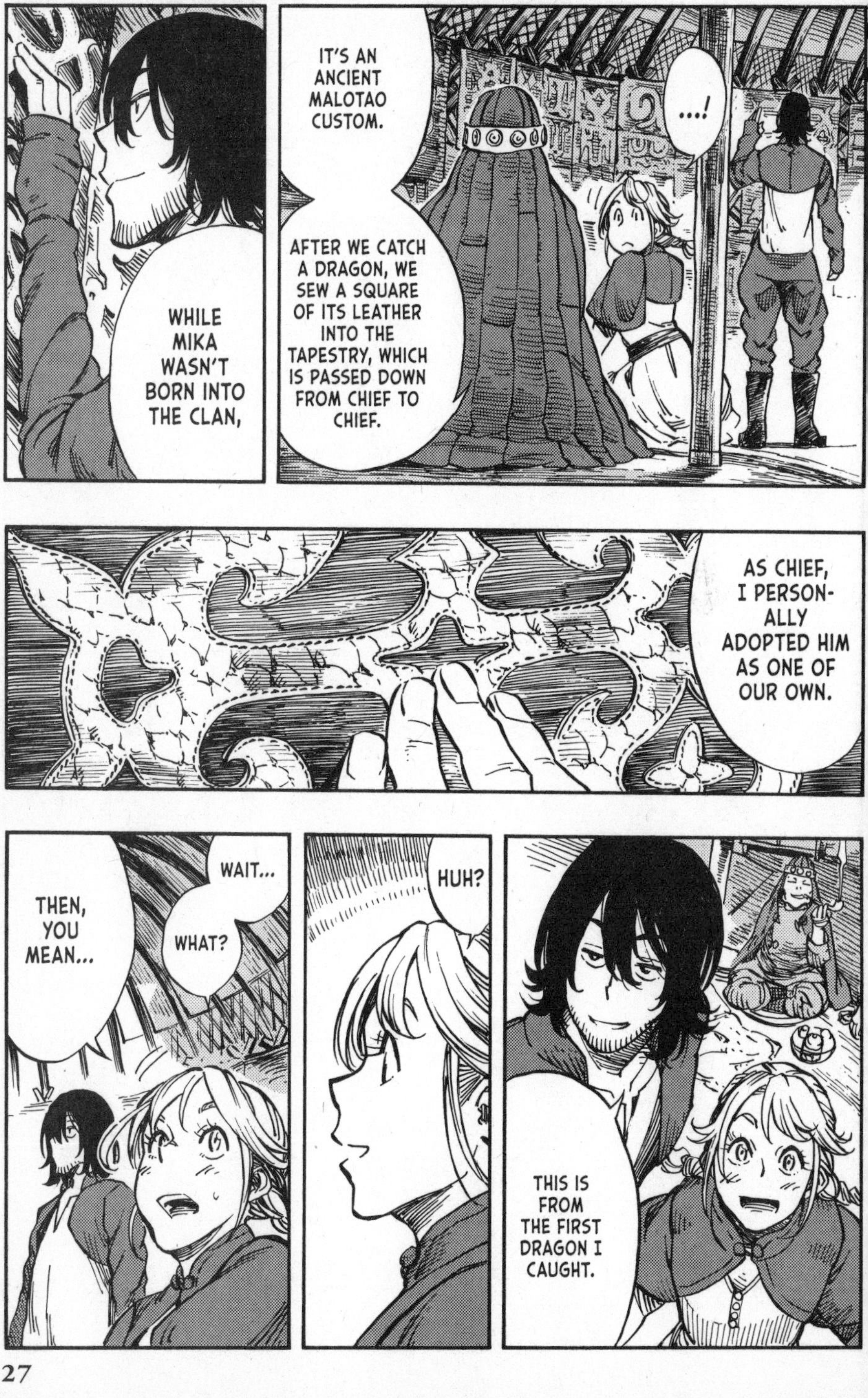
...!
IT'S AN ANCIENT MALOTAO CUSTOM.
AFTER WE CATCH A DRAGON, WE SEW A SQUARE OF ITS LEATHER INTO THE TAPESTRY, WHICH IS PASSED DOWN FROM CHIEF TO CHIEF.
WHILE MIKA WASN'T BORN INTO THE CLAN,
AS CHIEF, I PERSON-ALLY ADOPTED HIM AS ONE OF OUR OWN.
THIS IS FROM THE FIRST DRAGON I CAUGHT.
HUH?
WAIT...
WHAT?
THEN, YOU MEAN...

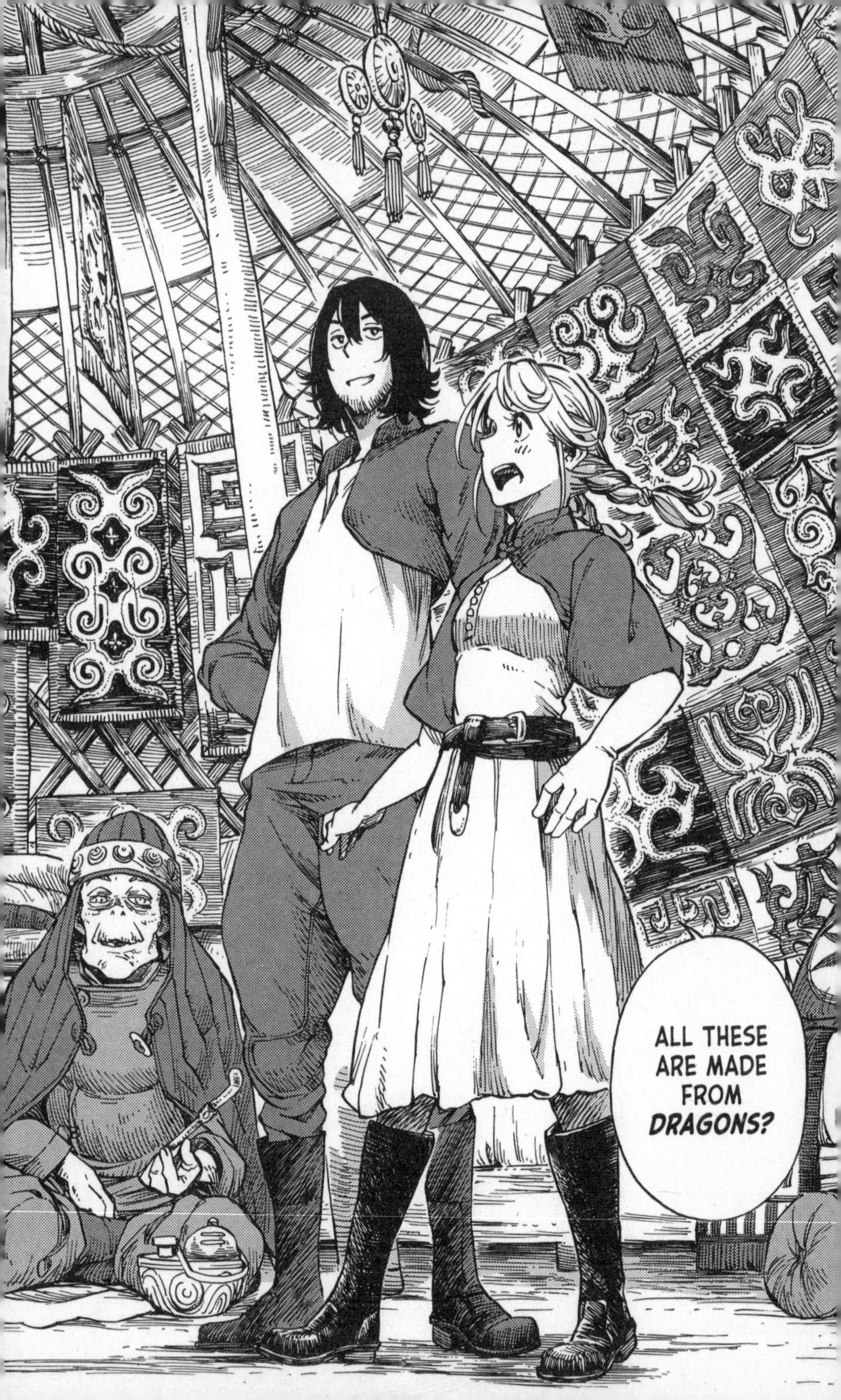
ALL THESE ARE MADE FROM *DRAGONS?*

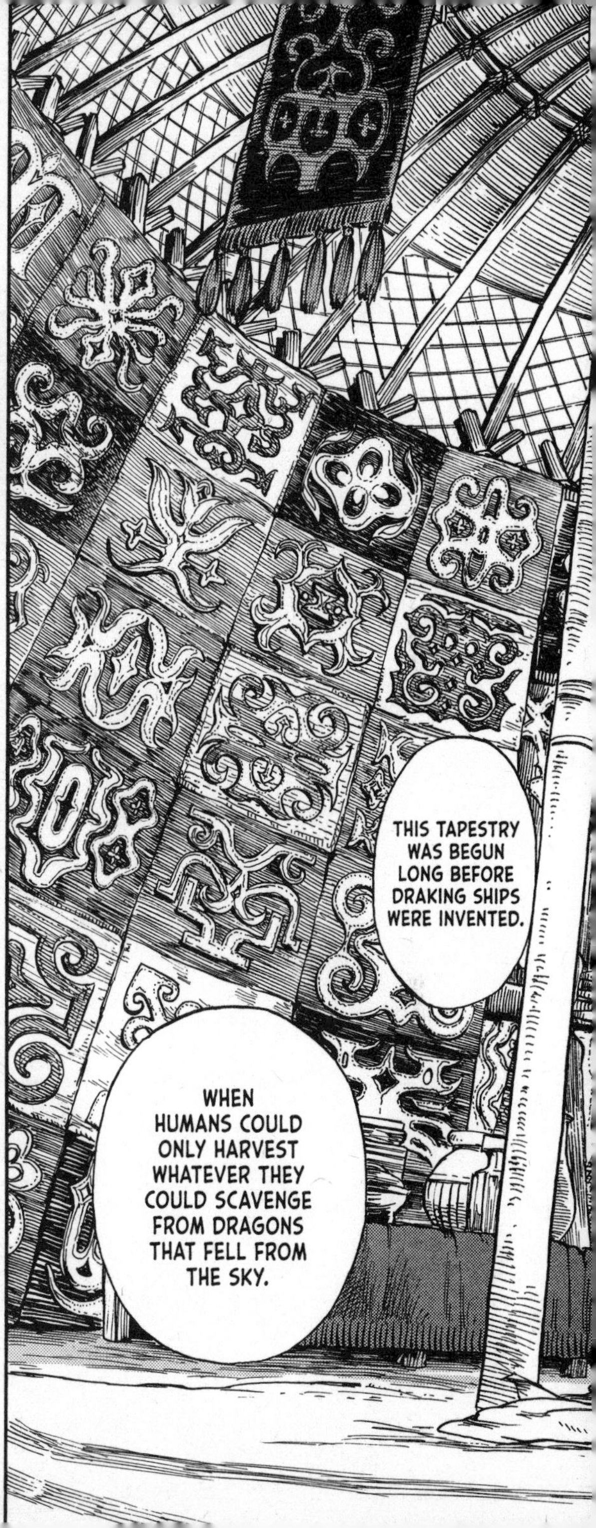
THIS TAPESTRY WAS BEGUN LONG BEFORE DRAKING SHIPS WERE INVENTED.
WHEN HUMANS COULD ONLY HARVEST WHATEVER THEY COULD SCAVENGE FROM DRAGONS THAT FELL FROM THE SKY.

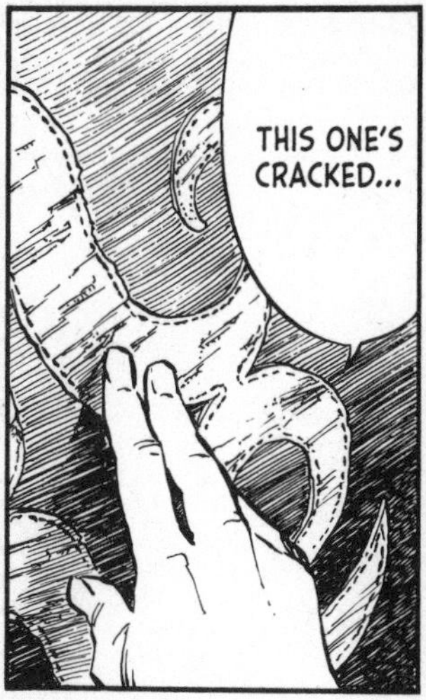
THIS ONE'S CRACKED...

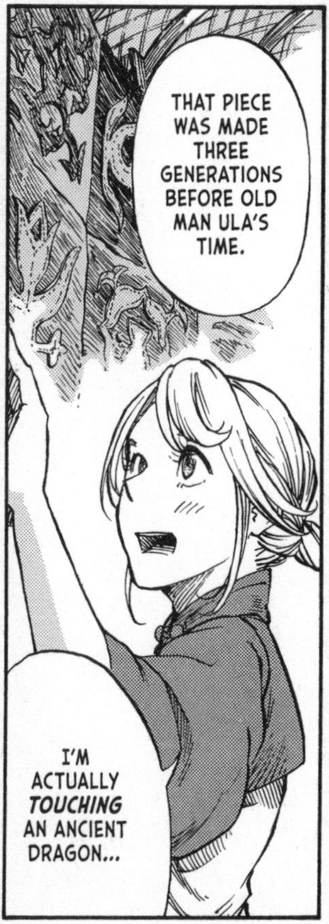
THAT PIECE WAS MADE THREE GENERATIONS BEFORE OLD MAN ULA'S TIME.
I'M ACTUALLY *TOUCHING* AN ANCIENT DRAGON...

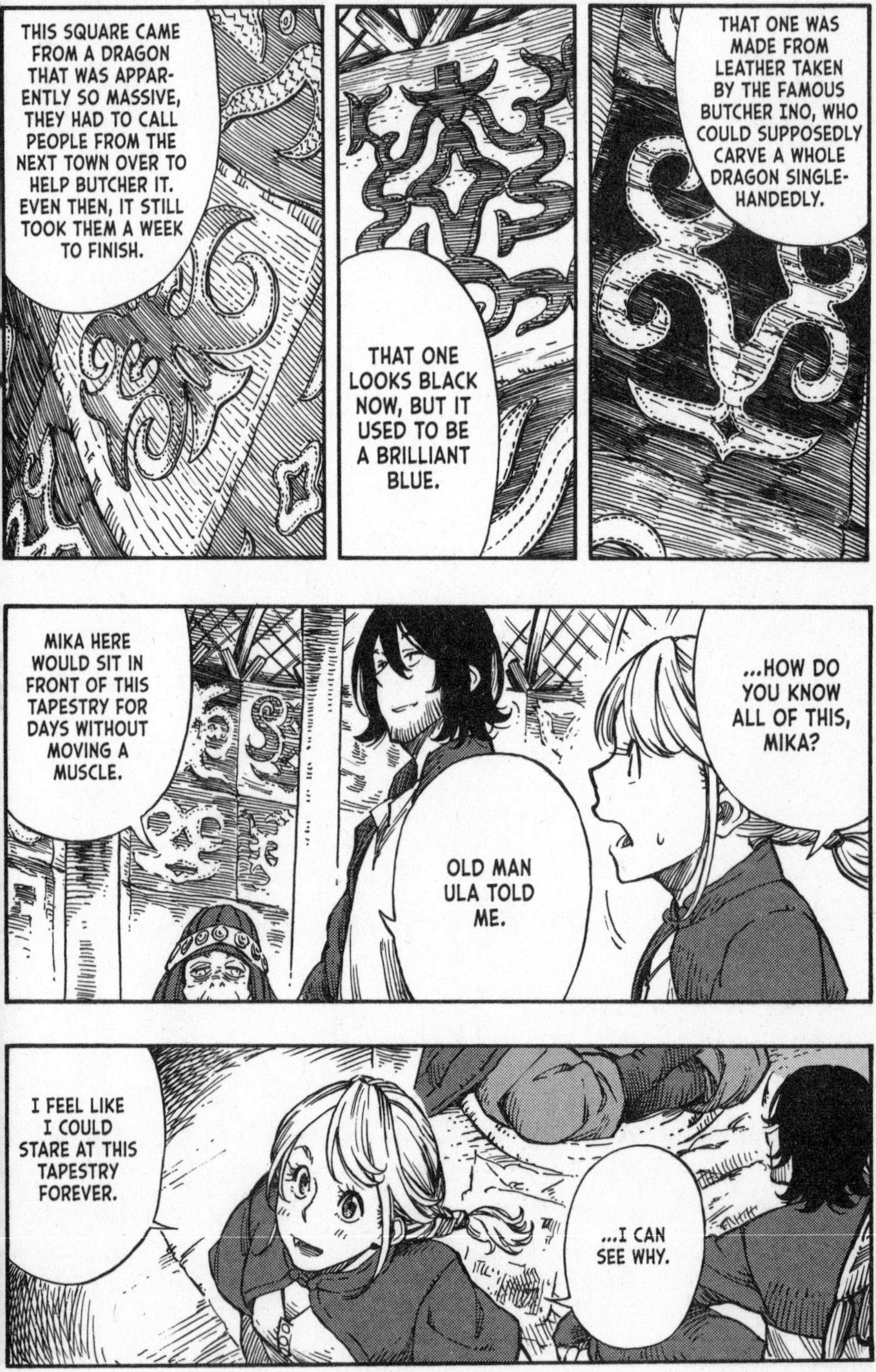
THAT ONE WAS MADE FROM LEATHER TAKEN BY THE FAMOUS BUTCHER INO, WHO COULD SUPPOSEDLY CARVE A WHOLE DRAGON SINGLE-HANDEDLY.
THAT ONE LOOKS BLACK NOW, BUT IT USED TO BE A BRILLIANT BLUE.
THIS SQUARE CAME FROM A DRAGON THAT WAS APPARENTLY SO MASSIVE, THEY HAD TO CALL PEOPLE FROM THE NEXT TOWN OVER TO HELP BUTCHER IT. EVEN THEN, IT STILL TOOK THEM A WEEK TO FINISH.
...HOW DO YOU KNOW ALL OF THIS, MIKA?
MIKA HERE WOULD SIT IN FRONT OF THIS TAPESTRY FOR DAYS WITHOUT MOVING A MUSCLE.
OLD MAN ULA TOLD ME.
I FEEL LIKE I COULD STARE AT THIS TAPESTRY FOREVER.
...I CAN SEE WHY.

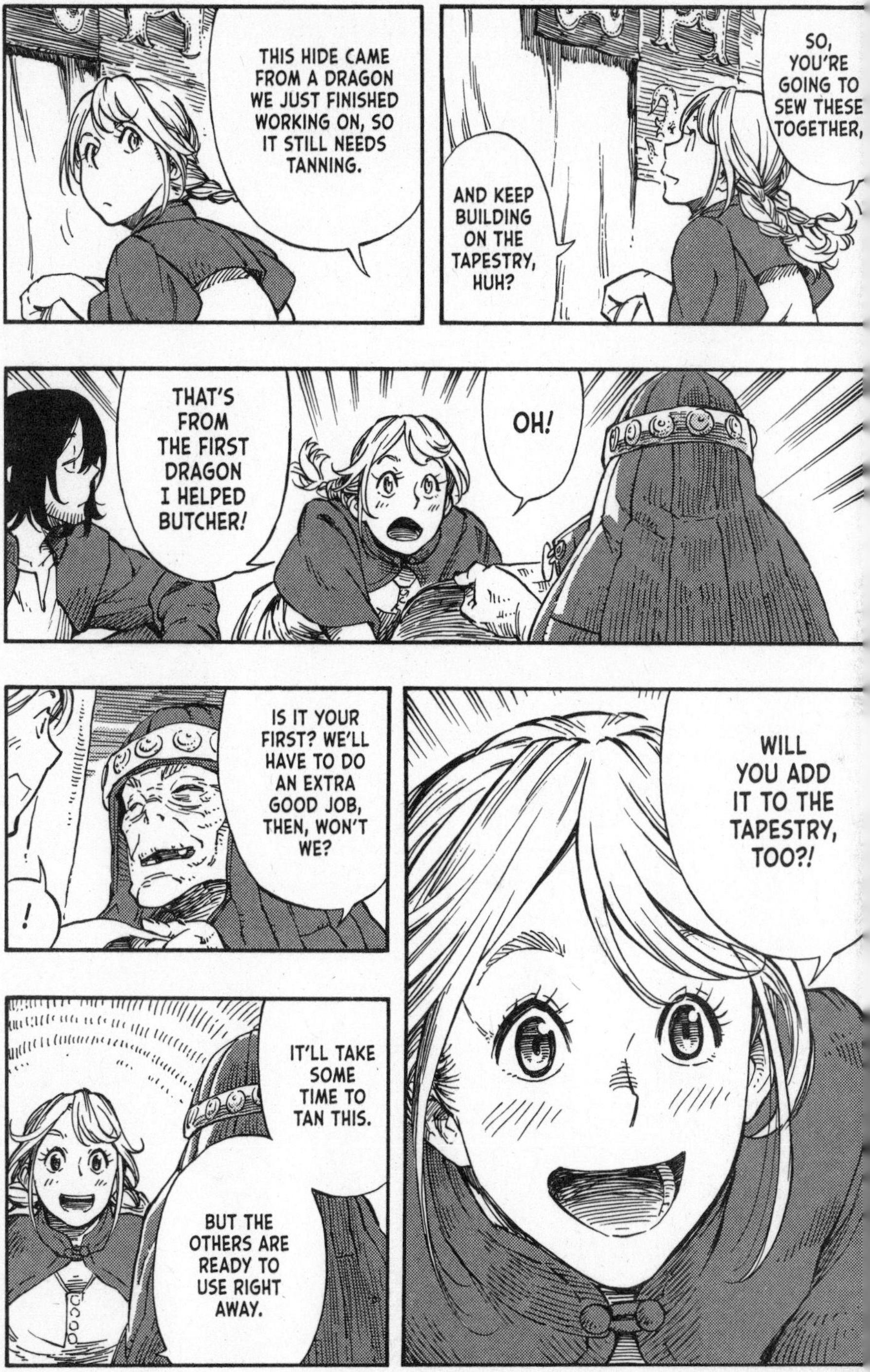
SO, YOU'RE GOING TO SEW THESE TOGETHER,
AND KEEP BUILDING ON THE TAPESTRY, HUH?
THIS HIDE CAME FROM A DRAGON WE JUST FINISHED WORKING ON, SO IT STILL NEEDS TANNING.
OH!
THAT'S FROM THE FIRST DRAGON I HELPED BUTCHER!
WILL YOU ADD IT TO THE TAPESTRY, TOO?!
!
IS IT YOUR FIRST? WE'LL HAVE TO DO AN EXTRA GOOD JOB, THEN, WON'T WE?
IT'LL TAKE SOME TIME TO TAN THIS.
BUT THE OTHERS ARE READY TO USE RIGHT AWAY.

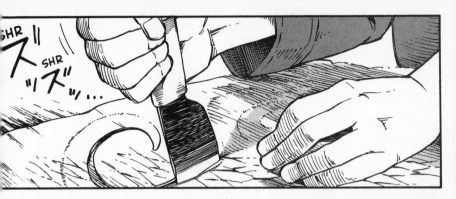

...

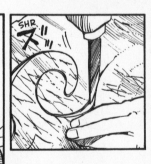

IS THERE ANY PARTICULAR MEANING TO THE DESIGN YOU'RE CUTTING?

HMM...

THE LEATHER TELLS US HOW IT WANTS TO BE CUT.

?

THE COLOR AND FEEL OF THE LEATHER. THE PRESENCE OF SCALES OR HAIR. ROUGH OR DAMAGED AREAS...

ALL OF THE LEATHER'S CHARACTERISTICS GUIDE MY HAND TO THE RIGHT DESIGN.

I SEE...

AFTER THE PATTERN HAS BEEN CUT, I USE A STITCHING CHISEL TO PUNCH HOLES ALONG THE EDGE.

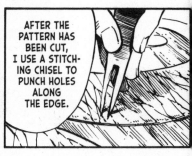

THNK

ドン

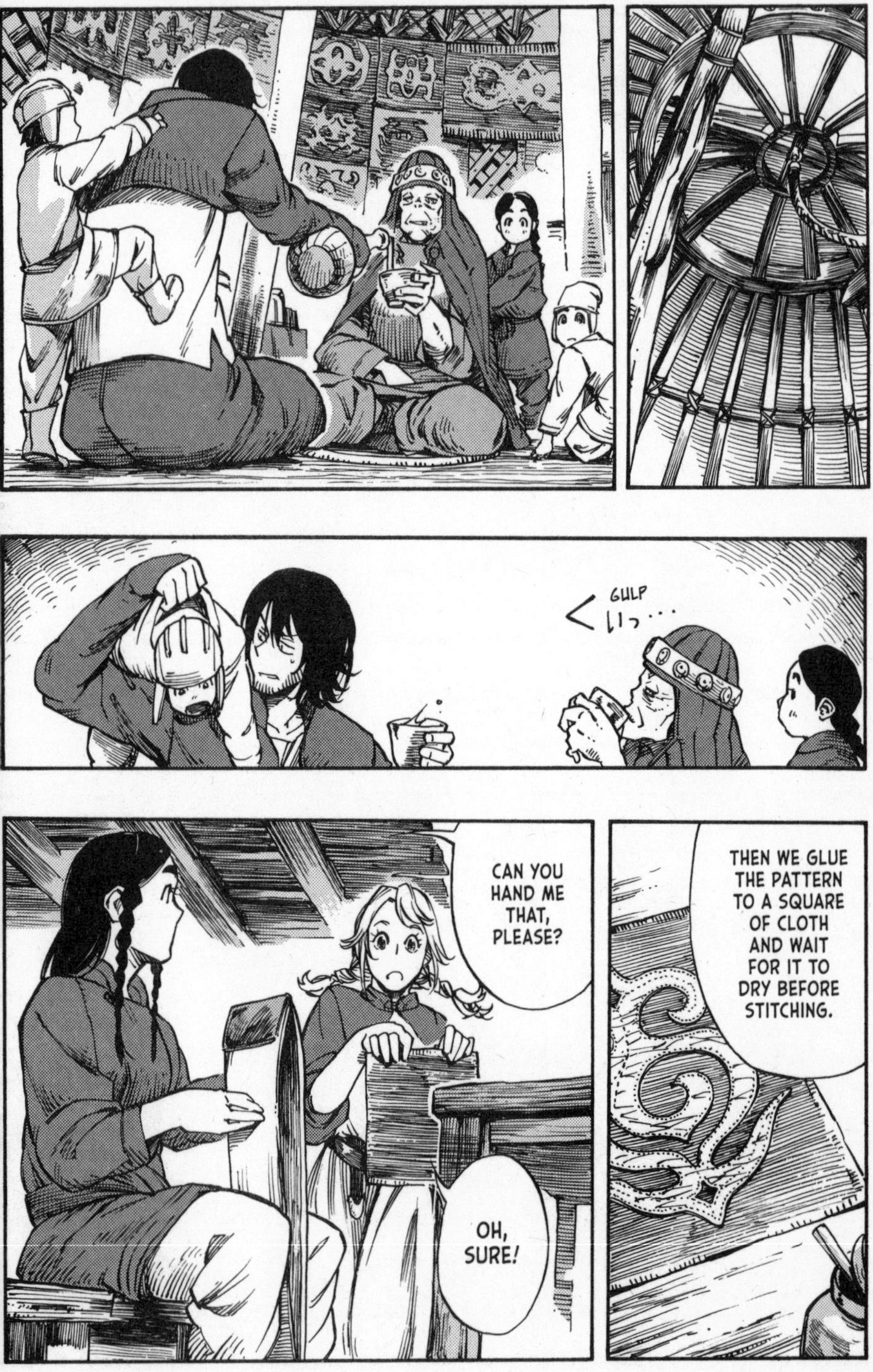
GULP
くいっ…
THEN WE GLUE THE PATTERN TO A SQUARE OF CLOTH AND WAIT FOR IT TO DRY BEFORE STITCHING.
CAN YOU HAND ME THAT, PLEASE?
OH, SURE!

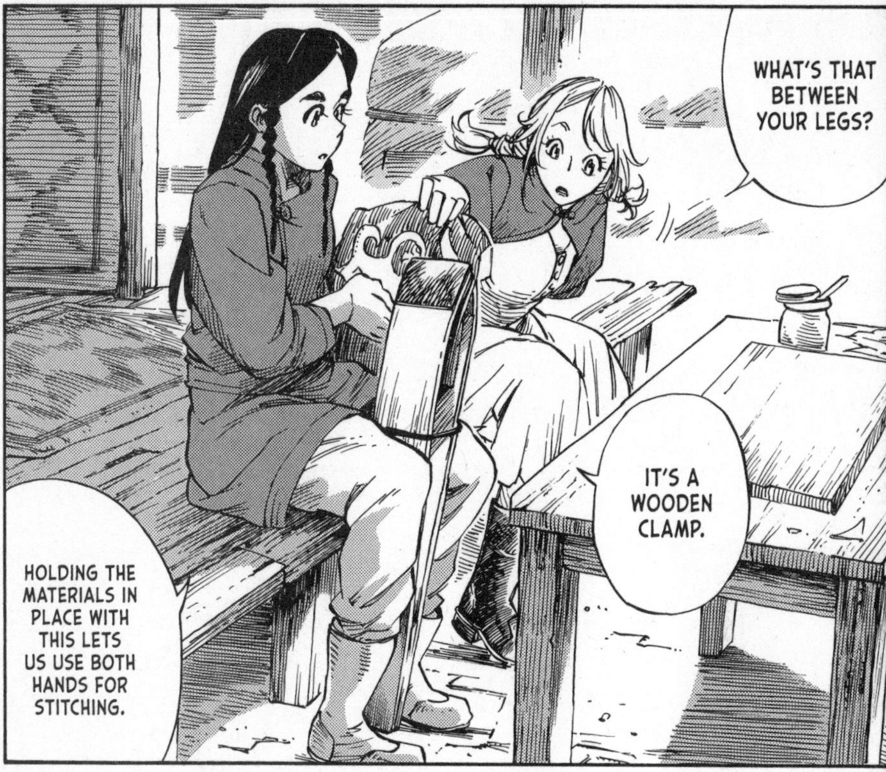
WHAT'S THAT BETWEEN YOUR LEGS?
IT'S A WOODEN CLAMP.
HOLDING THE MATERIALS IN PLACE WITH THIS LETS US USE BOTH HANDS FOR STITCHING.

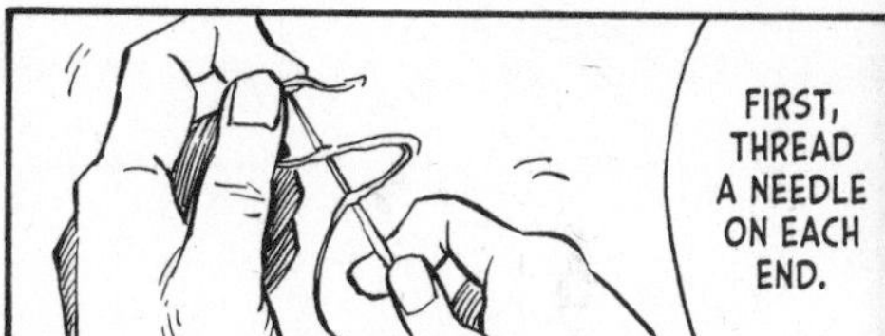
FIRST, THREAD A NEEDLE ON EACH END.

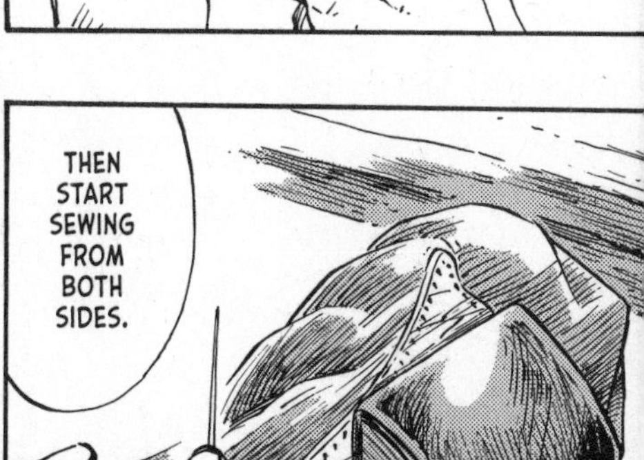
THEN START SEWING FROM BOTH SIDES.

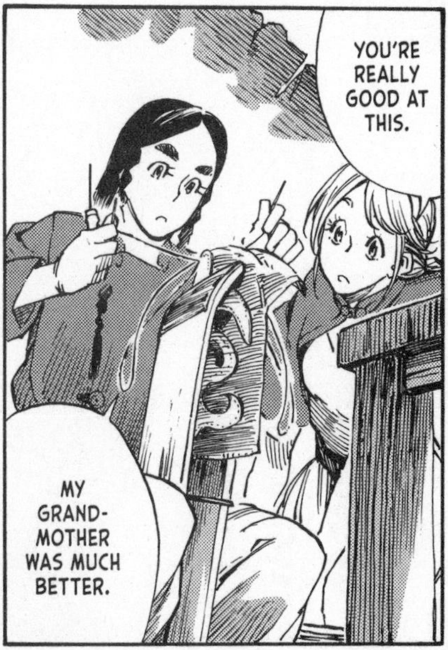
YOU'RE REALLY GOOD AT THIS.
MY GRAND-MOTHER WAS MUCH BETTER.

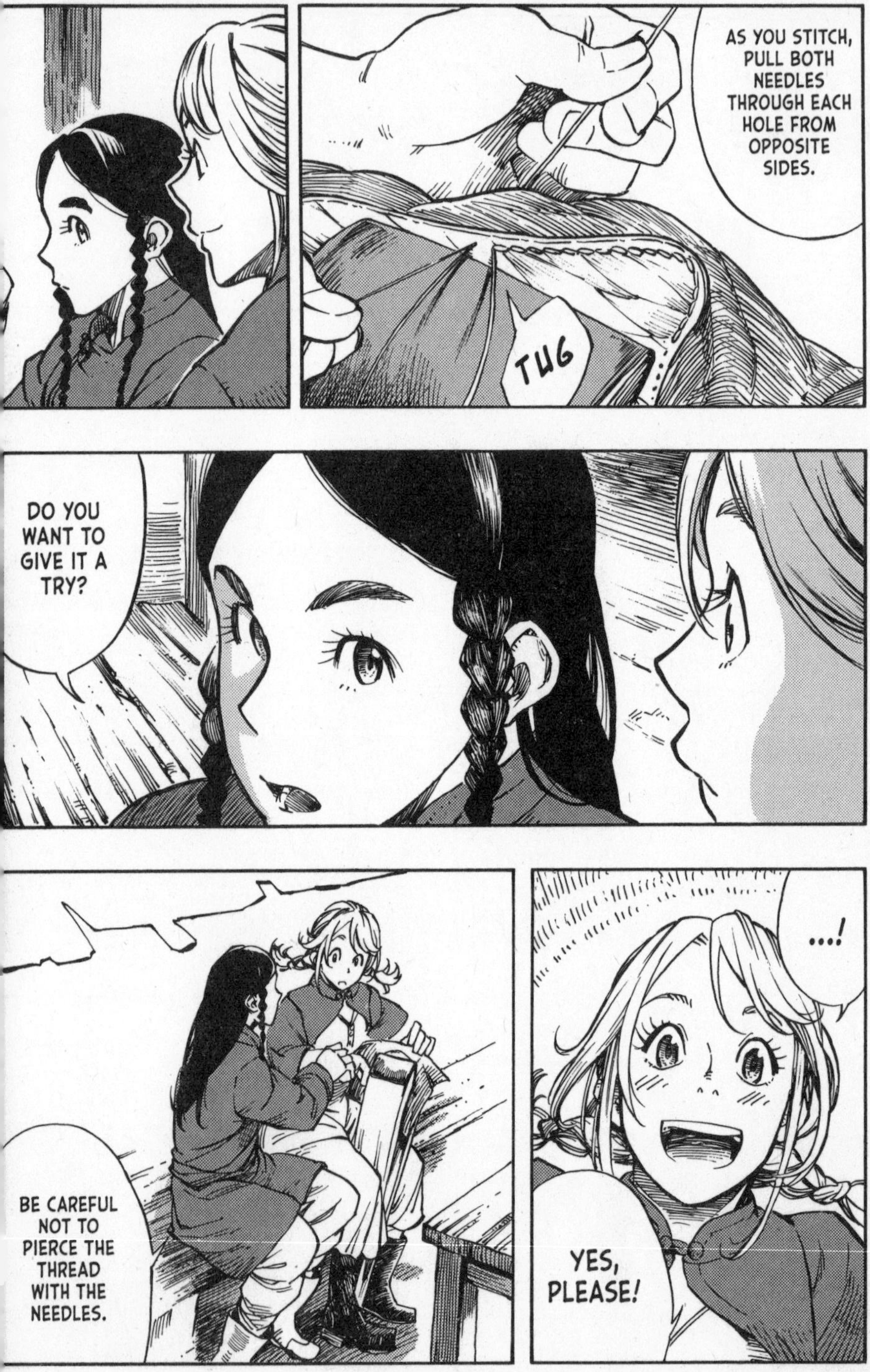
AS YOU STITCH, PULL BOTH NEEDLES THROUGH EACH HOLE FROM OPPOSITE SIDES.
TUG
DO YOU WANT TO GIVE IT A TRY?
...!
YES, PLEASE!
BE CAREFUL NOT TO PIERCE THE THREAD WITH THE NEEDLES.

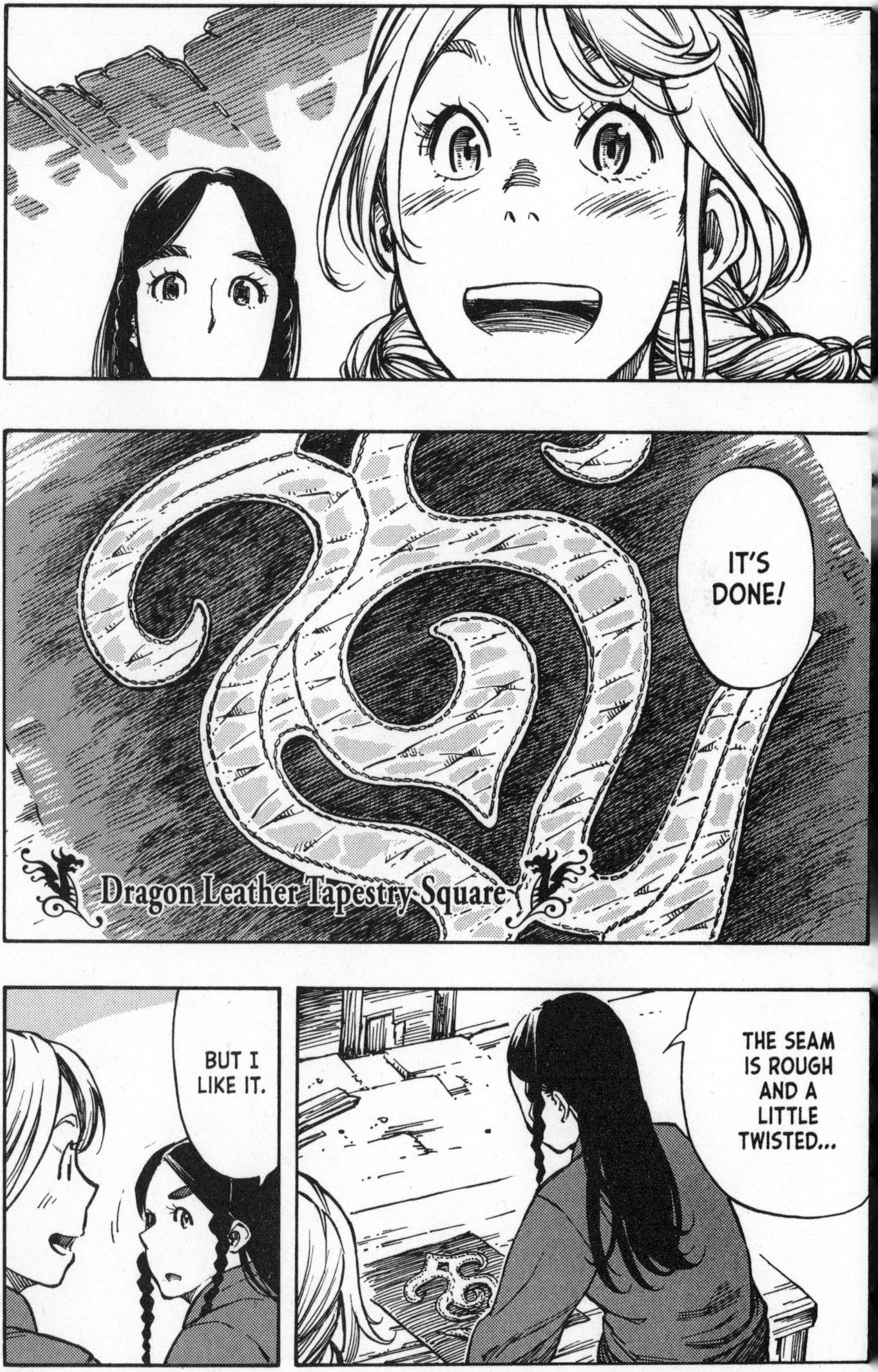
IT'S DONE!
Dragon Leather Tapestry Square
THE SEAM IS ROUGH AND A LITTLE TWISTED...
BUT I LIKE IT.

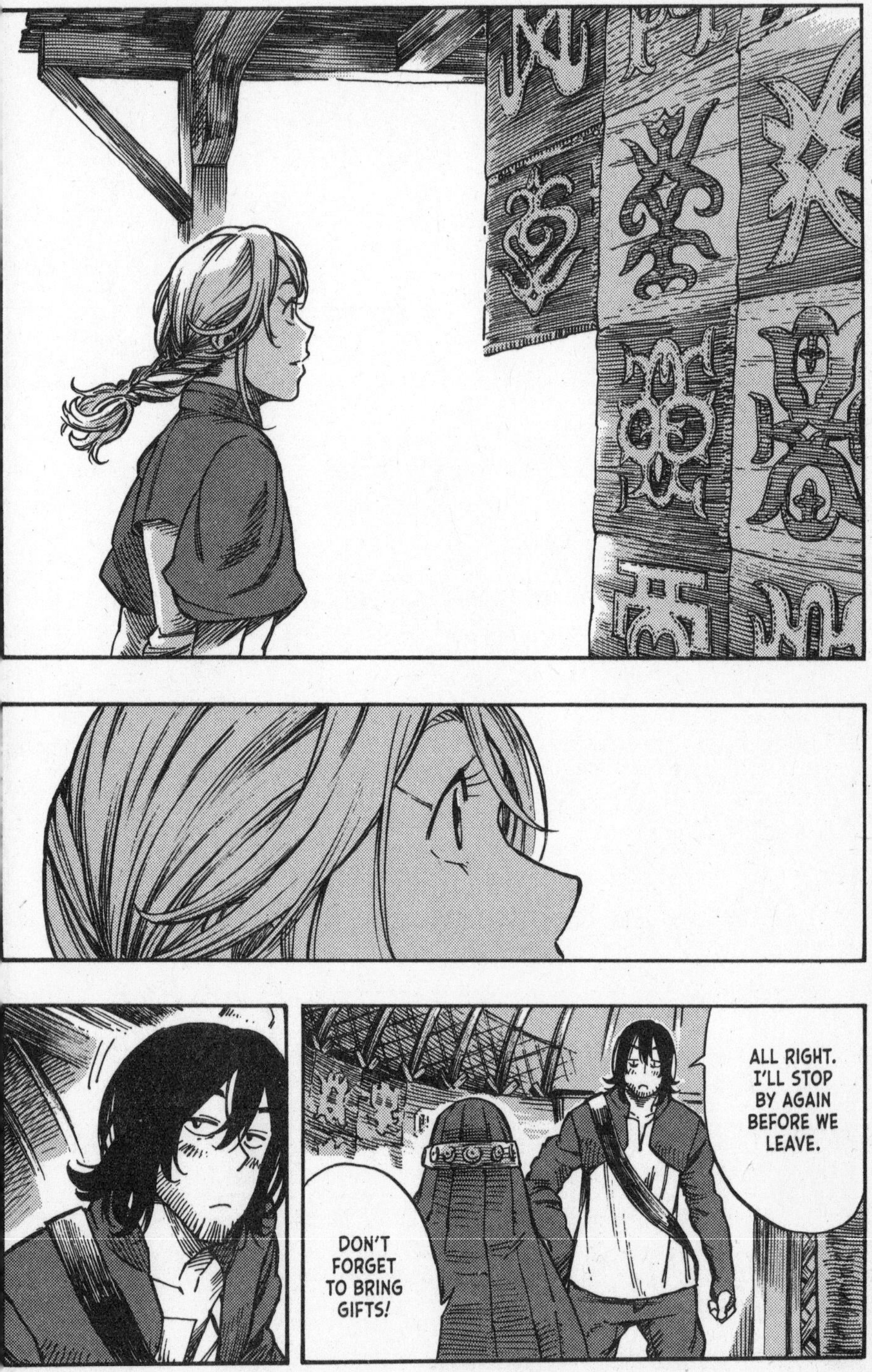
ALL RIGHT. I'LL STOP BY AGAIN BEFORE WE LEAVE.
DON'T FORGET TO BRING GIFTS!

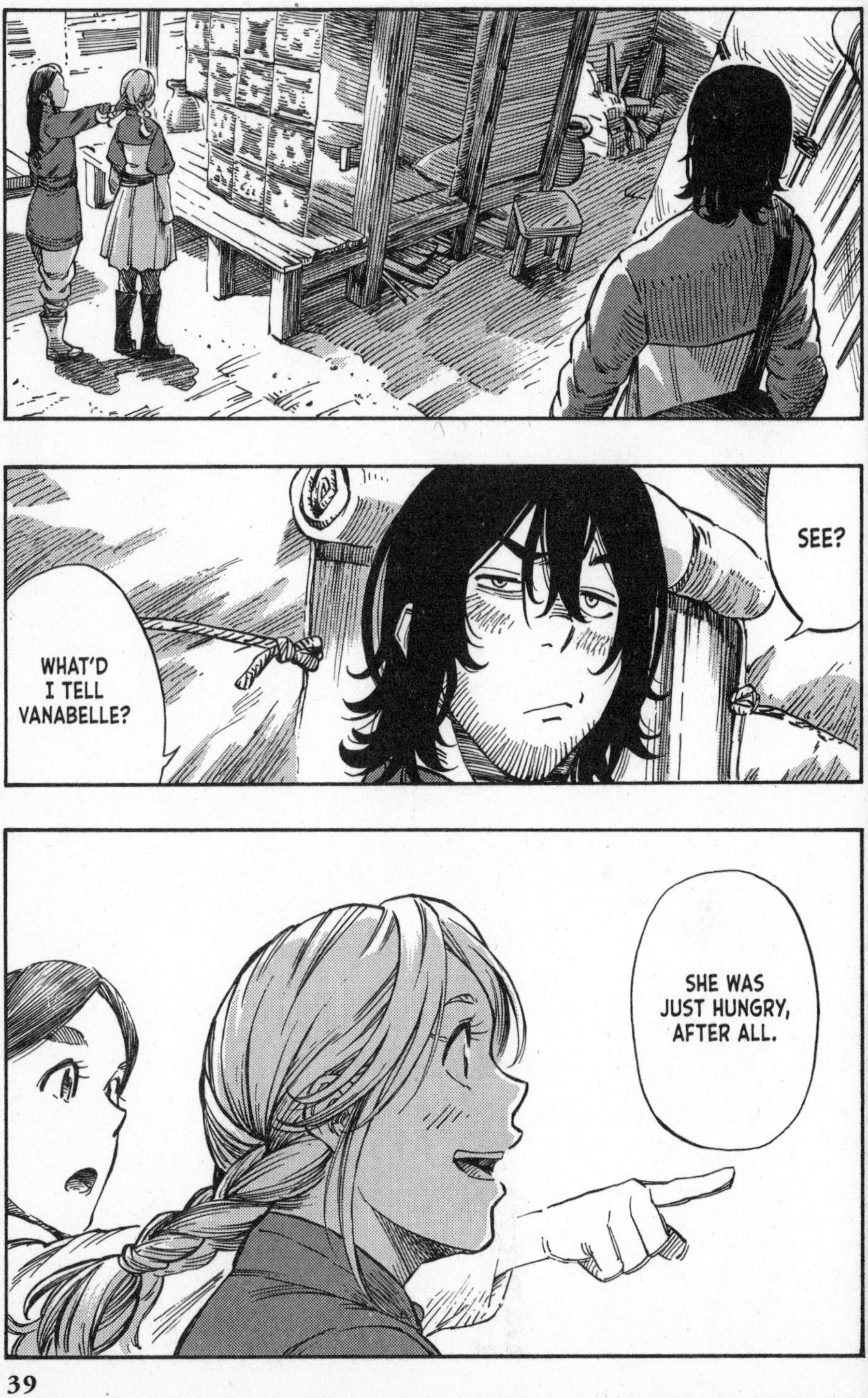
SEE?
WHAT'D I TELL VANABELLE?
SHE WAS JUST HUNGRY, AFTER ALL.

Dragon Leather Tapestry

IT'S
DONE!

Materials

✦ Cloth (400 x 400 mm)

✦ Dragon leather

✦ Sinew thread

✦ Glue

01

Wax the sinew thread.

02

Draw the pattern on a piece of paper and place it on the leather. Using a stylus, trace the design through the paper onto the leather.

03

Use a leatherworking knife to carefully cut out the pattern, then use a stitching chisel to punch holes in the leather.

04

Glue the cut pattern to a square of cloth and allow to dry.

WHAT'S THAT BETWEEN YOUR LEGS?

IT'S A WOODEN CLAMP.

05

Use a clamp (also known as a "stitching pony") to keep the tapestry square in place, thread a needle on each end of the thread, and sew a saddle stitch. Keep the front of the pattern facing right, and begin the stitch from the far end, working towards yourself (if right-handed).

06

When you reach the last hole, take the right-side needle and pull it through the left side of the tapestry (back). Tie the thread on the back side of the cloth, apply glue to the knot, and pull taut.

07

Cut the loose thread, press the knot with the bottom of a wooden mallet or something similar, and it's done.

IT'S SURPRISINGLY STRENUOUS WORK, SO BEGINNERS WILL HAVE A TOUGH TIME.

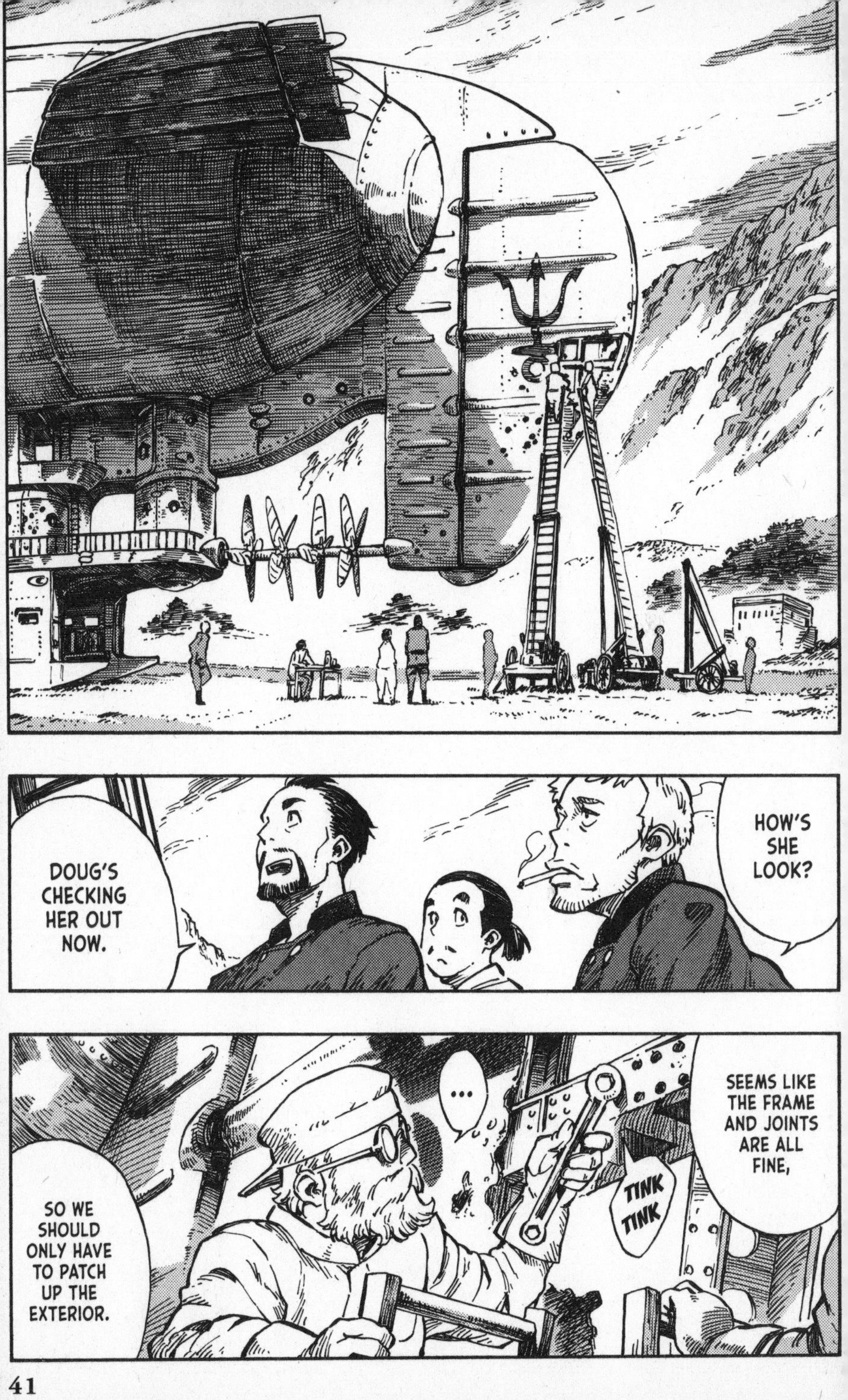
HOW'S SHE LOOK?
DOUG'S CHECKING HER OUT NOW.
SEEMS LIKE THE FRAME AND JOINTS ARE ALL FINE,
TINK TINK
...
SO WE SHOULD ONLY HAVE TO PATCH UP THE EXTERIOR.

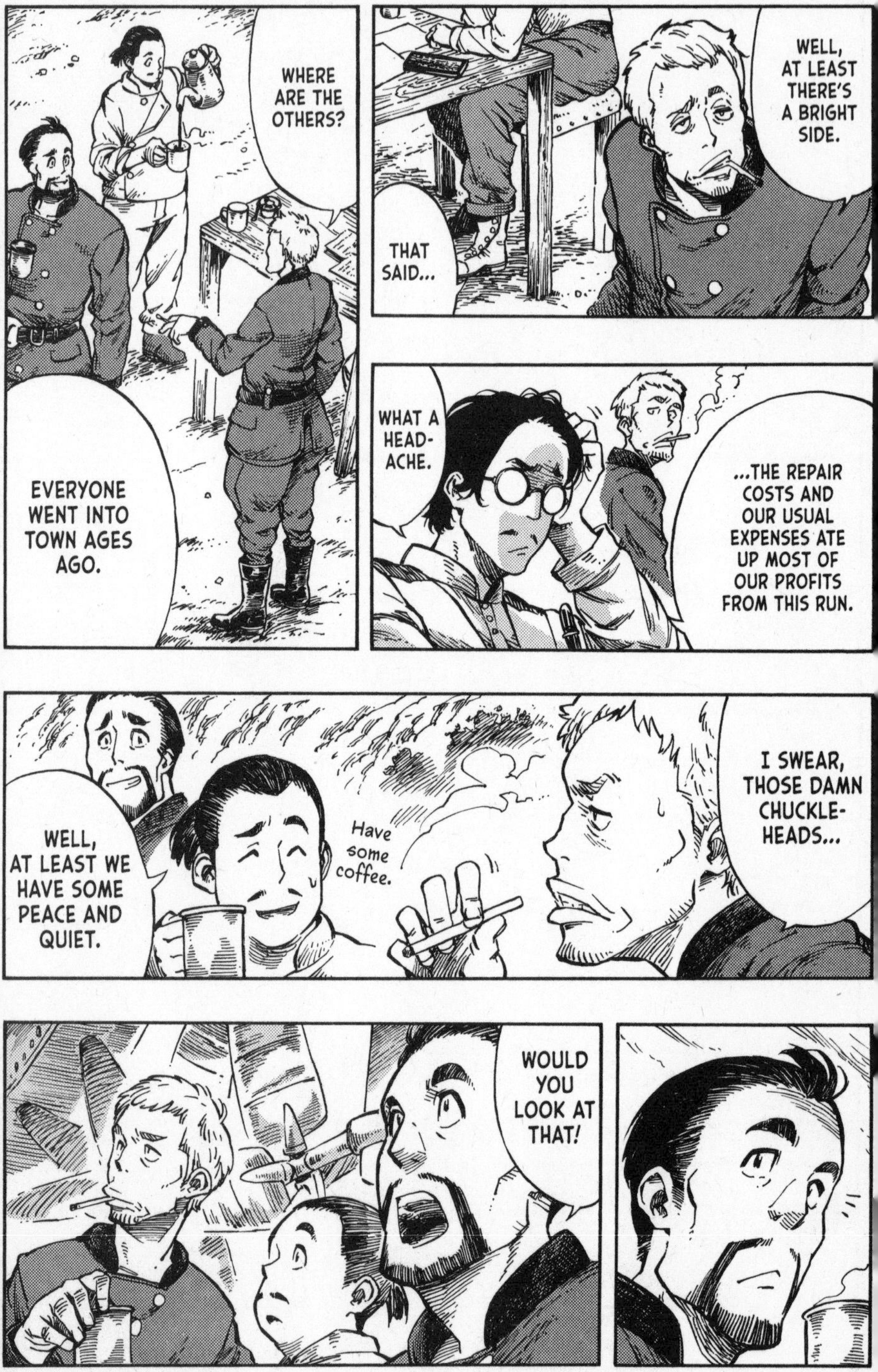
WELL, AT LEAST THERE'S A BRIGHT SIDE.
THAT SAID...
...THE REPAIR COSTS AND OUR USUAL EXPENSES ATE UP MOST OF OUR PROFITS FROM THIS RUN.
WHAT A HEAD-ACHE.
WHERE ARE THE OTHERS?
EVERYONE WENT INTO TOWN AGES AGO.
I SWEAR, THOSE DAMN CHUCKLE-HEADS...
Have some coffee.
WELL, AT LEAST WE HAVE SOME PEACE AND QUIET.
WOULD YOU LOOK AT THAT!

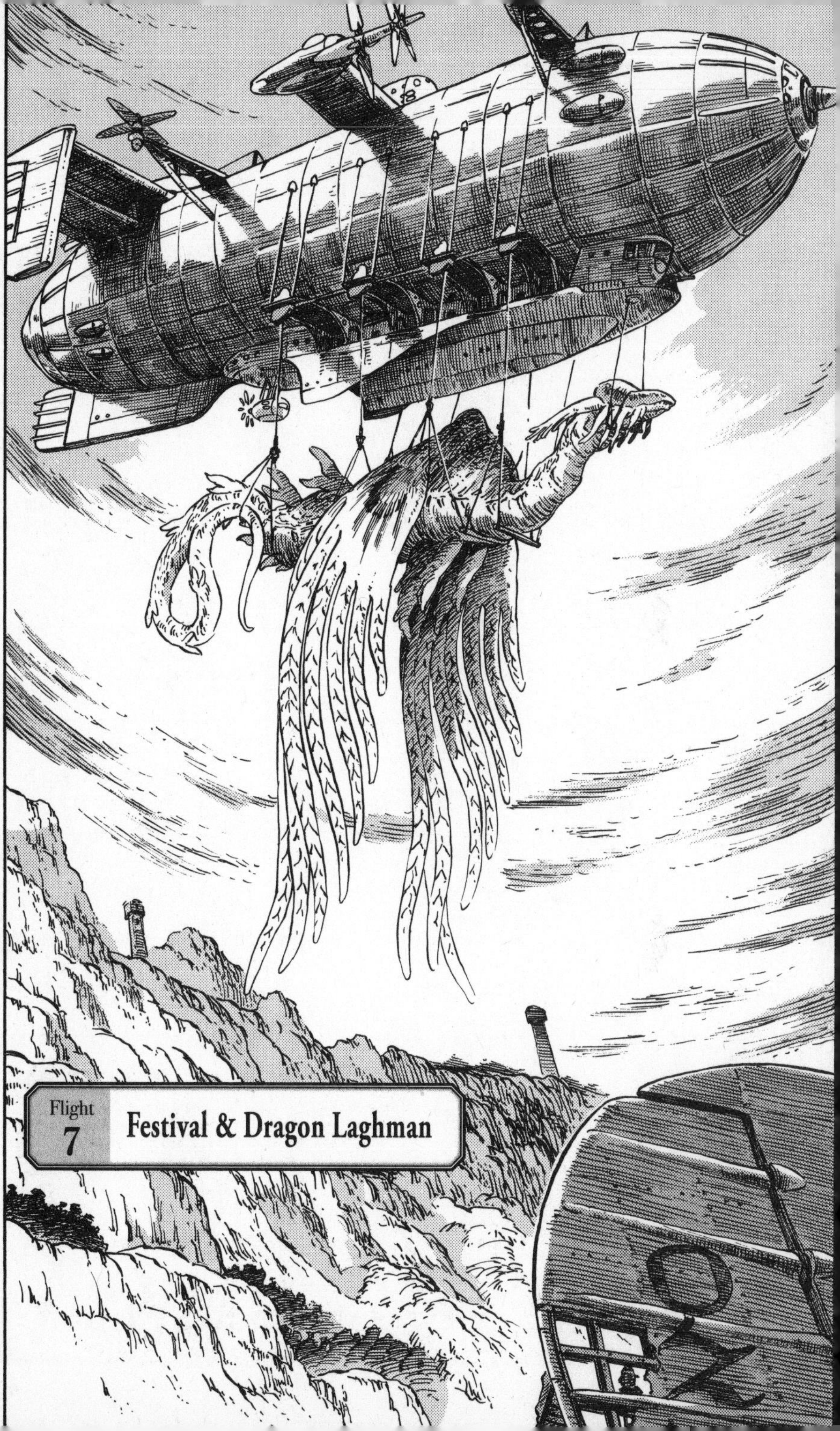
Flight
7
Festival & Dragon Laghman

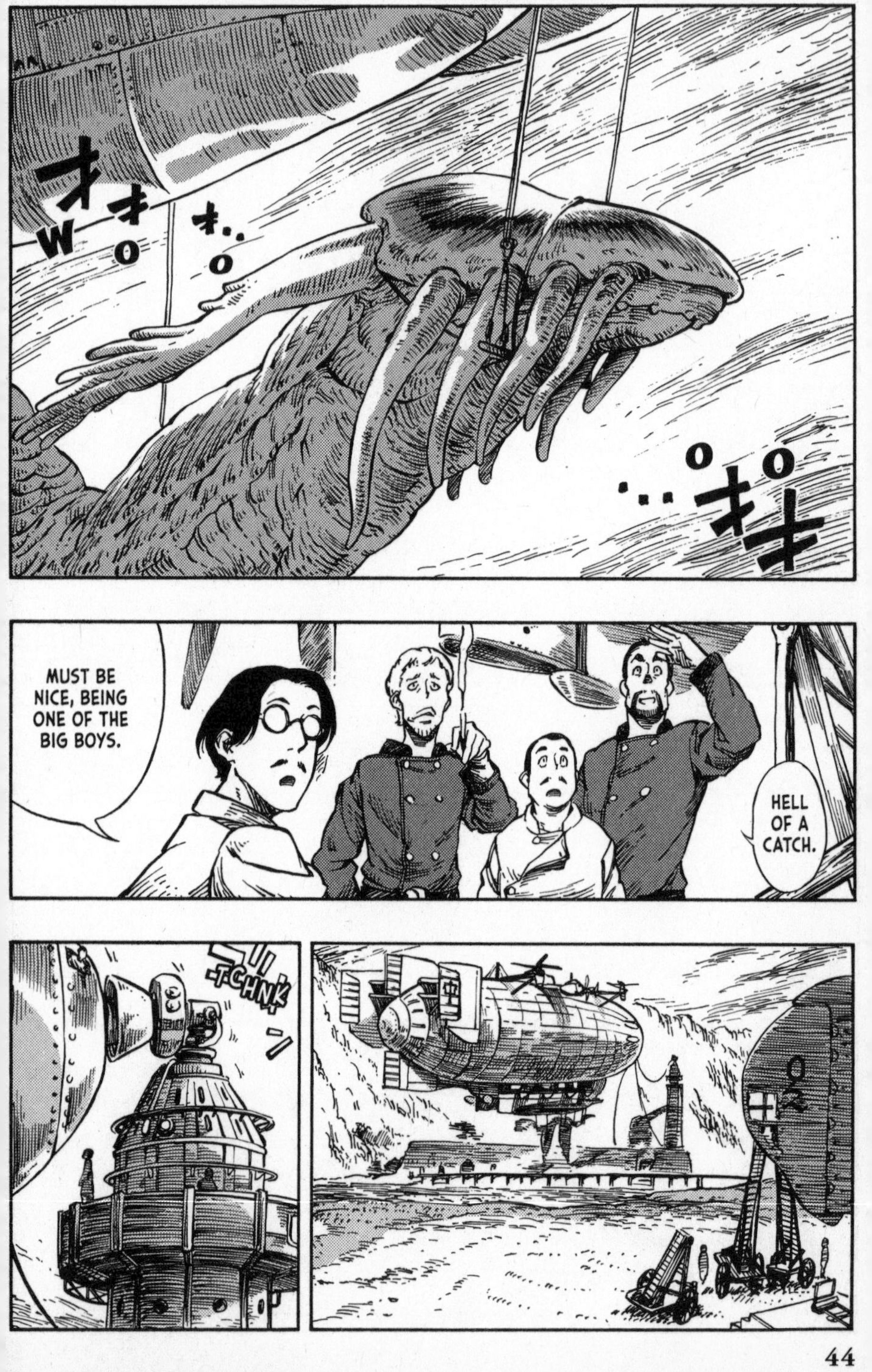
オオ WO
オ.. O
...O O オオ
HELL OF A CATCH.
MUST BE NICE, BEING ONE OF THE BIG BOYS.
TCHNK

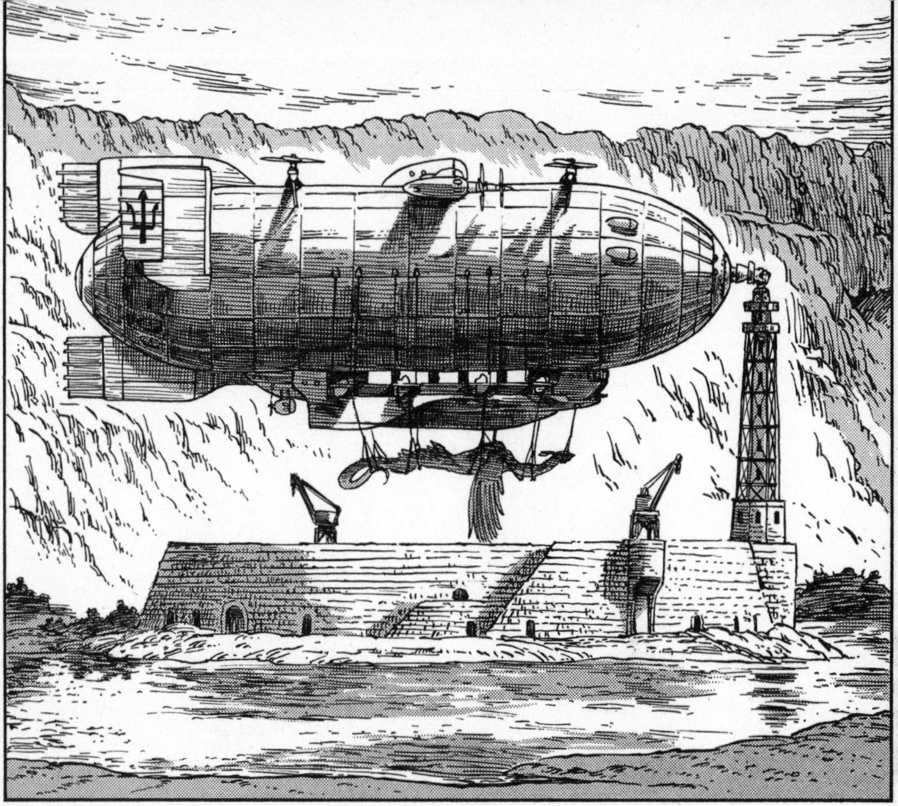

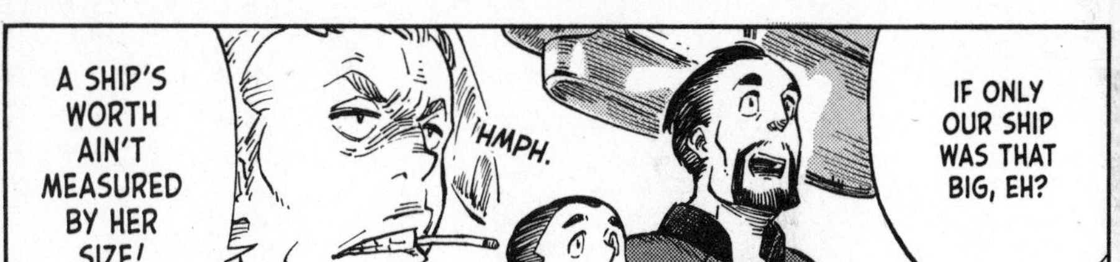
IF ONLY OUR SHIP WAS THAT BIG, EH?
HMPH.
A SHIP'S WORTH AIN'T MEASURED BY HER SIZE!

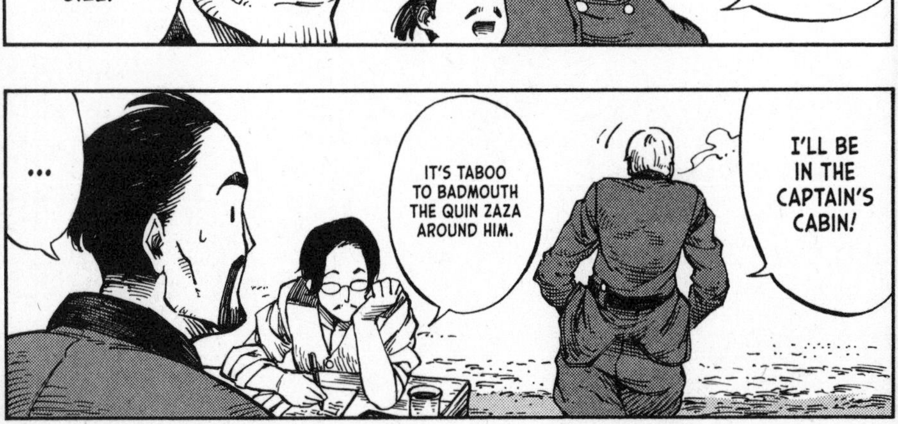
I'LL BE IN THE CAPTAIN'S CABIN!
IT'S TABOO TO BADMOUTH THE QUIN ZAZA AROUND HIM.
...

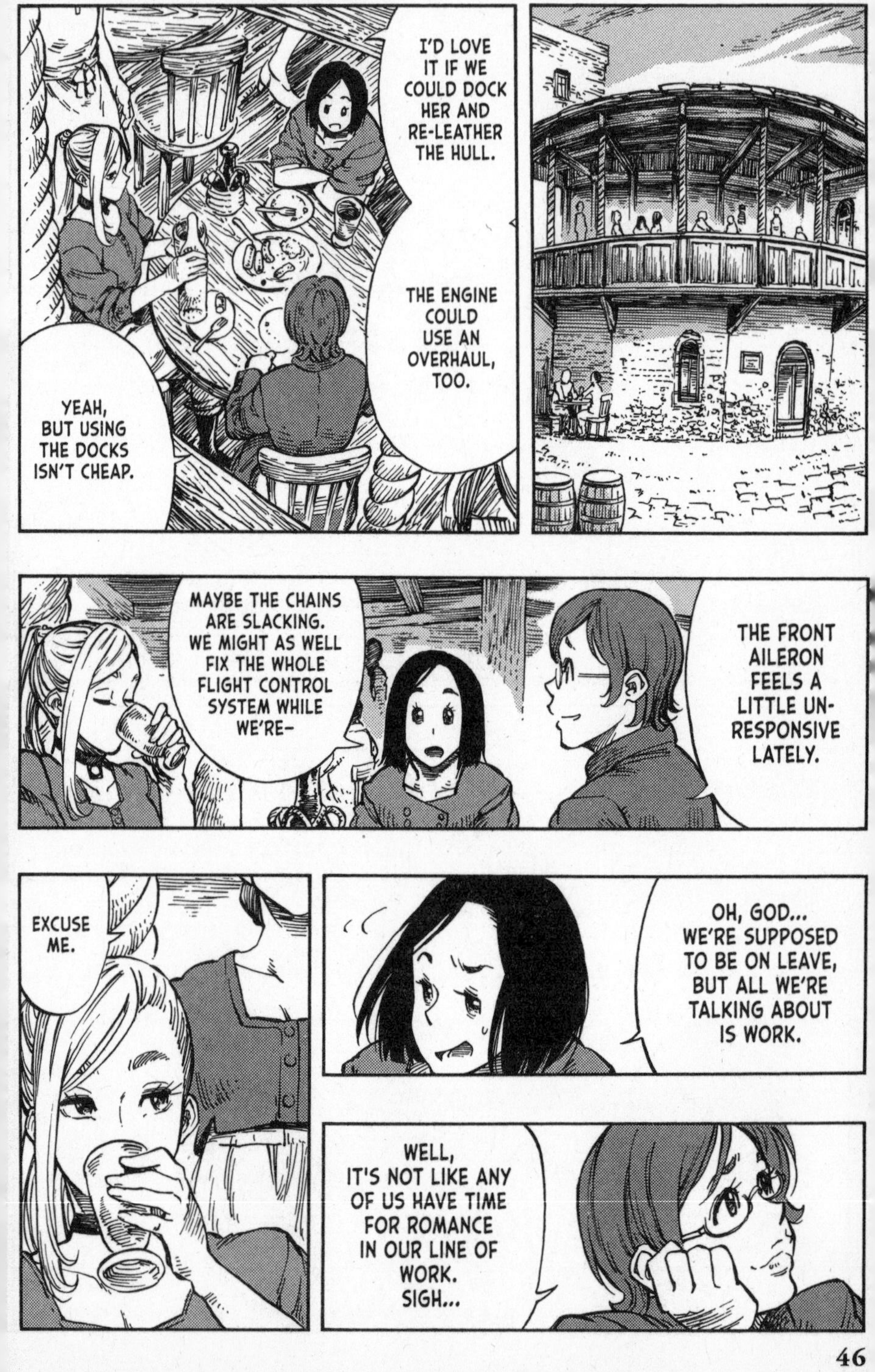
I'D LOVE IT IF WE COULD DOCK HER AND RE-LEATHER THE HULL.
THE ENGINE COULD USE AN OVERHAUL, TOO.
YEAH, BUT USING THE DOCKS ISN'T CHEAP.
THE FRONT AILERON FEELS A LITTLE UN-RESPONSIVE LATELY.
MAYBE THE CHAINS ARE SLACKING. WE MIGHT AS WELL FIX THE WHOLE FLIGHT CONTROL SYSTEM WHILE WE'RE–
OH, GOD... WE'RE SUPPOSED TO BE ON LEAVE, BUT ALL WE'RE TALKING ABOUT IS WORK.
WELL, IT'S NOT LIKE ANY OF US HAVE TIME FOR ROMANCE IN OUR LINE OF WORK. SIGH...
EXCUSE ME.

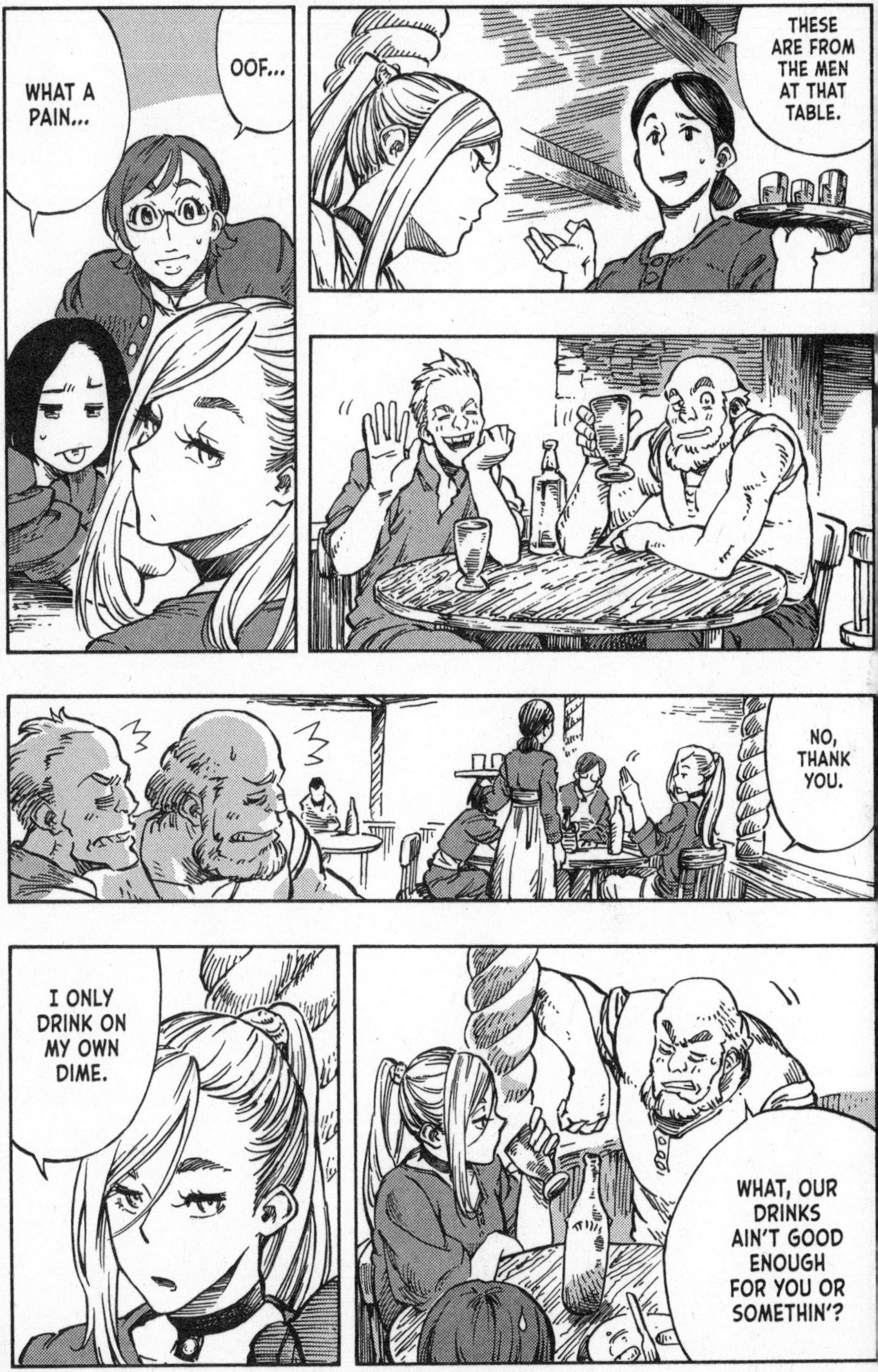

WHAT A PAIN...
OOF...
THESE ARE FROM THE MEN AT THAT TABLE.
NO, THANK YOU.
I ONLY DRINK ON MY OWN DIME.
WHAT, OUR DRINKS AIN'T GOOD ENOUGH FOR YOU OR SOMETHIN'?

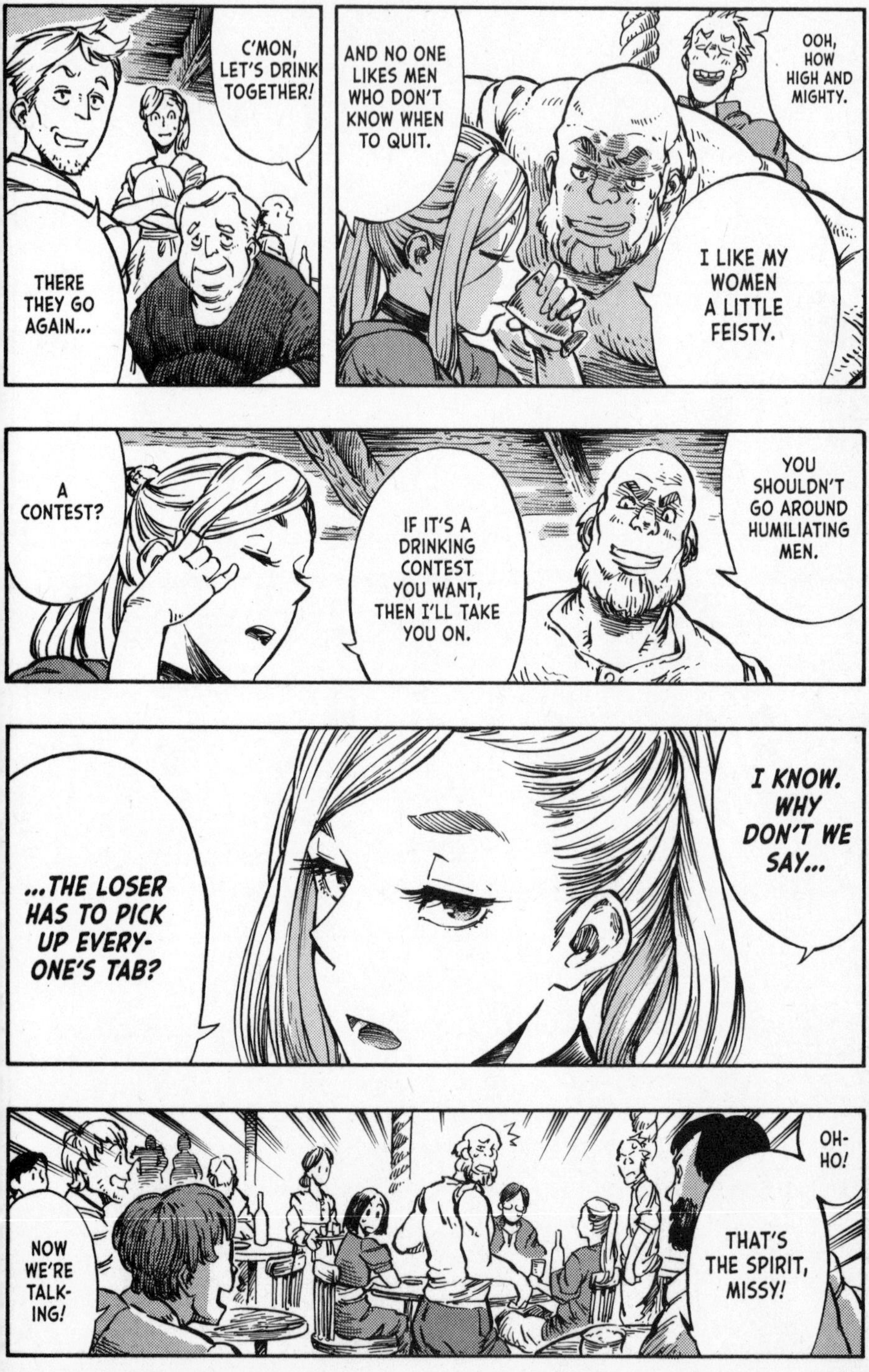
OOH, HOW HIGH AND MIGHTY.
I LIKE MY WOMEN A LITTLE FEISTY.
AND NO ONE LIKES MEN WHO DON'T KNOW WHEN TO QUIT.
C'MON, LET'S DRINK TOGETHER!
THERE THEY GO AGAIN...
YOU SHOULDN'T GO AROUND HUMILIATING MEN.
IF IT'S A DRINKING CONTEST YOU WANT, THEN I'LL TAKE YOU ON.
A CONTEST?
I KNOW. WHY DON'T WE SAY...
...THE LOSER HAS TO PICK UP EVERY-ONE'S TAB?
OH-HO!
THAT'S THE SPIRIT, MISSY!
NOW WE'RE TALK-ING!

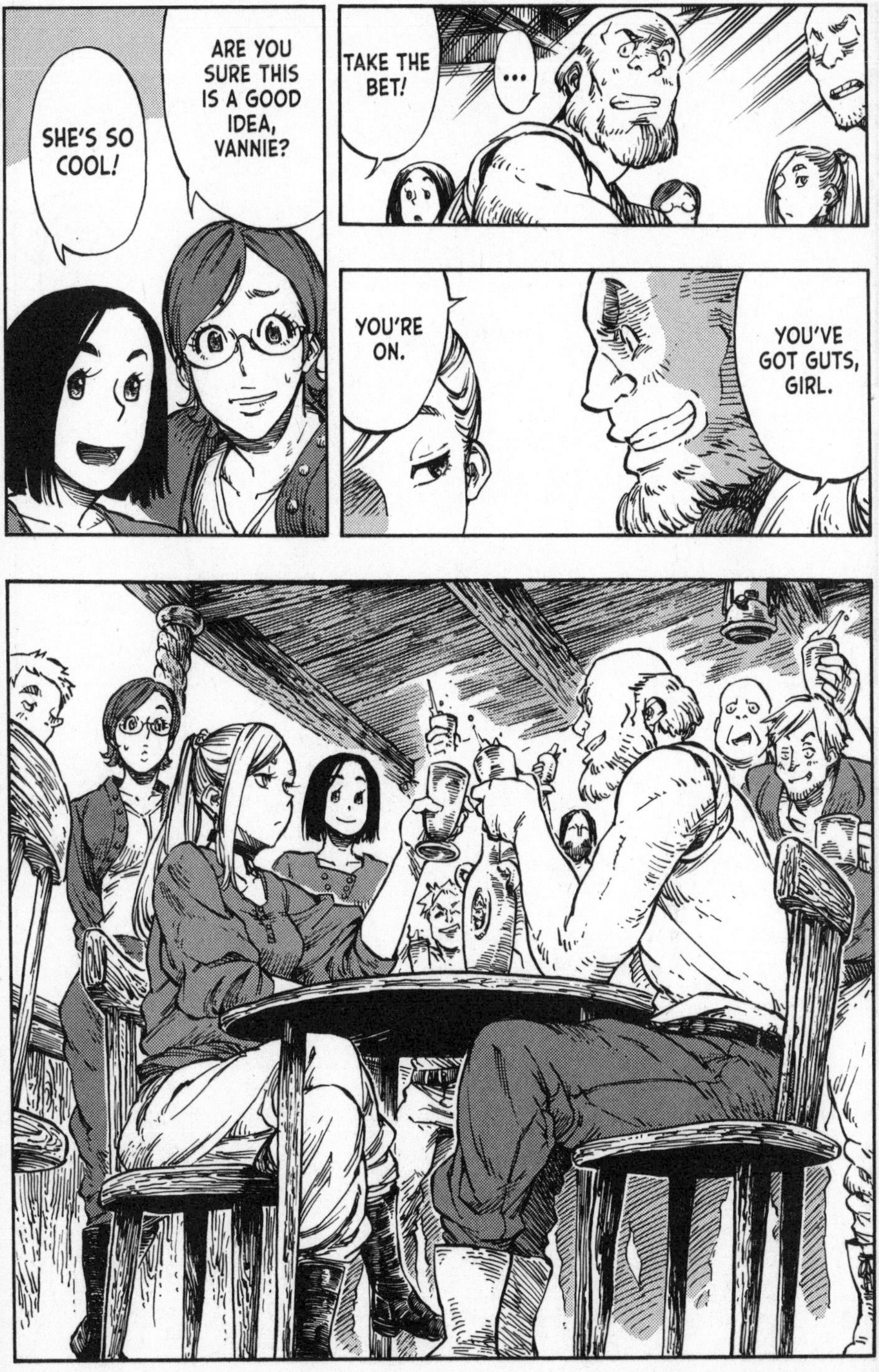
...
TAKE THE BET!
YOU'VE GOT GUTS, GIRL.
YOU'RE ON.
ARE YOU SURE THIS IS A GOOD IDEA, VANNIE?
SHE'S SO COOL!

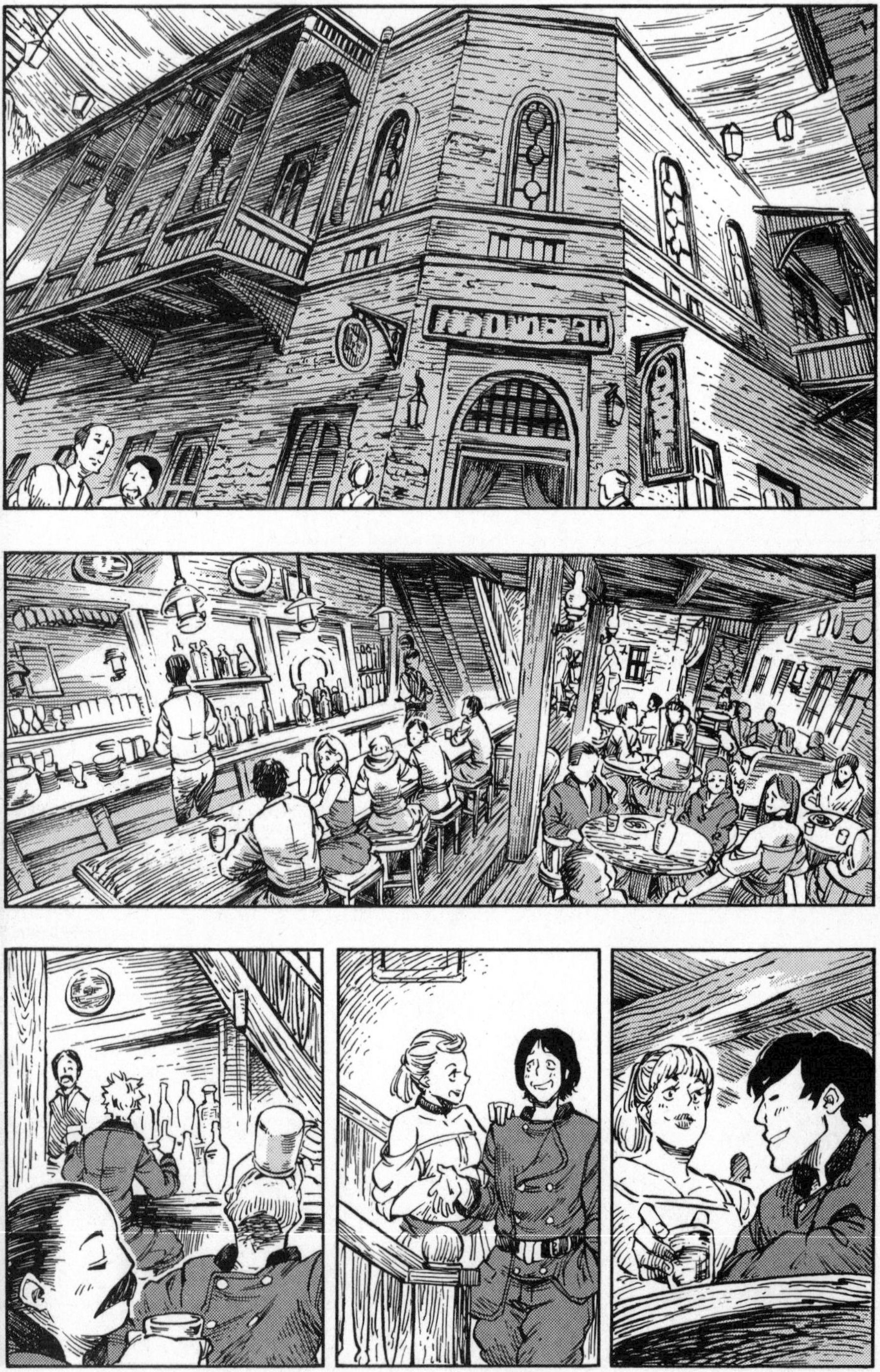

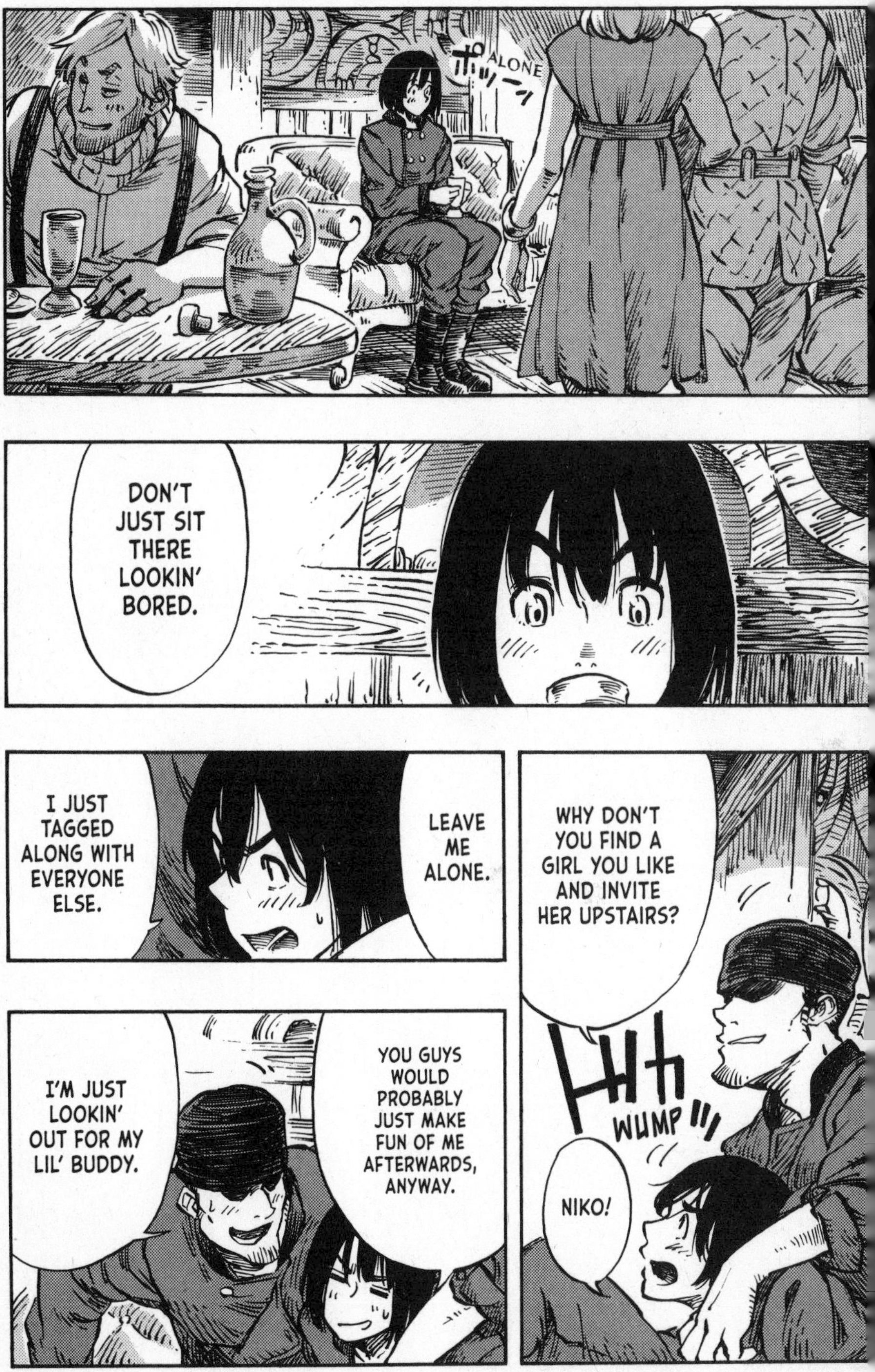
ALONE
DON'T JUST SIT THERE LOOKIN' BORED.
WHY DON'T YOU FIND A GIRL YOU LIKE AND INVITE HER UPSTAIRS?
WUMP
NIKO!
LEAVE ME ALONE.
I JUST TAGGED ALONG WITH EVERYONE ELSE.
YOU GUYS WOULD PROBABLY JUST MAKE FUN OF ME AFTERWARDS, ANYWAY.
I'M JUST LOOKIN' OUT FOR MY LIL' BUDDY.

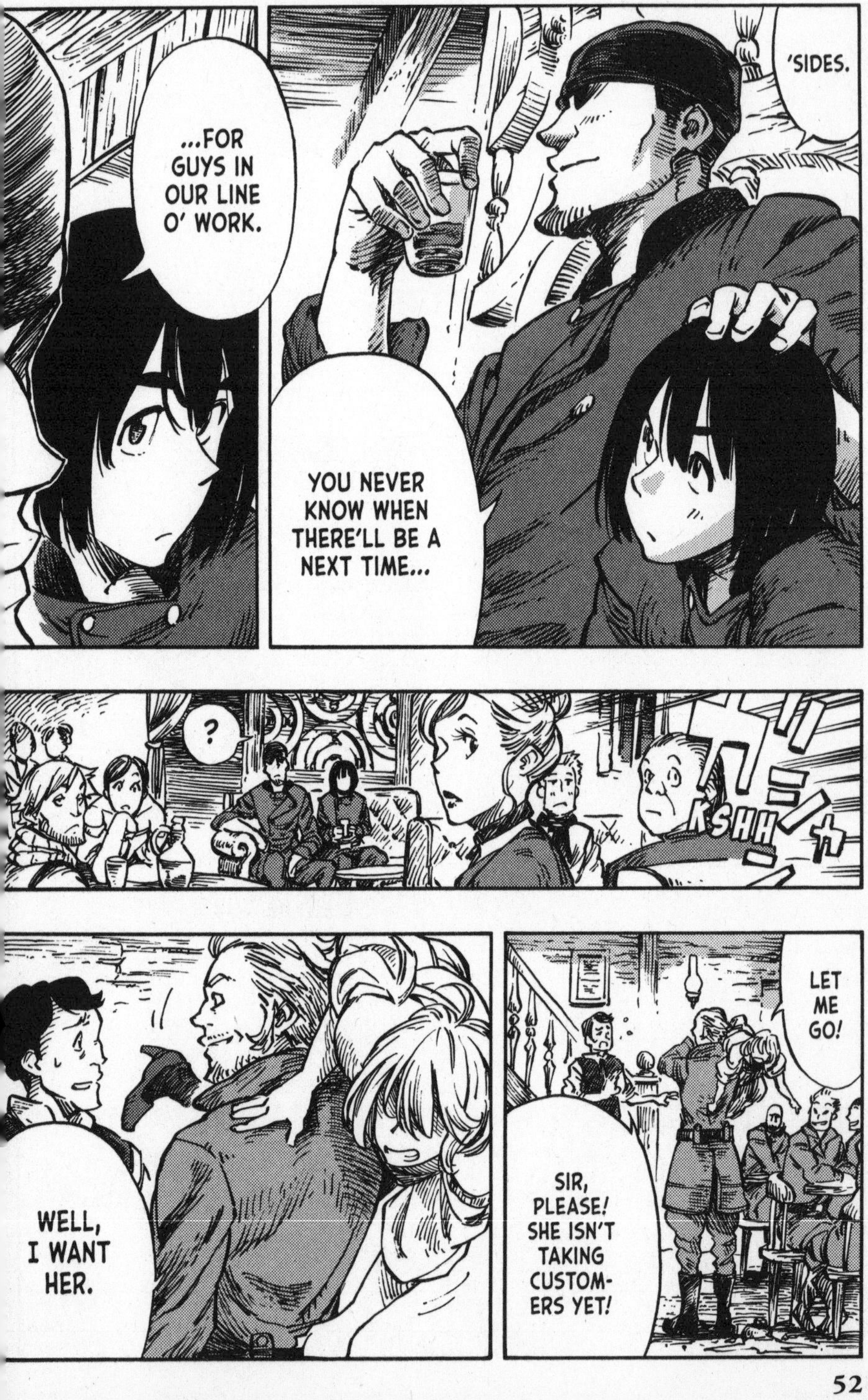
'SIDES.
YOU NEVER KNOW WHEN THERE'LL BE A NEXT TIME...
...FOR GUYS IN OUR LINE O' WORK.
?
KSHH
LET ME GO!
SIR, PLEASE! SHE ISN'T TAKING CUSTOM-ERS YET!
WELL, I WANT HER.

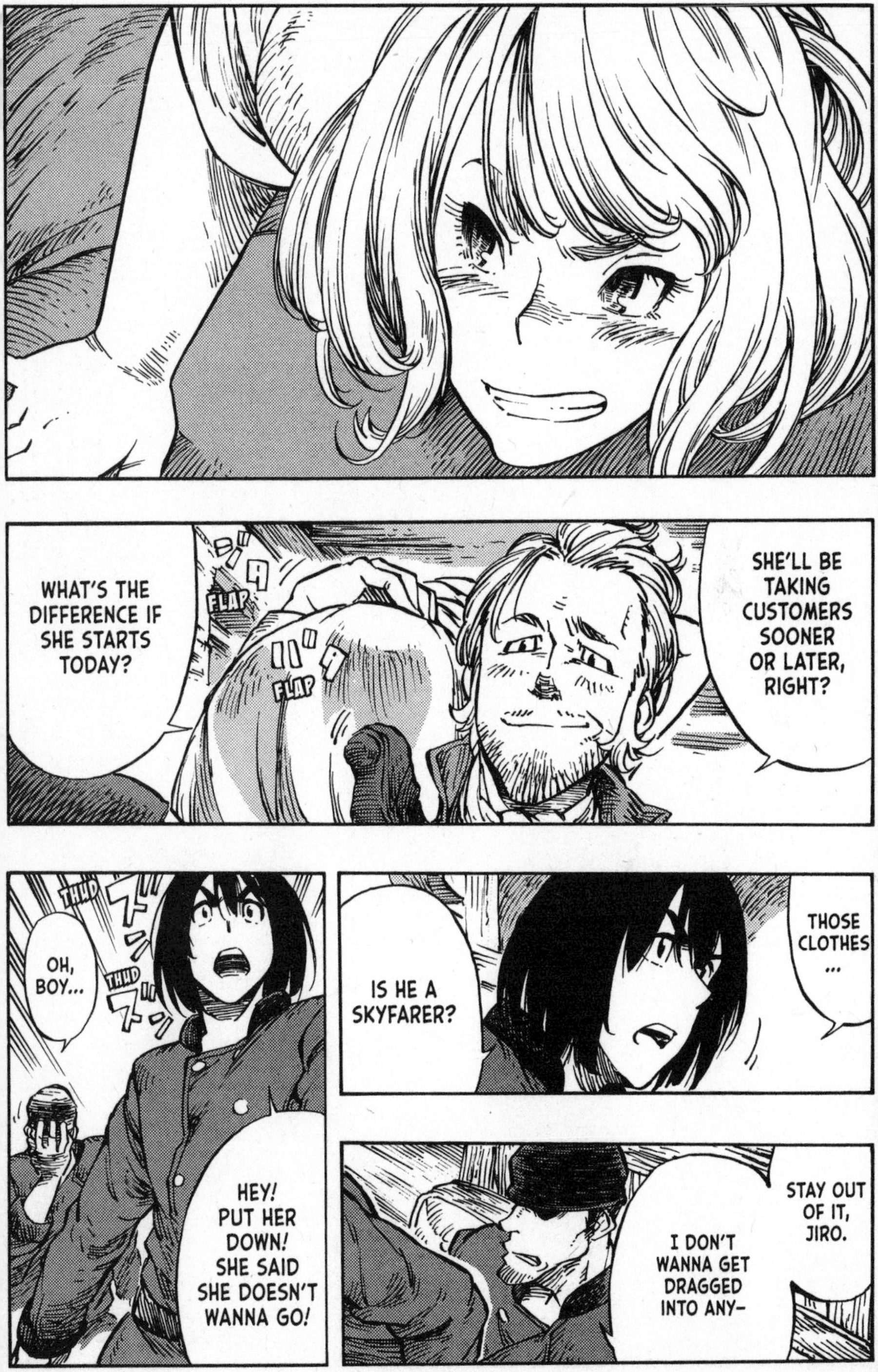
SHE'LL BE TAKING CUSTOMERS SOONER OR LATER, RIGHT?
FLAP
FLAP
WHAT'S THE DIFFERENCE IF SHE STARTS TODAY?
THOSE CLOTHES ...
IS HE A SKYFARER?
STAY OUT OF IT, JIRO.
I DON'T WANNA GET DRAGGED INTO ANY–
THUD
THUD
OH, BOY...
HEY! PUT HER DOWN! SHE SAID SHE DOESN'T WANNA GO!

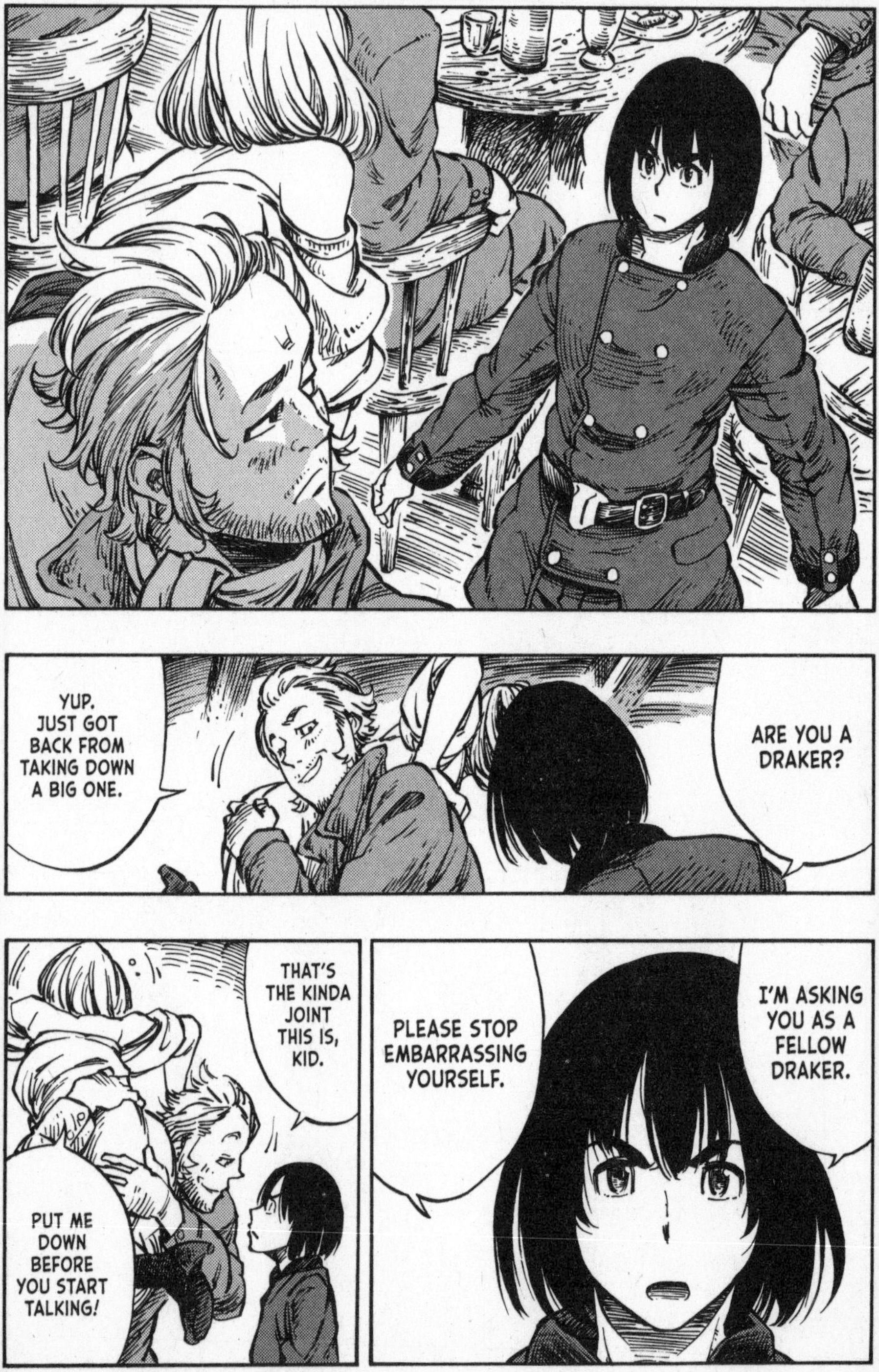
ARE YOU A DRAKER?
YUP. JUST GOT BACK FROM TAKING DOWN A BIG ONE.
I'M ASKING YOU AS A FELLOW DRAKER.
PLEASE STOP EMBARRASSING YOURSELF.
THAT'S THE KINDA JOINT THIS IS, KID.
PUT ME DOWN BEFORE YOU START TALKING!

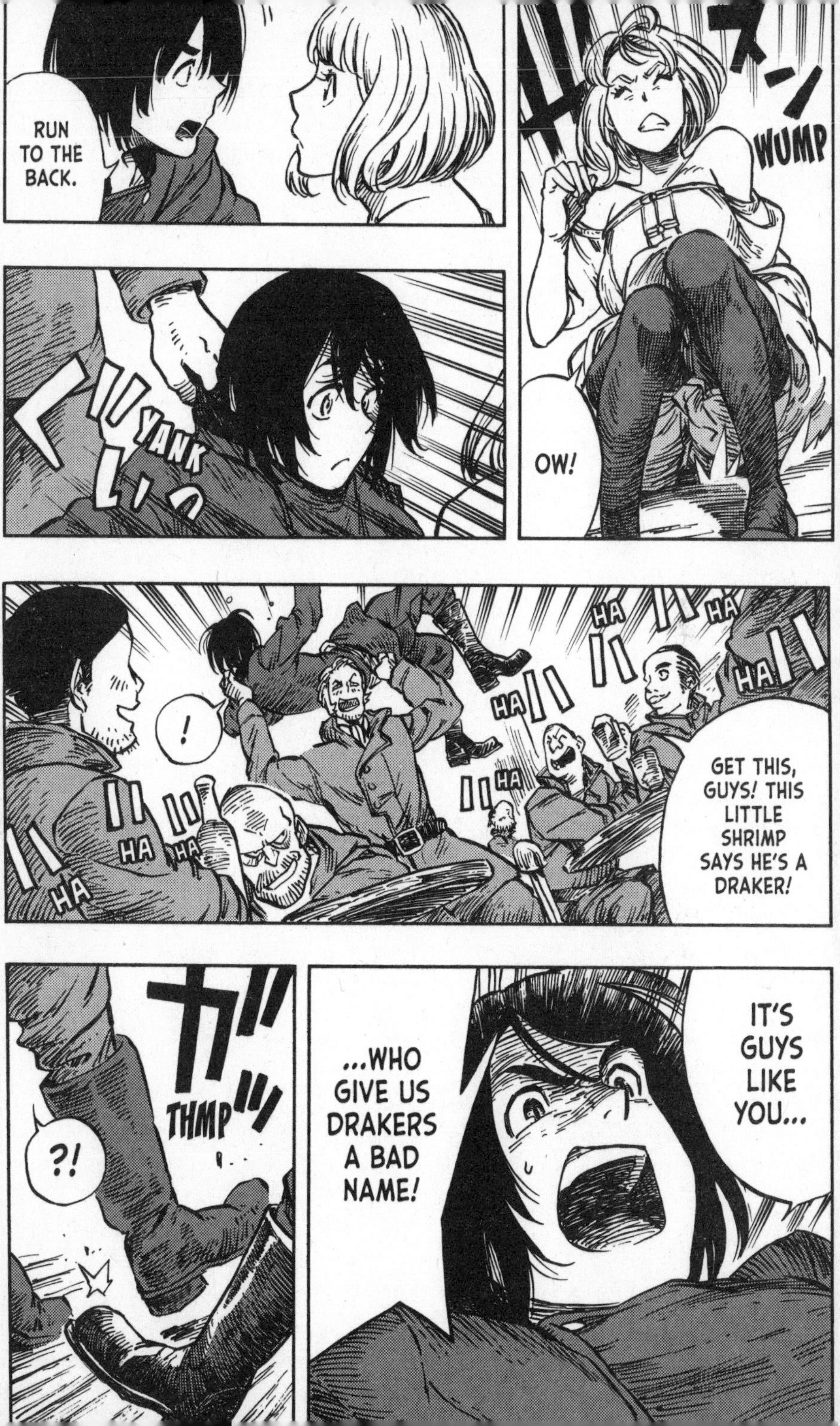
WUMP
OW!
RUN TO THE BACK.
YANK
GET THIS, GUYS! THIS LITTLE SHRIMP SAYS HE'S A DRAKER!
HA HA
HA
HA
HA
HA HA
HA
!
IT'S GUYS LIKE YOU...
...WHO GIVE US DRAKERS A BAD NAME!
THMP
?!

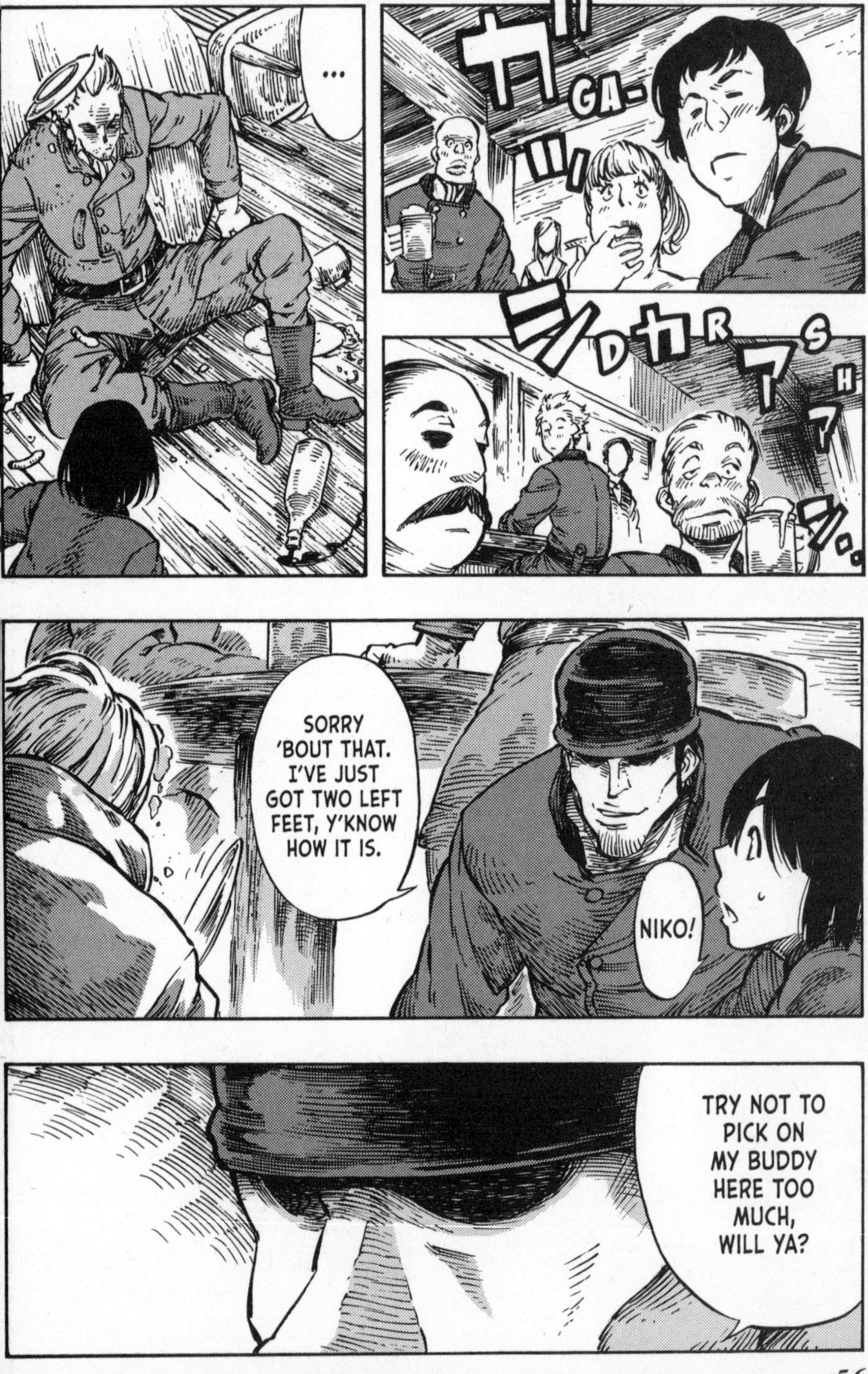
GA-
DRSH
...
SORRY 'BOUT THAT. I'VE JUST GOT TWO LEFT FEET, Y'KNOW HOW IT IS.
NIKO!
TRY NOT TO PICK ON MY BUDDY HERE TOO MUCH, WILL YA?

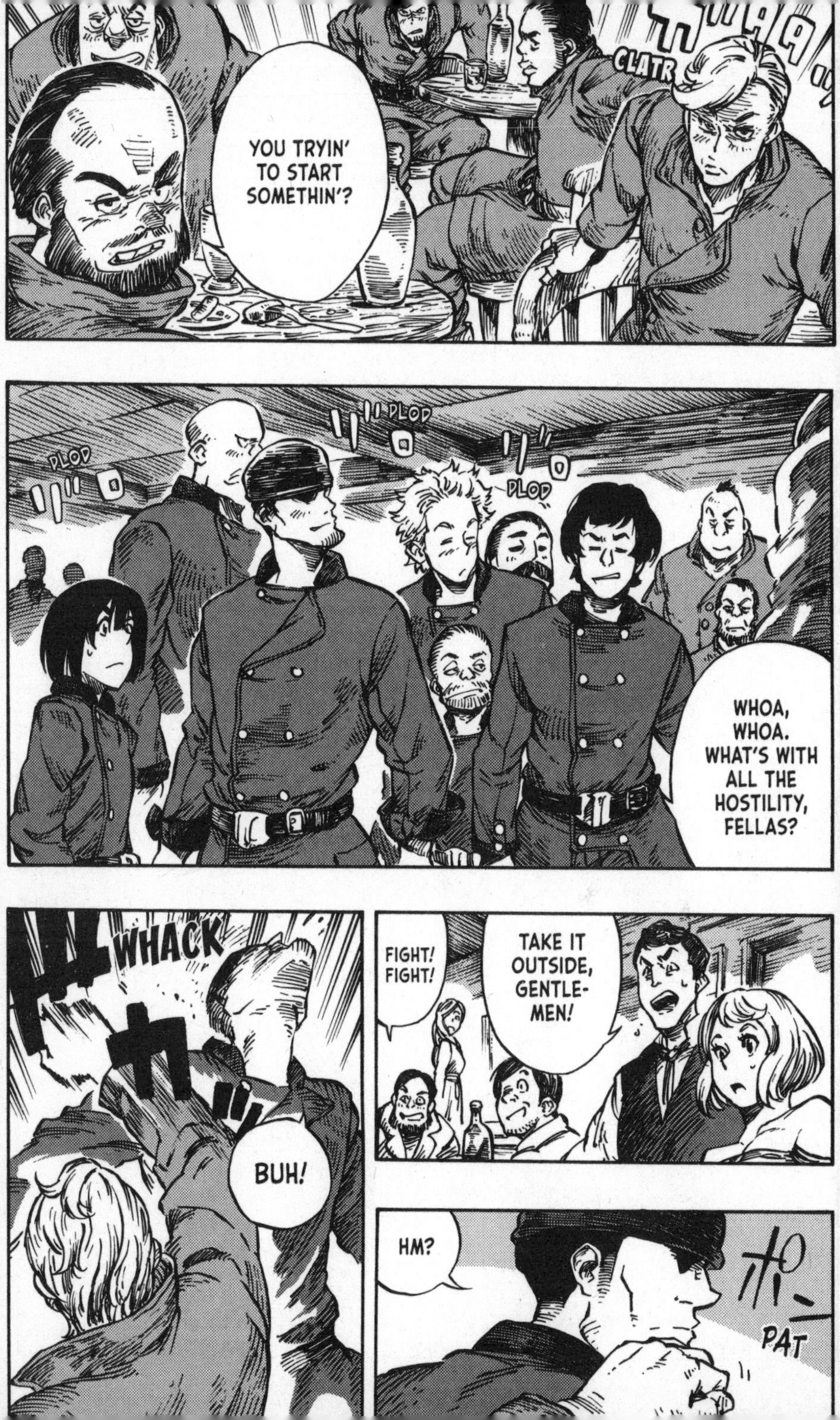
CLATR
YOU TRYIN' TO START SOMETHIN'?
PLOD
PLOD
PLOD
WHOA, WHOA. WHAT'S WITH ALL THE HOSTILITY, FELLAS?
TAKE IT OUTSIDE, GENTLE-MEN!
FIGHT! FIGHT!
HM?
PAT
WHACK
BUH!

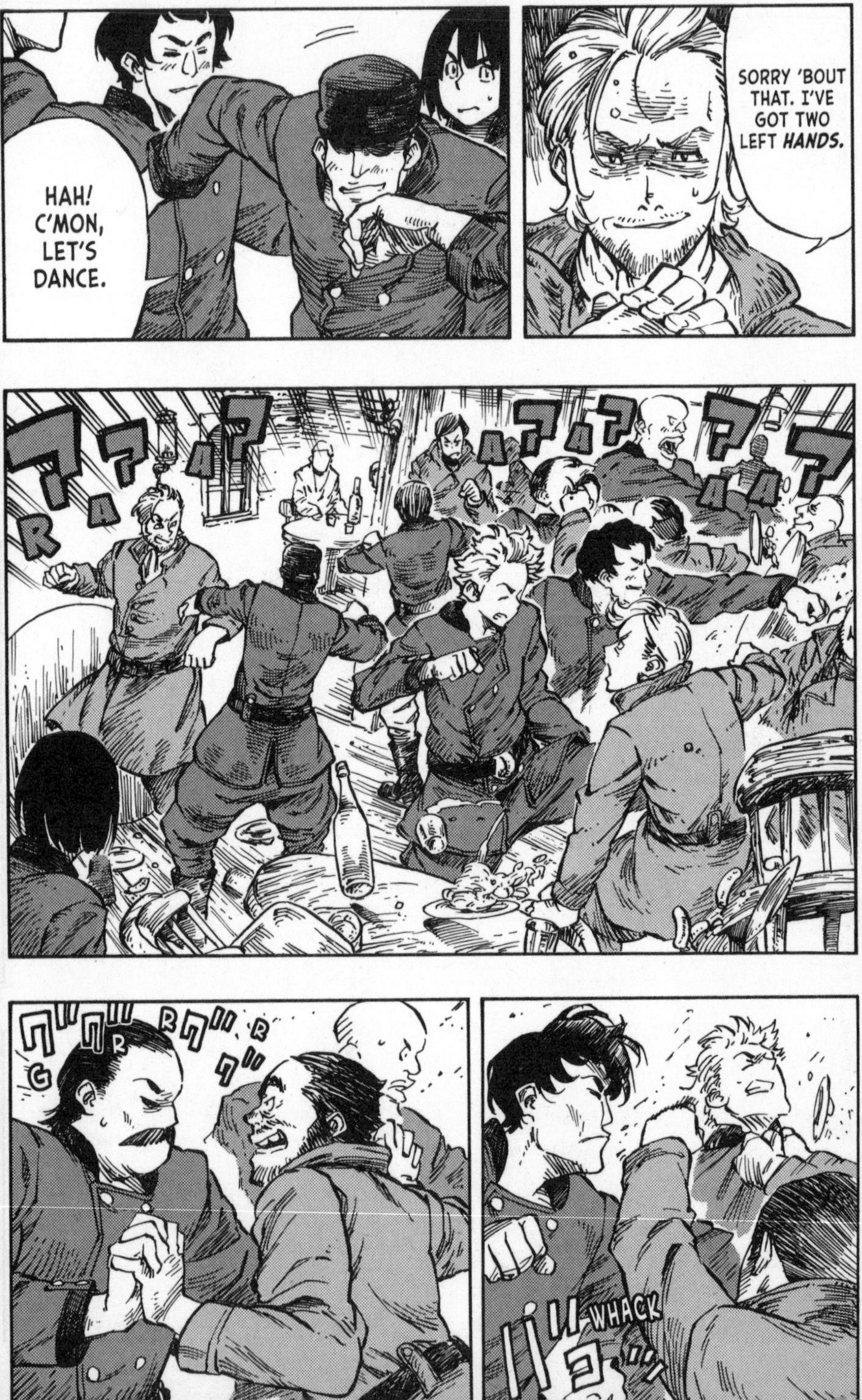
SORRY 'BOUT THAT. I'VE GOT TWO LEFT *HANDS.*
HAH! C'MON, LET'S DANCE.
WHACK

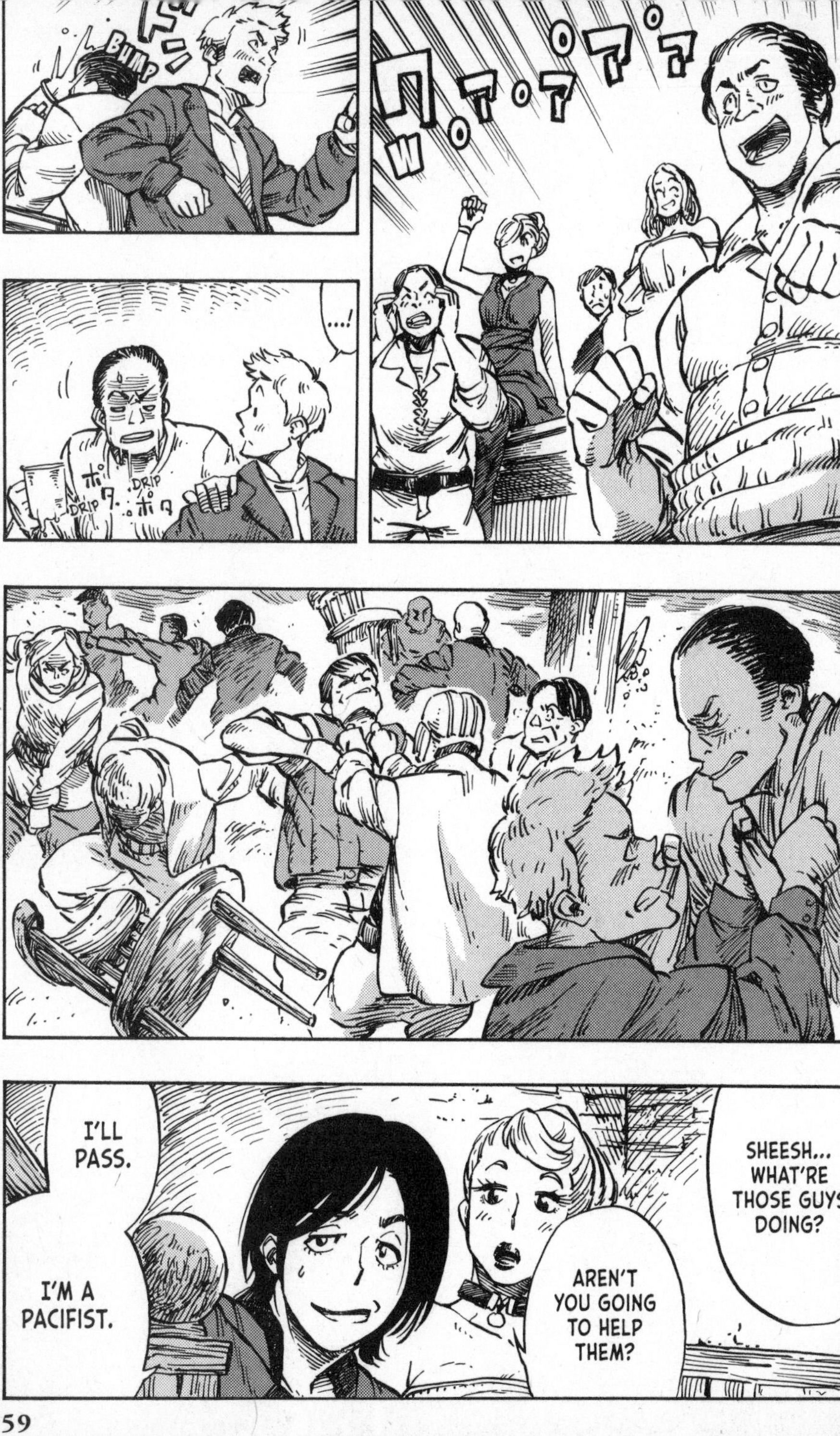
ワァァァァ
W
ドン
BUMP
...!
ポタ ポタ
DRIP DRIP
SHEESH... WHAT'RE THOSE GUYS DOING?
AREN'T YOU GOING TO HELP THEM?
I'LL PASS.
I'M A PACIFIST.

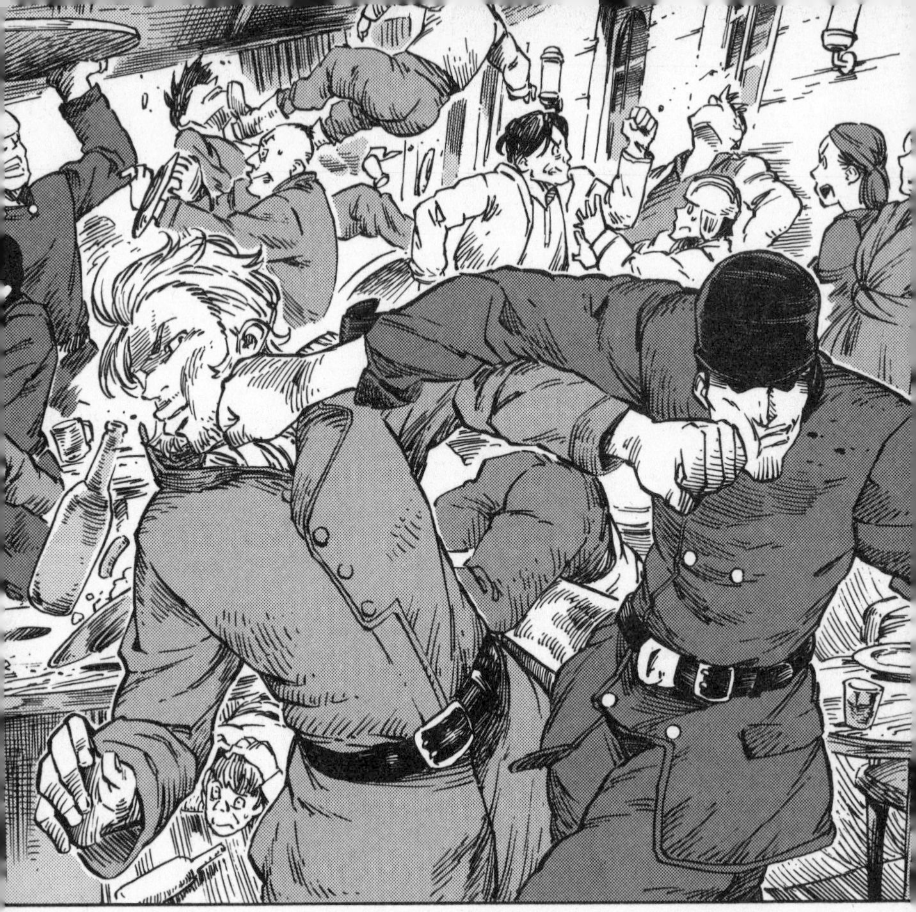

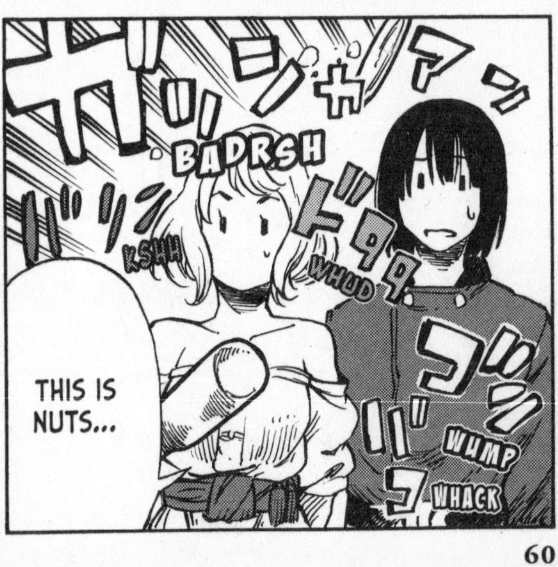
BADRSH
WHUD
KSHH
WHMP
WHACK
THIS IS NUTS...

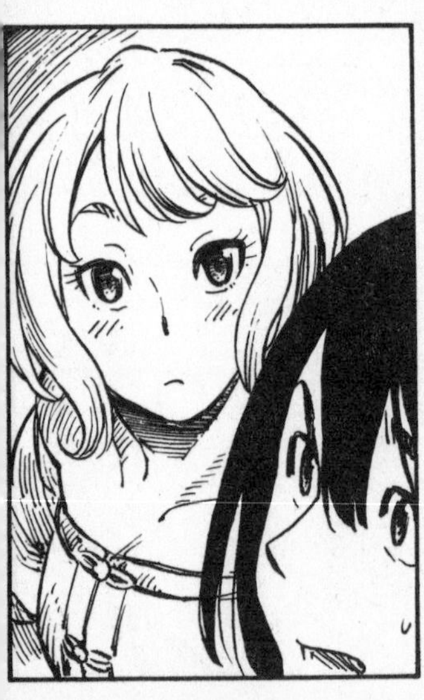

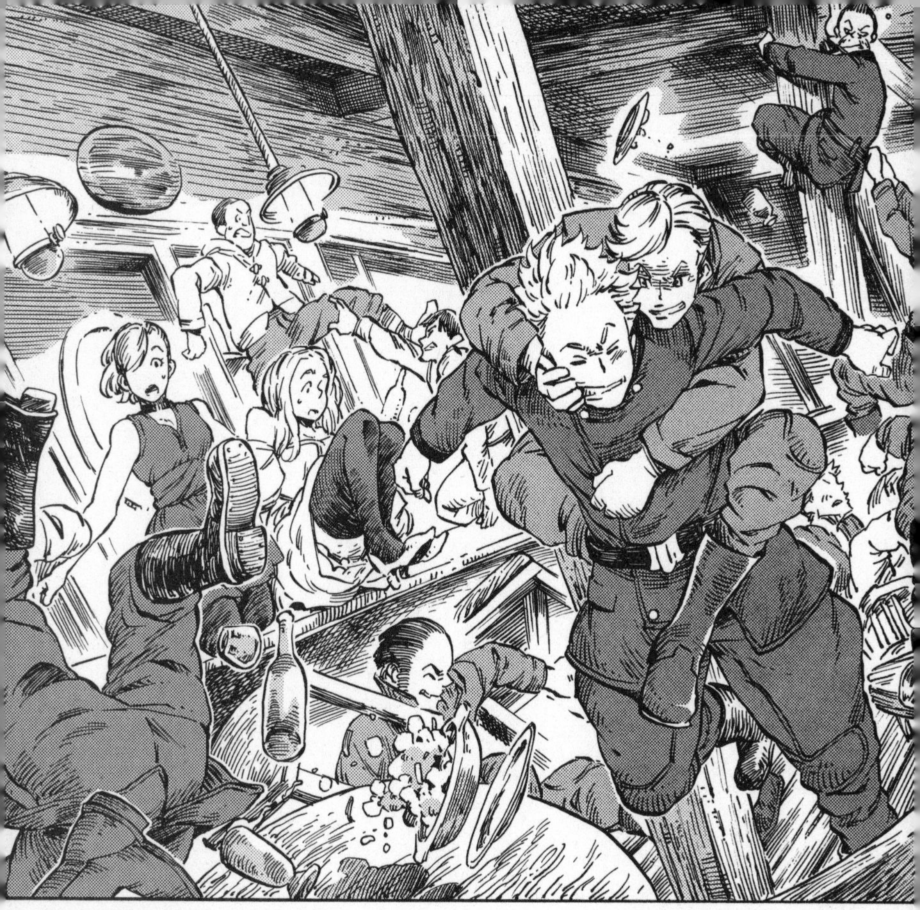

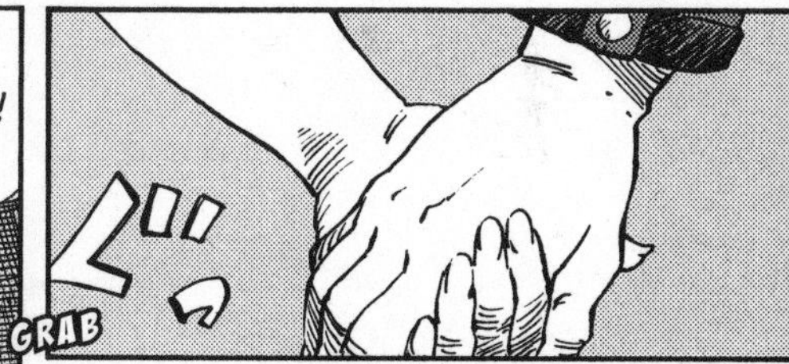
GRAB

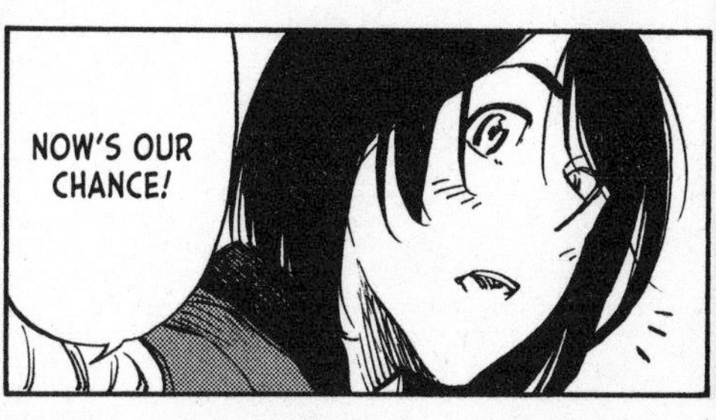
NOW'S OUR CHANCE!

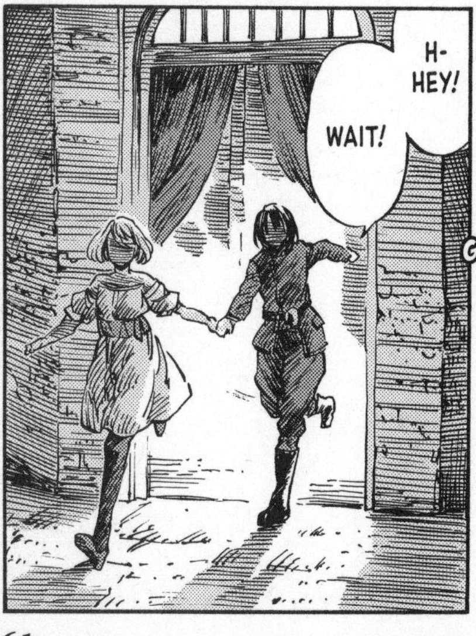
H- HEY!
WAIT!

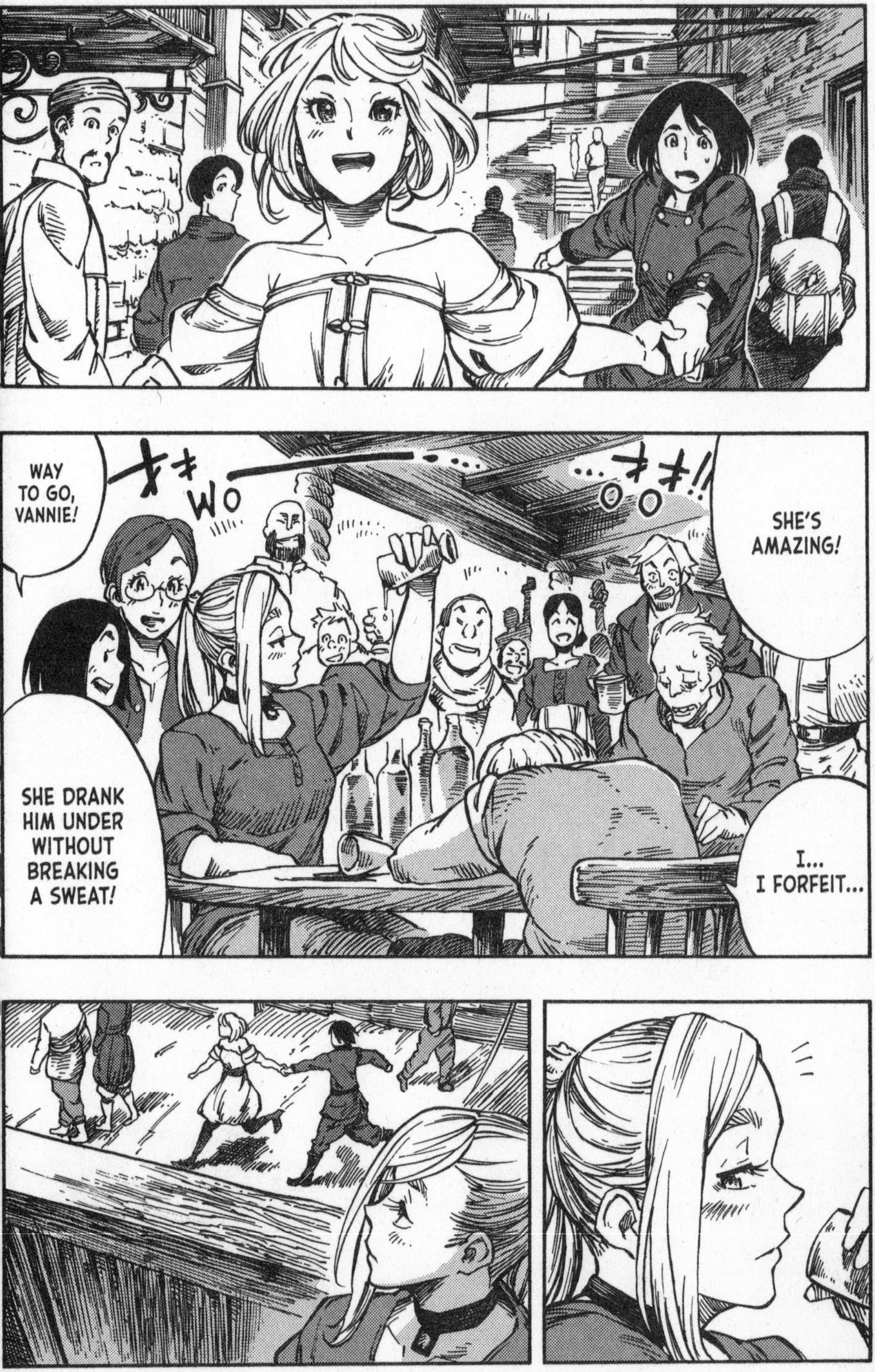
SHE'S AMAZING!
WO
WAY TO GO, VANNIE!
I... I FORFEIT...
SHE DRANK HIM UNDER WITHOUT BREAKING A SWEAT!

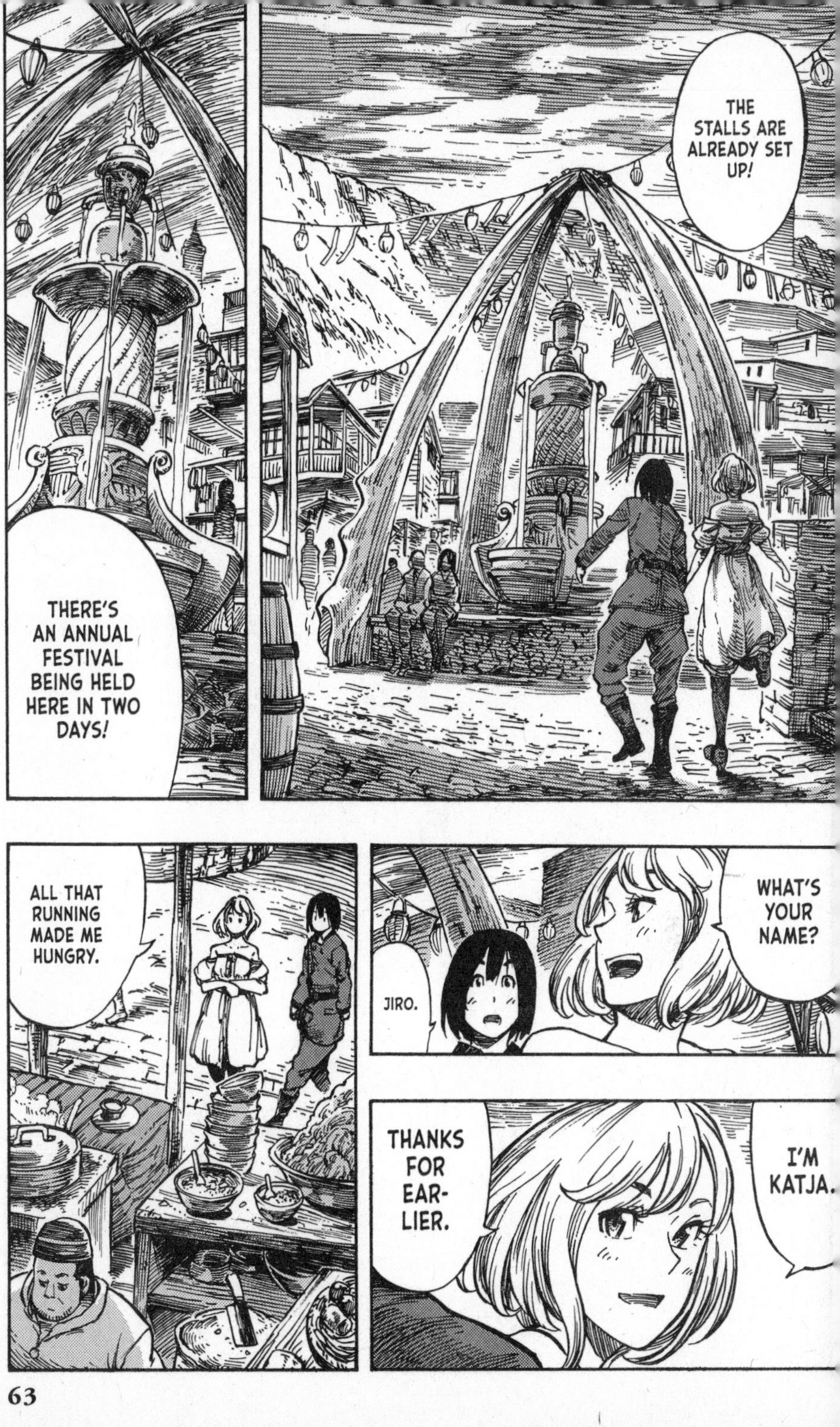
THE STALLS ARE ALREADY SET UP!
THERE'S AN ANNUAL FESTIVAL BEING HELD HERE IN TWO DAYS!
WHAT'S YOUR NAME?
JIRO.
I'M KATJA.
THANKS FOR EAR-LIER.
ALL THAT RUNNING MADE ME HUNGRY.

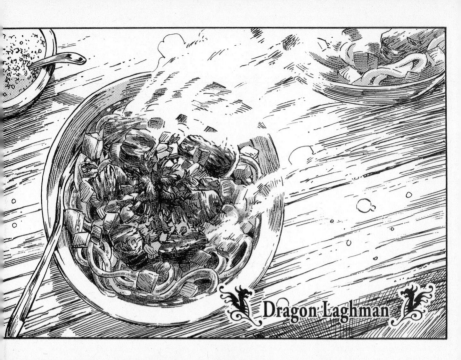

Dragon Laghman

I LIKE MINE WITH LOTS OF CRUSHED PEANUTS.

SHFF

パ
ラ
ラ

HEY, MISTER. IS IT OKAY IF WE EAT OVER THERE?

JUST MAKE SURE YOU BRING BACK THE DISHES.

64

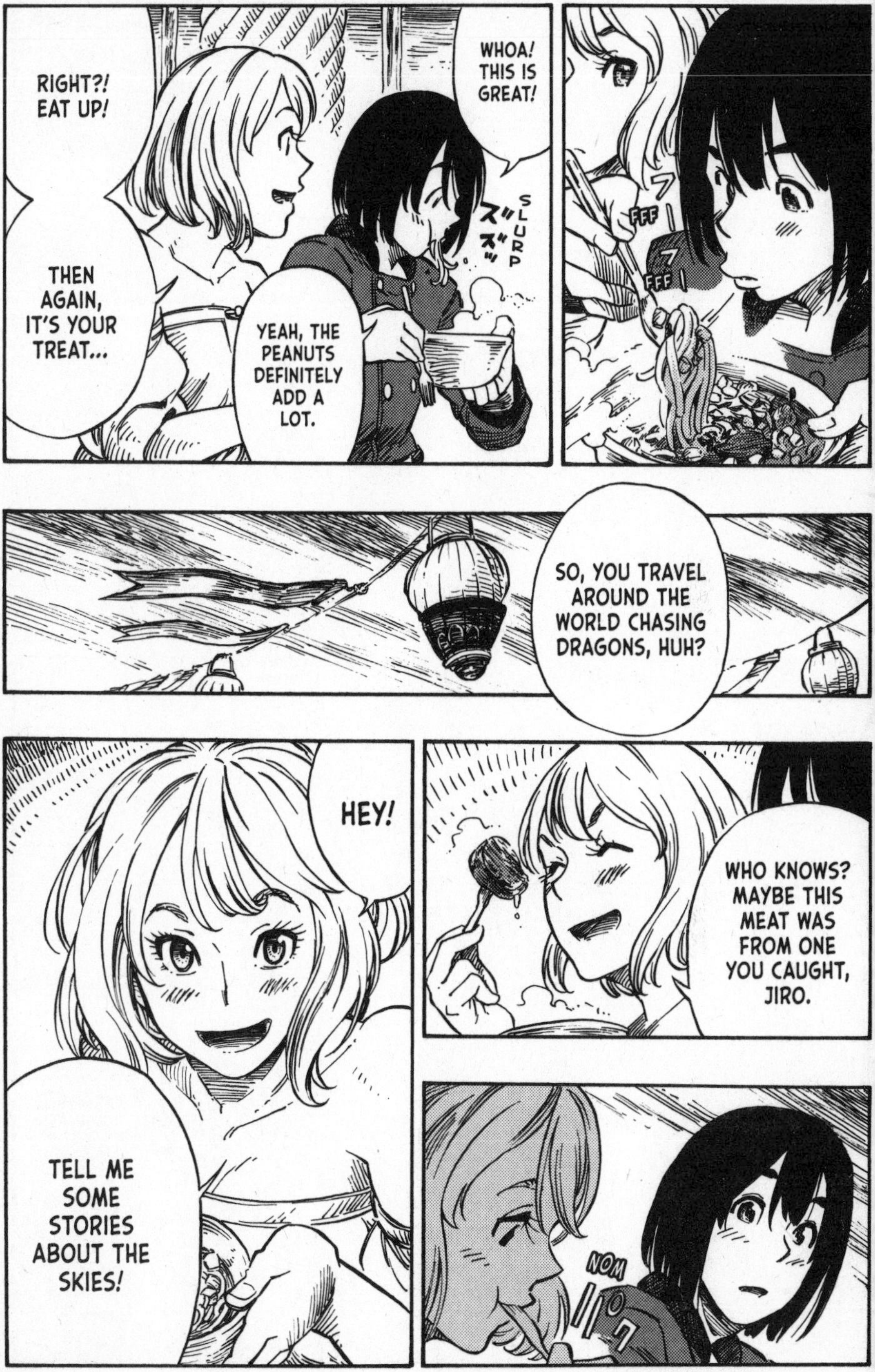
FFF
FFF
WHOA! THIS IS GREAT!
SLURP
RIGHT?! EAT UP!
YEAH, THE PEANUTS DEFINITELY ADD A LOT.
THEN AGAIN, IT'S YOUR TREAT...
SO, YOU TRAVEL AROUND THE WORLD CHASING DRAGONS, HUH?
WHO KNOWS? MAYBE THIS MEAT WAS FROM ONE YOU CAUGHT, JIRO.
NOM
HEY!
TELL ME SOME STORIES ABOUT THE SKIES!

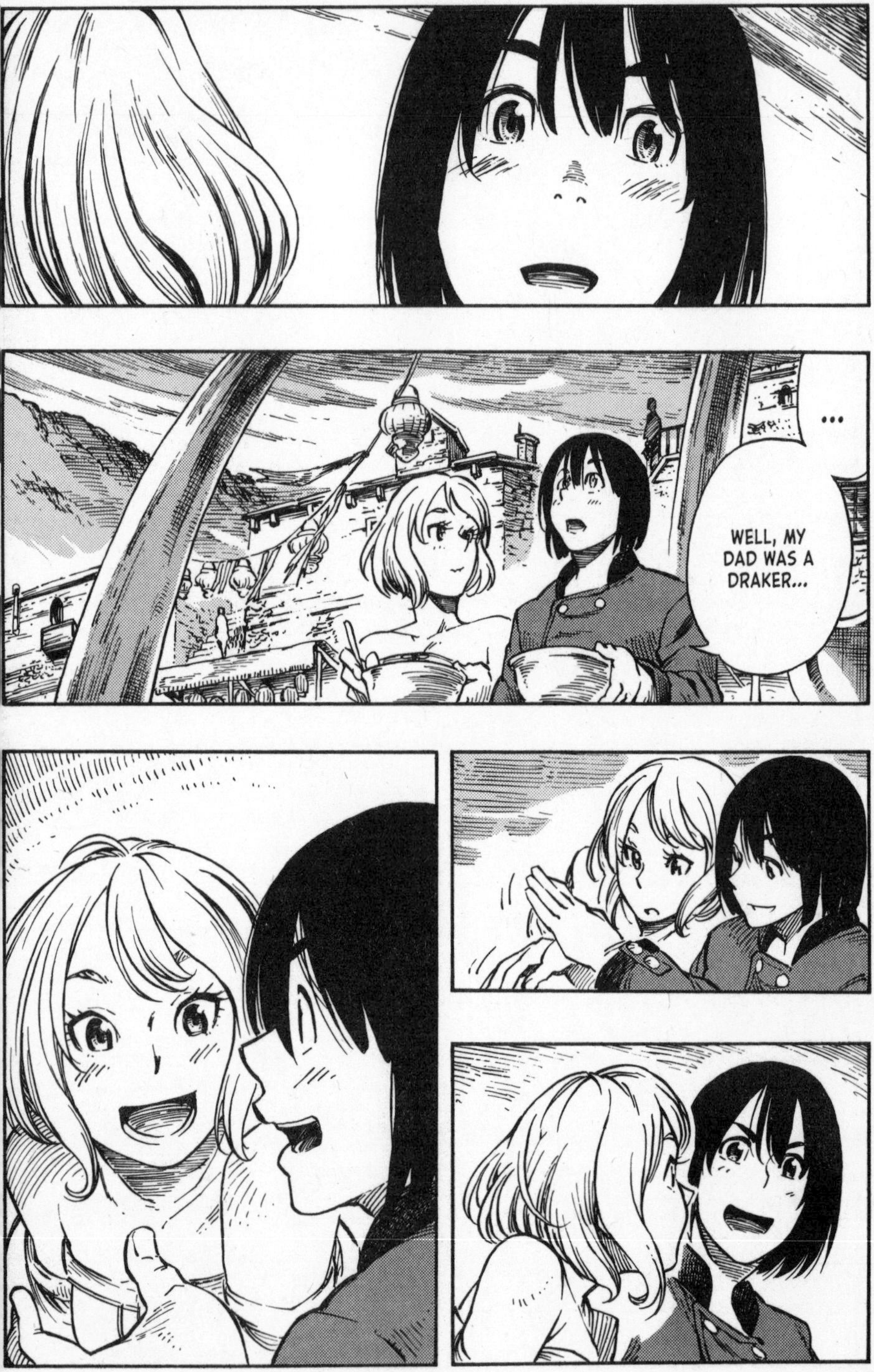
...
WELL, MY DAD WAS A DRAKER...

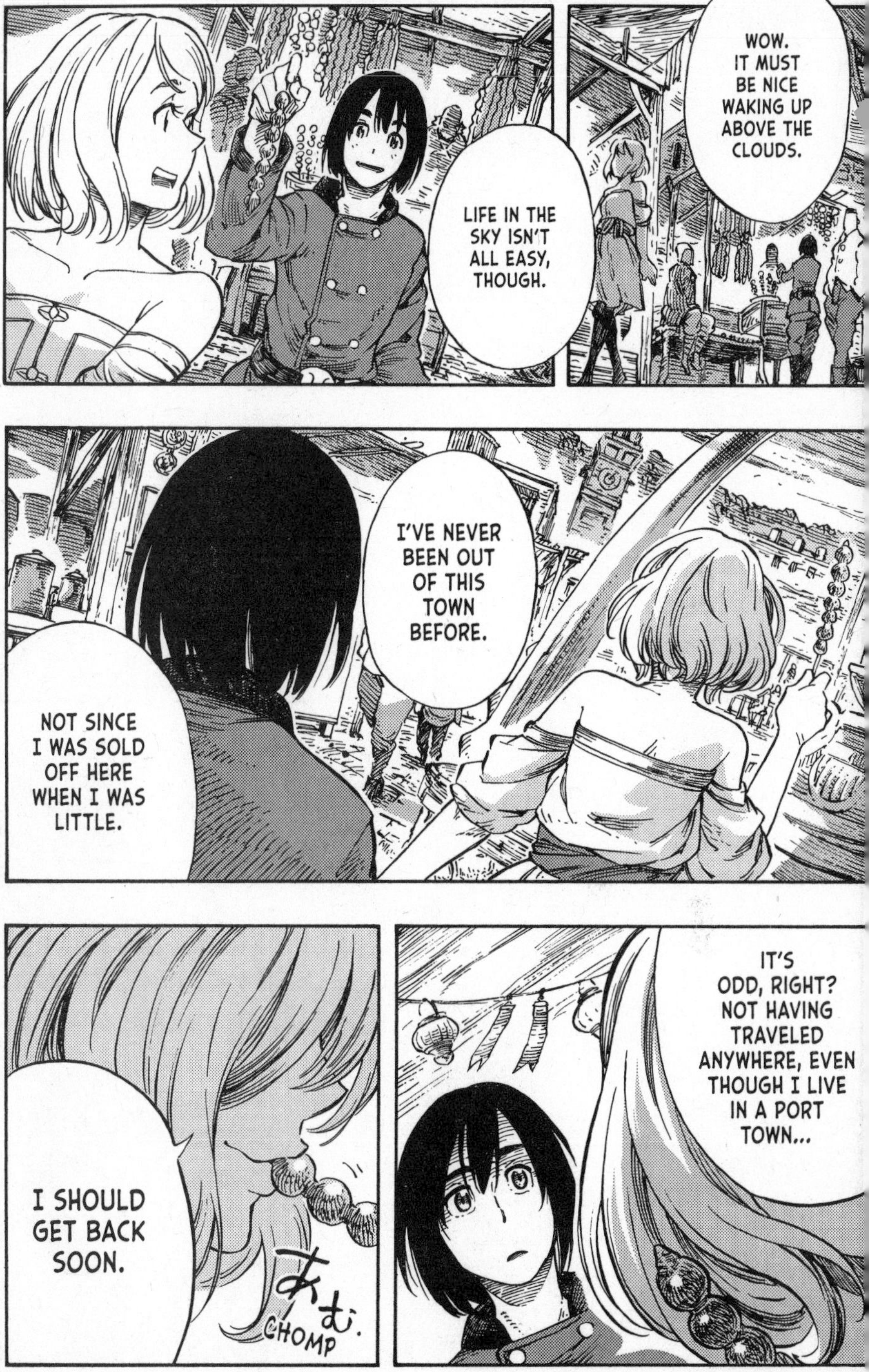
WOW. IT MUST BE NICE WAKING UP ABOVE THE CLOUDS.
LIFE IN THE SKY ISN'T ALL EASY, THOUGH.
I'VE NEVER BEEN OUT OF THIS TOWN BEFORE.
NOT SINCE I WAS SOLD OFF HERE WHEN I WAS LITTLE.
IT'S ODD, RIGHT? NOT HAVING TRAVELED ANYWHERE, EVEN THOUGH I LIVE IN A PORT TOWN...
I SHOULD GET BACK SOON.
あむ
CHOMP

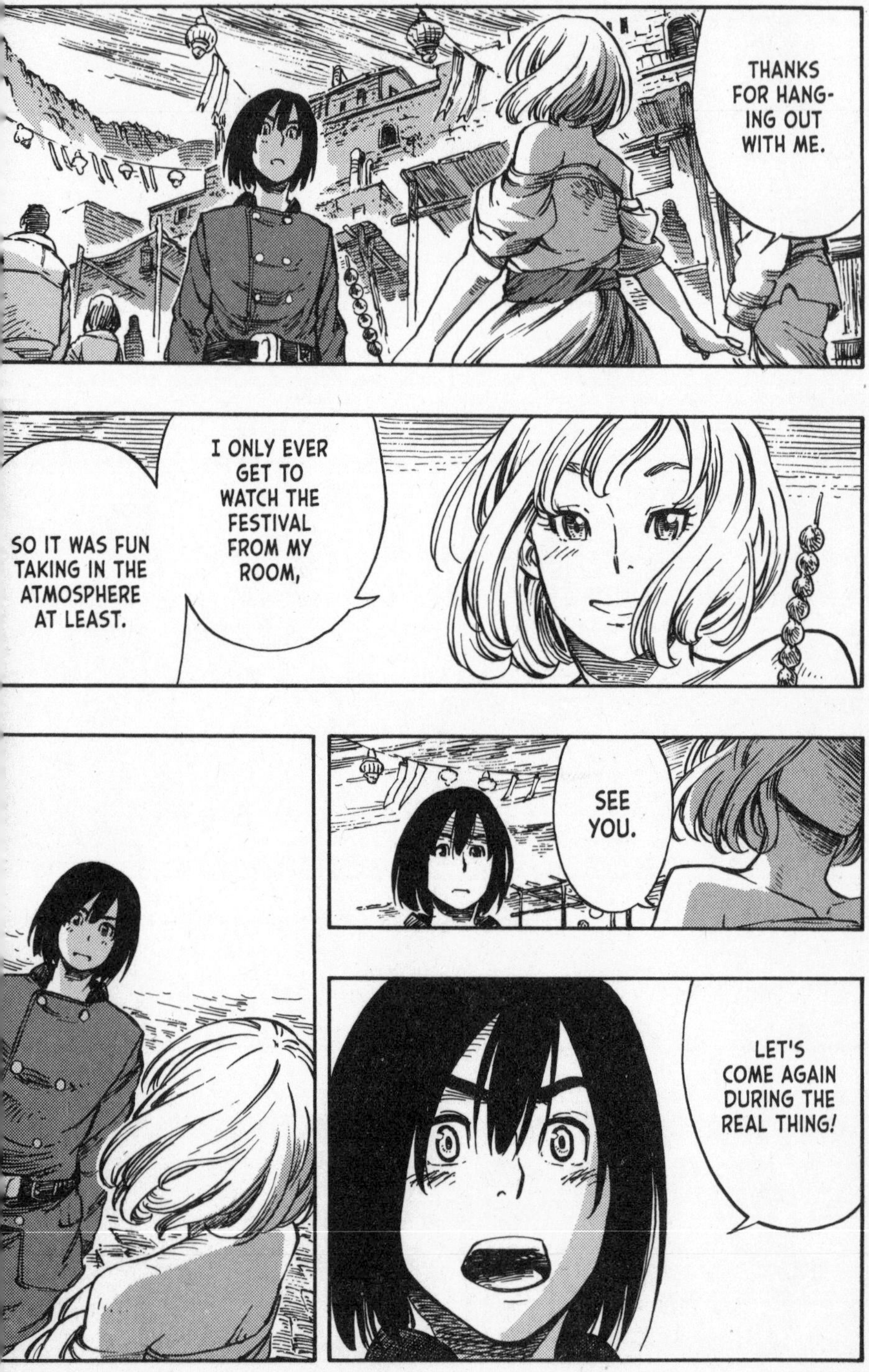
THANKS FOR HANG-ING OUT WITH ME.
I ONLY EVER GET TO WATCH THE FESTIVAL FROM MY ROOM,
SO IT WAS FUN TAKING IN THE ATMOSPHERE AT LEAST.
SEE YOU.
LET'S COME AGAIN DURING THE REAL THING!

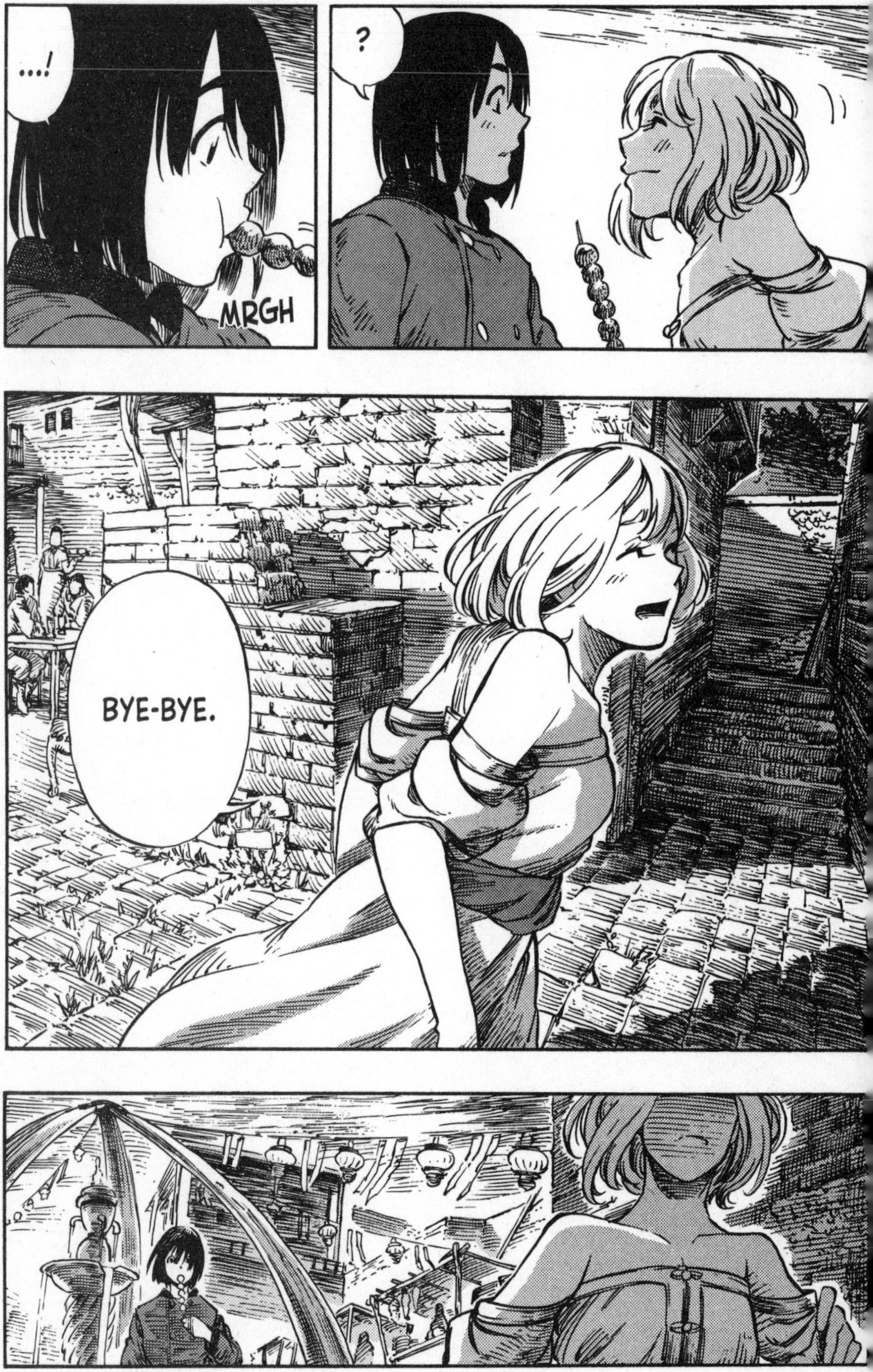
?
...!
MRGH
BYE-BYE.

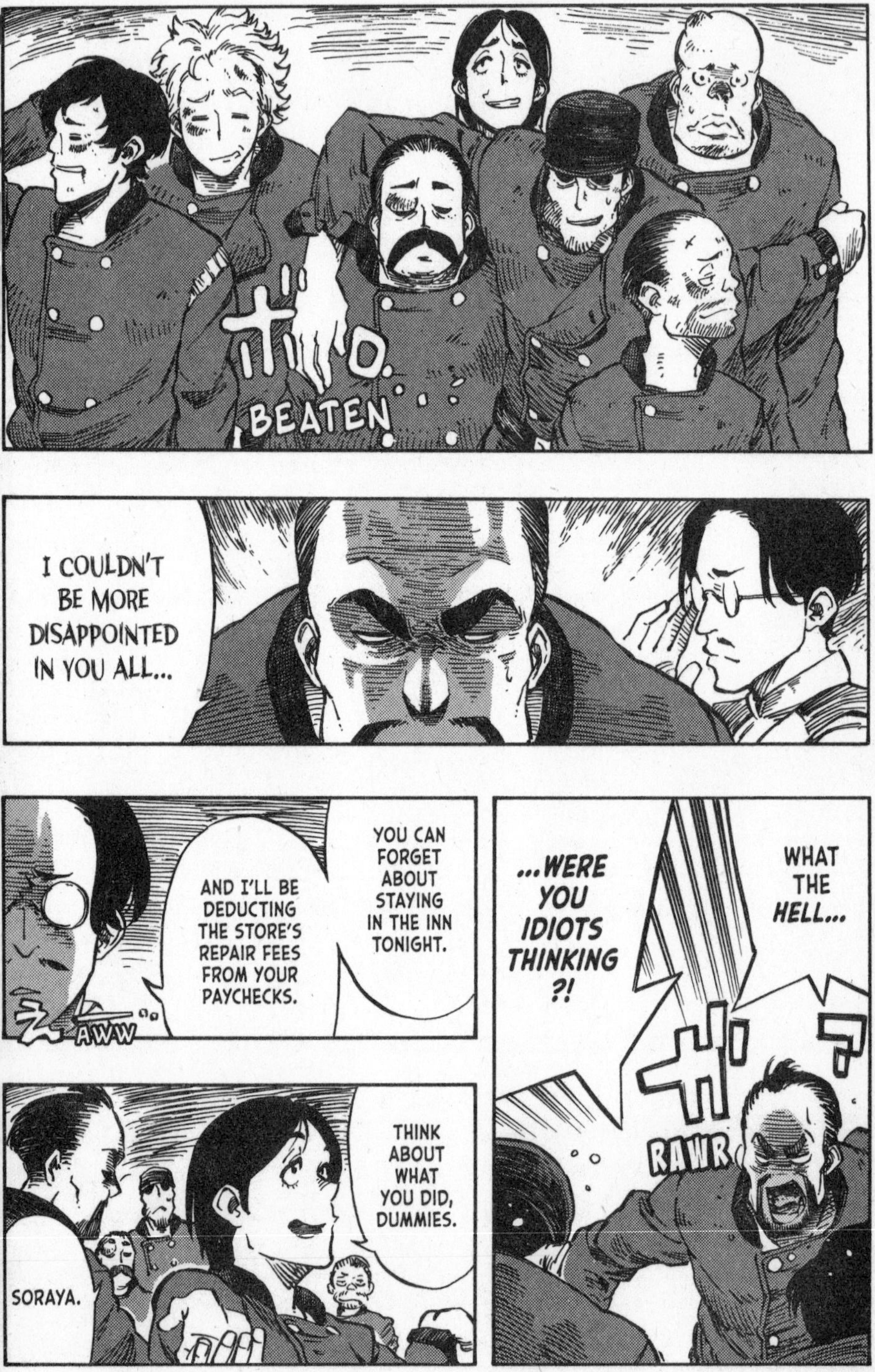
BEATEN
I COULDN'T BE MORE DISAPPOINTED IN YOU ALL...
WHAT THE HELL...
...WERE YOU IDIOTS THINKING?!
RAWR
YOU CAN FORGET ABOUT STAYING IN THE INN TONIGHT.
AND I'LL BE DEDUCTING THE STORE'S REPAIR FEES FROM YOUR PAYCHECKS.
AWW
THINK ABOUT WHAT YOU DID, DUMMIES.
SORAYA.

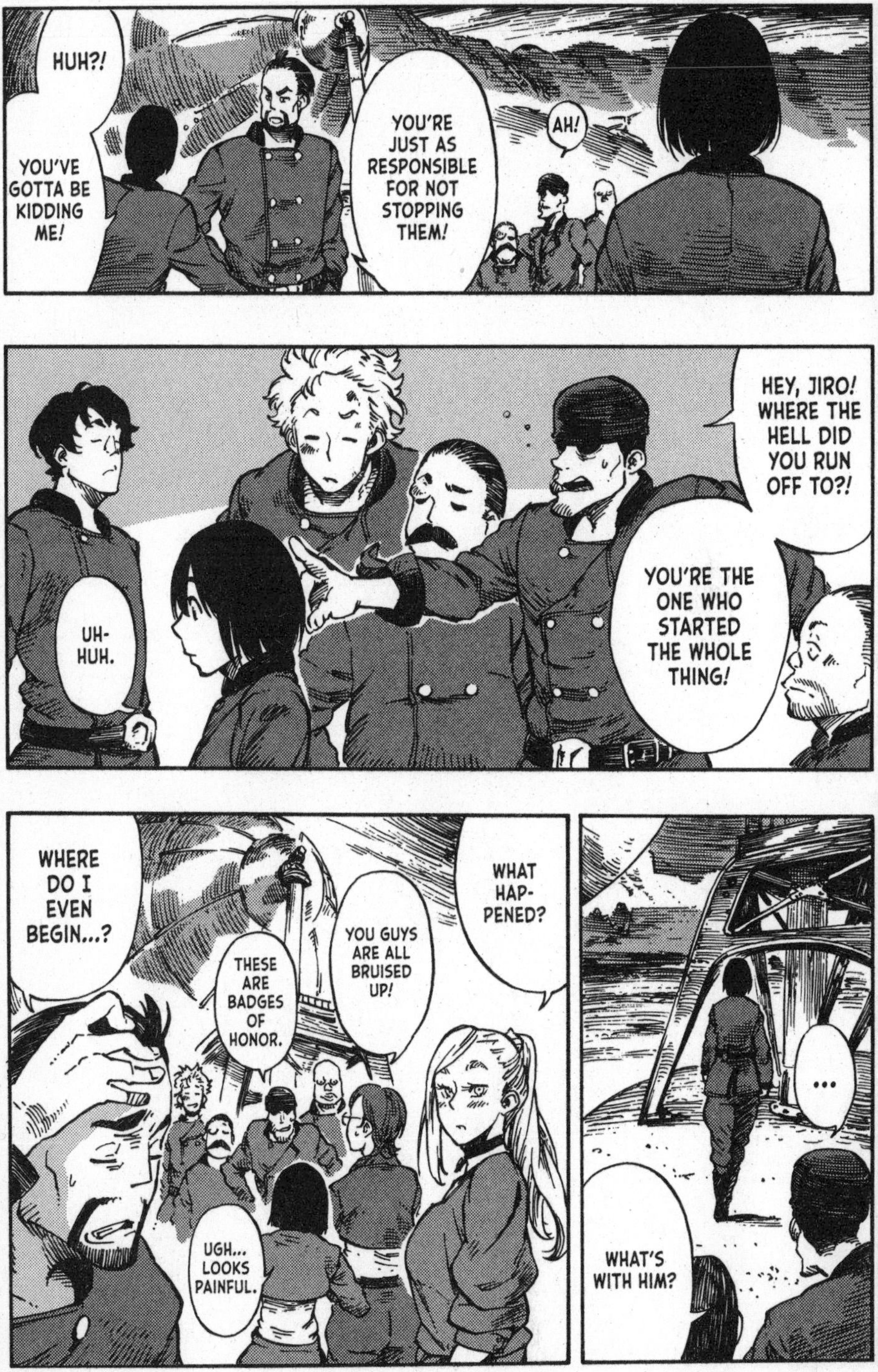
AH!
YOU'RE JUST AS RESPONSIBLE FOR NOT STOPPING THEM!
HUH?!
YOU'VE GOTTA BE KIDDING ME!
HEY, JIRO! WHERE THE HELL DID YOU RUN OFF TO?!
YOU'RE THE ONE WHO STARTED THE WHOLE THING!
UH-HUH.
...
WHAT'S WITH HIM?
WHAT HAP-PENED?
YOU GUYS ARE ALL BRUISED UP!
THESE ARE BADGES OF HONOR.
WHERE DO I EVEN BEGIN...?
UGH... LOOKS PAINFUL.

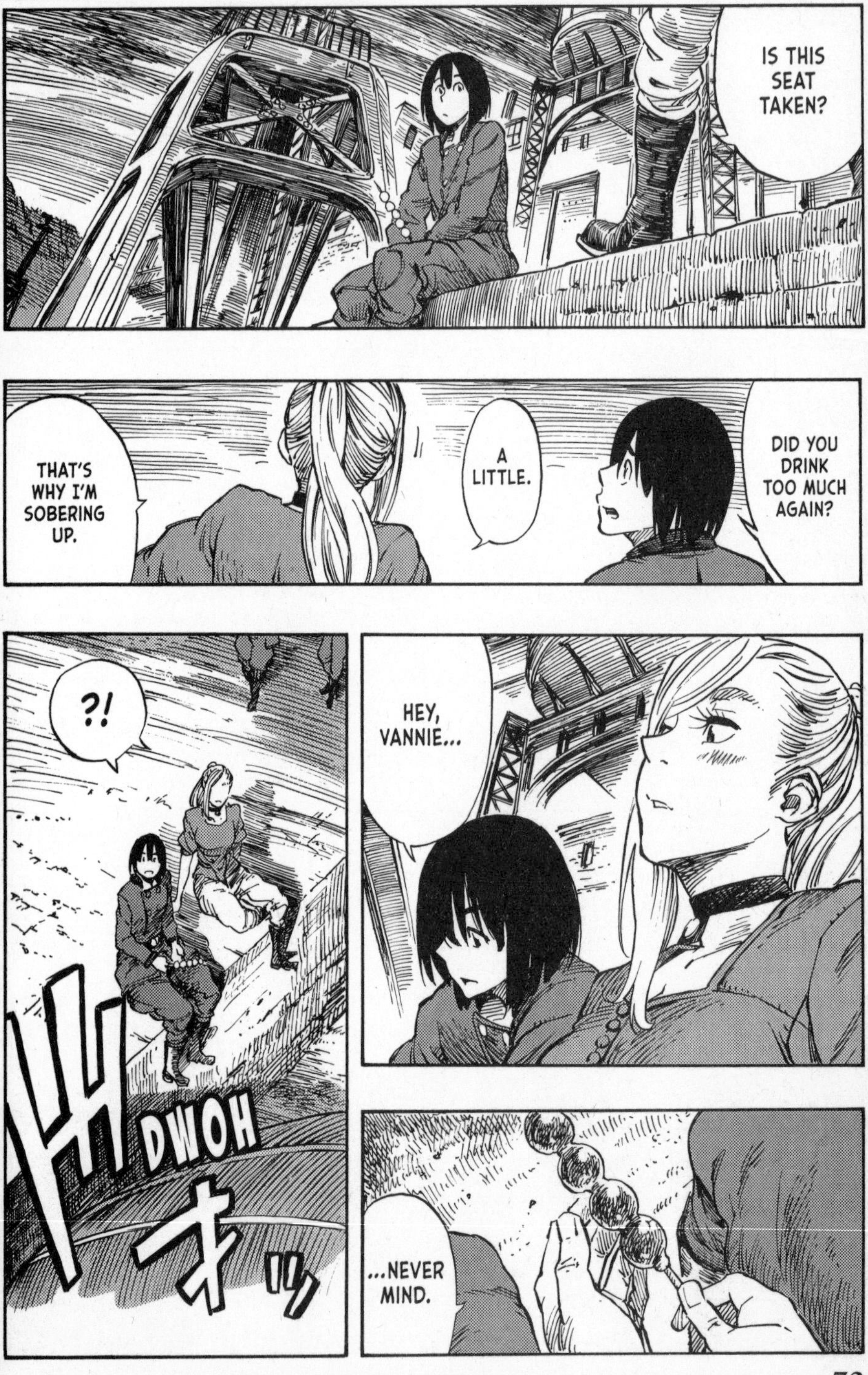
IS THIS SEAT TAKEN?
DID YOU DRINK TOO MUCH AGAIN?
A LITTLE.
THAT'S WHY I'M SOBERING UP.
HEY, VANNIE...
...NEVER MIND.
?!
DWOH

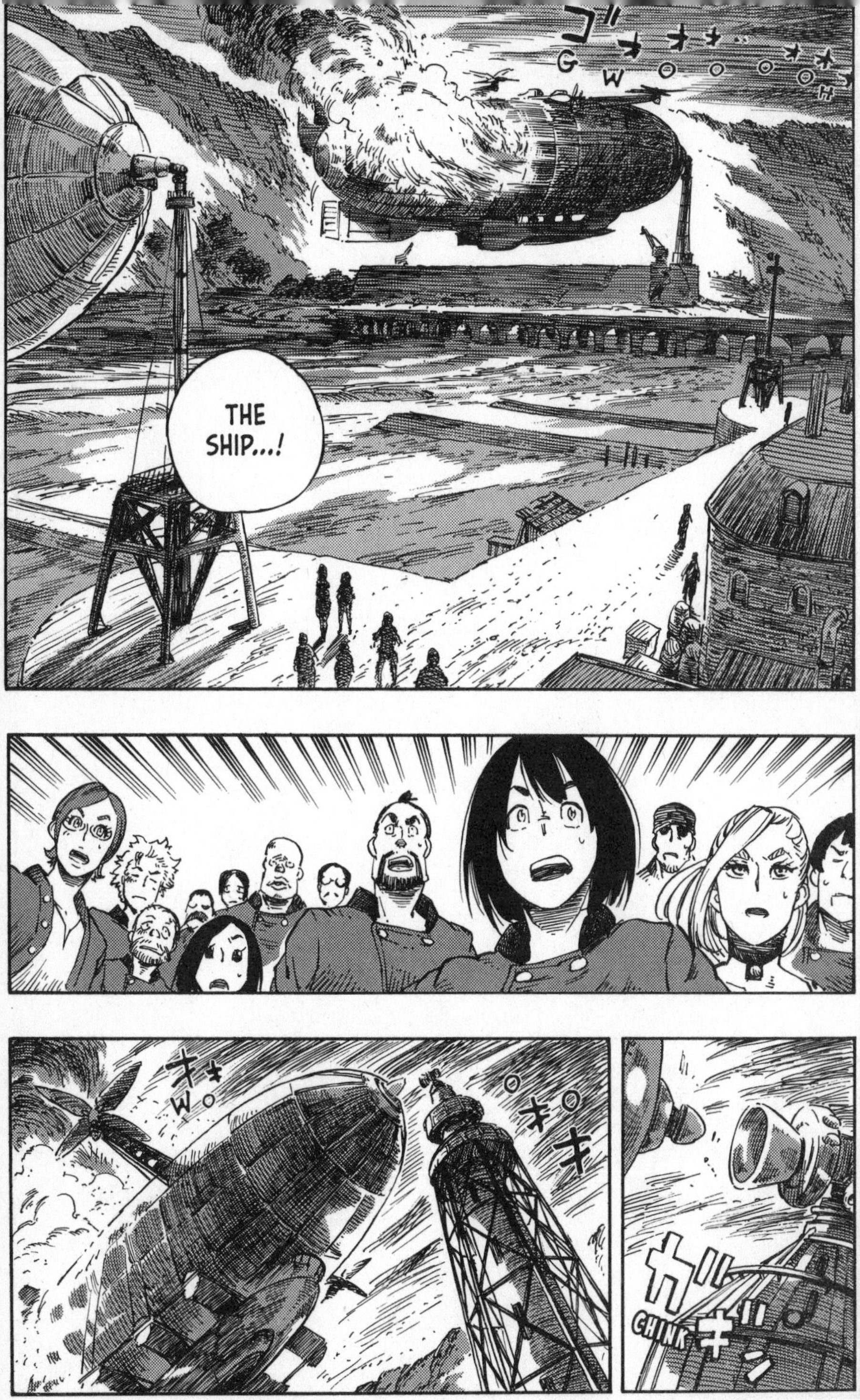
GWOOOOOH
THE SHIP...!
CHINK

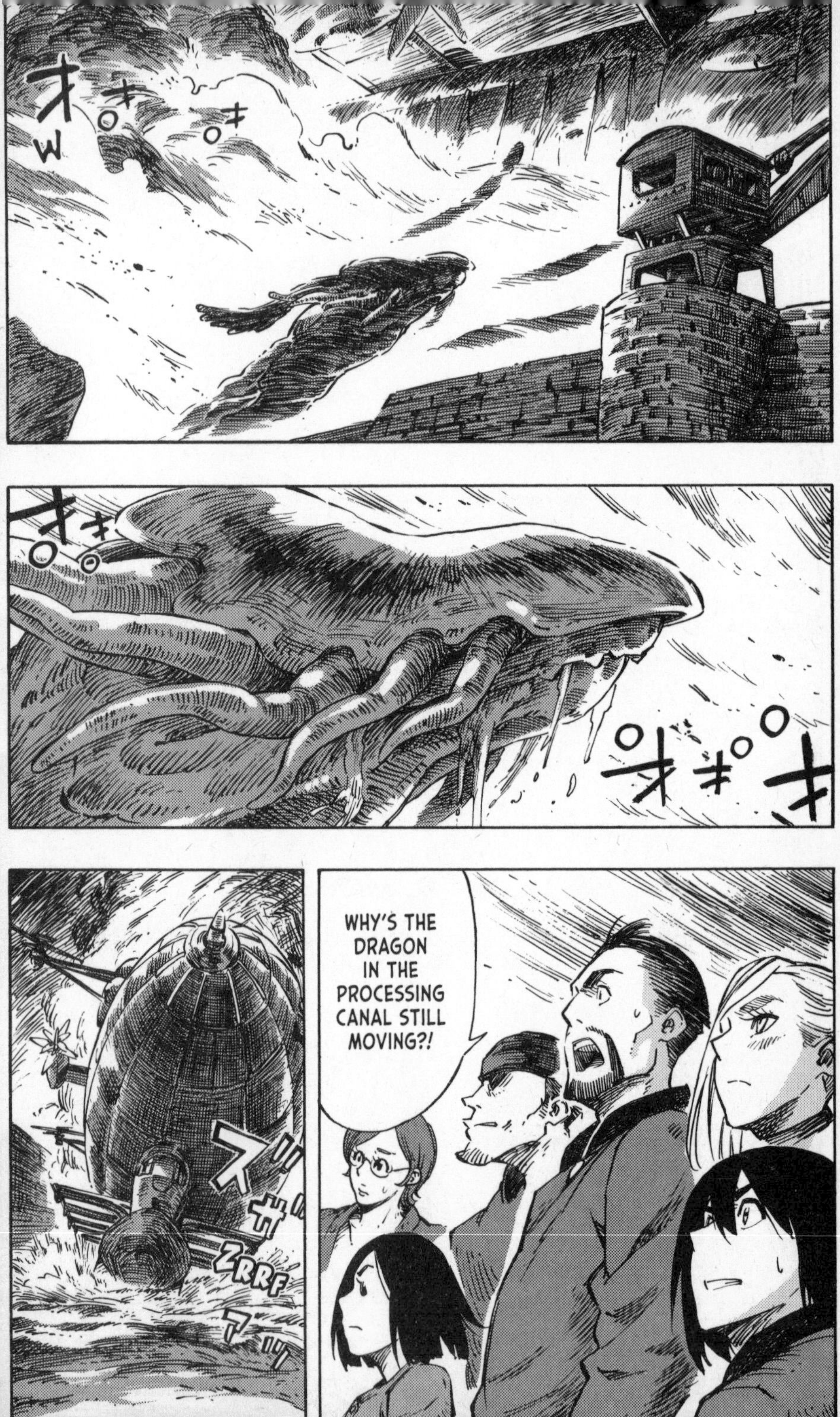
WHY'S THE DRAGON IN THE PROCESSING CANAL STILL MOVING?!
ZRRF

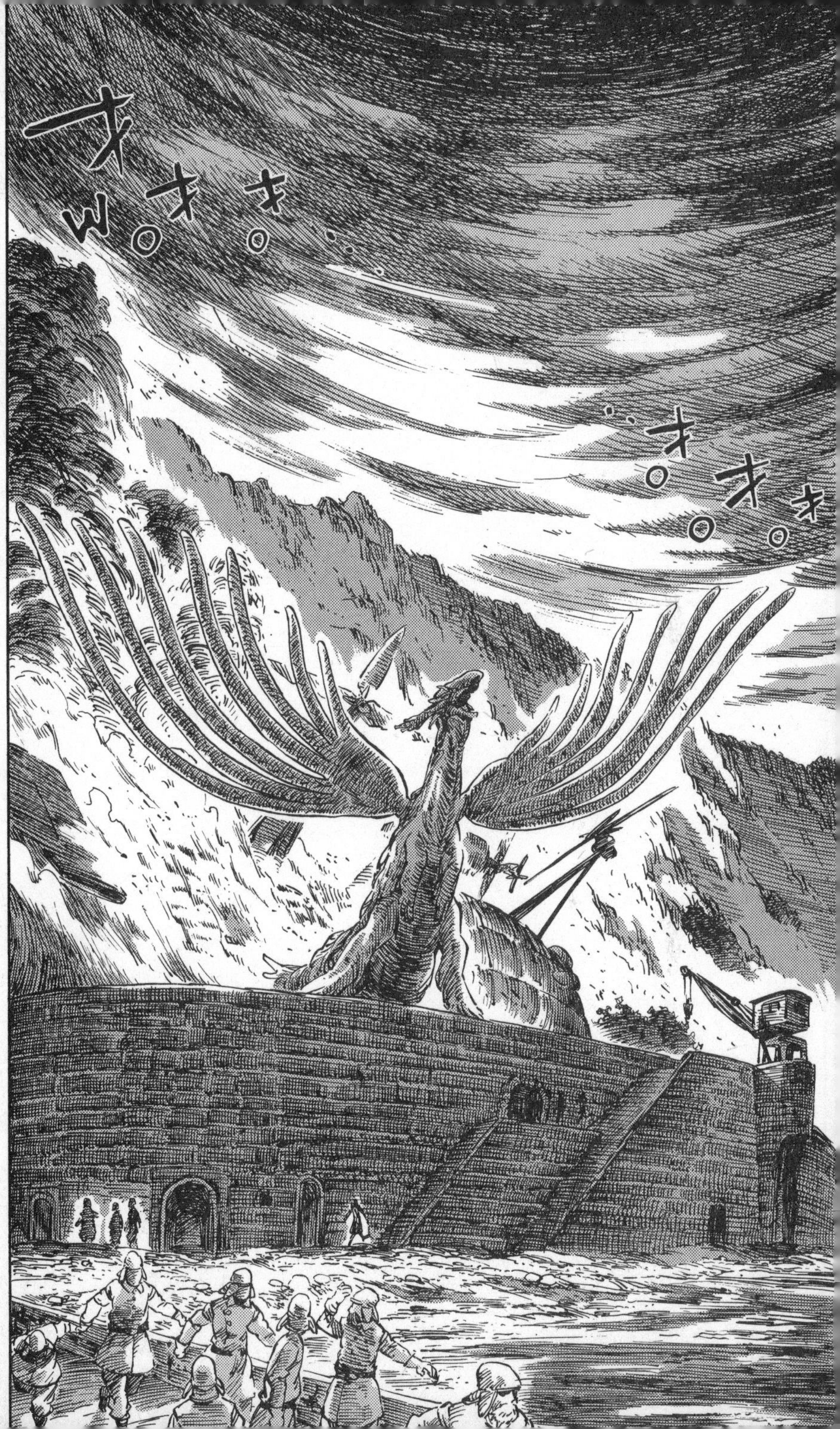
WOO...
...OOO

Dragon Laghman

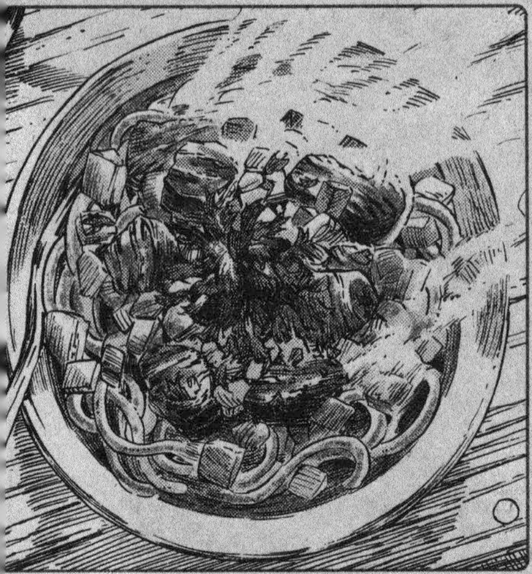

Ingredients (serves 4)	
★ Noodles	
300g bread flour	
¾ cup water	
½ tsp salt	
★ Soup	
200g dragon meat	1 clove garlic
½ onion	½ tbsp + a pinch salt
½ carrot stick	½ tsp cumin powder
½ celery stick	½ tsp coriander powder
1 potato	½ tsp chili powder
1-2 tomatoes	Cilantro to taste
2 red bell peppers	

1

ı a bowl, mix water, salt, and our. Once incorporated, knead ıe dough until smooth and set side to rest for 15 minutes.

02

Once the dough has softened, cut into several portions and stretch each section into rods about 1 cm in diameter. Starting from the center of a large tray or plate, lay the dough pieces down, spiraling outward across the surface. Brush with vegetable oil to prevent the dough from drying out.

03

Slice the dragon meat into large bite-sized pieces and cube vegetables into 1.5-cm pieces.

4

leat a generous amount of oil in pan until smoking, then add arlic and meat. Once cooked ırough, add the vegetables, ıixing in the tomatoes last.

05

Add 10 cups of water, salt, and spices and bring to a boil. Turn the heat down to low and simmer the mixture for 20 minutes until the ingredients are tender.

06

With one hand holding down one end of the dough pieces, stretch the dough into thin noodles with your other hand.

7

lold the noodles with both hands nd, while pulling from both ends, lap the noodles down onto the utting board, further stretching ıe noodles. Boil the finished oodles in a pot of water.

08

When the noodles rise to the surface, remove from pot, drain thoroughly with a sieve, then place in a bowl. Pour soup over the noodles and sprinkle with cilantro to garnish.

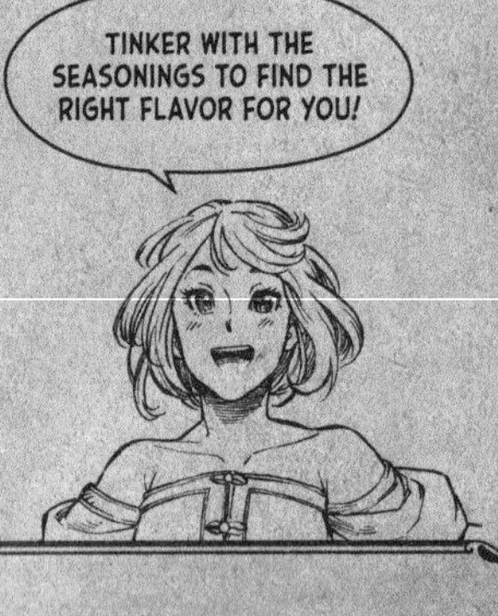
TINKER WITH THE SEASONINGS TO FIND THE RIGHT FLAVOR FOR YOU!

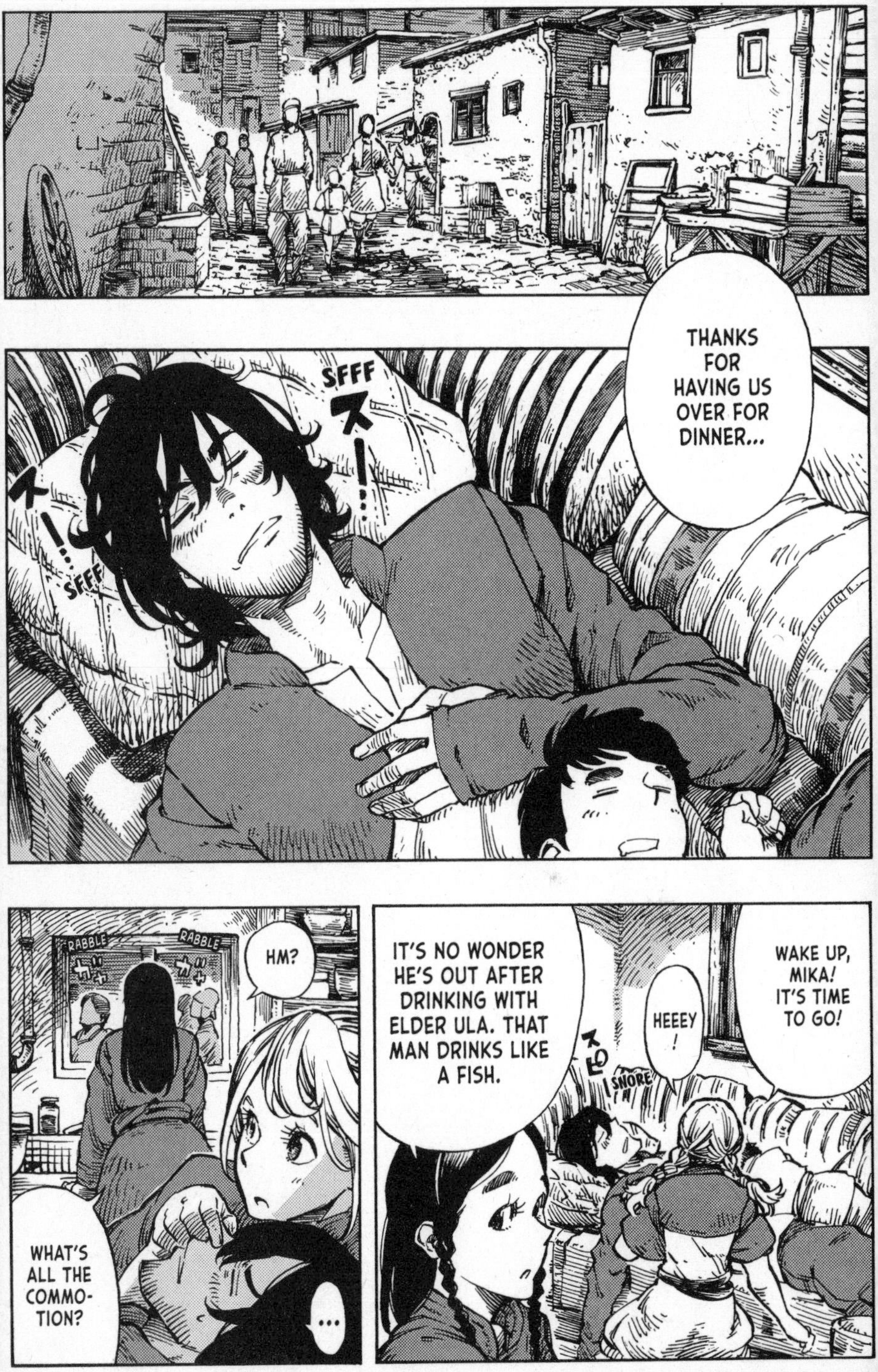
THANKS FOR HAVING US OVER FOR DINNER...
SFFF
SFFF
WAKE UP, MIKA! IT'S TIME TO GO!
HEEEY!
SNORE
IT'S NO WONDER HE'S OUT AFTER DRINKING WITH ELDER ULA. THAT MAN DRINKS LIKE A FISH.
RABBLE
RABBLE
HM?
WHAT'S ALL THE COMMOTION?
...

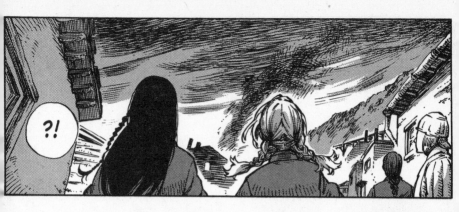

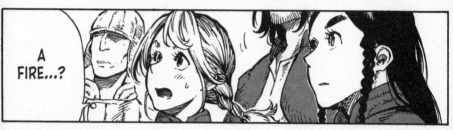

?!
A FIRE...?
MIKA!
You're awake.
IT'S COMING FROM THE PORT.
...
LET'S GO, TAKITA.

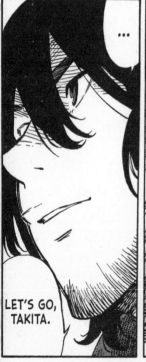

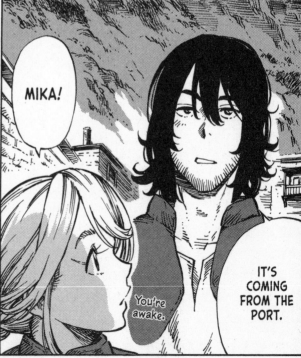

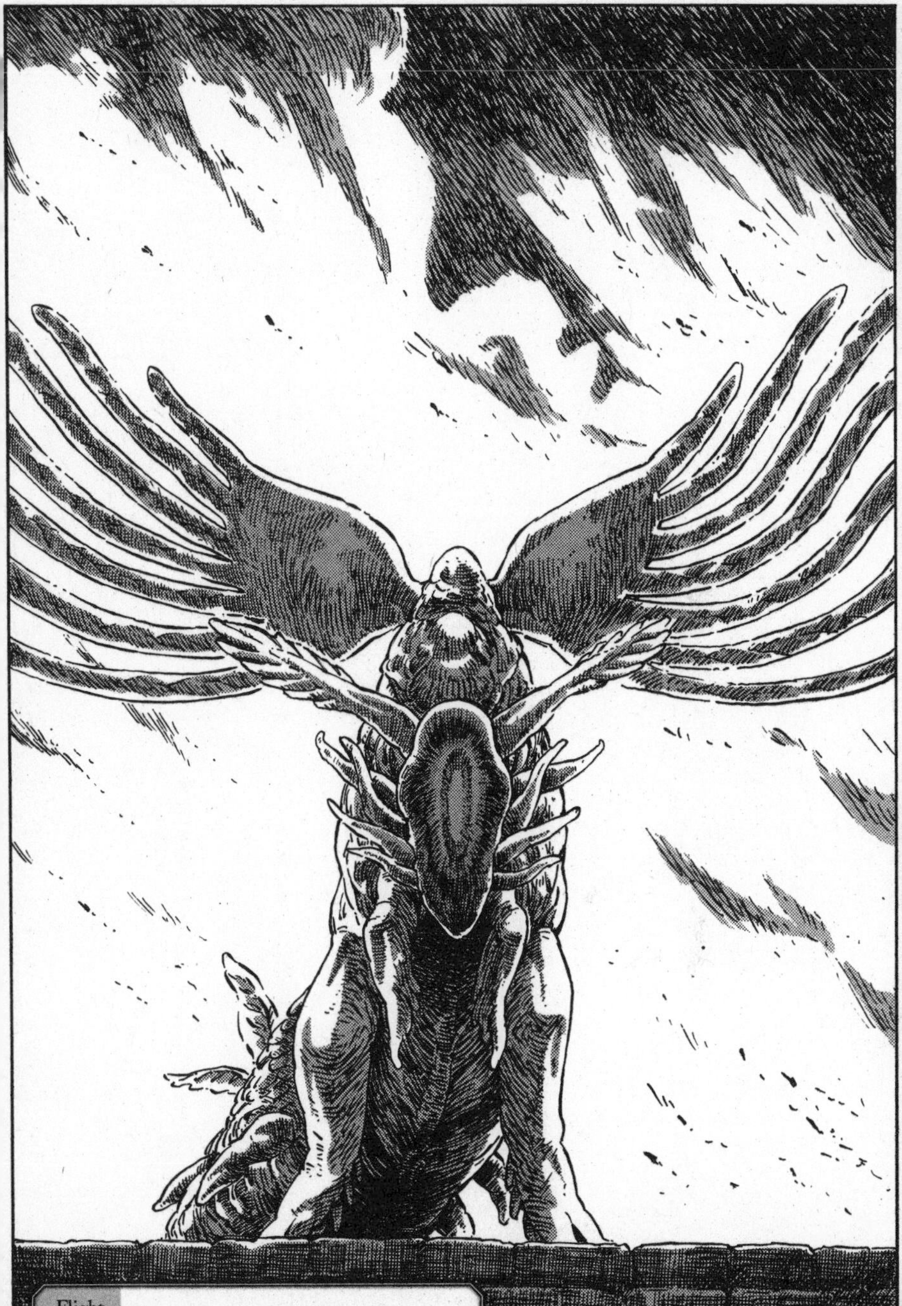
Flight
8
Disaster & Edible Dragons

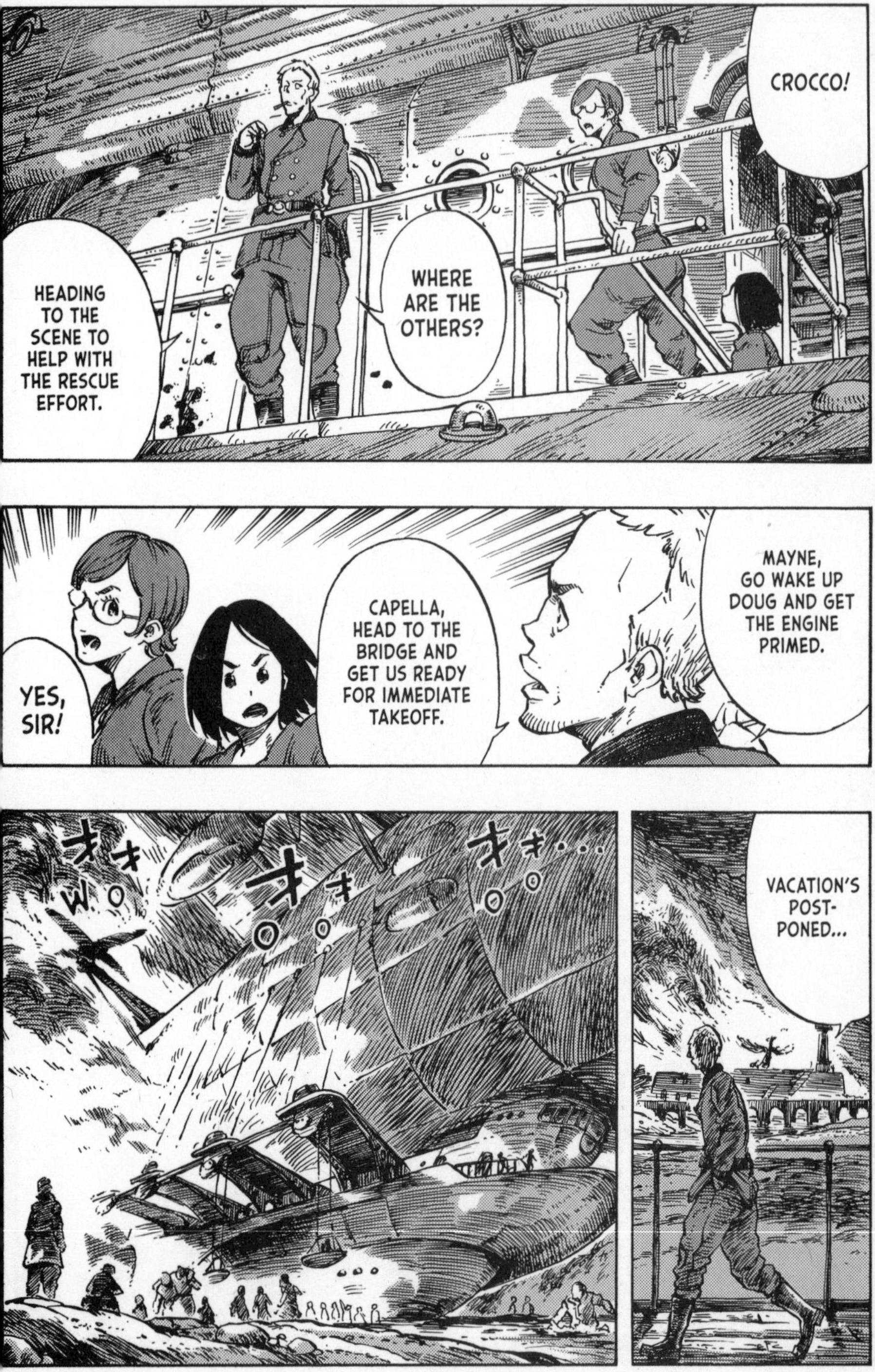
CROCCO!
WHERE ARE THE OTHERS?
HEADING TO THE SCENE TO HELP WITH THE RESCUE EFFORT.
MAYNE, GO WAKE UP DOUG AND GET THE ENGINE PRIMED.
CAPELLA, HEAD TO THE BRIDGE AND GET US READY FOR IMMEDIATE TAKEOFF.
YES, SIR!
VACATION'S POST-PONED...
WO
OO
OO...

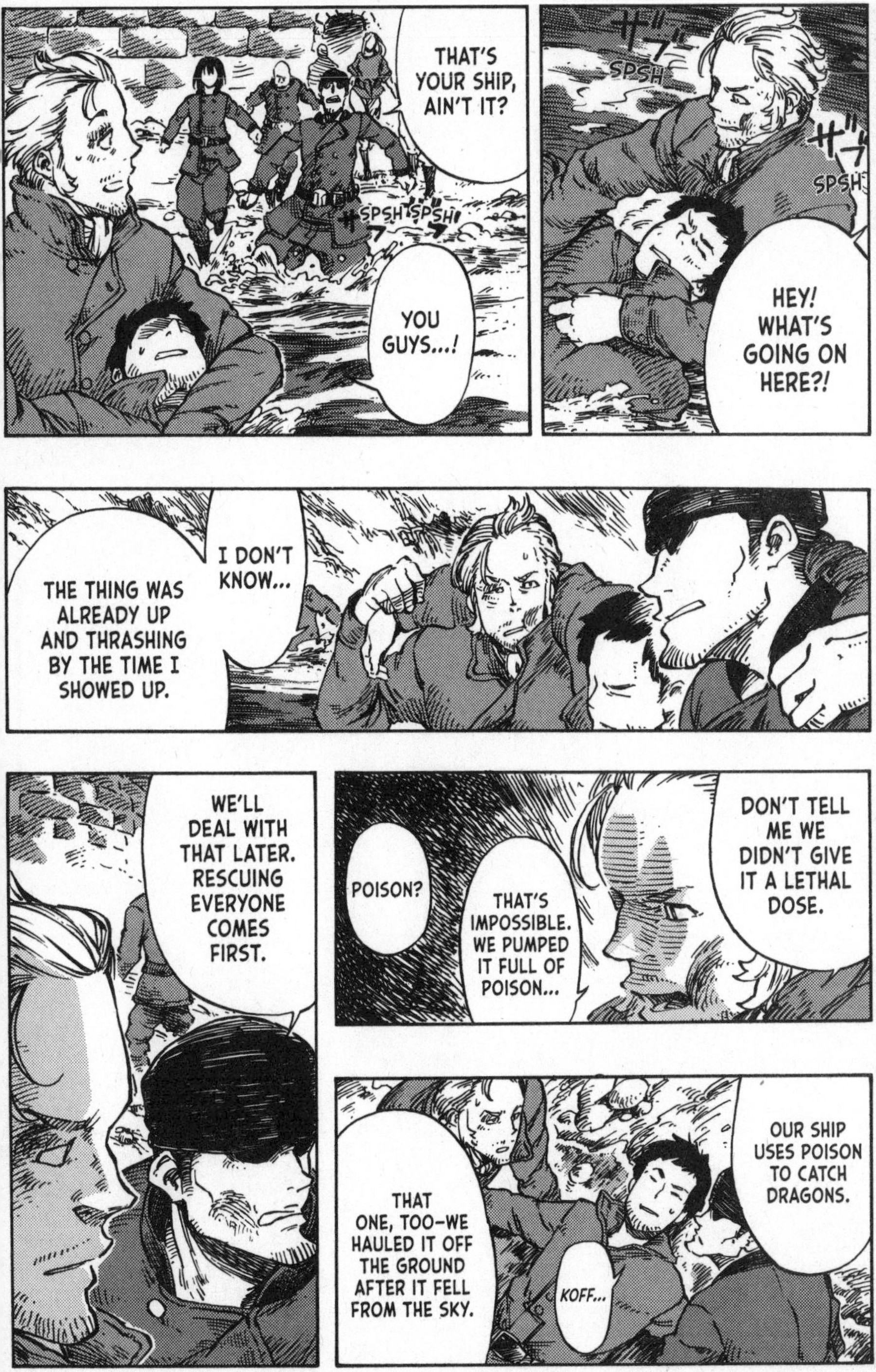
THAT'S YOUR SHIP, AIN'T IT?
SPSH SPSH
YOU GUYS...!
SPSH
SPSH
HEY! WHAT'S GOING ON HERE?!
I DON'T KNOW...
THE THING WAS ALREADY UP AND THRASHING BY THE TIME I SHOWED UP.
WE'LL DEAL WITH THAT LATER. RESCUING EVERYONE COMES FIRST.
DON'T TELL ME WE DIDN'T GIVE IT A LETHAL DOSE.
THAT'S IMPOSSIBLE. WE PUMPED IT FULL OF POISON...
POISON?
OUR SHIP USES POISON TO CATCH DRAGONS.
THAT ONE, TOO—WE HAULED IT OFF THE GROUND AFTER IT FELL FROM THE SKY.
KOFF...

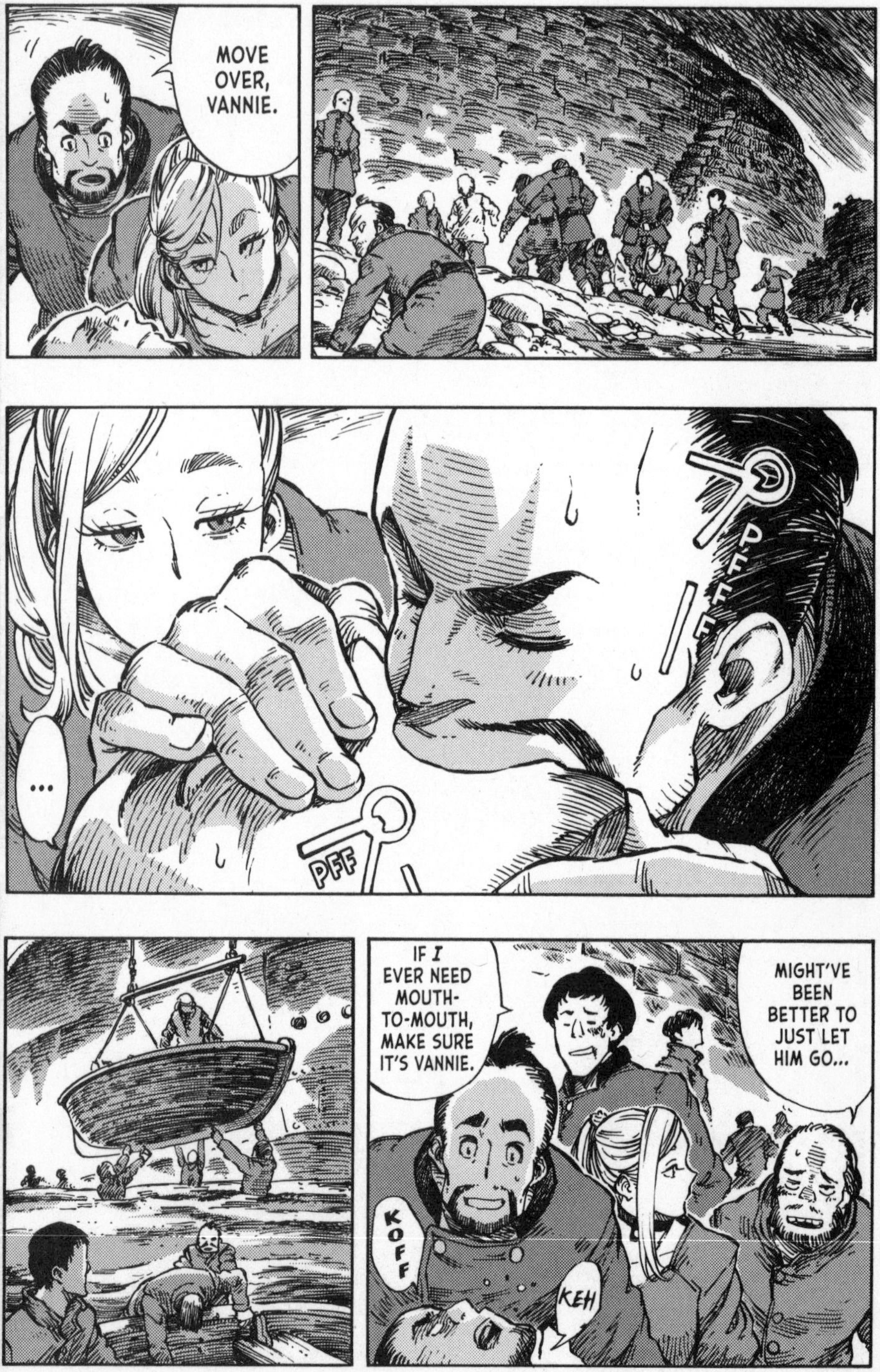
MOVE OVER, VANNIE.
PFFFF
PFF
...
MIGHT'VE BEEN BETTER TO JUST LET HIM GO...
IF *I* EVER NEED MOUTH-TO-MOUTH, MAKE SURE IT'S VANNIE.
KOFF
KEH

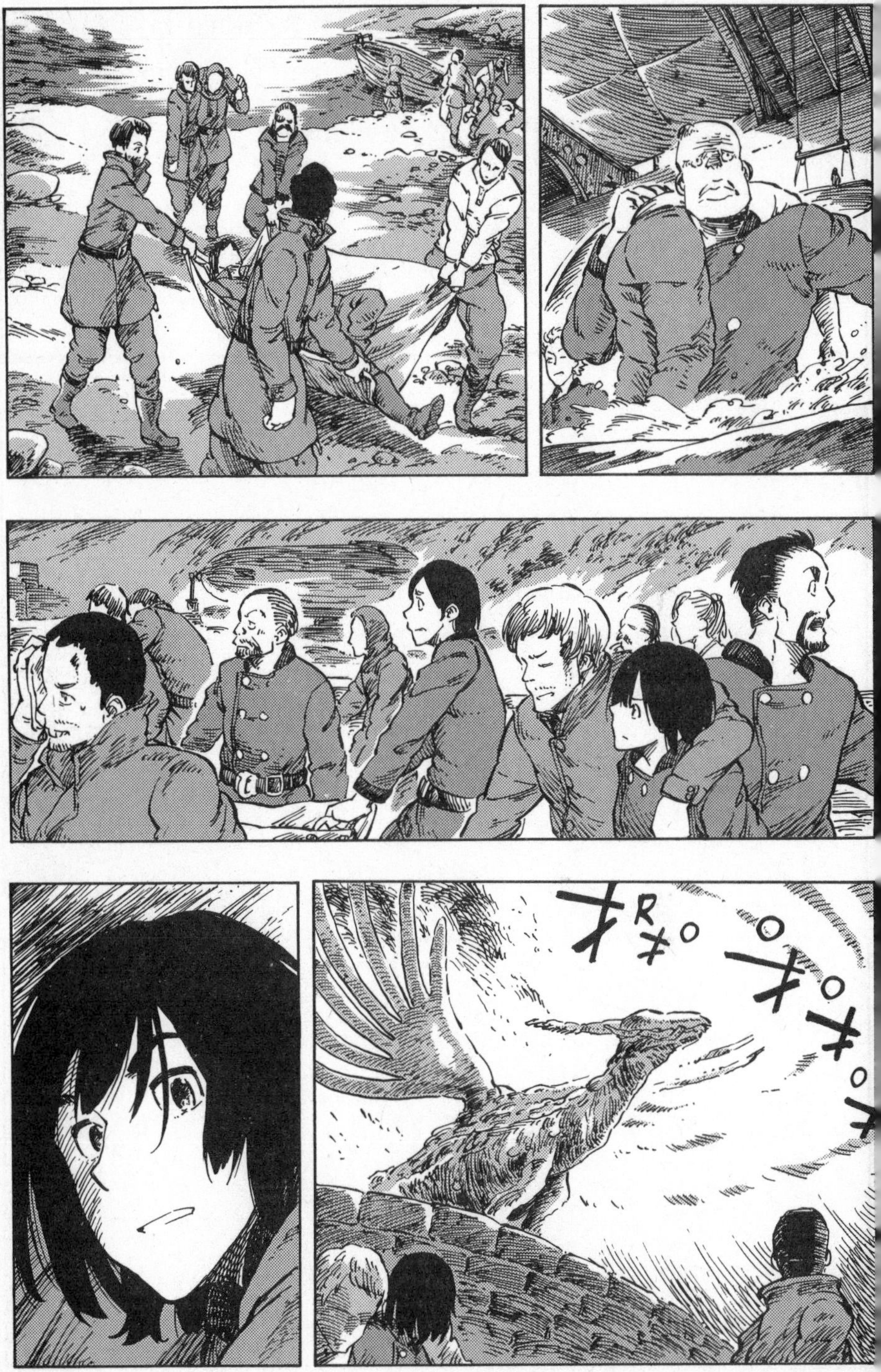

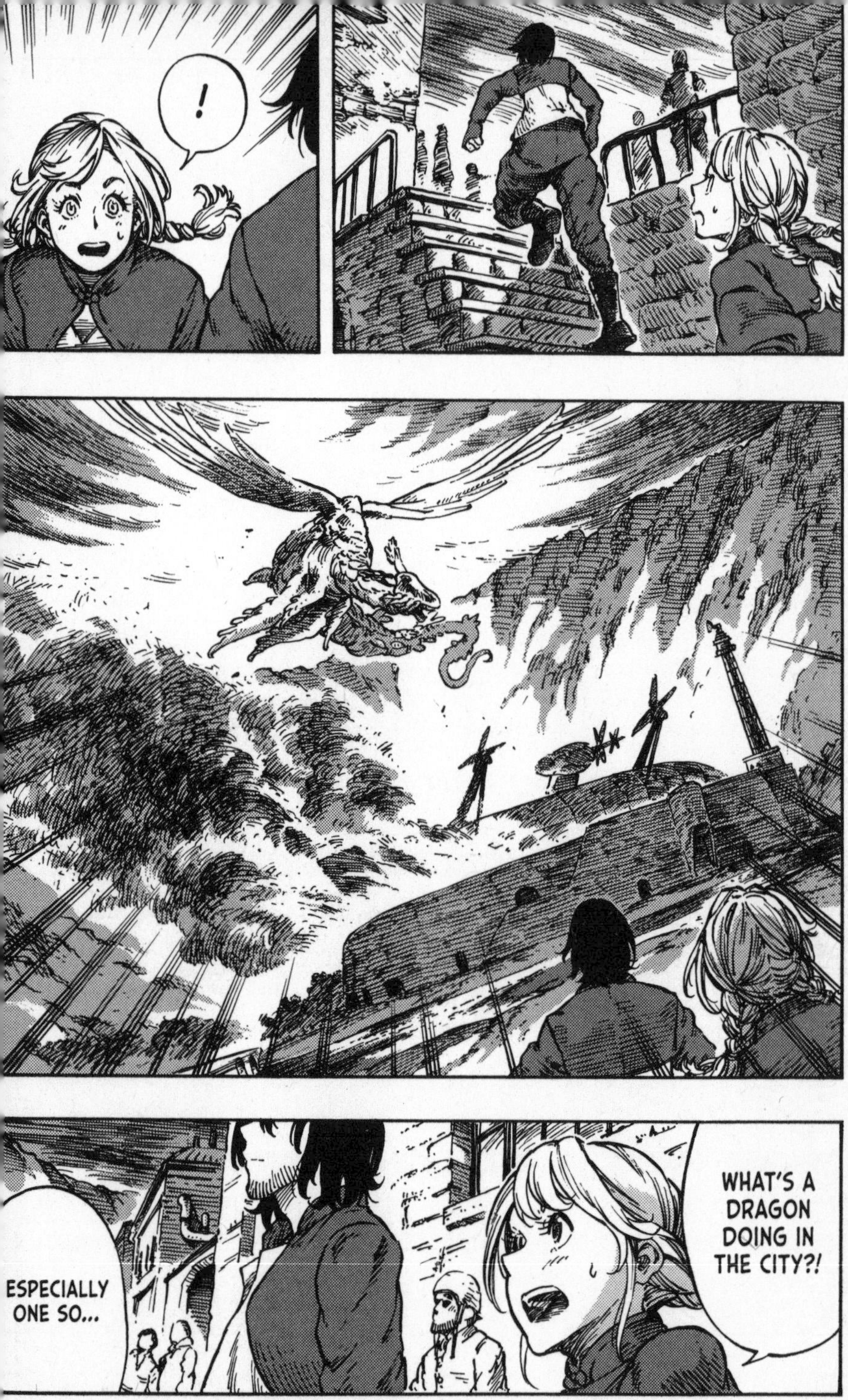
!
WHAT'S A DRAGON DOING IN THE CITY?!
ESPECIALLY ONE SO...

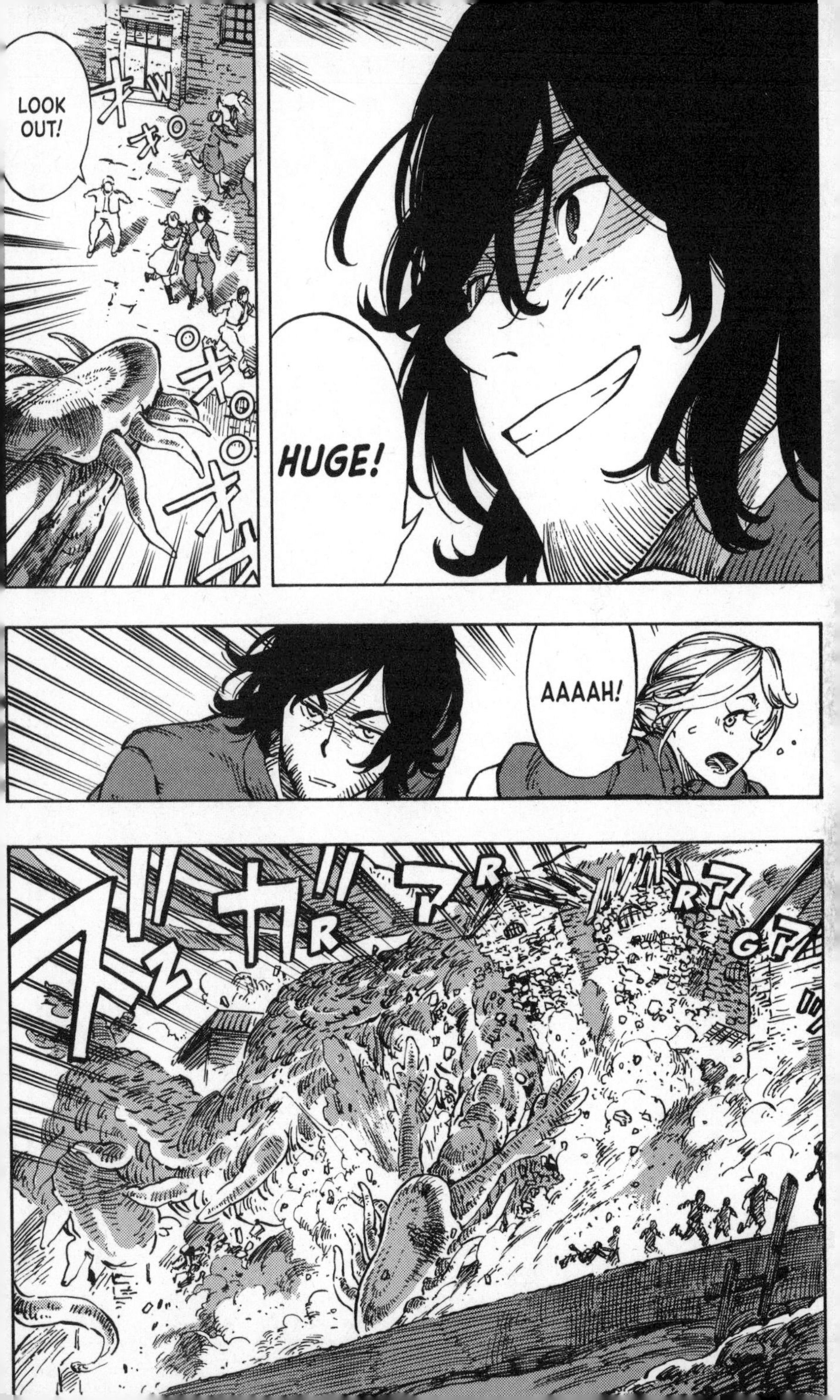
HUGE!
LOOK OUT!
AAAAH!

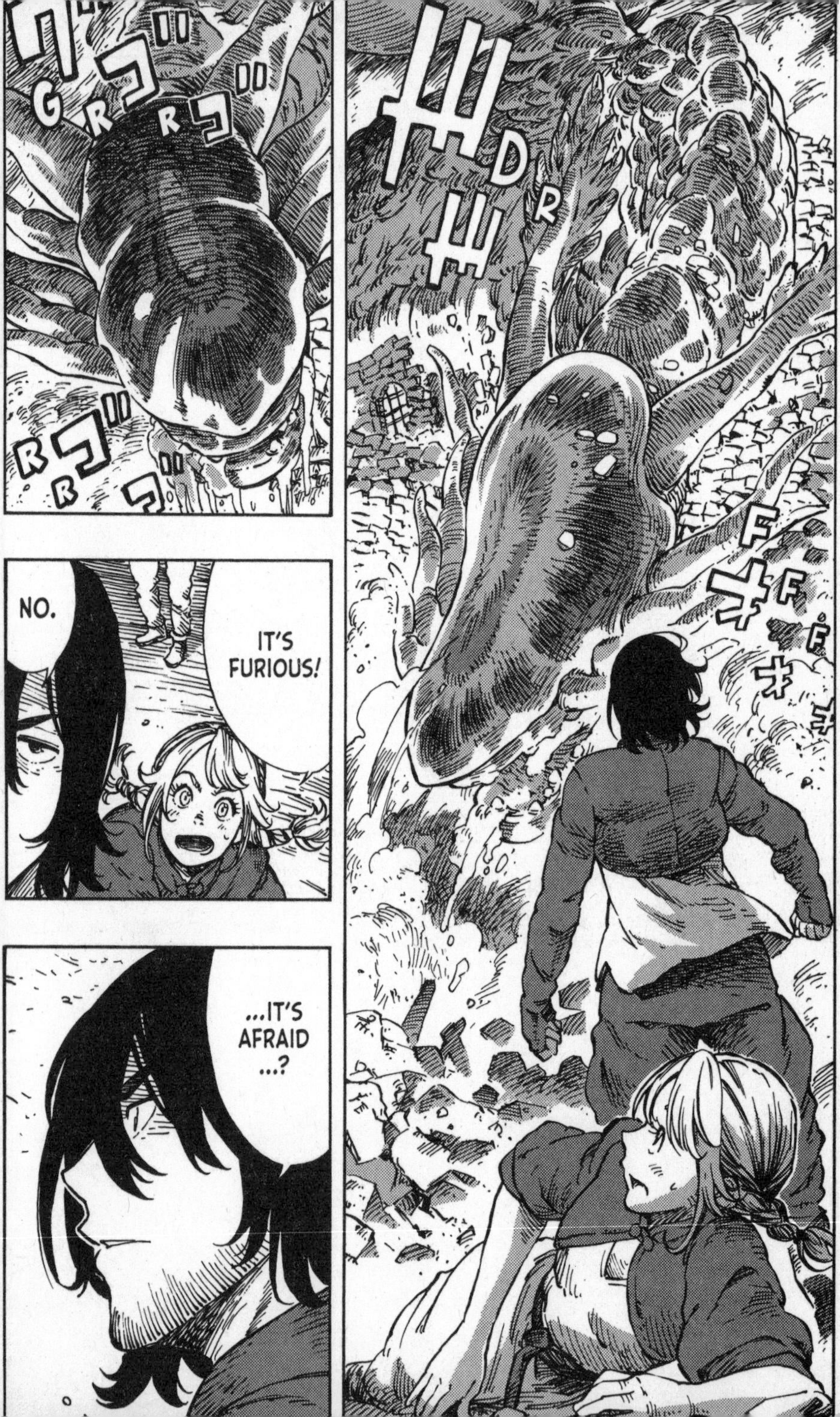
DR
FFF
GRR
RR
NO.
IT'S FURIOUS!
...IT'S AFRAID ...?

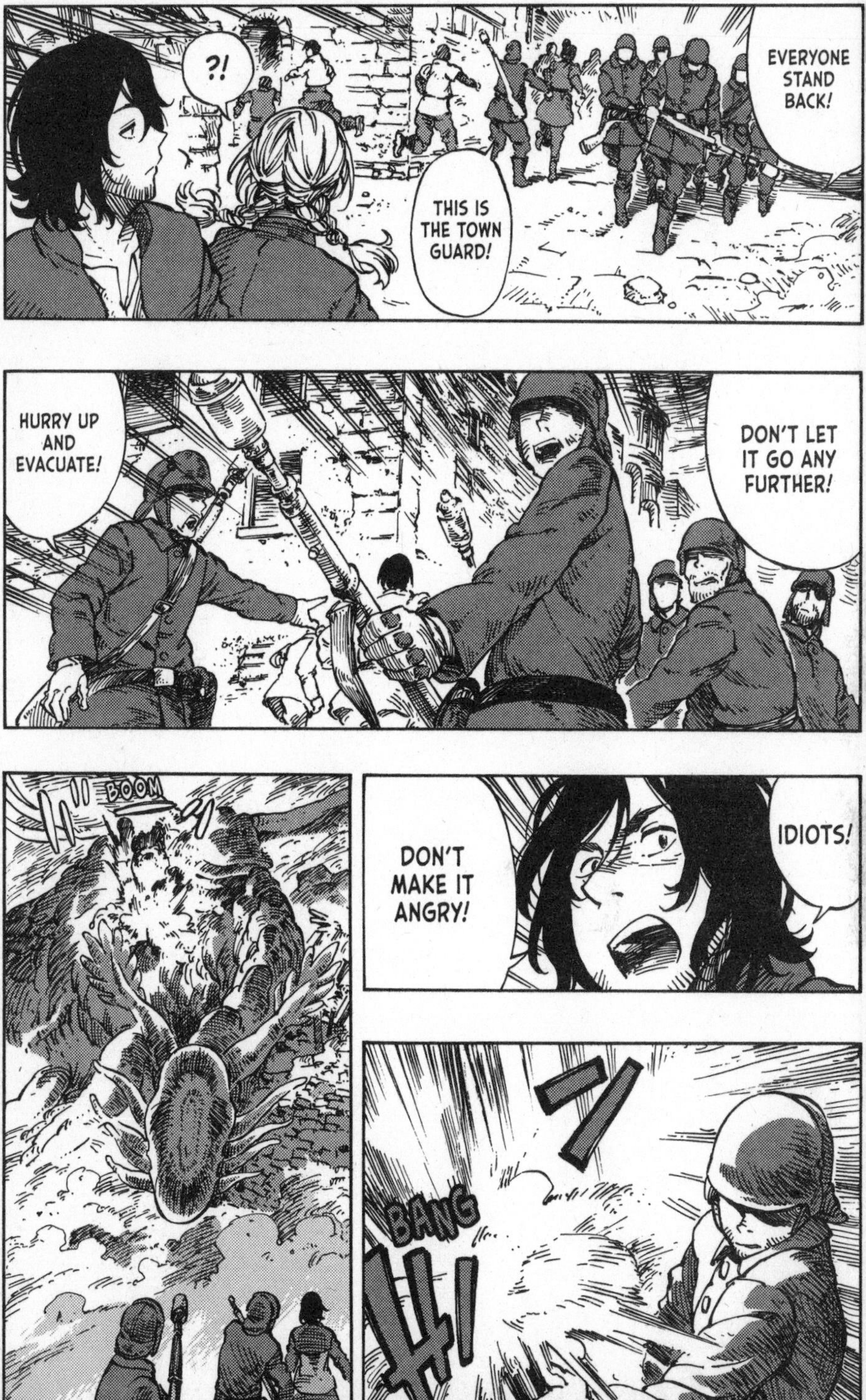
EVERYONE STAND BACK!
THIS IS THE TOWN GUARD!
?!
DON'T LET IT GO ANY FURTHER!
HURRY UP AND EVACUATE!
IDIOTS!
DON'T MAKE IT ANGRY!
BANG
BOOM

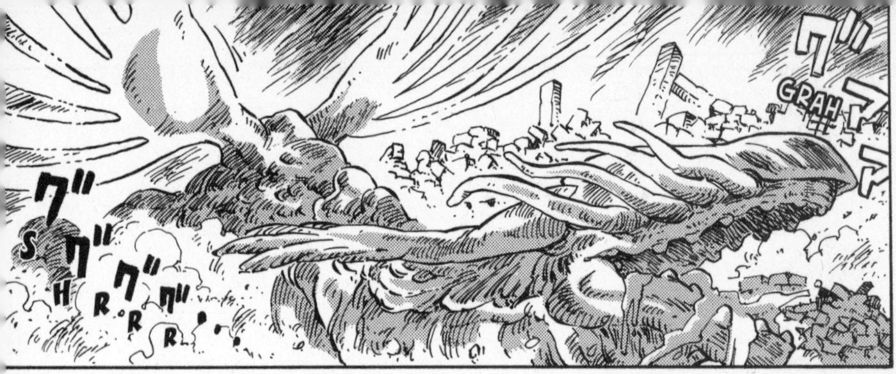
GRAH
SHRRRR
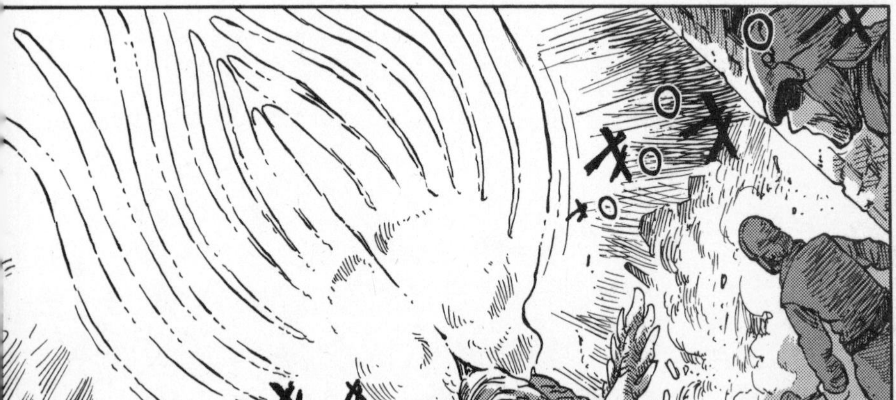
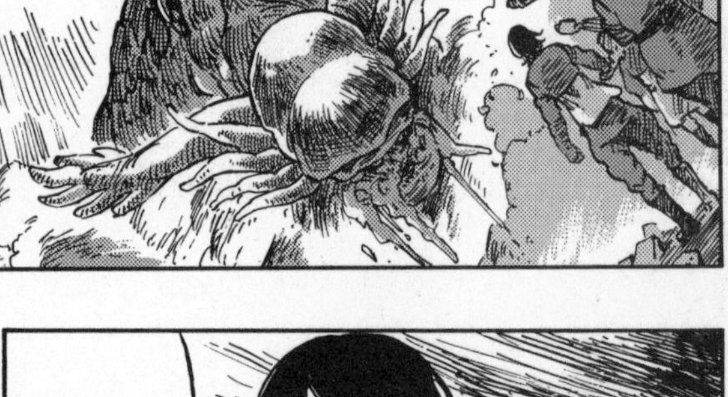
WHAT'S IT DOING?!
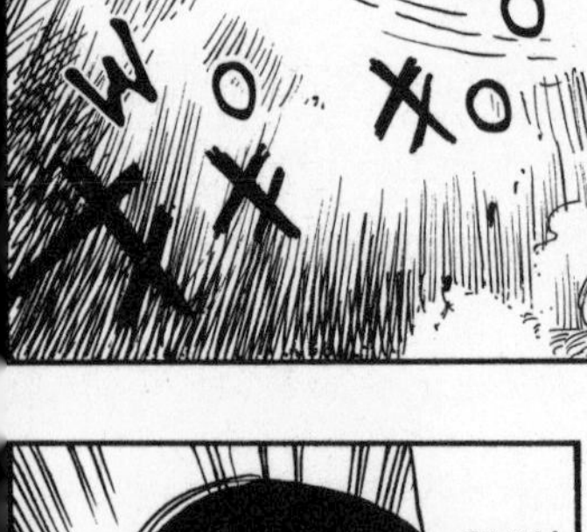
RUN!
GET THE HELL OUT OF HERE!

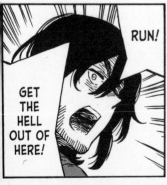

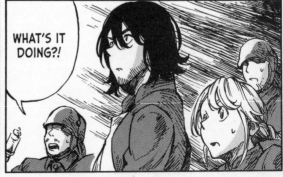

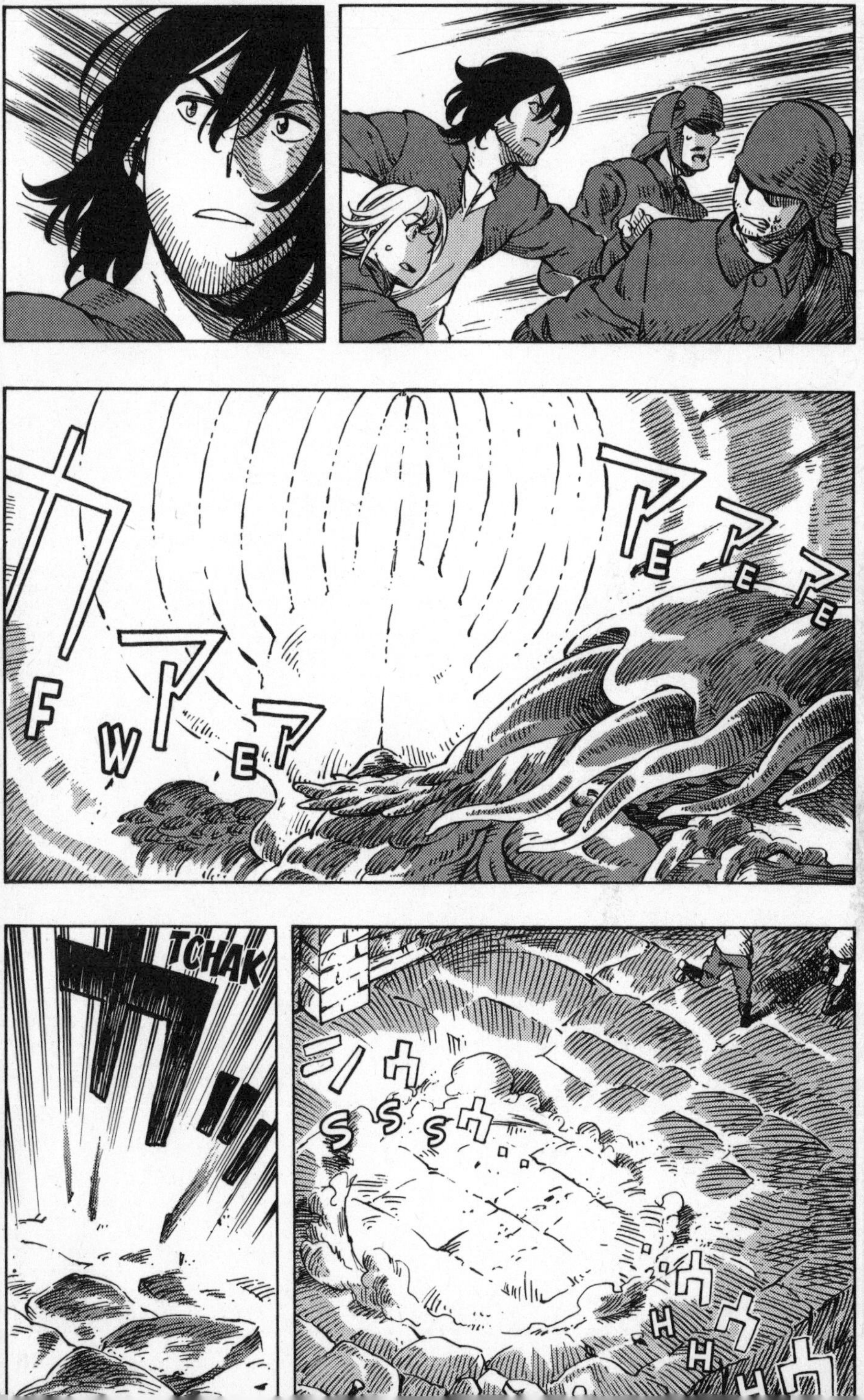
E E E
F W E
S S S
H H
TCHAK

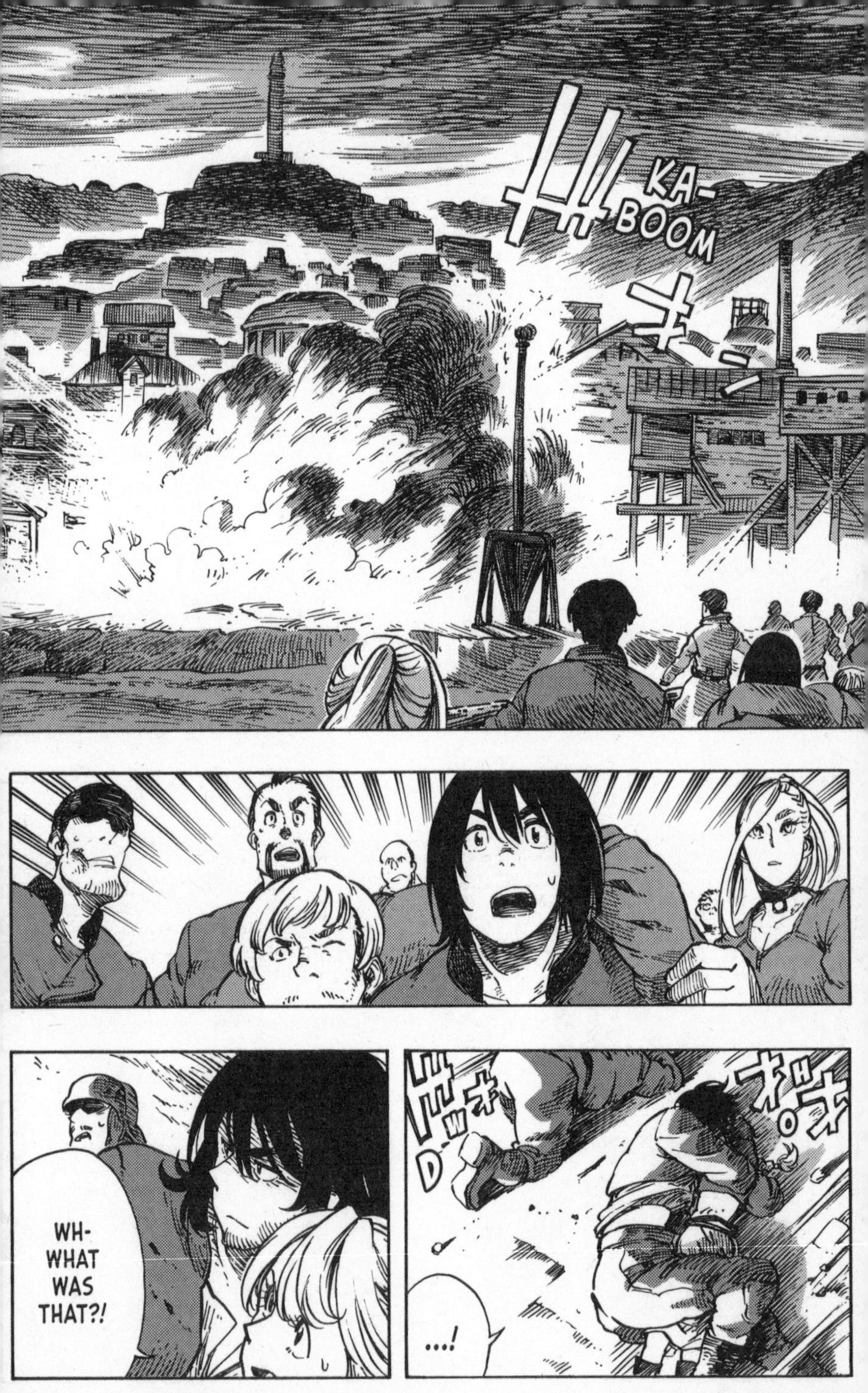
KA-BOOM
...!
WH- WHAT WAS THAT?!

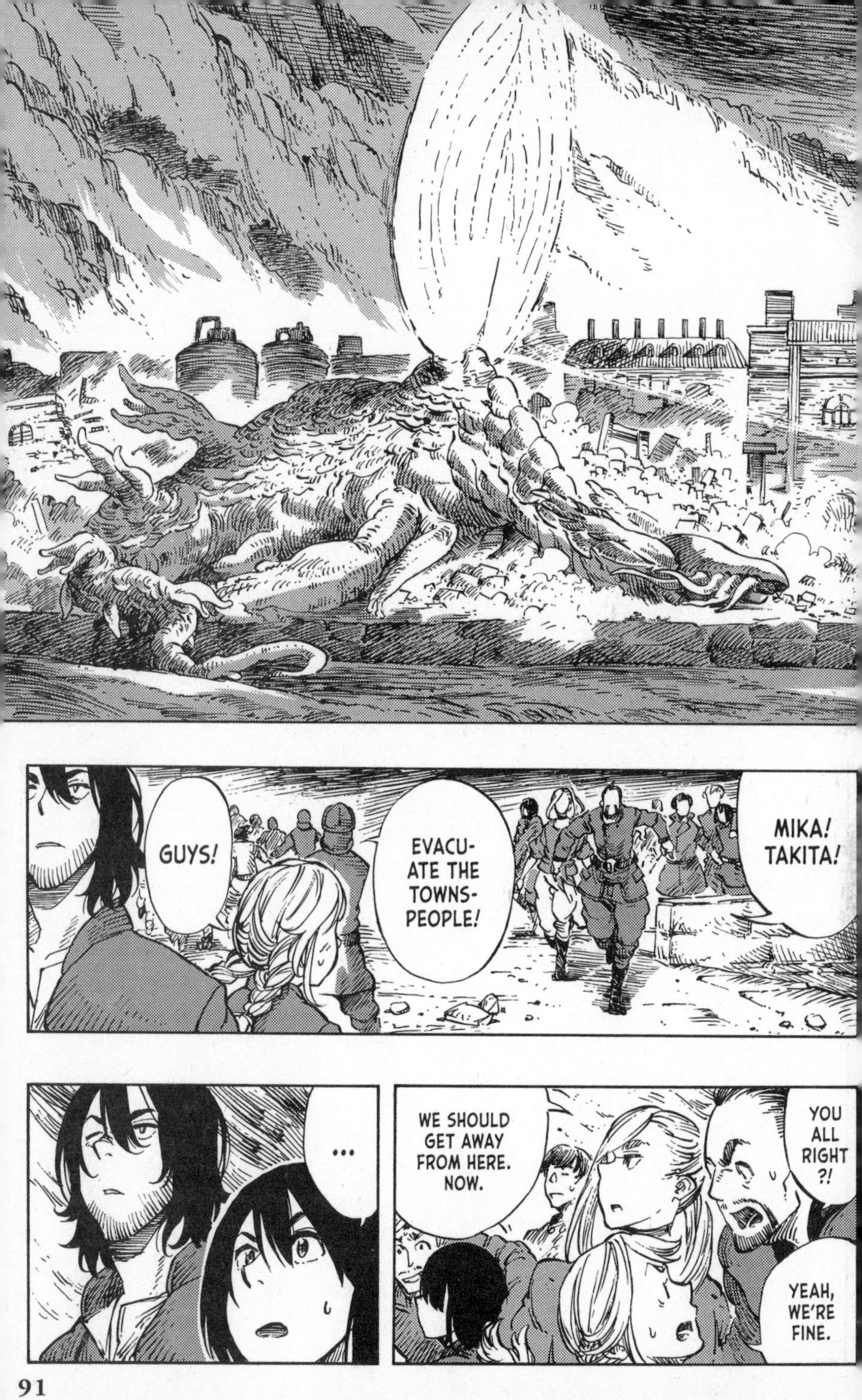
MIKA! TAKITA!
EVACU-ATE THE TOWNS-PEOPLE!
GUYS!
YOU ALL RIGHT ?!
YEAH, WE'RE FINE.
WE SHOULD GET AWAY FROM HERE. NOW.
...

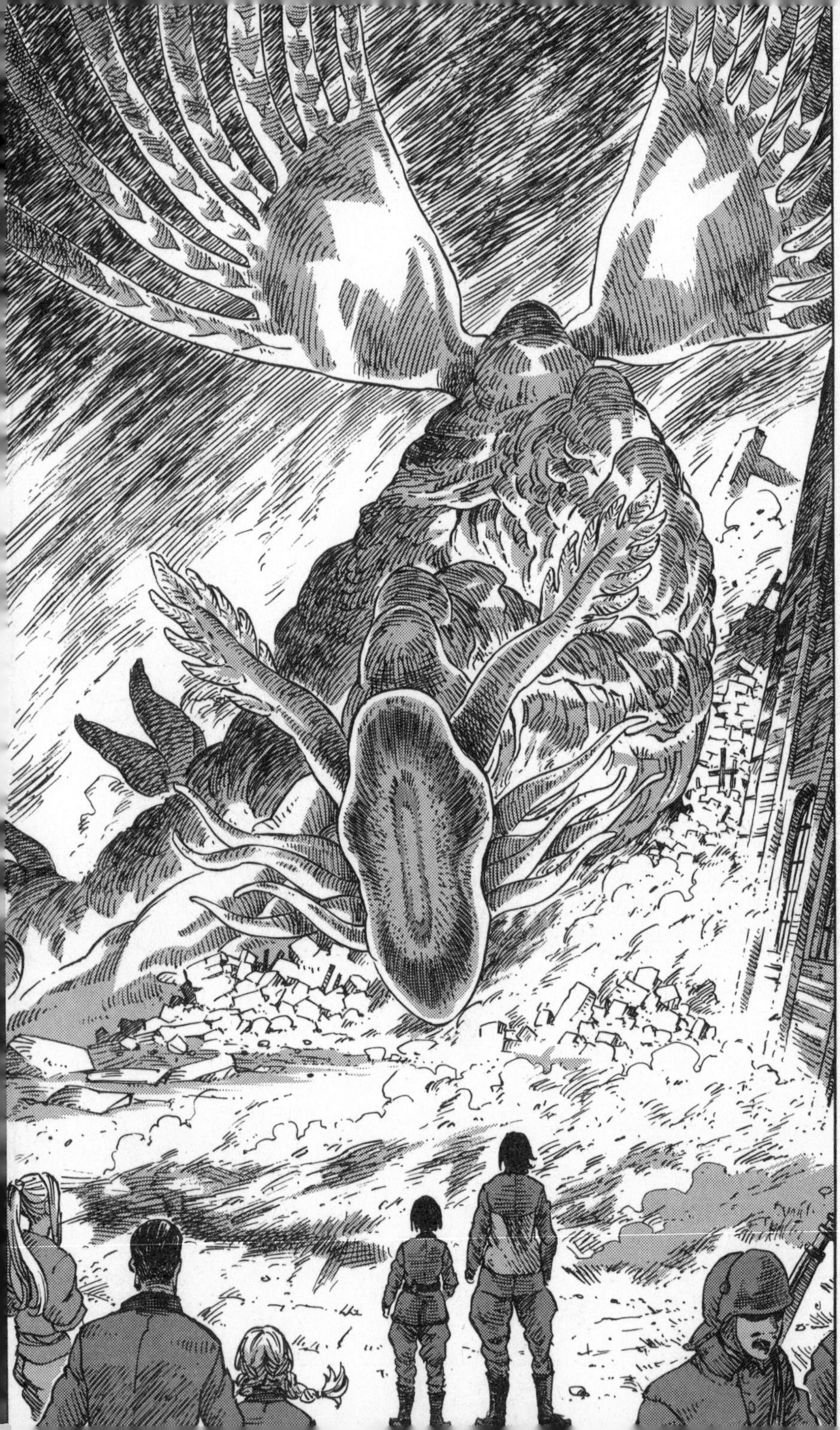

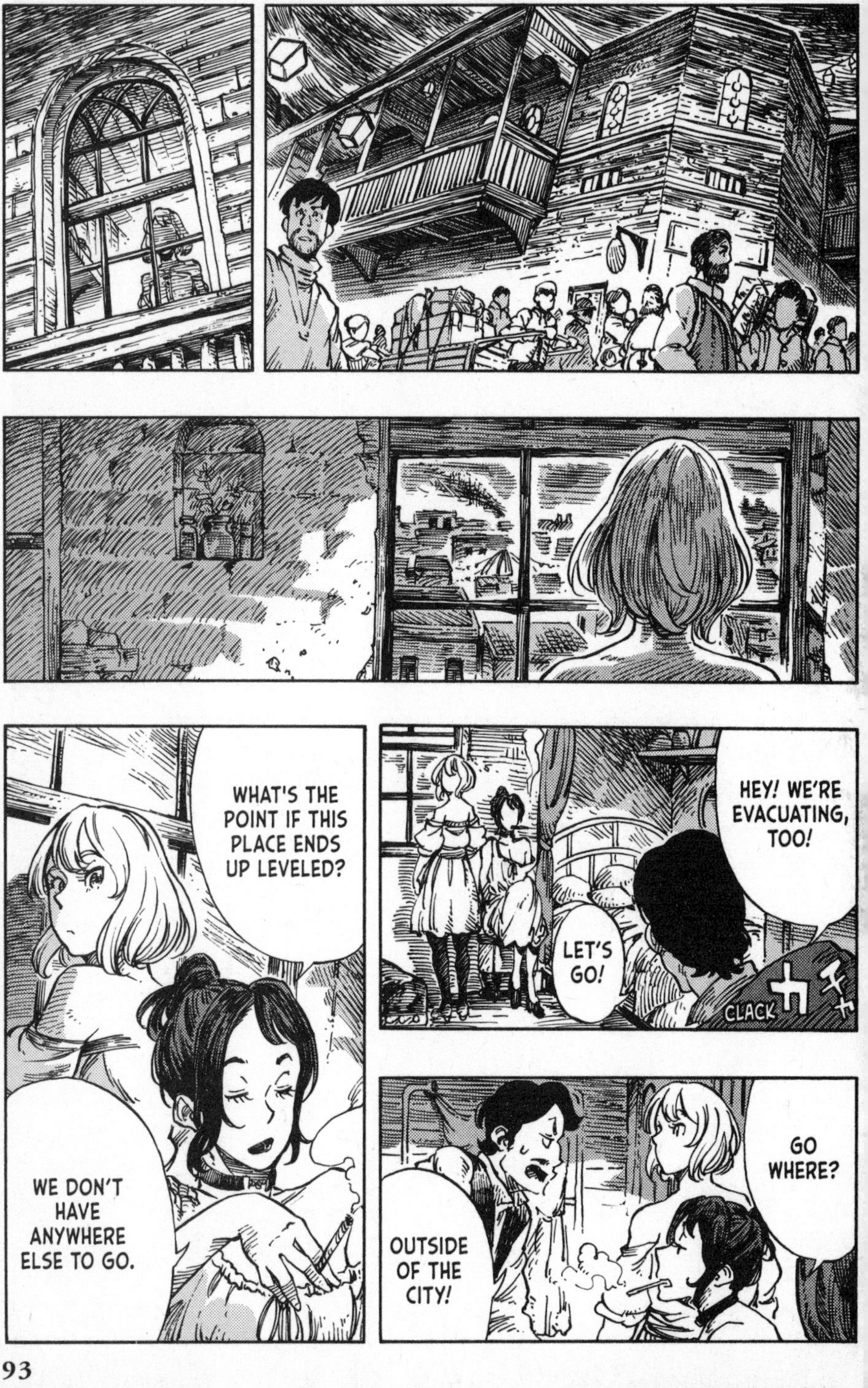
HEY! WE'RE EVACUATING, TOO!
LET'S GO!
CLACK
GO WHERE?
OUTSIDE OF THE CITY!
WHAT'S THE POINT IF THIS PLACE ENDS UP LEVELED?
WE DON'T HAVE ANYWHERE ELSE TO GO.

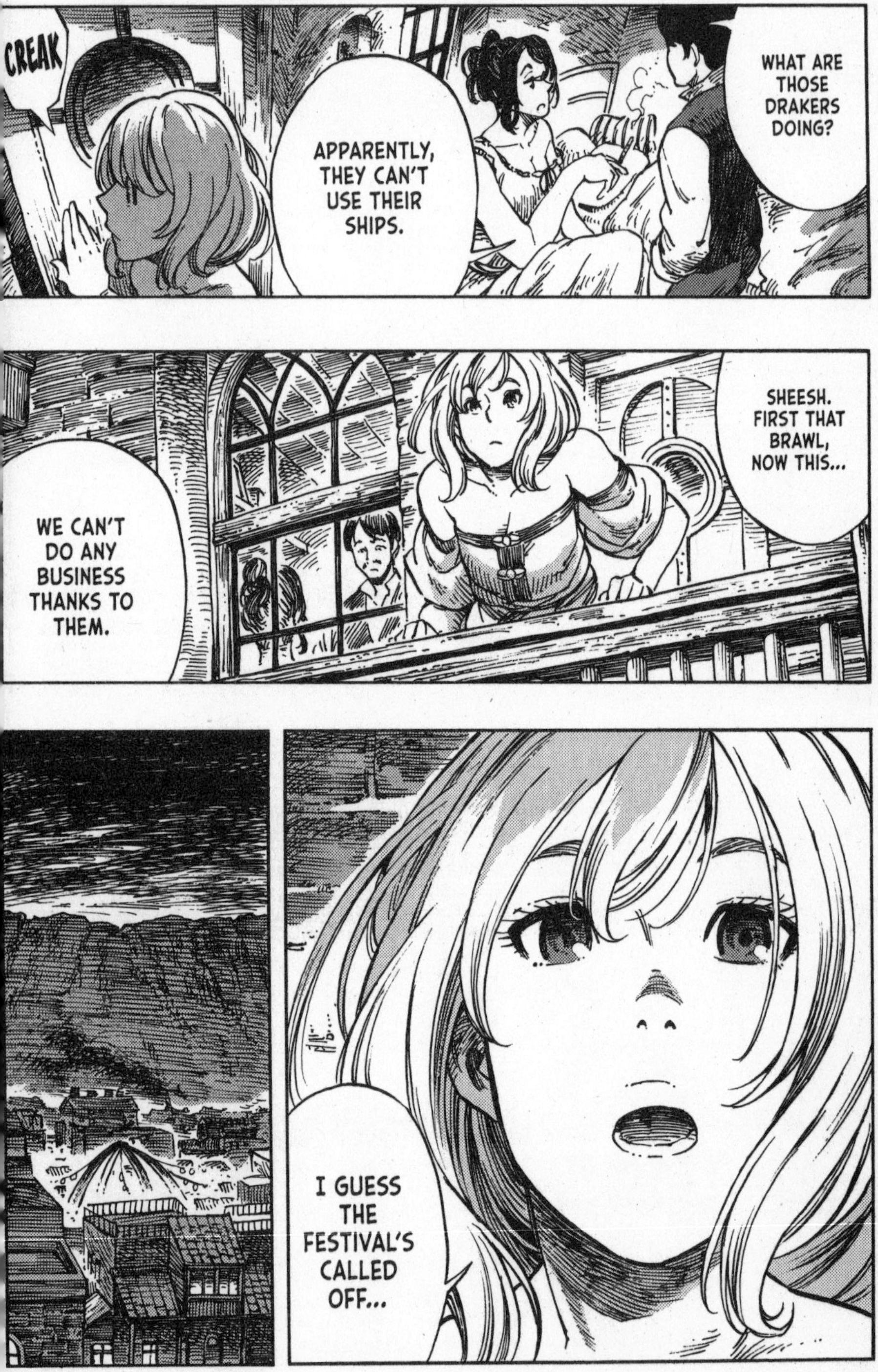
WHAT ARE THOSE DRAKERS DOING?
APPARENTLY, THEY CAN'T USE THEIR SHIPS.
CREAK
SHEESH. FIRST THAT BRAWL, NOW THIS...
WE CAN'T DO ANY BUSINESS THANKS TO THEM.
I GUESS THE FESTIVAL'S CALLED OFF...

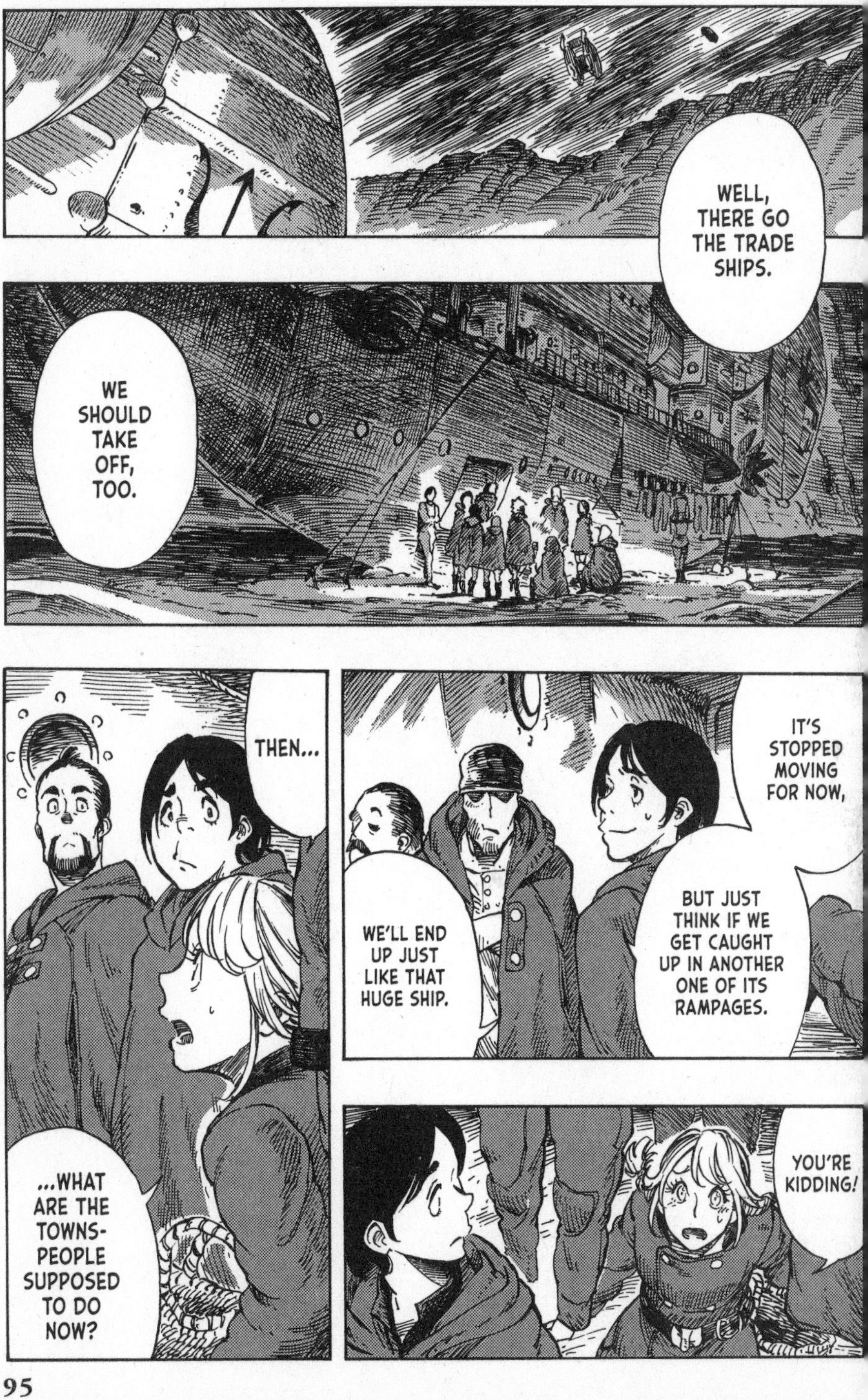
WELL, THERE GO THE TRADE SHIPS.
WE SHOULD TAKE OFF, TOO.
IT'S STOPPED MOVING FOR NOW,
BUT JUST THINK IF WE GET CAUGHT UP IN ANOTHER ONE OF ITS RAMPAGES.
WE'LL END UP JUST LIKE THAT HUGE SHIP.
YOU'RE KIDDING!
THEN...
...WHAT ARE THE TOWNS-PEOPLE SUPPOSED TO DO NOW?

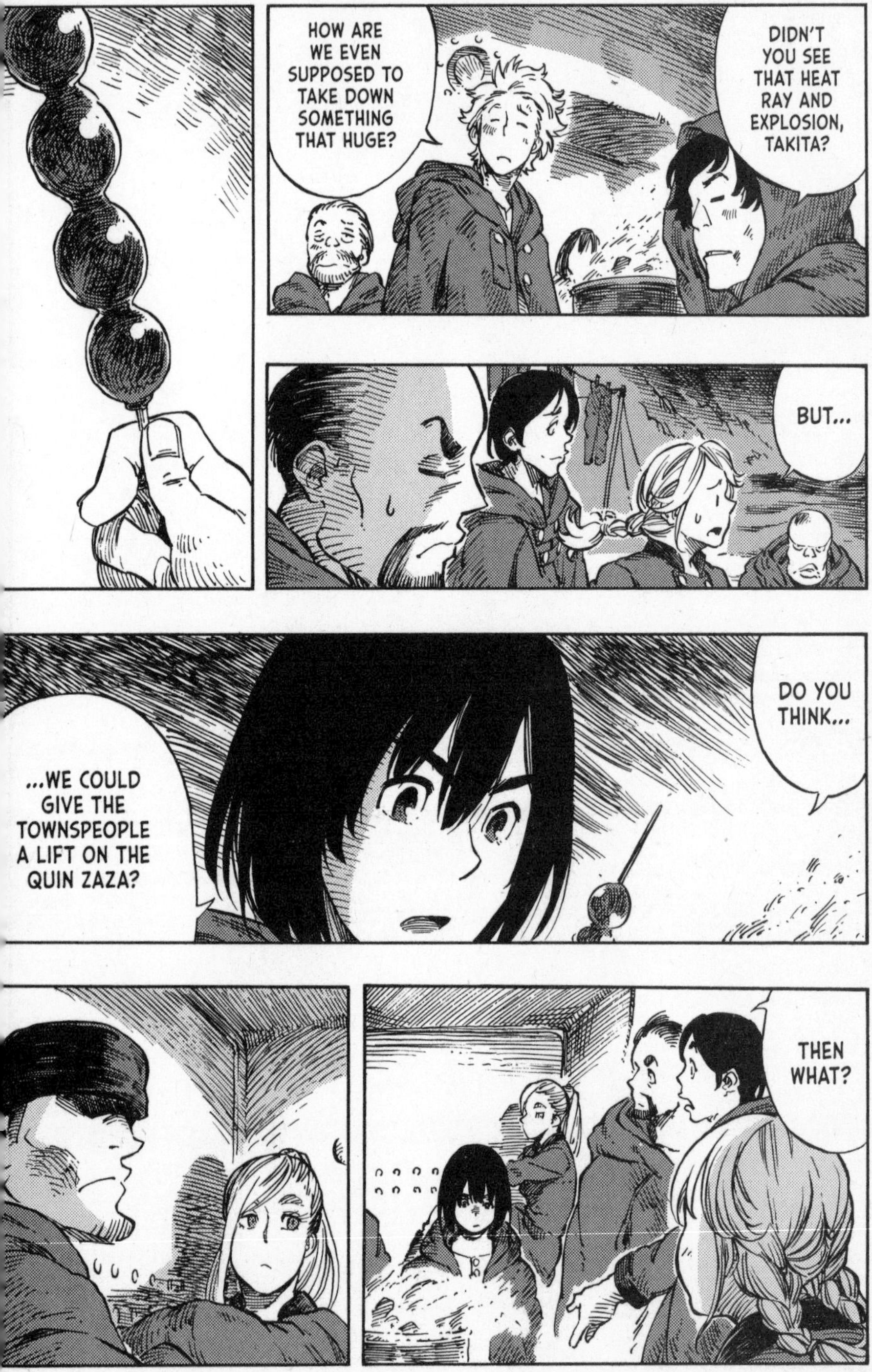
DIDN'T YOU SEE THAT HEAT RAY AND EXPLOSION, TAKITA?
HOW ARE WE EVEN SUPPOSED TO TAKE DOWN SOMETHING THAT HUGE?
BUT...
DO YOU THINK...
...WE COULD GIVE THE TOWNSPEOPLE A LIFT ON THE QUIN ZAZA?
THEN WHAT?

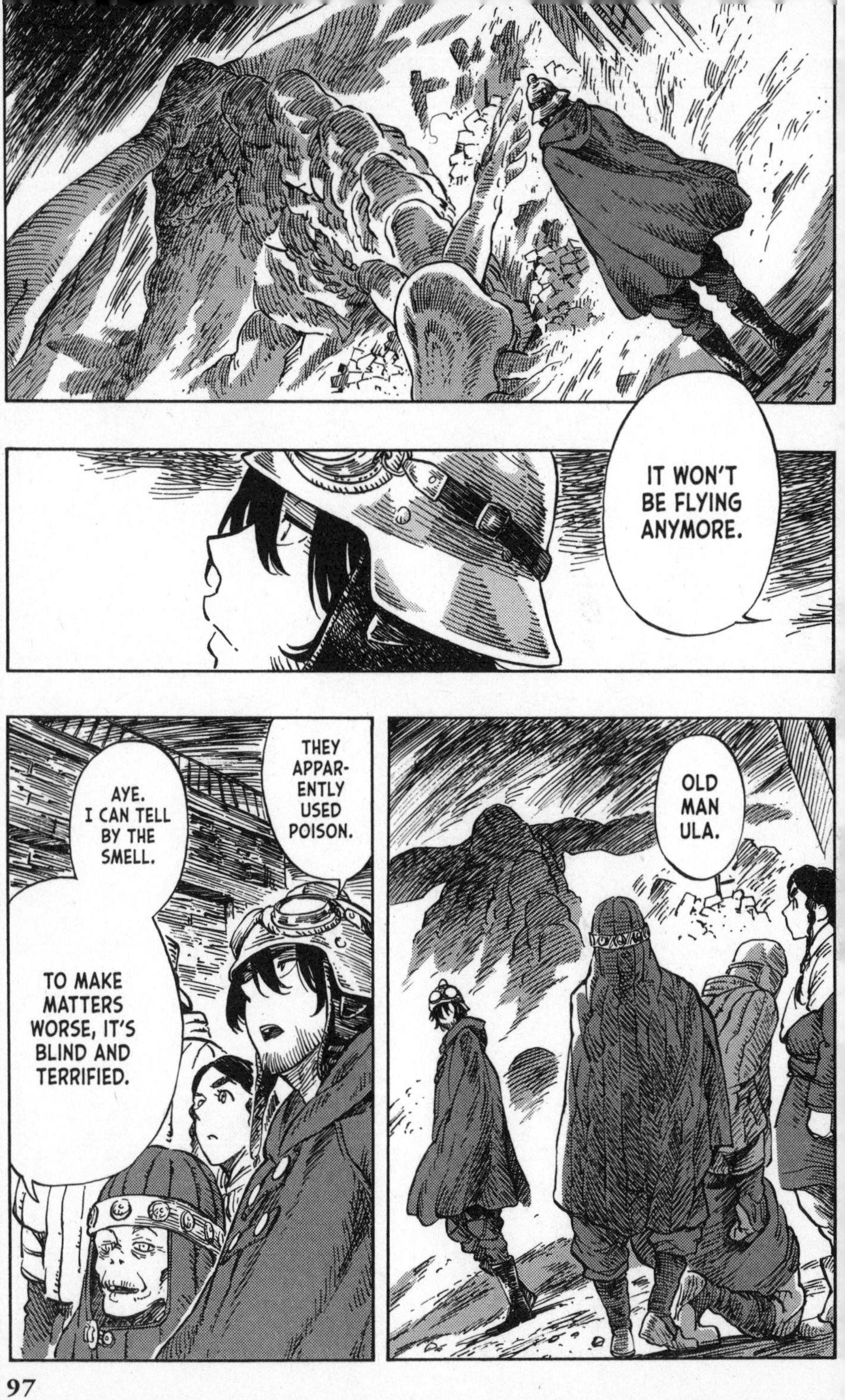
IT WON'T BE FLYING ANYMORE.
OLD MAN ULA.
THEY APPAR-ENTLY USED POISON.
AYE. I CAN TELL BY THE SMELL.
TO MAKE MATTERS WORSE, IT'S BLIND AND TERRIFIED.

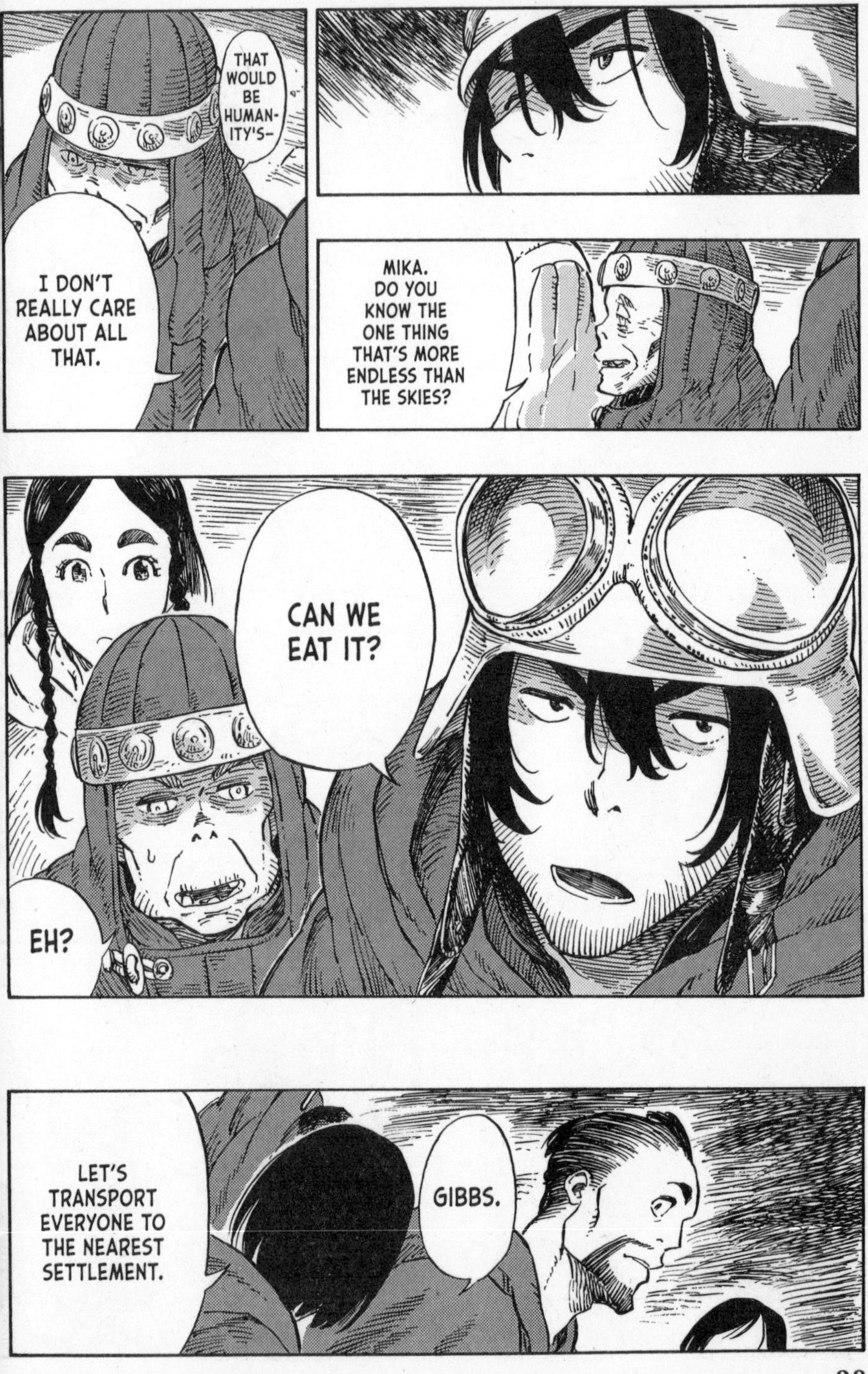
THAT WOULD BE HUMANITY'S—
I DON'T REALLY CARE ABOUT ALL THAT.
MIKA. DO YOU KNOW THE ONE THING THAT'S MORE ENDLESS THAN THE SKIES?
CAN WE EAT IT?
EH?
GIBBS.
LET'S TRANSPORT EVERYONE TO THE NEAREST SETTLEMENT.

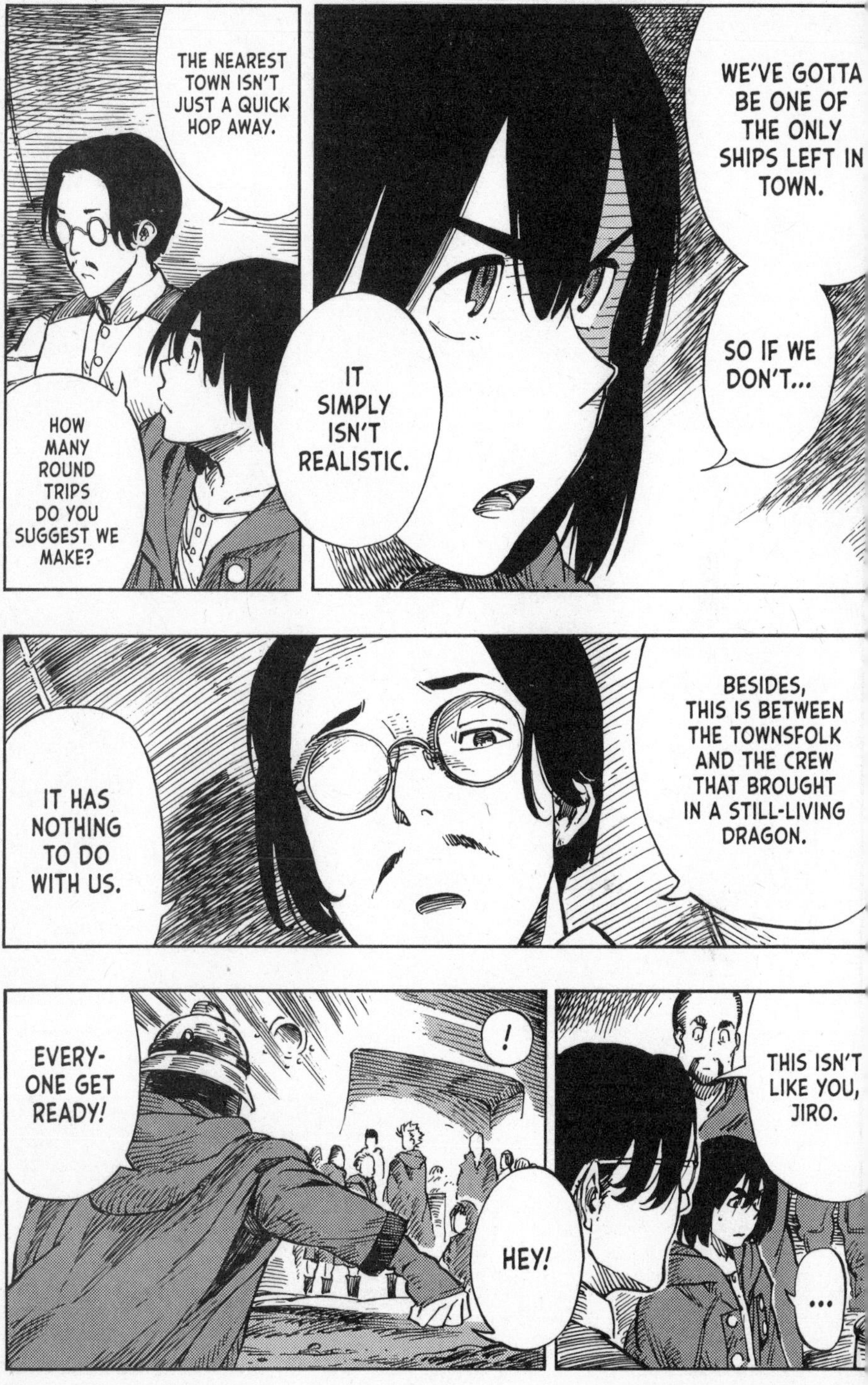
WE'VE GOTTA BE ONE OF THE ONLY SHIPS LEFT IN TOWN.
SO IF WE DON'T...
IT SIMPLY ISN'T REALISTIC.
THE NEAREST TOWN ISN'T JUST A QUICK HOP AWAY.
HOW MANY ROUND TRIPS DO YOU SUGGEST WE MAKE?
BESIDES, THIS IS BETWEEN THE TOWNSFOLK AND THE CREW THAT BROUGHT IN A STILL-LIVING DRAGON.
IT HAS NOTHING TO DO WITH US.
THIS ISN'T LIKE YOU, JIRO.
...
!
EVERY-ONE GET READY!
HEY!

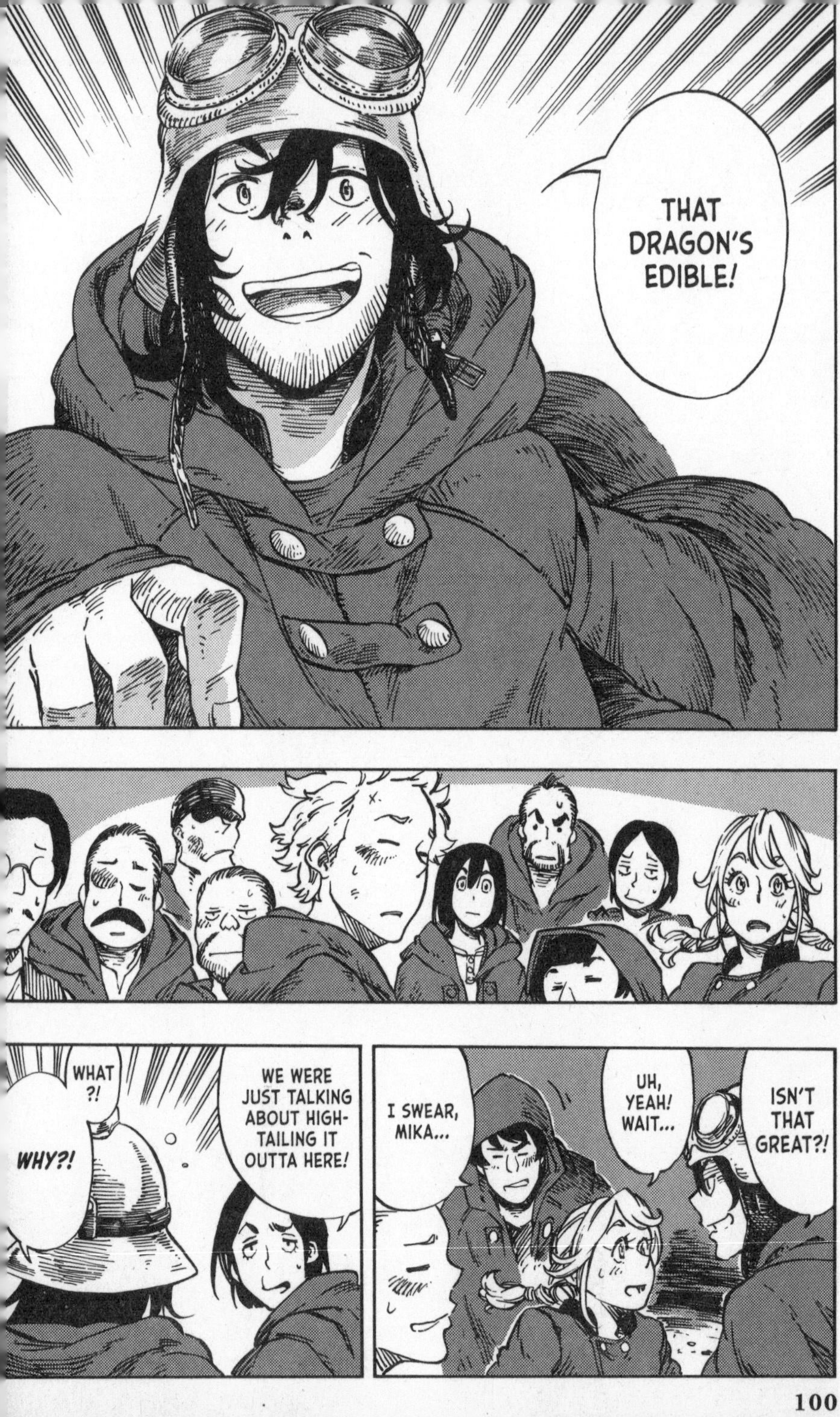
THAT DRAGON'S EDIBLE!
ISN'T THAT GREAT?!
UH, YEAH! WAIT...
I SWEAR, MIKA...
WE WERE JUST TALKING ABOUT HIGH-TAILING IT OUTTA HERE!
WHAT?!
WHY?!

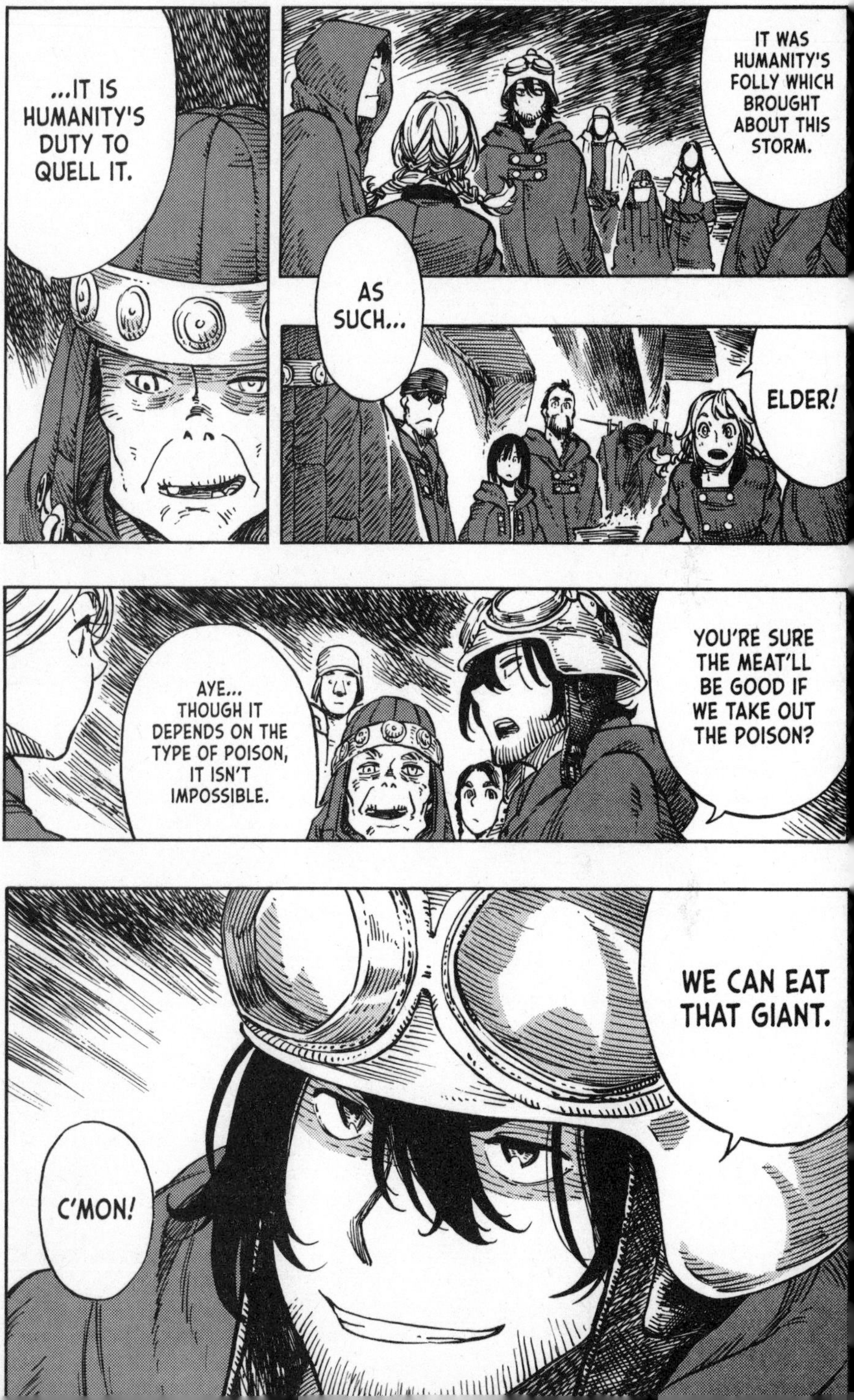
IT WAS HUMANITY'S FOLLY WHICH BROUGHT ABOUT THIS STORM.
AS SUCH...
ELDER!
...IT IS HUMANITY'S DUTY TO QUELL IT.
YOU'RE SURE THE MEAT'LL BE GOOD IF WE TAKE OUT THE POISON?
AYE... THOUGH IT DEPENDS ON THE TYPE OF POISON, IT ISN'T IMPOSSIBLE.
WE CAN EAT THAT GIANT.
C'MON!

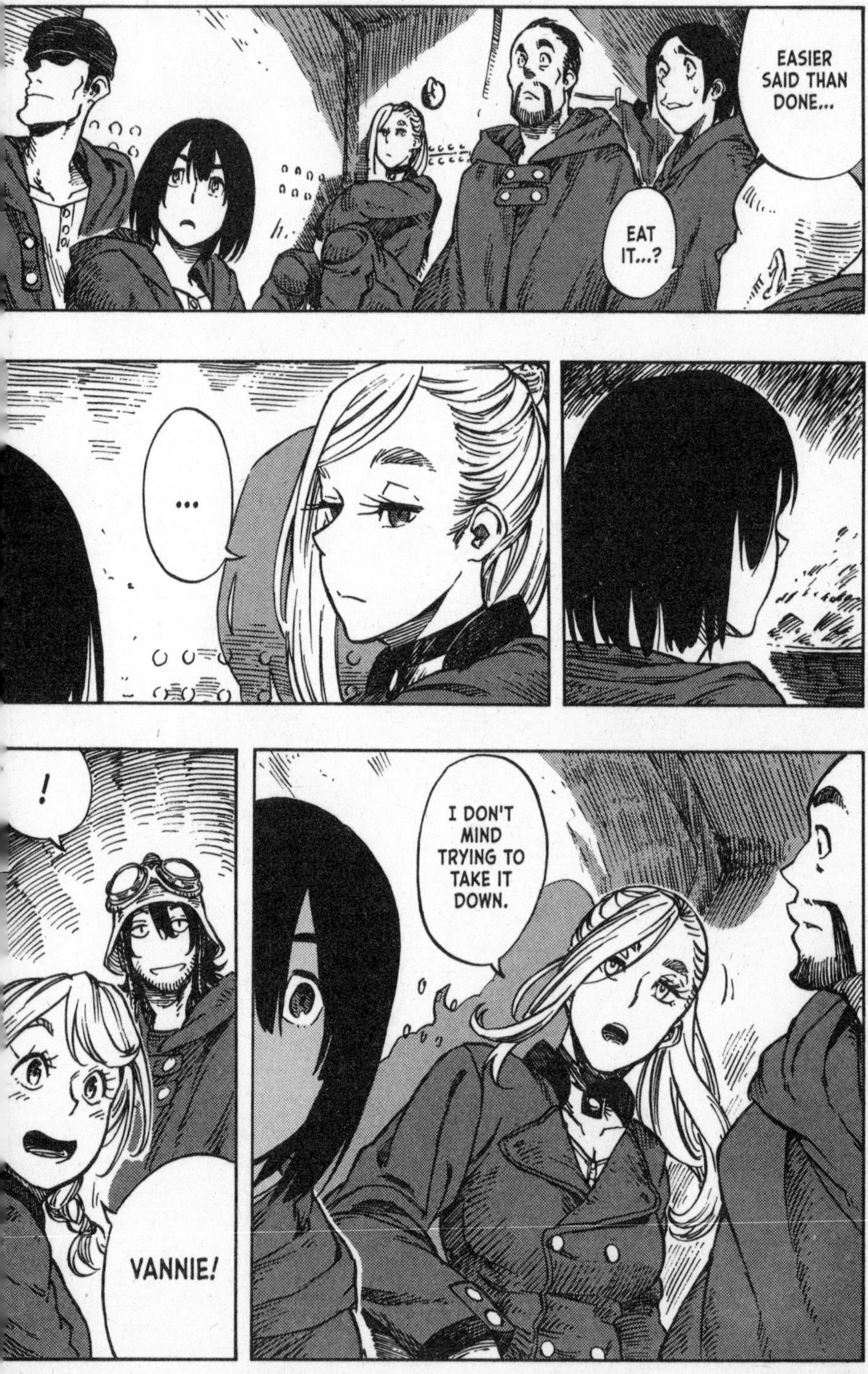
EASIER SAID THAN DONE...
EAT IT...?
...
I DON'T MIND TRYING TO TAKE IT DOWN.
!
VANNIE!

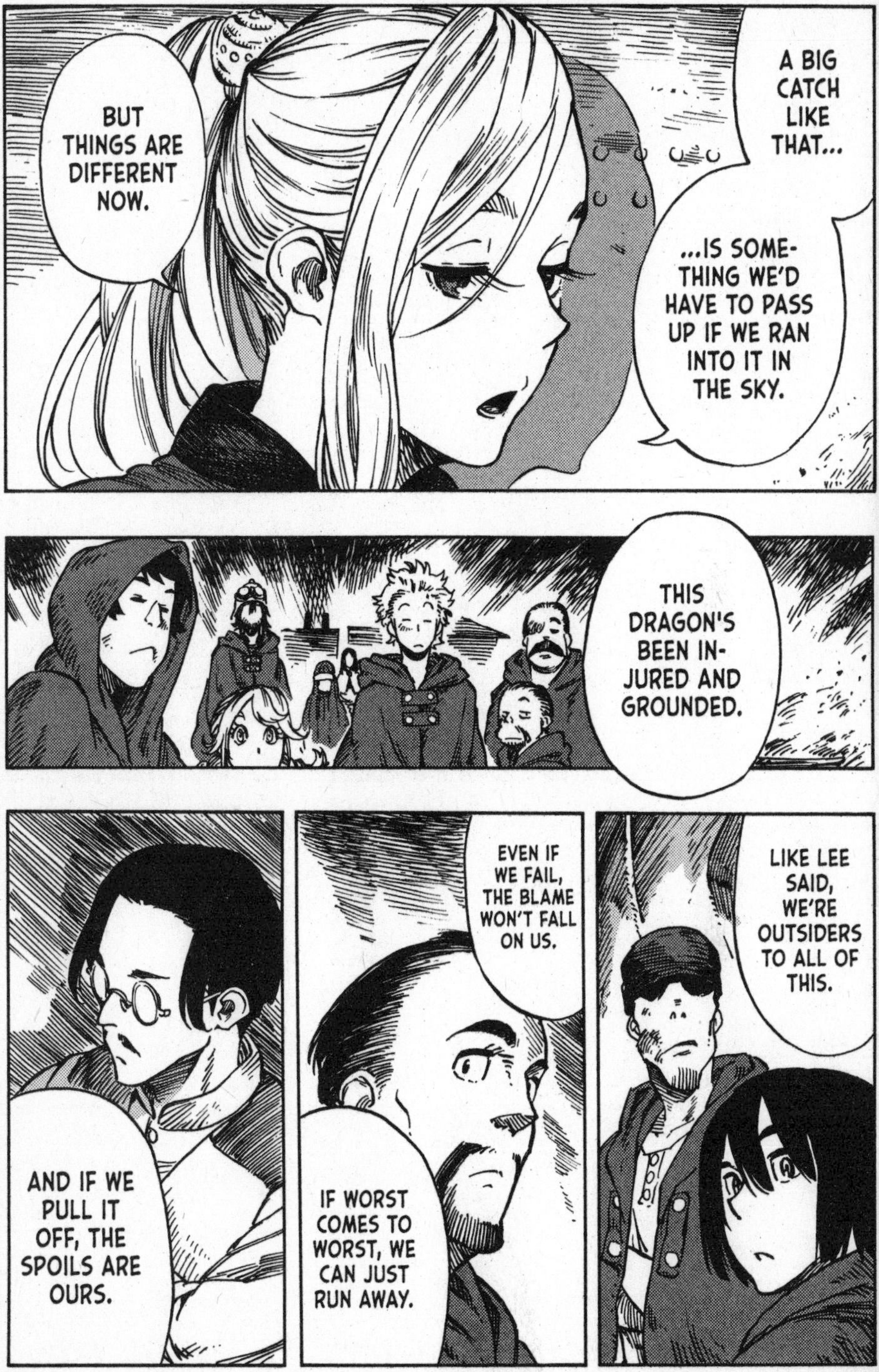
A BIG CATCH LIKE THAT...
...IS SOMETHING WE'D HAVE TO PASS UP IF WE RAN INTO IT IN THE SKY.
BUT THINGS ARE DIFFERENT NOW.
THIS DRAGON'S BEEN INJURED AND GROUNDED.
LIKE LEE SAID, WE'RE OUTSIDERS TO ALL OF THIS.
EVEN IF WE FAIL, THE BLAME WON'T FALL ON US.
IF WORST COMES TO WORST, WE CAN JUST RUN AWAY.
AND IF WE PULL IT OFF, THE SPOILS ARE OURS.

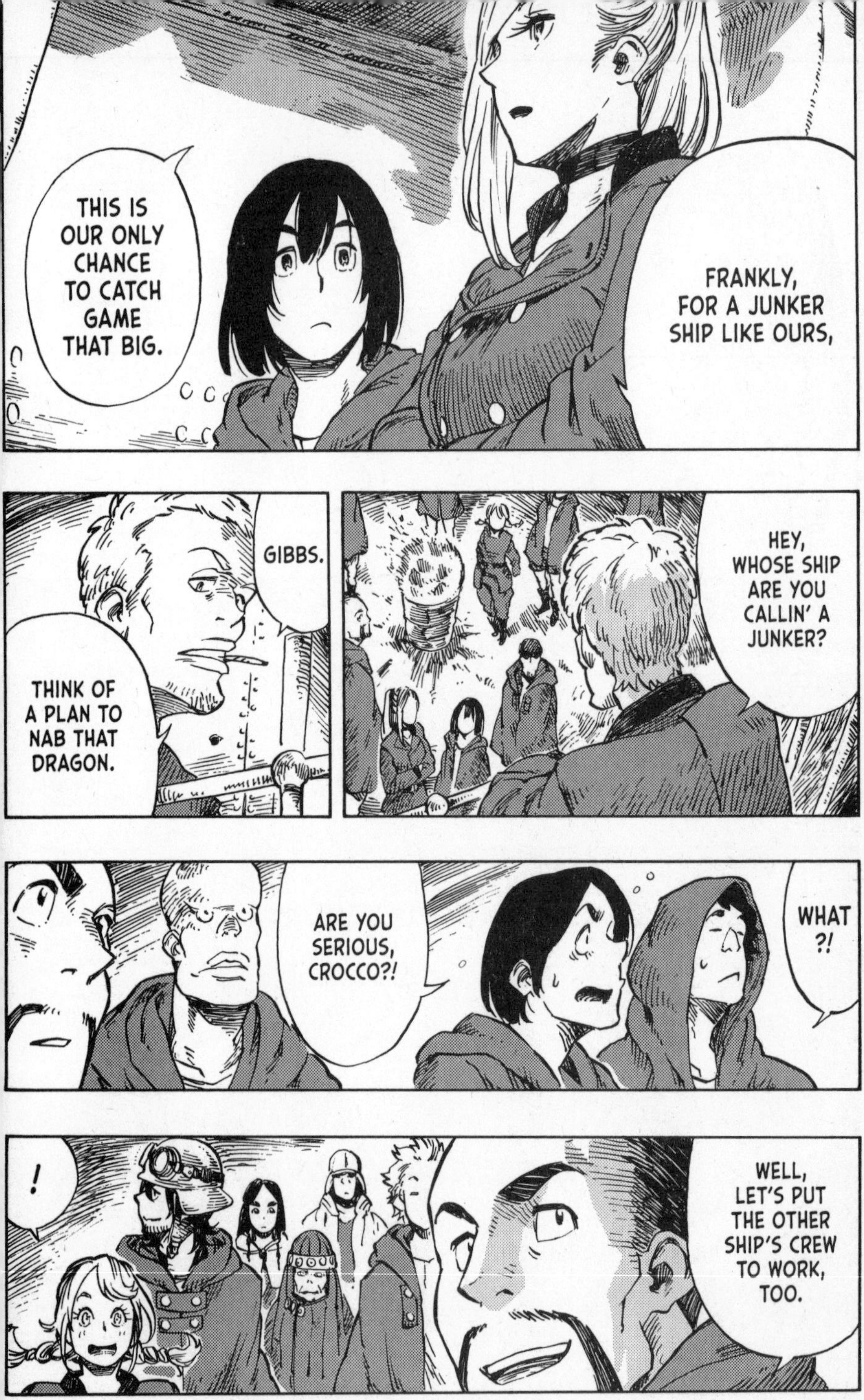
FRANKLY, FOR A JUNKER SHIP LIKE OURS,
THIS IS OUR ONLY CHANCE TO CATCH GAME THAT BIG.
HEY, WHOSE SHIP ARE YOU CALLIN' A JUNKER?
GIBBS.
THINK OF A PLAN TO NAB THAT DRAGON.
WHAT ?!
ARE YOU SERIOUS, CROCCO?!
WELL, LET'S PUT THE OTHER SHIP'S CREW TO WORK, TOO.
!

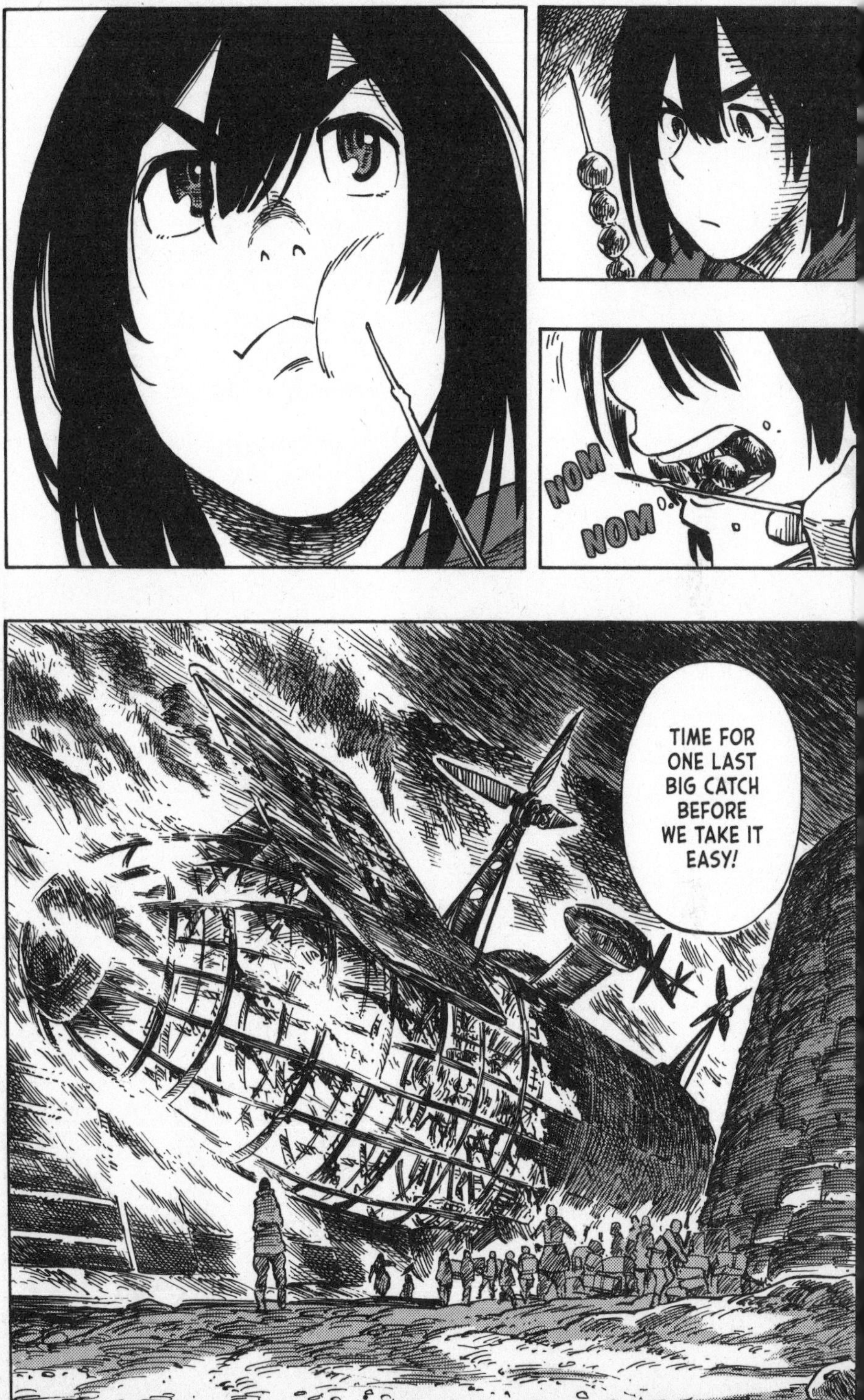
NOM
NOM
TIME FOR ONE LAST BIG CATCH BEFORE WE TAKE IT EASY!

Candied Grapes

Ingredients

✦ Grapes

✦ Grape juice

✦ Sugar

✦ Flour

✦ Skewers

01
Thicken sweetened grape juice with flour.

02
Dip grape skewers into the sauce and let dry.

03
Repeat the previous steps 2-3 times until the grapes are thoroughly coated.

YOU CAN'T GET THAT KIND OF FLAVOR ON THE *QUIN ZAZA.*

DRAGON's RECIPE

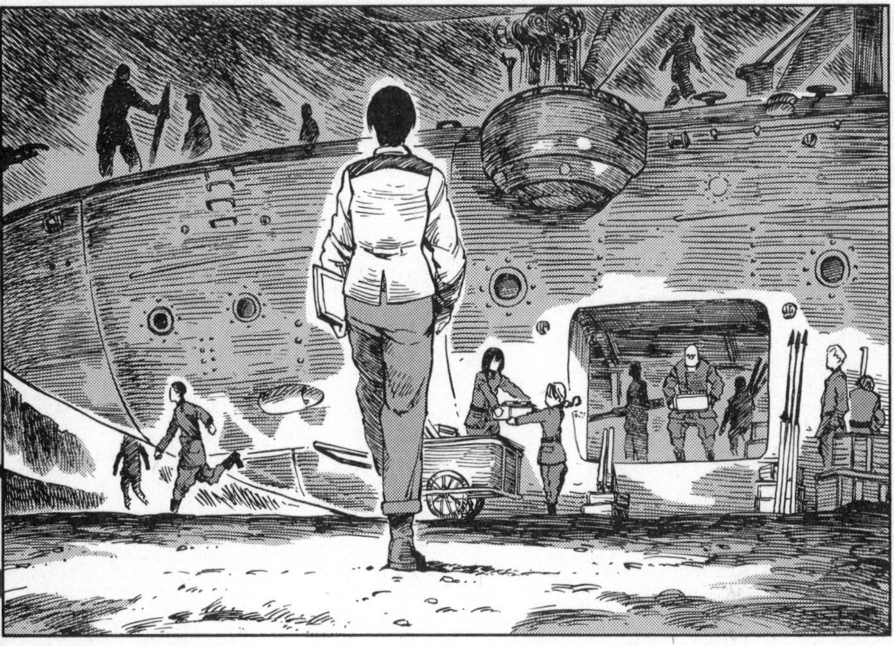

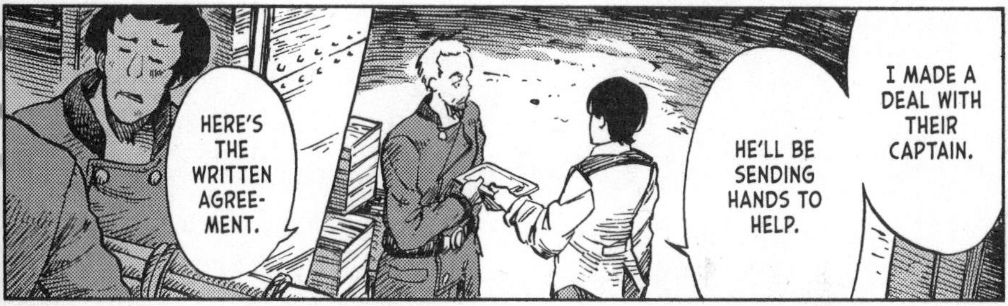
I MADE A DEAL WITH THEIR CAPTAIN.
HE'LL BE SENDING HANDS TO HELP.
HERE'S THE WRITTEN AGREEMENT.

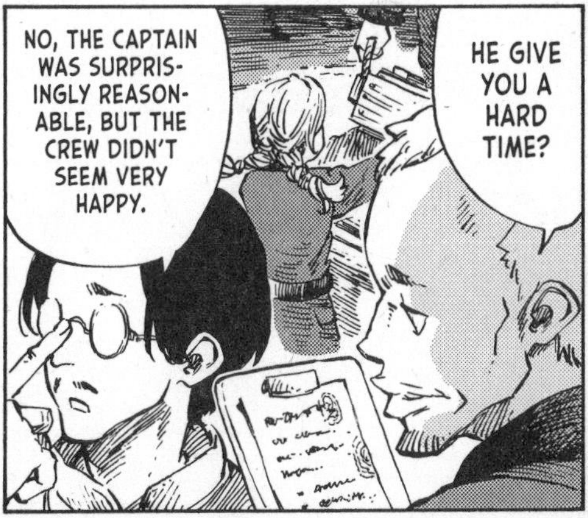
HE GIVE YOU A HARD TIME?
NO, THE CAPTAIN WAS SURPRISINGLY REASONABLE, BUT THE CREW DIDN'T SEEM VERY HAPPY.

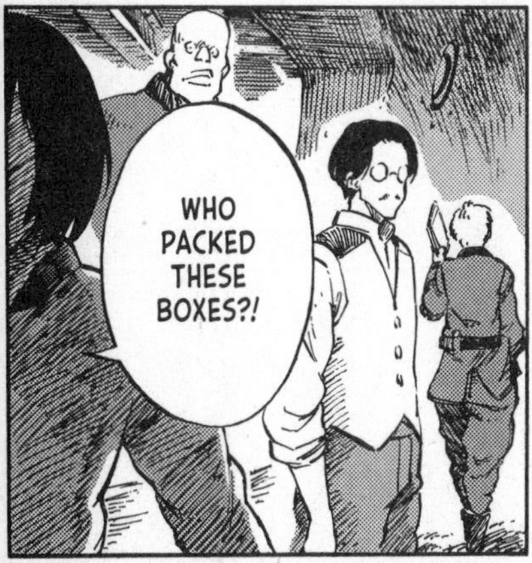
WHO PACKED THESE BOXES?!

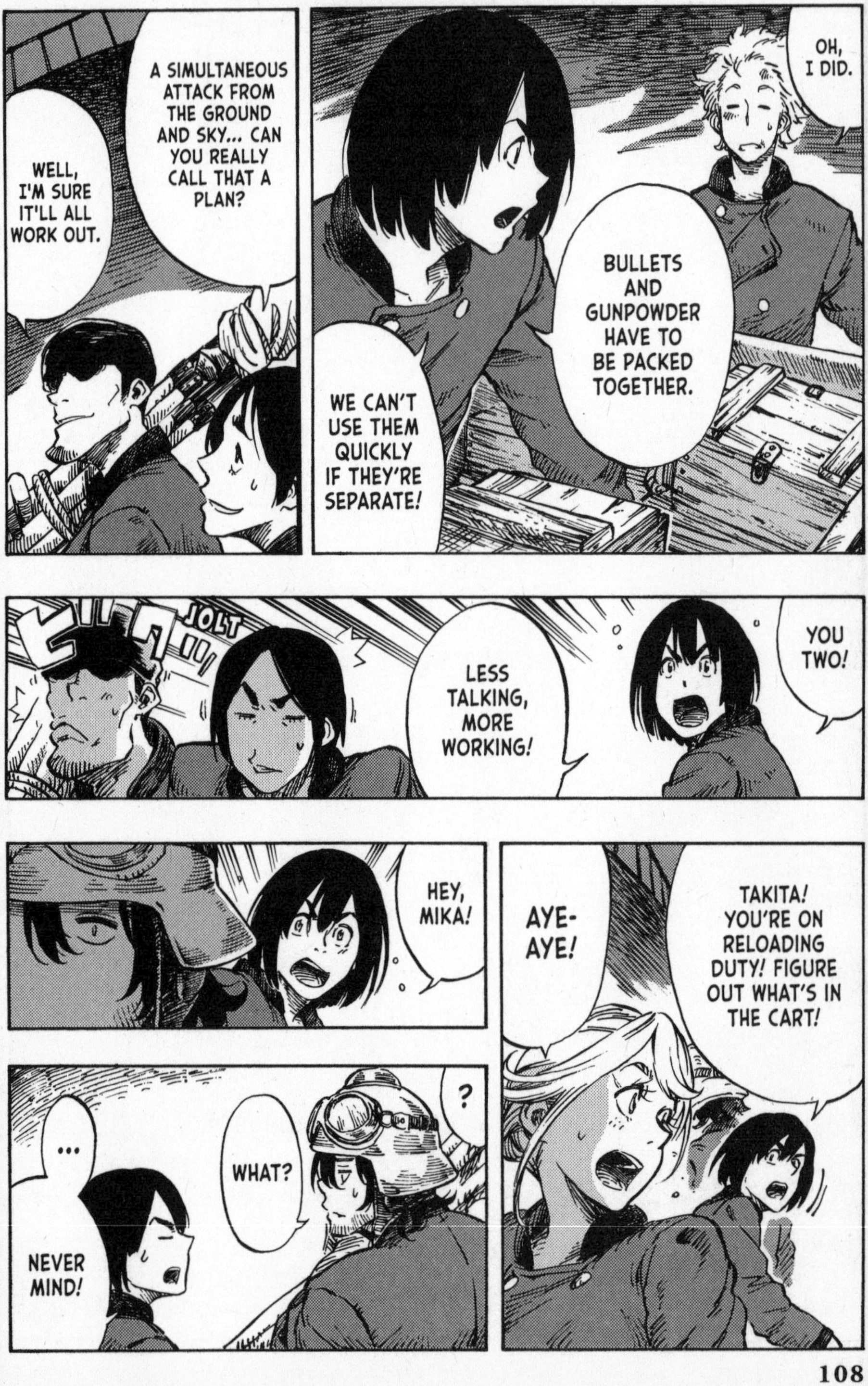
OH, I DID.
BULLETS AND GUNPOWDER HAVE TO BE PACKED TOGETHER.
WE CAN'T USE THEM QUICKLY IF THEY'RE SEPARATE!
A SIMULTANEOUS ATTACK FROM THE GROUND AND SKY... CAN YOU REALLY CALL THAT A PLAN?
WELL, I'M SURE IT'LL ALL WORK OUT.
YOU TWO!
LESS TALKING, MORE WORKING!
JOLT
TAKITA! YOU'RE ON RELOADING DUTY! FIGURE OUT WHAT'S IN THE CART!
AYE-AYE!
HEY, MIKA!
?
WHAT?
...
NEVER MIND!

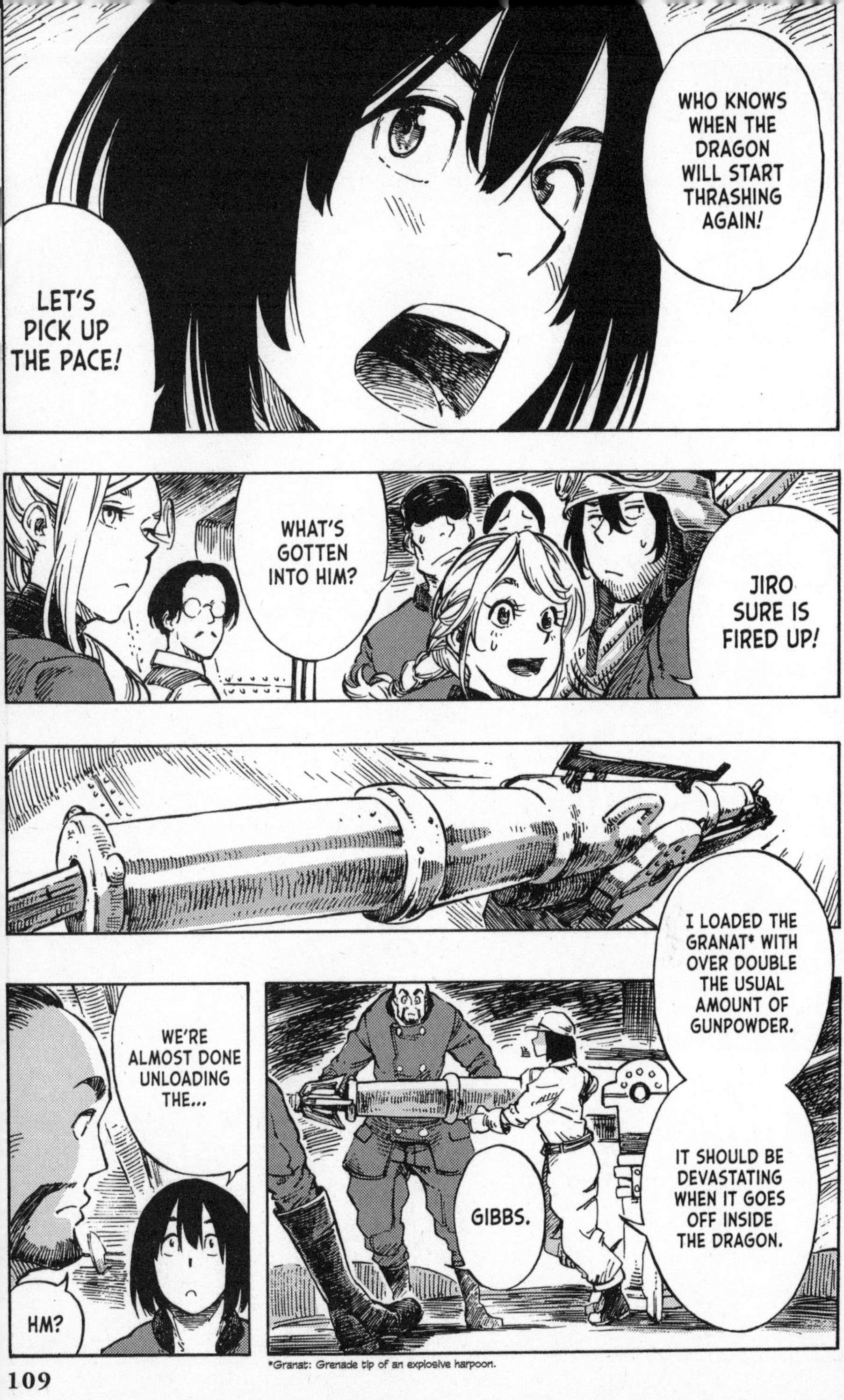
WHO KNOWS WHEN THE DRAGON WILL START THRASHING AGAIN!
LET'S PICK UP THE PACE!
JIRO SURE IS FIRED UP!
WHAT'S GOTTEN INTO HIM?
I LOADED THE GRANAT* WITH OVER DOUBLE THE USUAL AMOUNT OF GUNPOWDER.
IT SHOULD BE DEVASTATING WHEN IT GOES OFF INSIDE THE DRAGON.
GIBBS.
WE'RE ALMOST DONE UNLOADING THE...
HM?

*Granat: Grenade tip of an explosive harpoon.

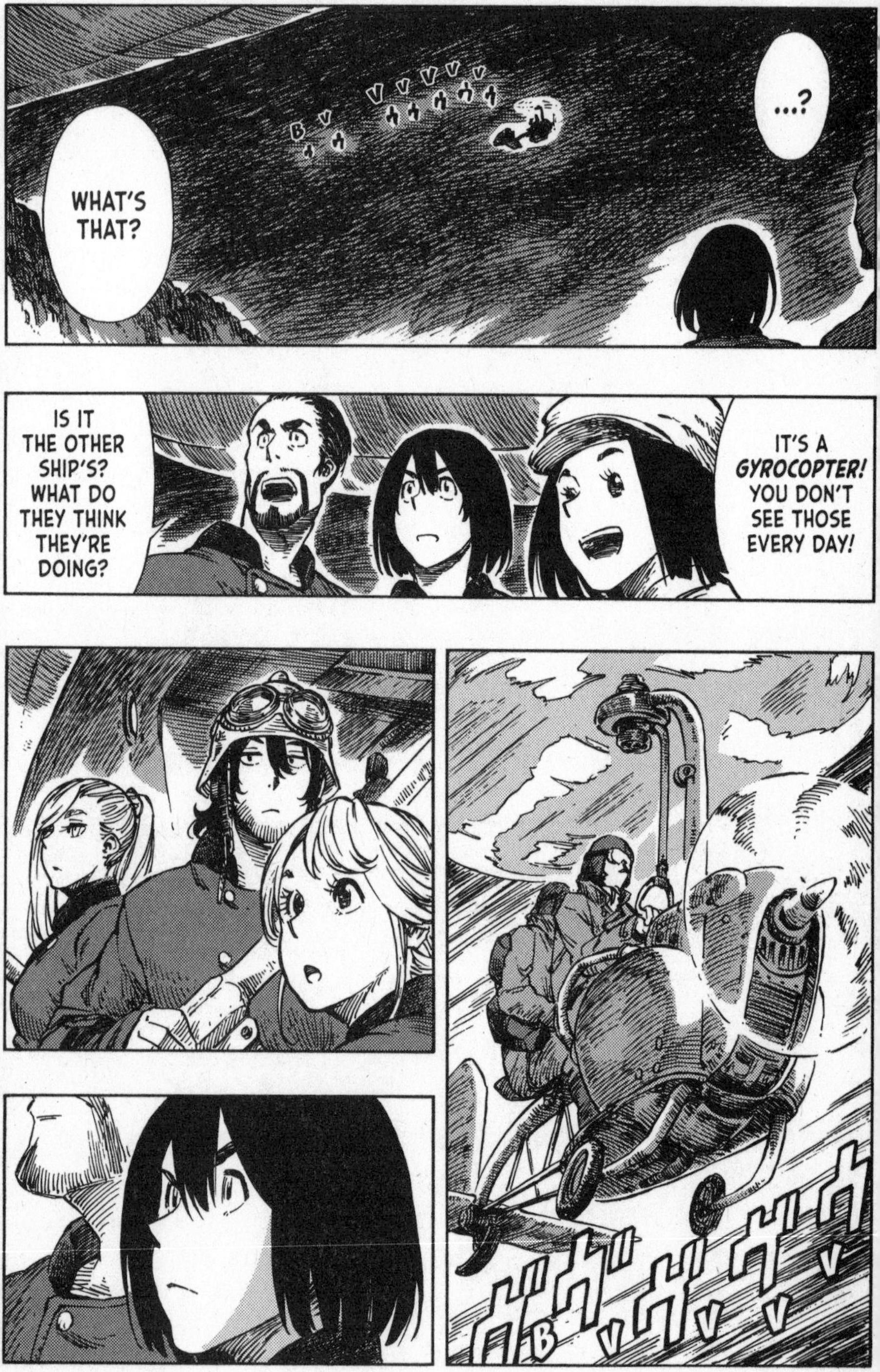
...?
WHAT'S THAT?
IT'S A *GYROCOPTER!* YOU DON'T SEE THOSE EVERY DAY!
IS IT THE OTHER SHIP'S? WHAT DO THEY THINK THEY'RE DOING?
BVVVV

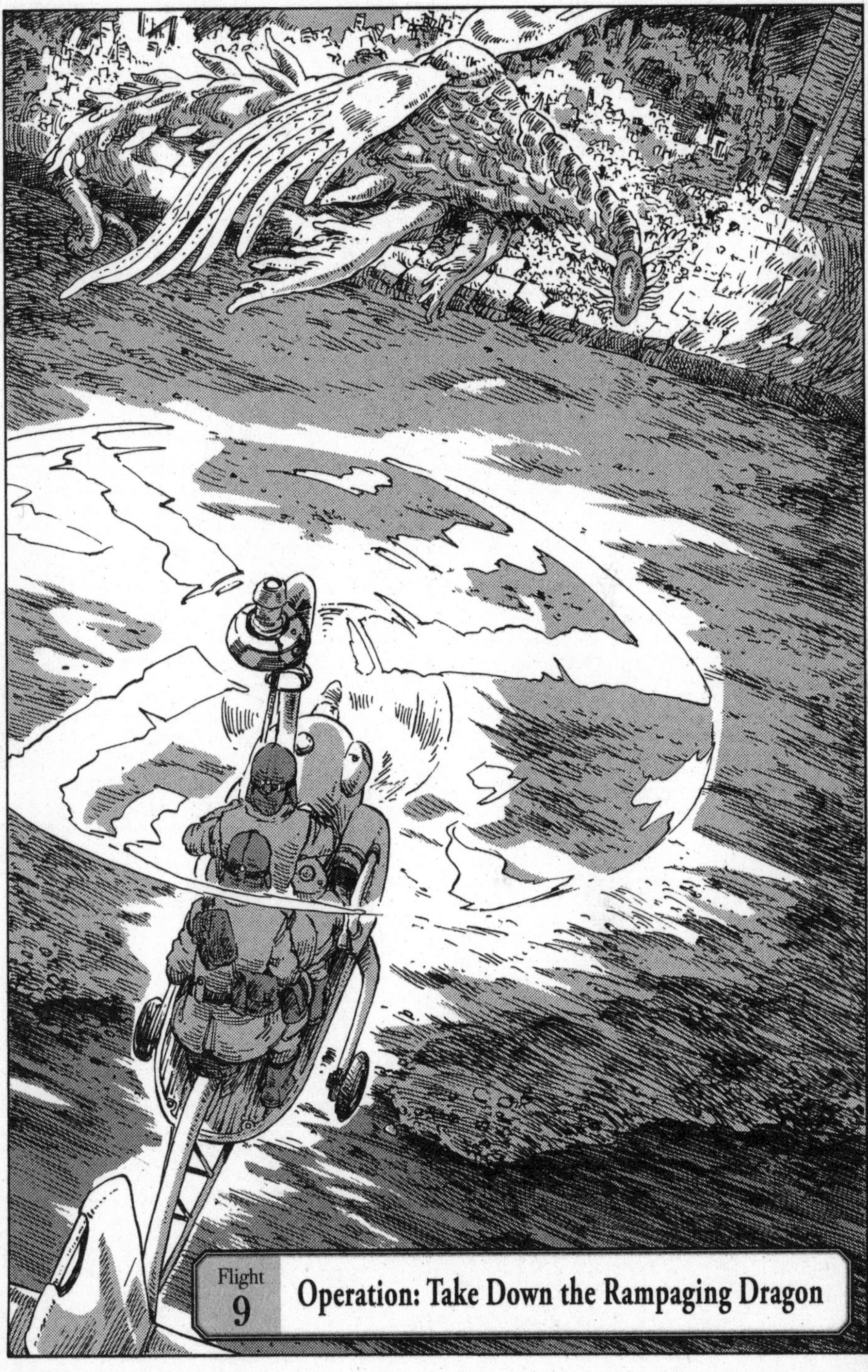

Flight 9 Operation: Take Down the Rampaging Dragon

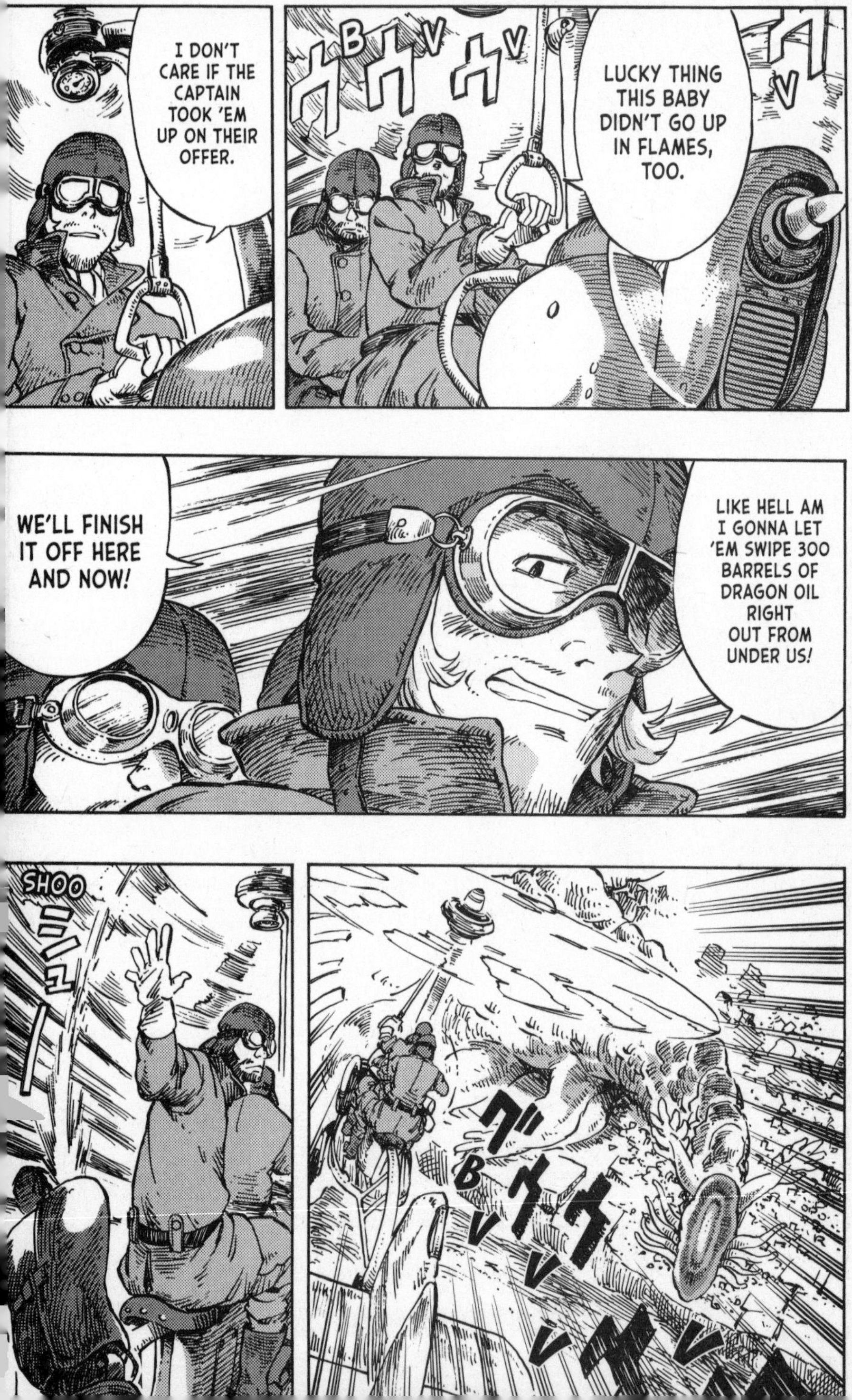
BVV
V
LUCKY THING THIS BABY DIDN'T GO UP IN FLAMES, TOO.
I DON'T CARE IF THE CAPTAIN TOOK 'EM UP ON THEIR OFFER.
LIKE HELL AM I GONNA LET 'EM SWIPE 300 BARRELS OF DRAGON OIL RIGHT OUT FROM UNDER US!
WE'LL FINISH IT OFF HERE AND NOW!
BVV
SHOO

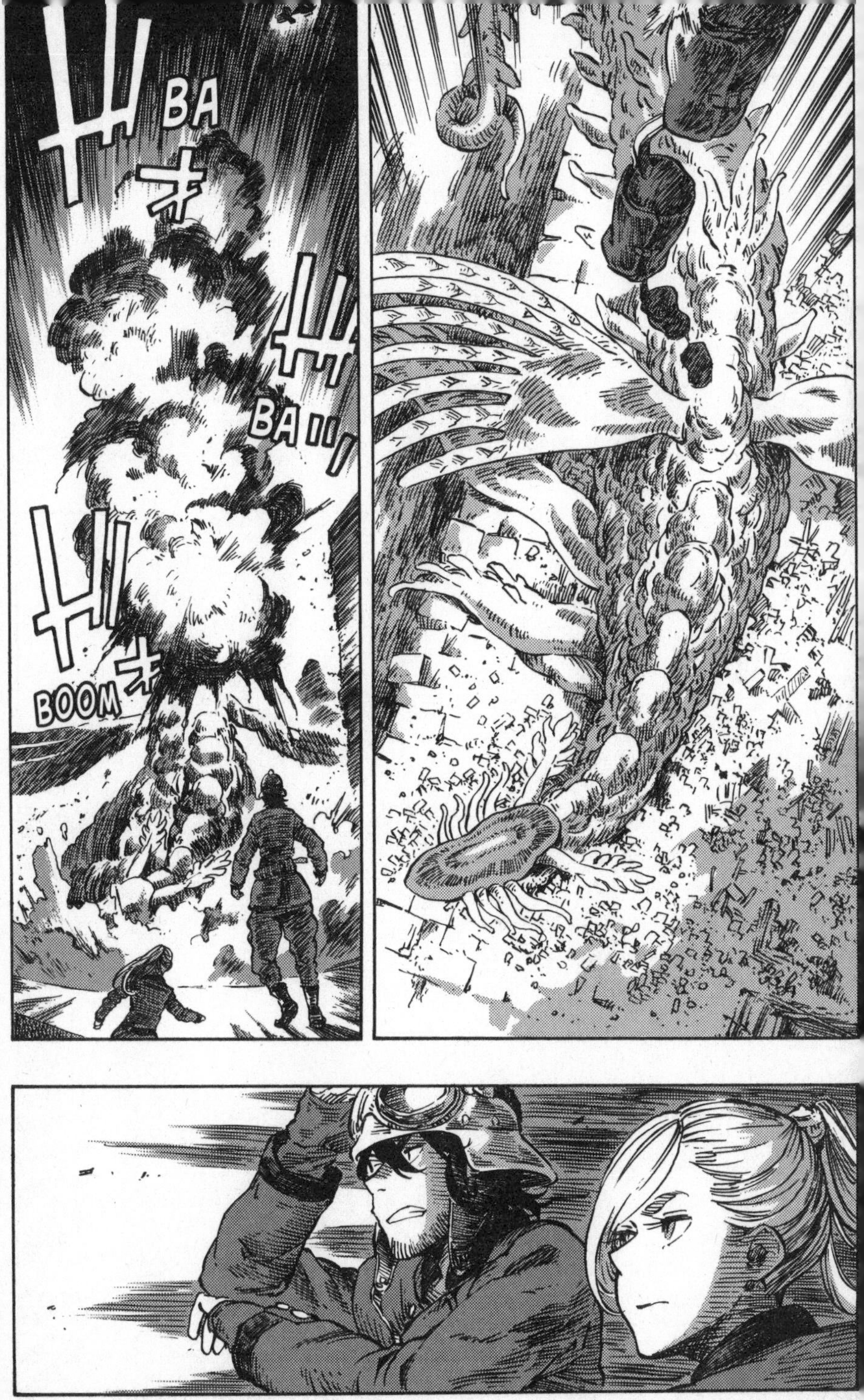
BA
BA
BOOM

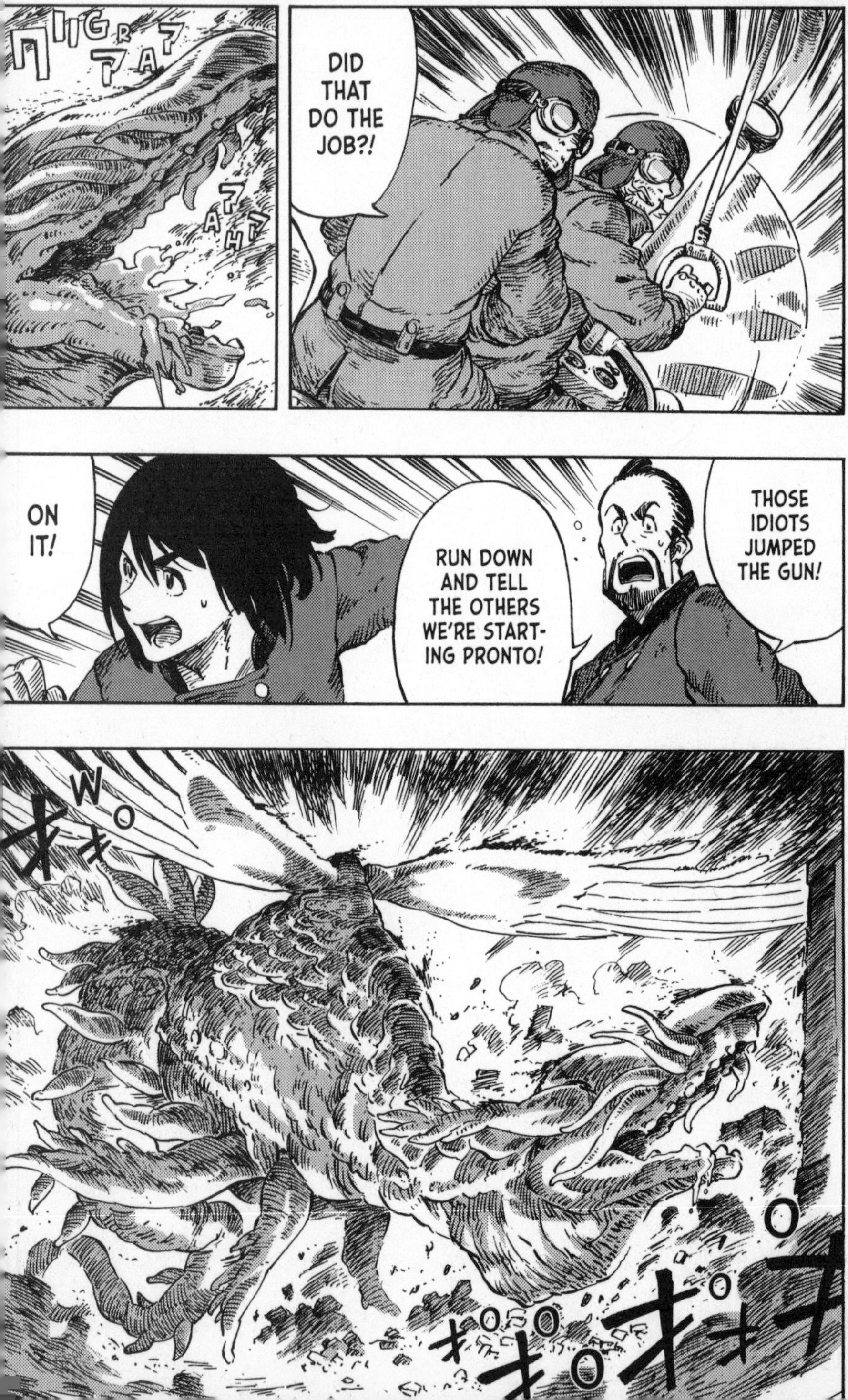
DID THAT DO THE JOB?!
THOSE IDIOTS JUMPED THE GUN!
RUN DOWN AND TELL THE OTHERS WE'RE START-ING PRONTO!
ON IT!
WO

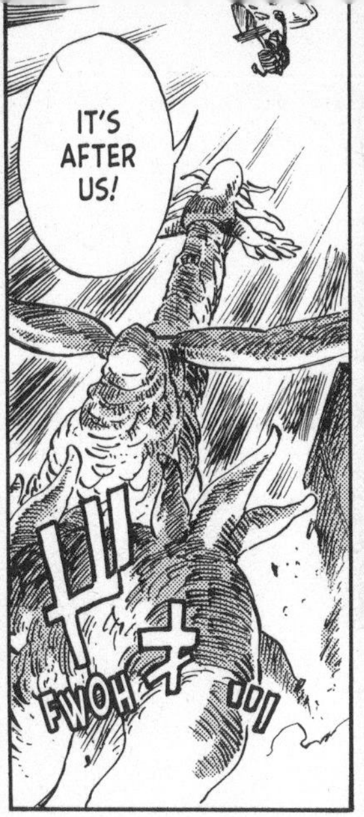
IT'S AFTER US!
FWOH

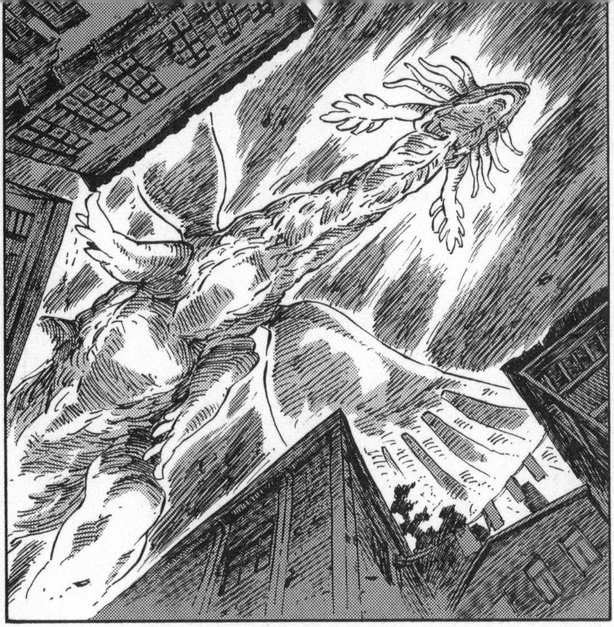

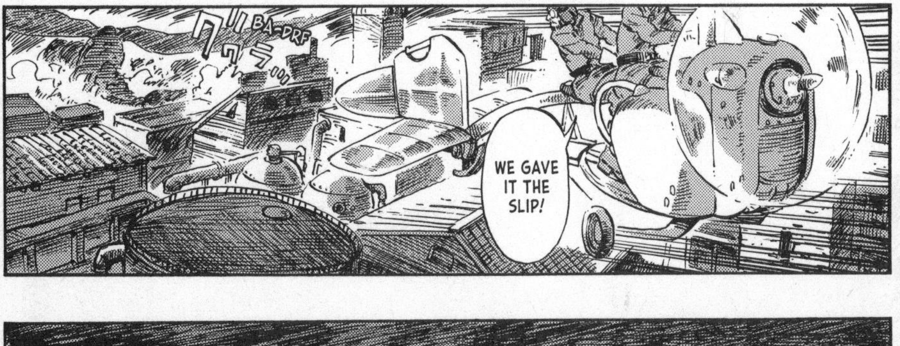
BA-DRF
WE GAVE IT THE SLIP!

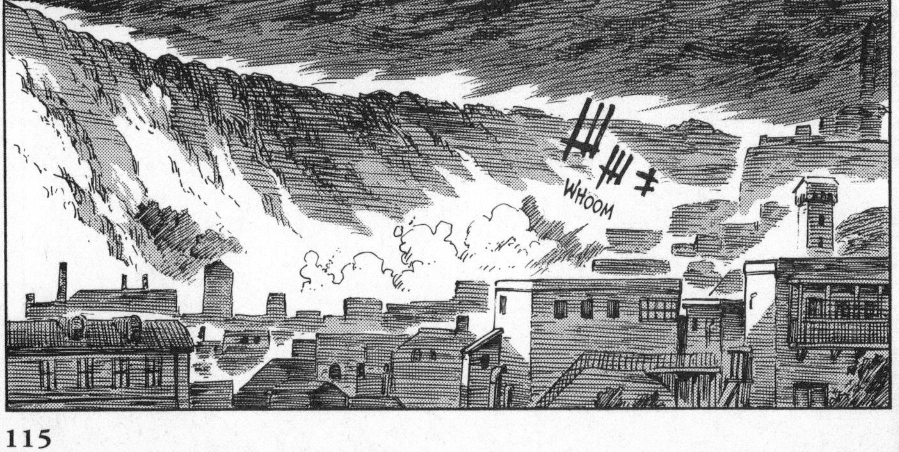
WHOOM

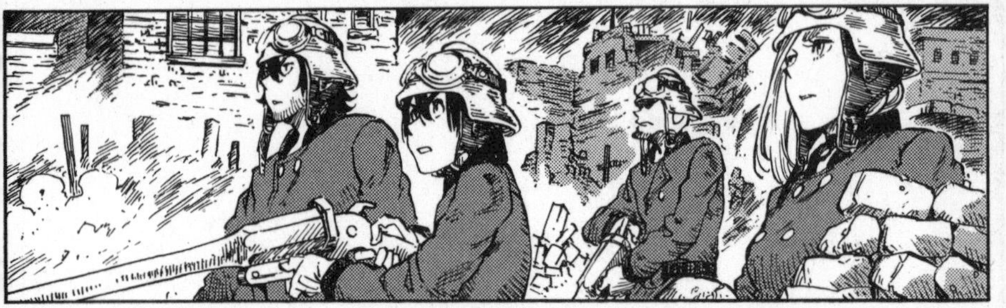
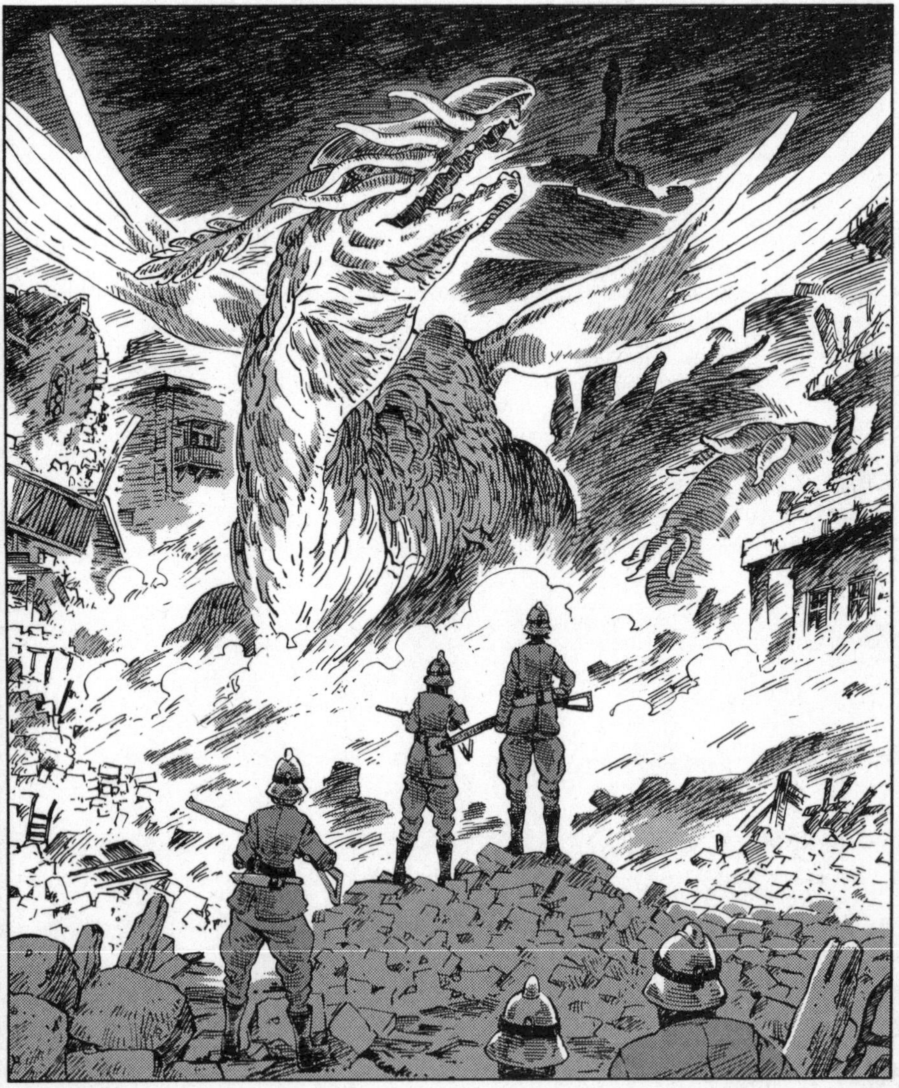

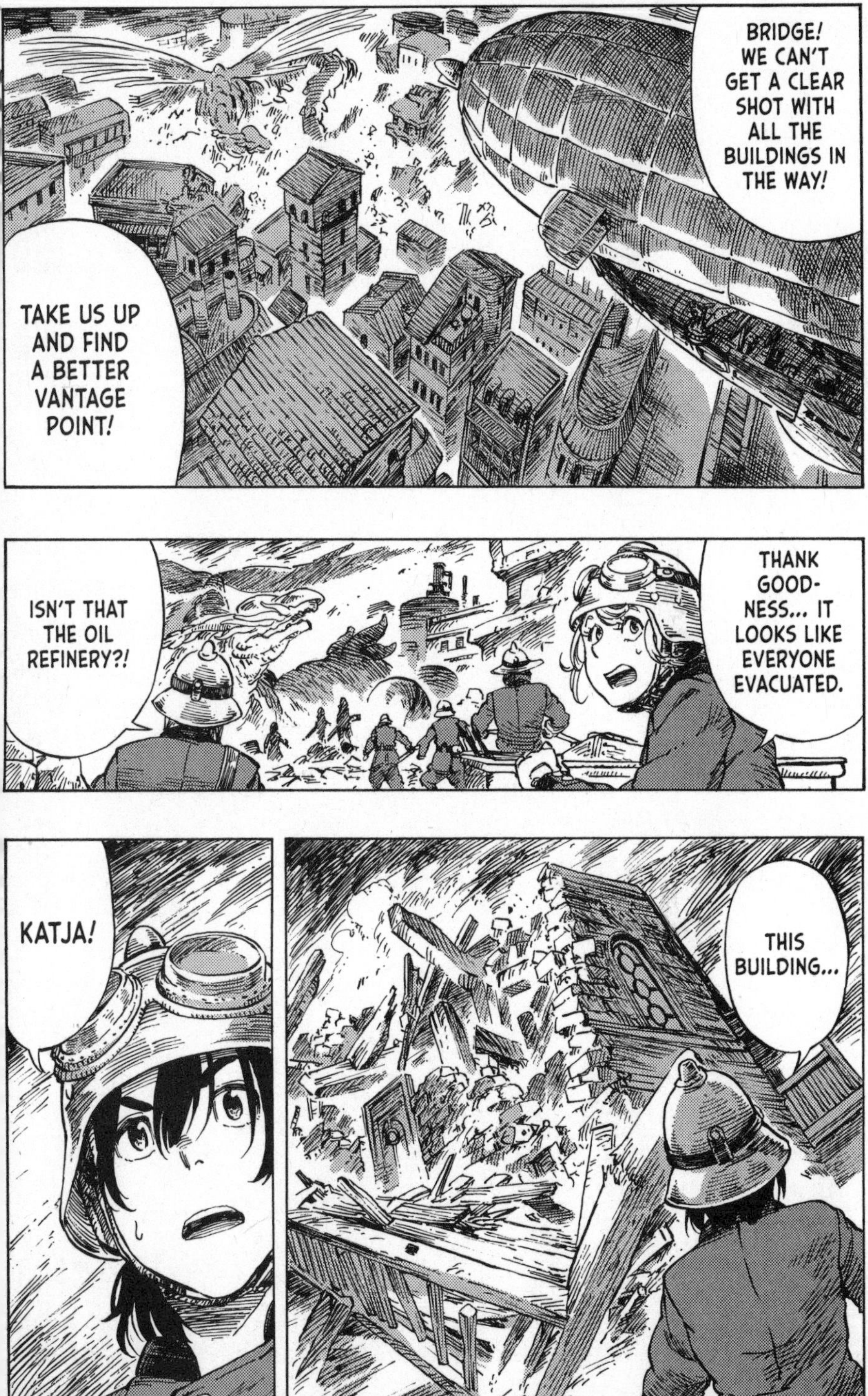
BRIDGE! WE CAN'T GET A CLEAR SHOT WITH ALL THE BUILDINGS IN THE WAY!
TAKE US UP AND FIND A BETTER VANTAGE POINT!
THANK GOODNESS... IT LOOKS LIKE EVERYONE EVACUATED.
ISN'T THAT THE OIL REFINERY?!
THIS BUILDING...
KATJA!

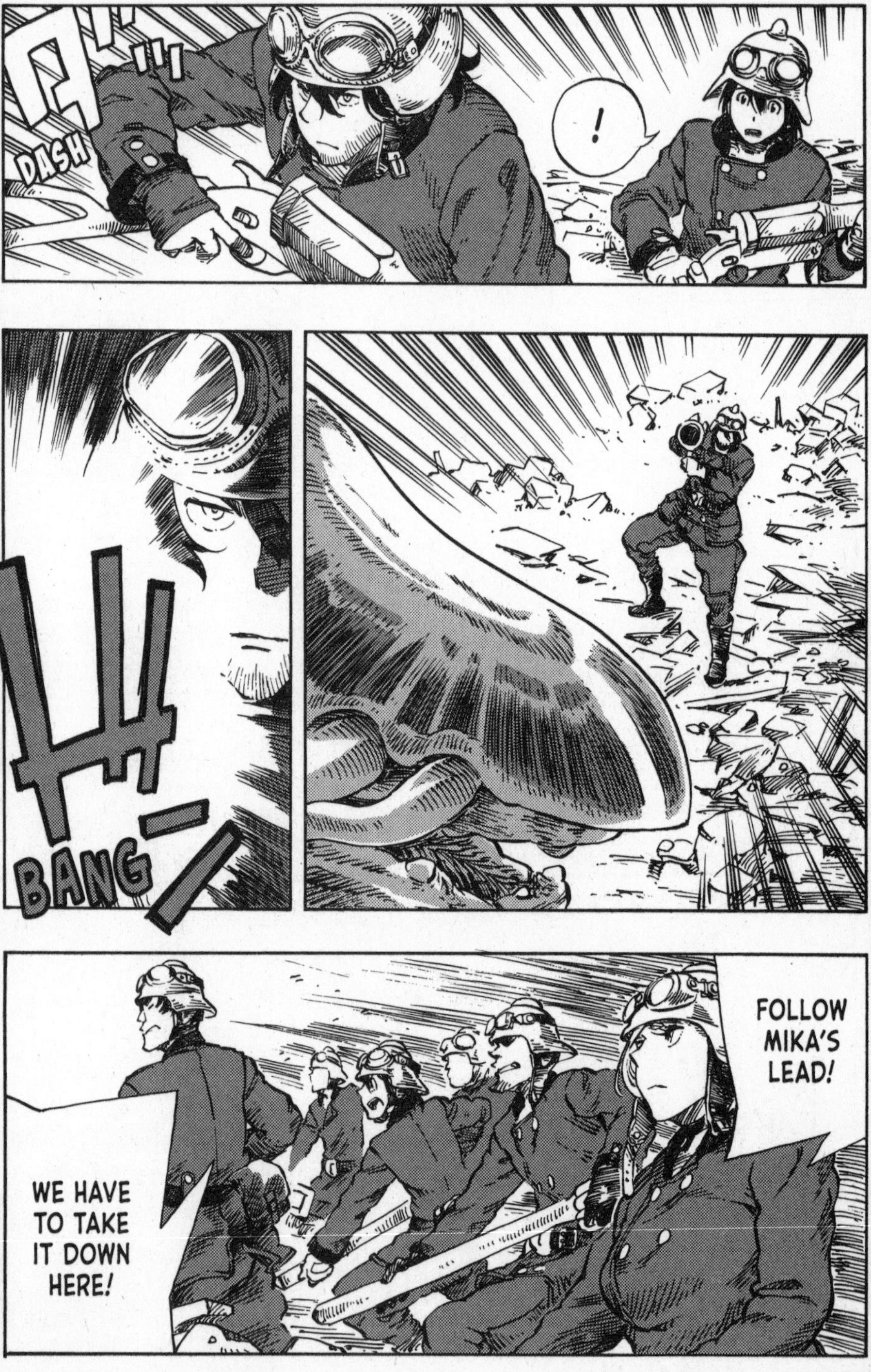
!
DASH
BANG
FOLLOW MIKA'S LEAD!
WE HAVE TO TAKE IT DOWN HERE!

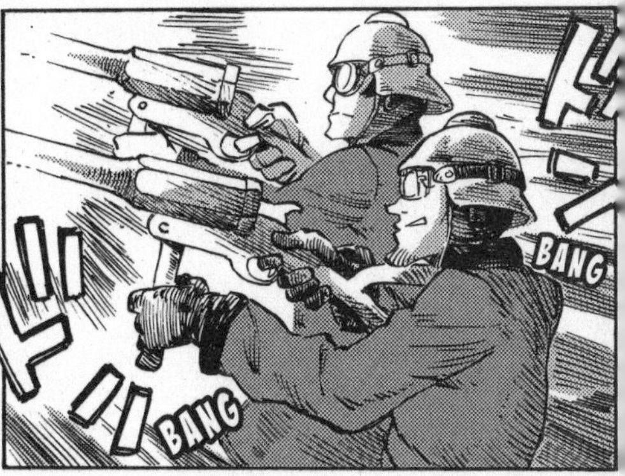
BANG
BANG

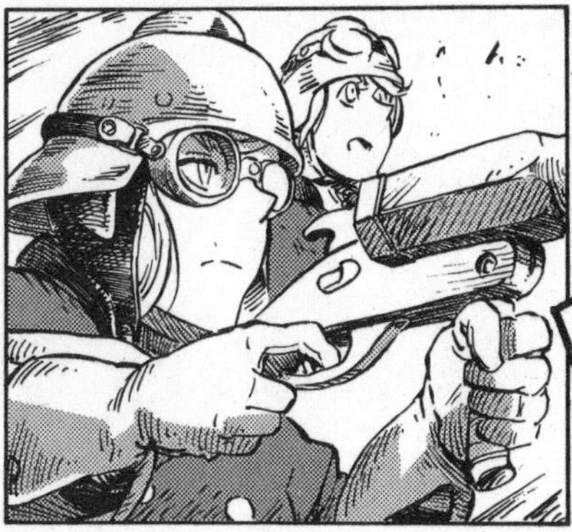

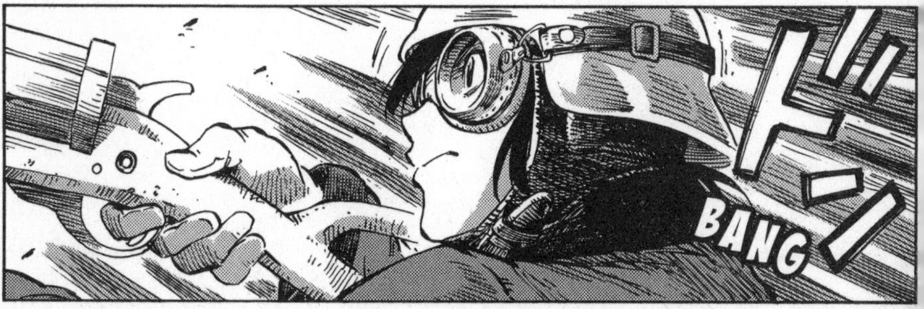
BANG

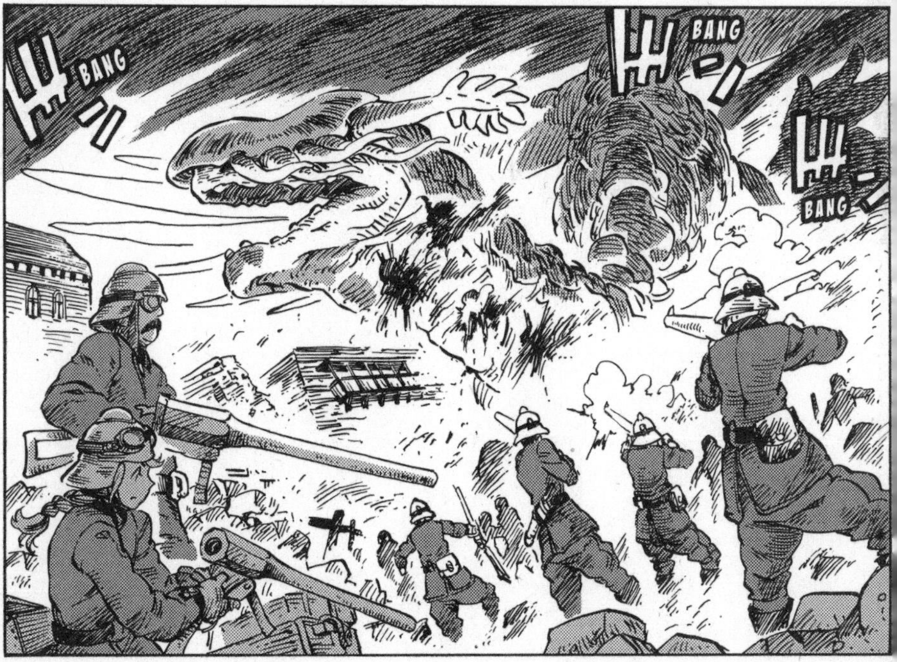
BANG
BANG
BANG
BANG

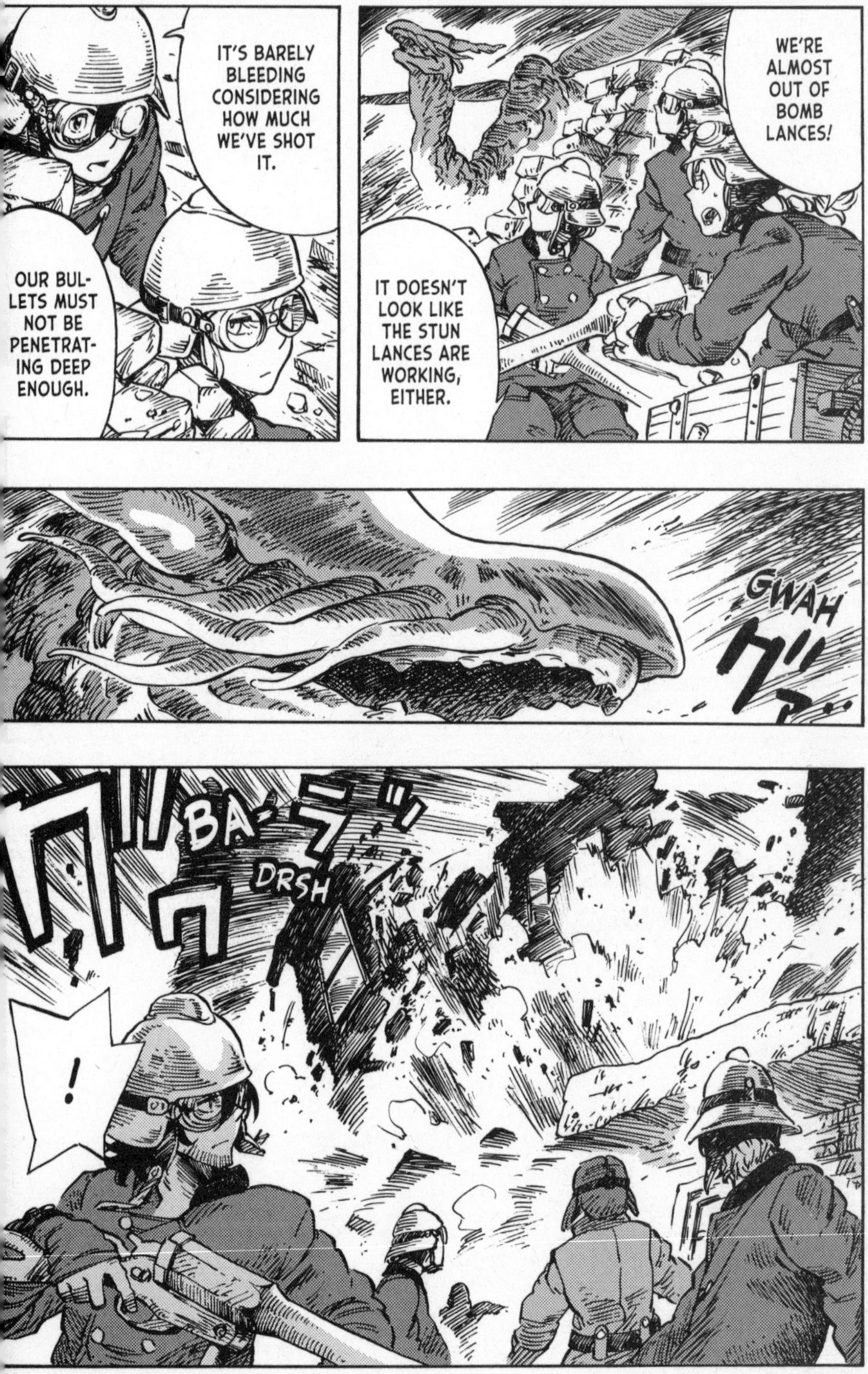
WE'RE ALMOST OUT OF BOMB LANCES!
IT DOESN'T LOOK LIKE THE STUN LANCES ARE WORKING, EITHER.
IT'S BARELY BLEEDING CONSIDERING HOW MUCH WE'VE SHOT IT.
OUR BULLETS MUST NOT BE PENETRATING DEEP ENOUGH.
GWAH
BA-
DRSH
!

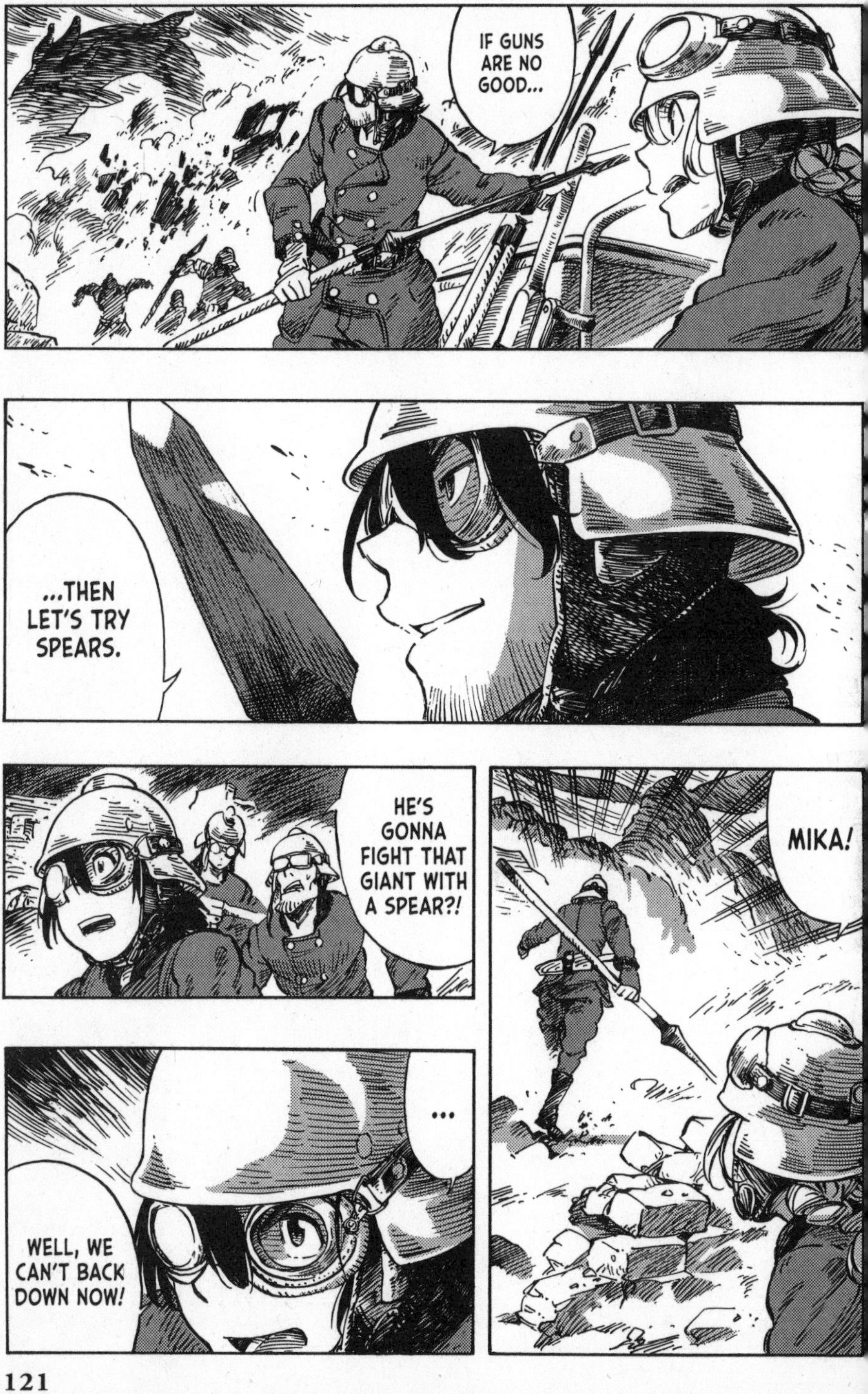
IF GUNS ARE NO GOOD...
...THEN LET'S TRY SPEARS.
MIKA!
HE'S GONNA FIGHT THAT GIANT WITH A SPEAR?!
...
WELL, WE CAN'T BACK DOWN NOW!

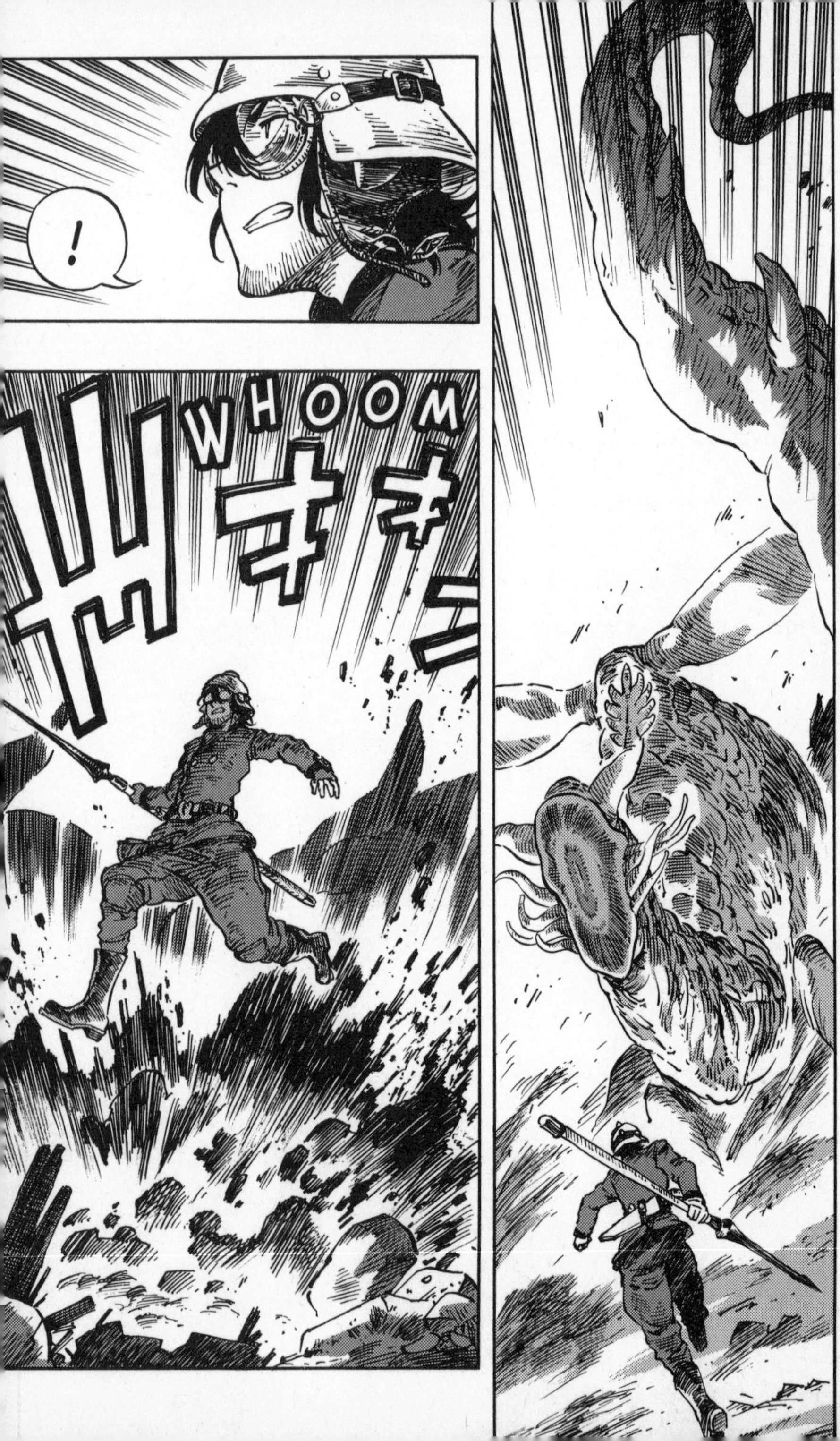
!
WHOOM

SCHINK

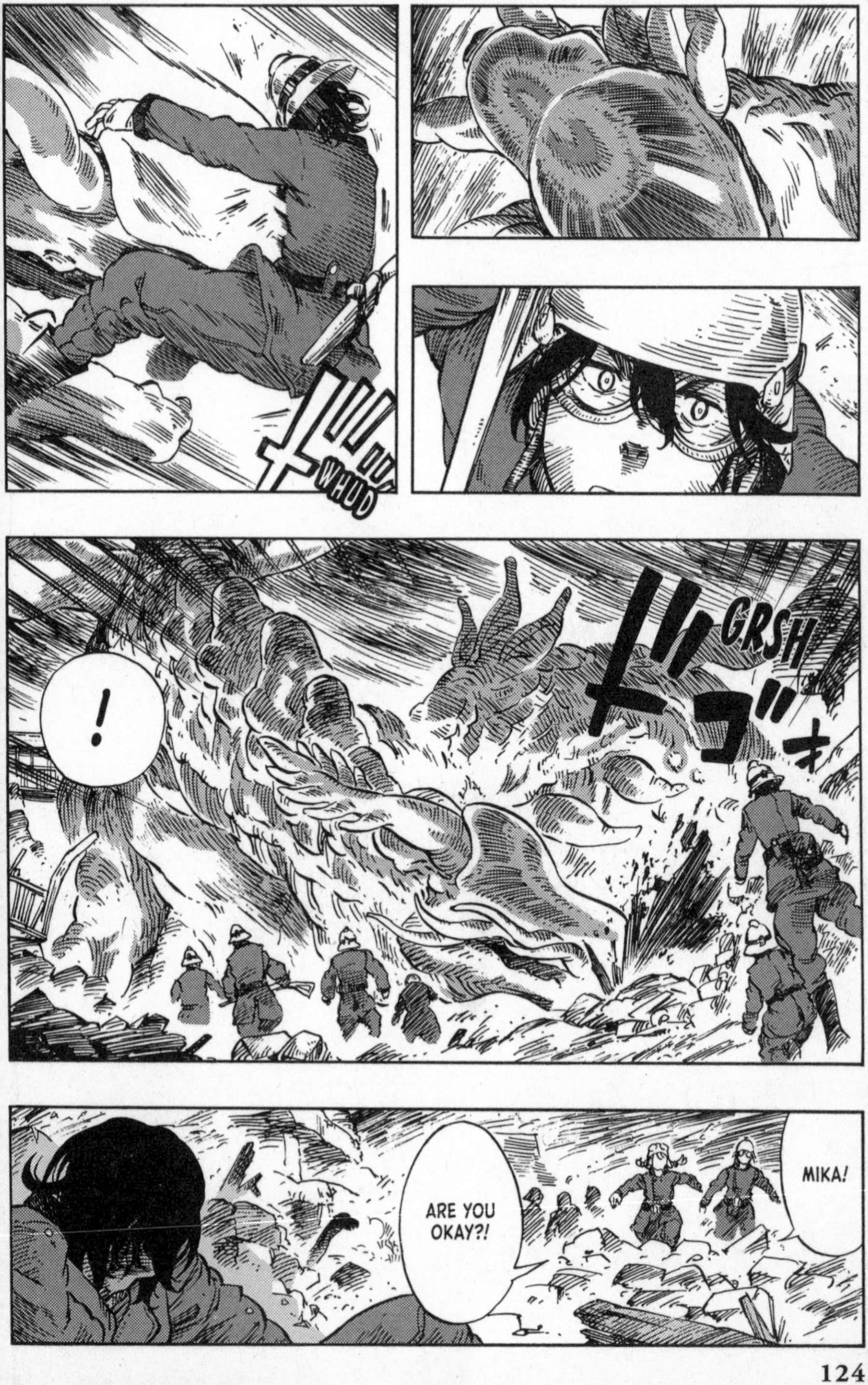
WHUD
GRSH
!
MIKA!
ARE YOU OKAY?!

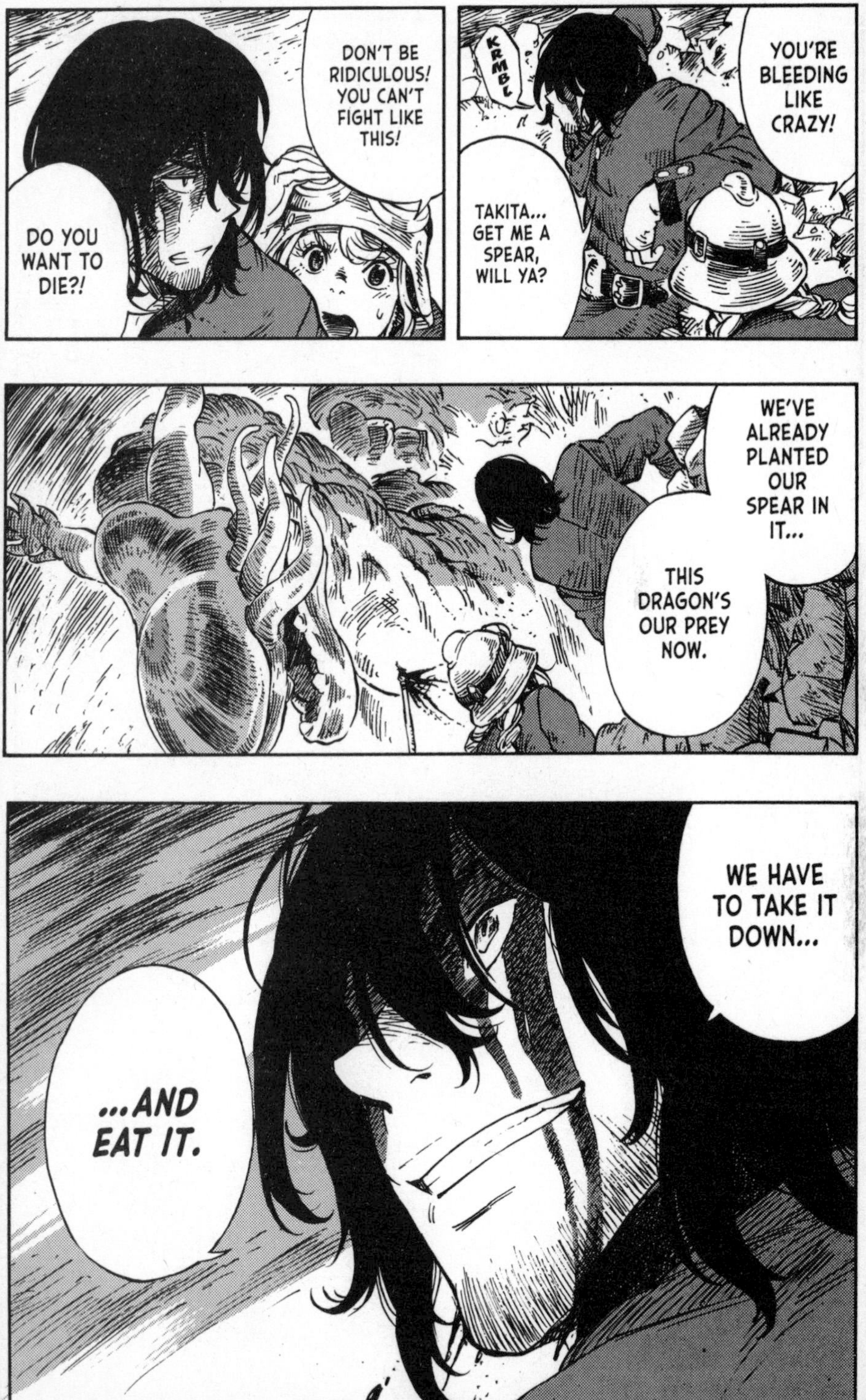
YOU'RE BLEEDING LIKE CRAZY!
KRMBL
TAKITA... GET ME A SPEAR, WILL YA?
DON'T BE RIDICULOUS! YOU CAN'T FIGHT LIKE THIS!
DO YOU WANT TO DIE?!
WE'VE ALREADY PLANTED OUR SPEAR IN IT...
THIS DRAGON'S OUR PREY NOW.
WE HAVE TO TAKE IT DOWN...
...AND EAT IT.

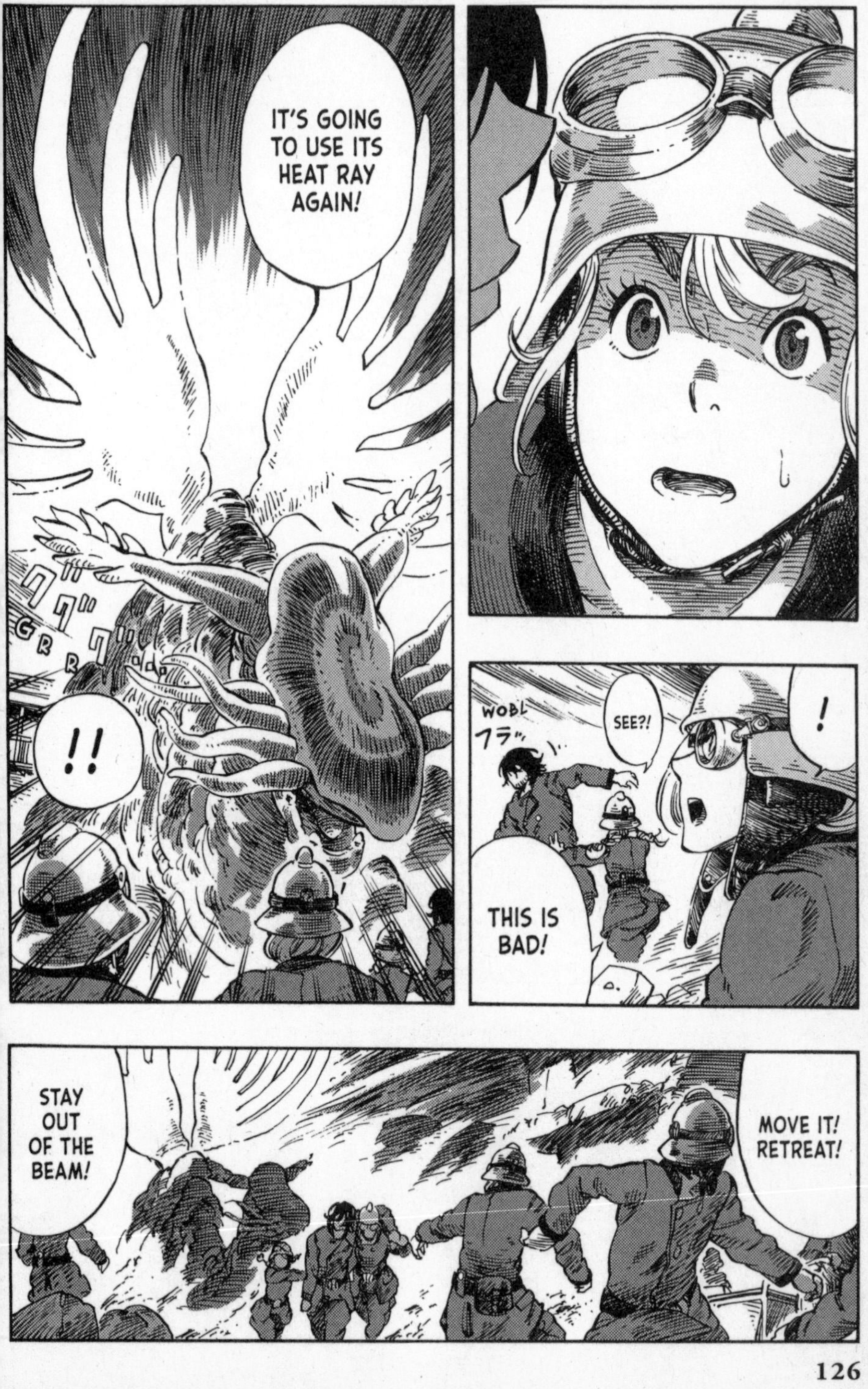
!
SEE?!
WOBL
THIS IS BAD!
IT'S GOING TO USE ITS HEAT RAY AGAIN!
GRRR
!!
MOVE IT! RETREAT!
STAY OUT OF THE BEAM!

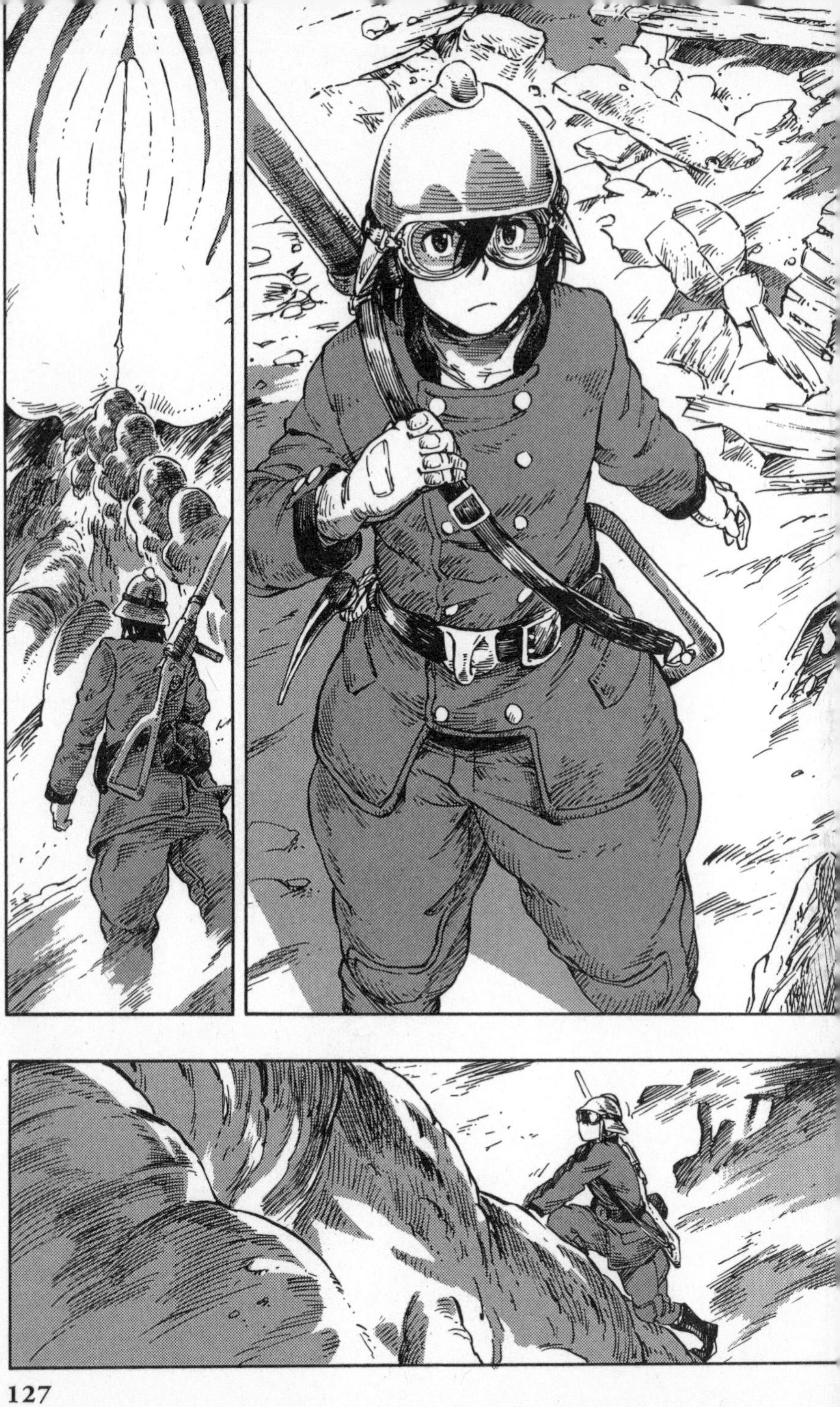

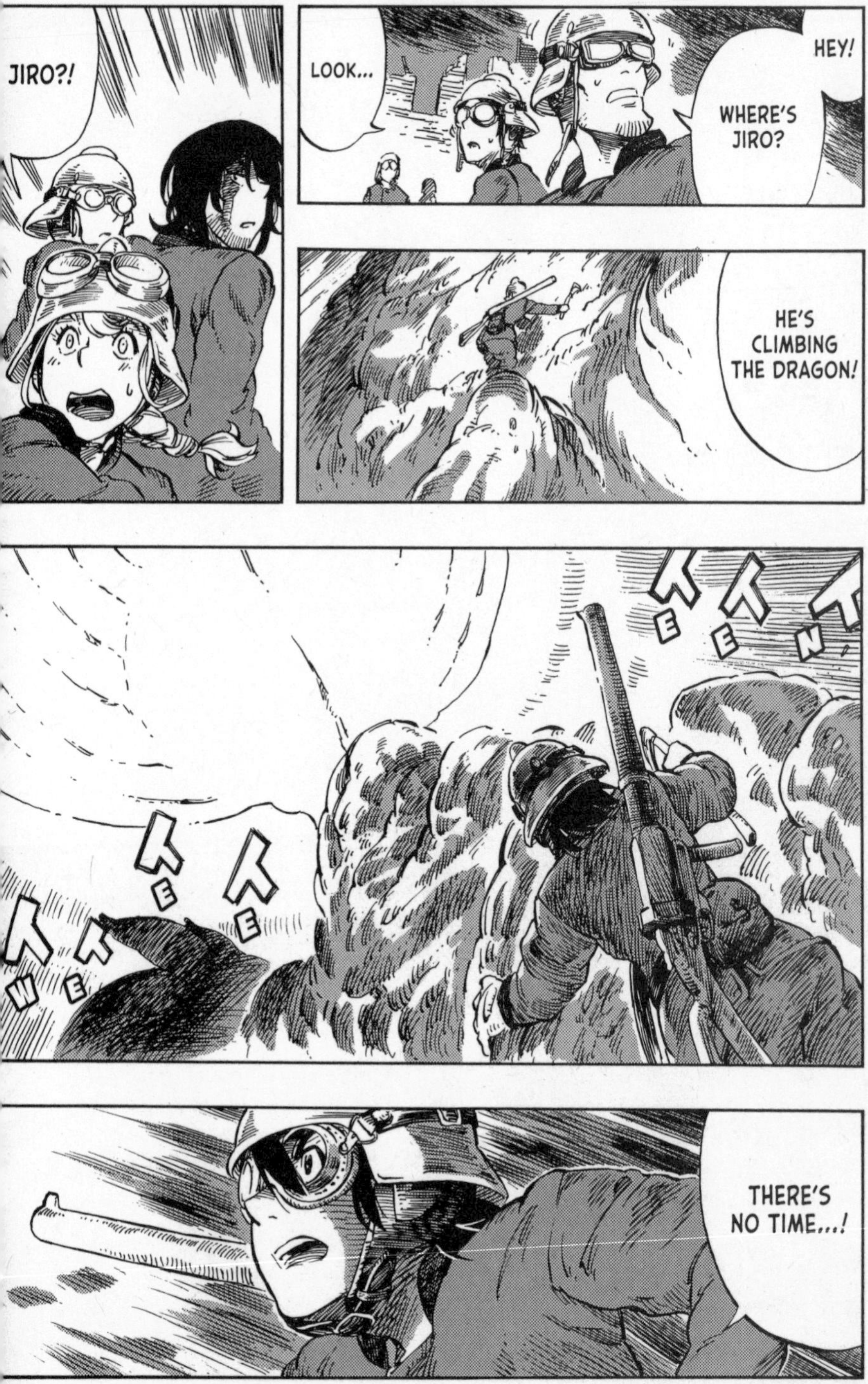
HEY!
WHERE'S JIRO?
LOOK...
HE'S CLIMBING THE DRAGON!
JIRO?!
EENT
WEEE
THERE'S NO TIME...!

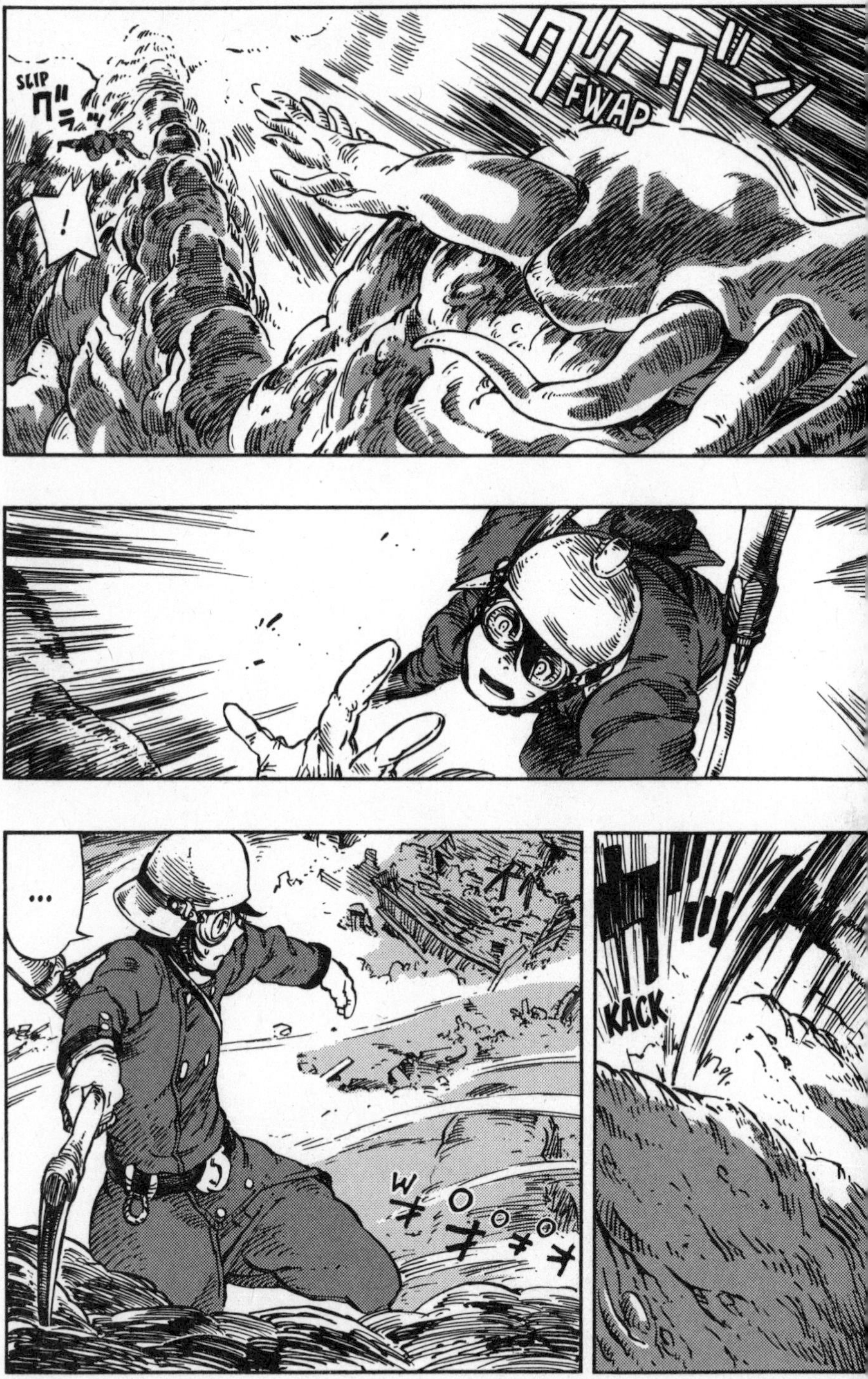
FWAP
SLIP
!
KACK
...
W

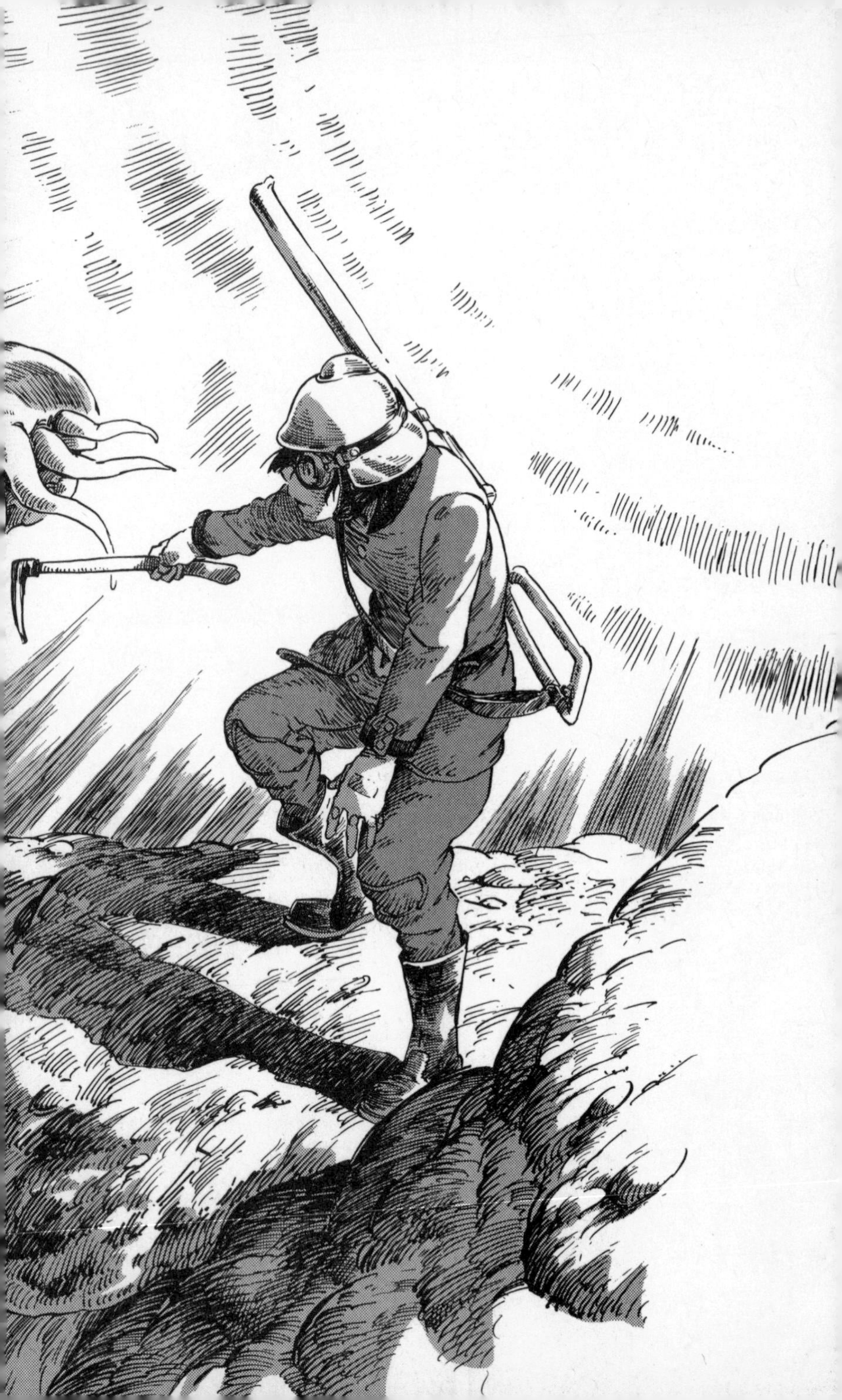

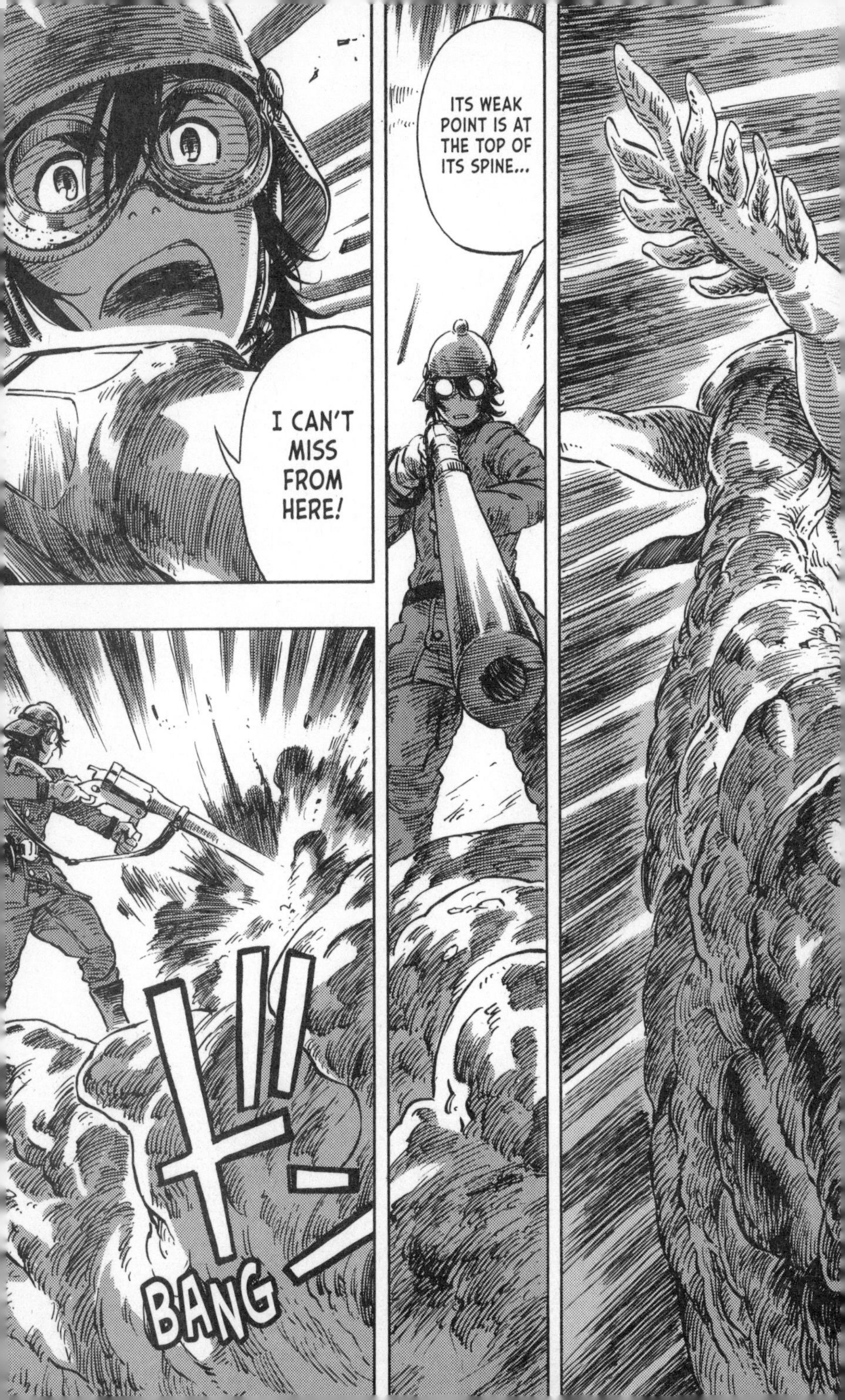
ITS WEAK POINT IS AT THE TOP OF ITS SPINE...
I CAN'T MISS FROM HERE!
BANG

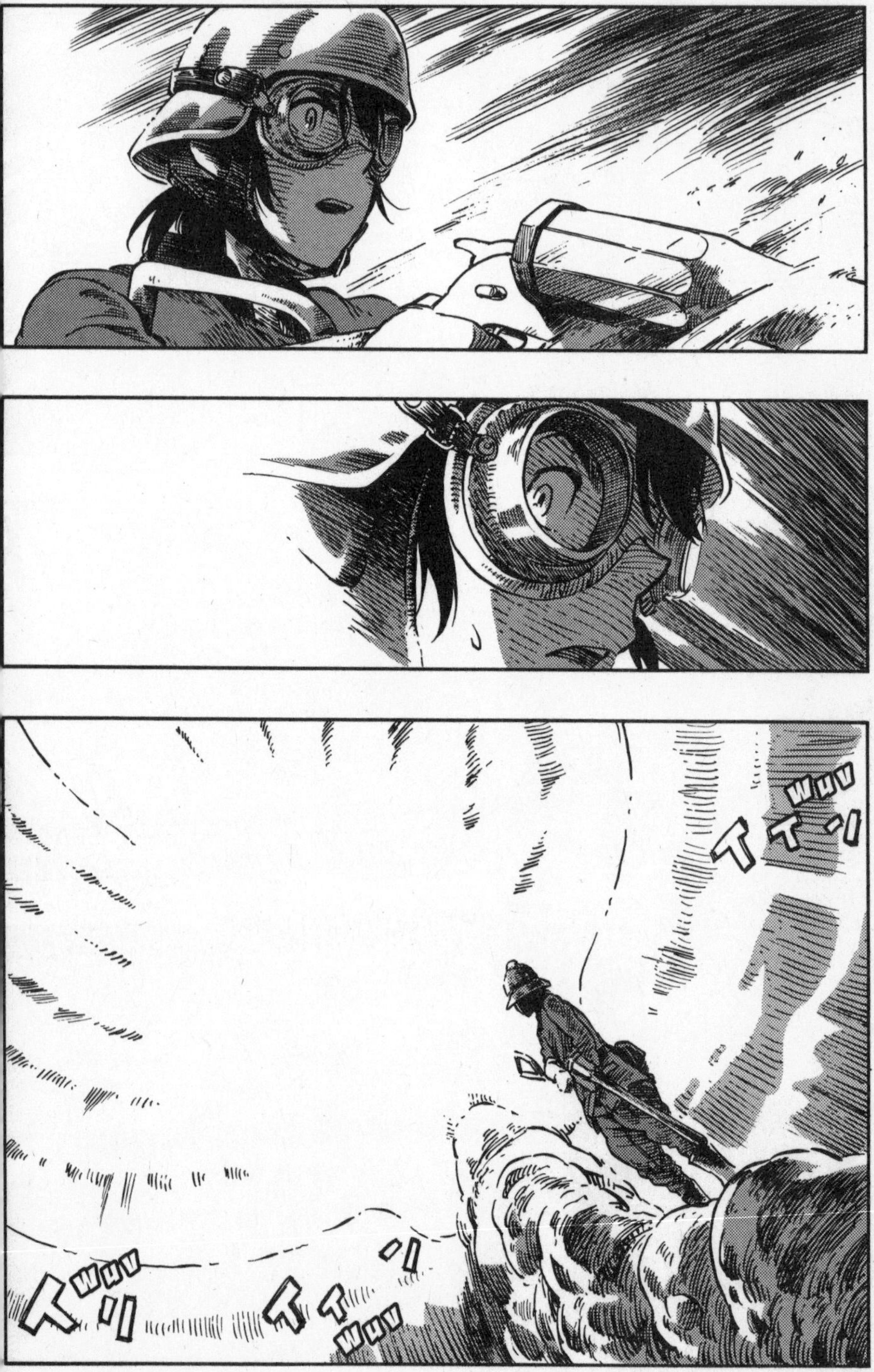

イイーー WHUV
イーー WHUV
イイー WHUV

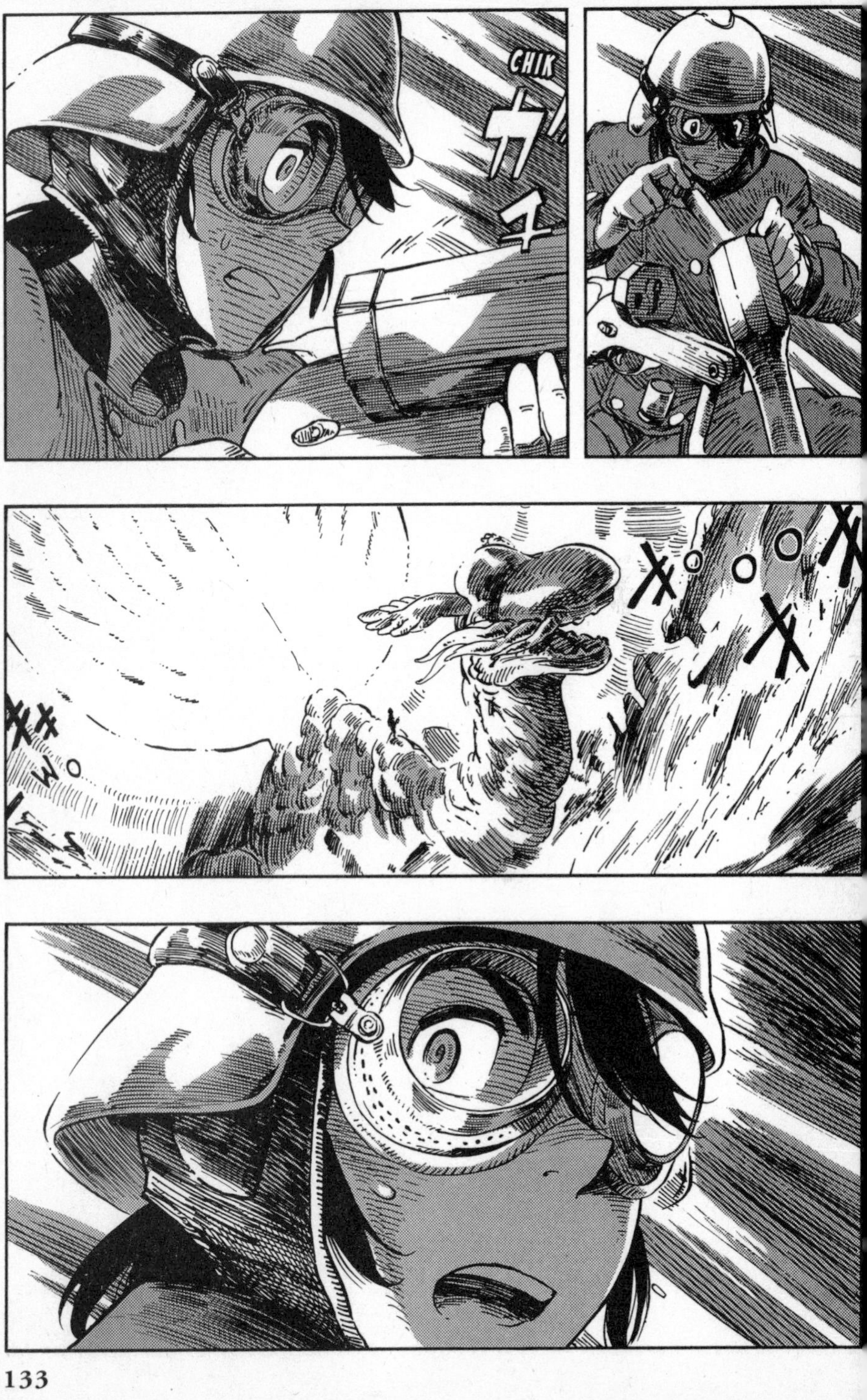
CHIK

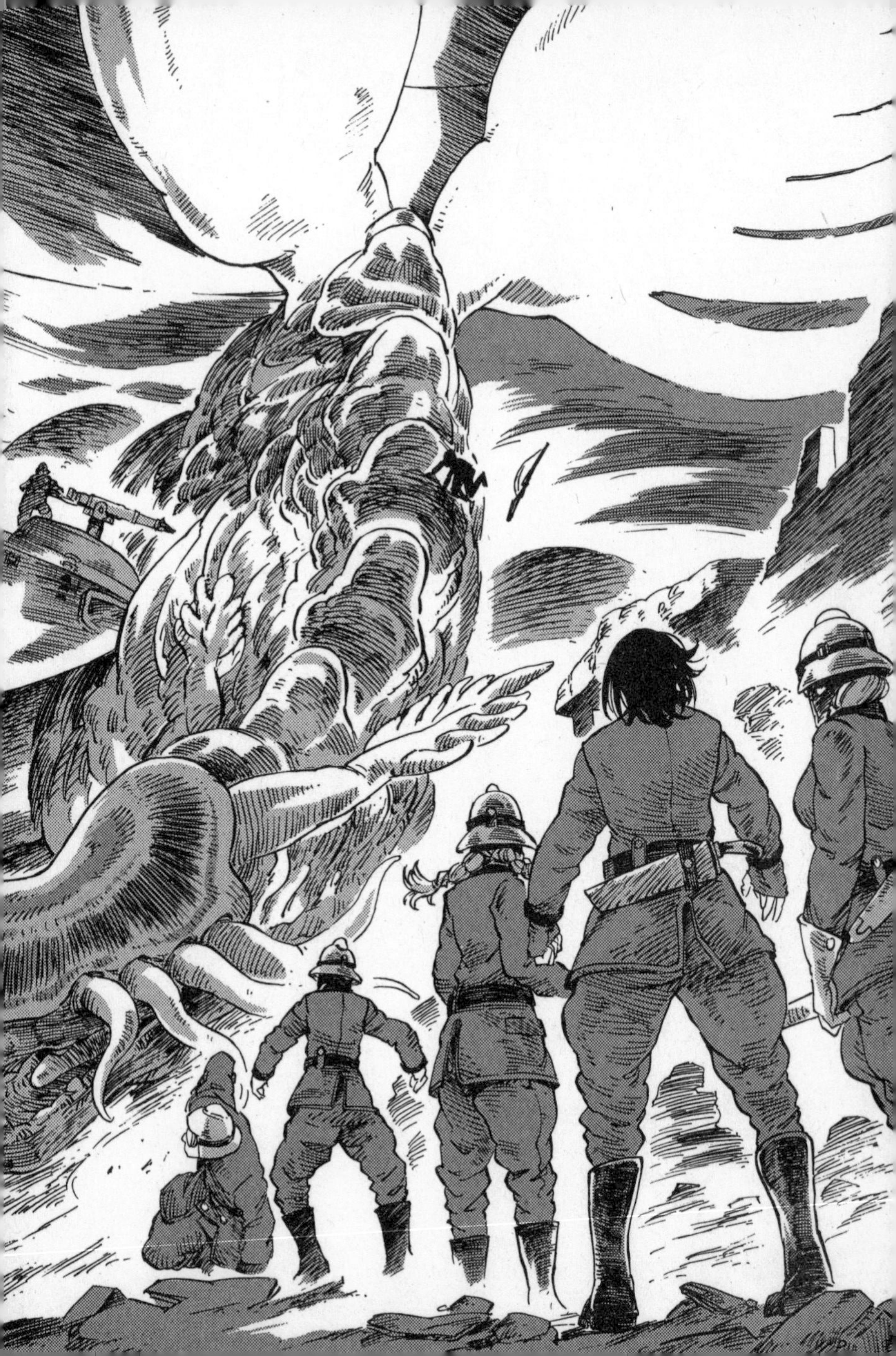

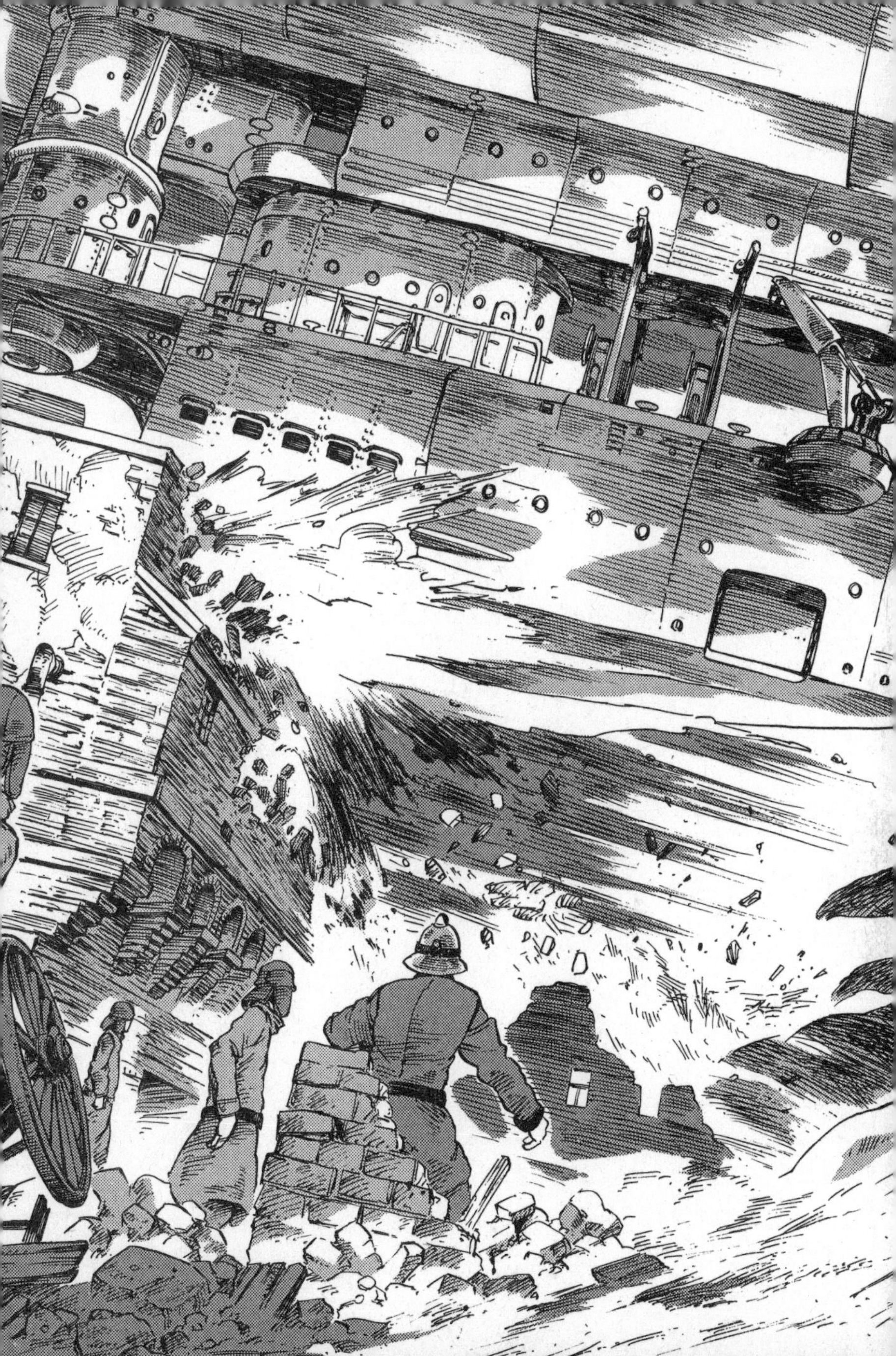

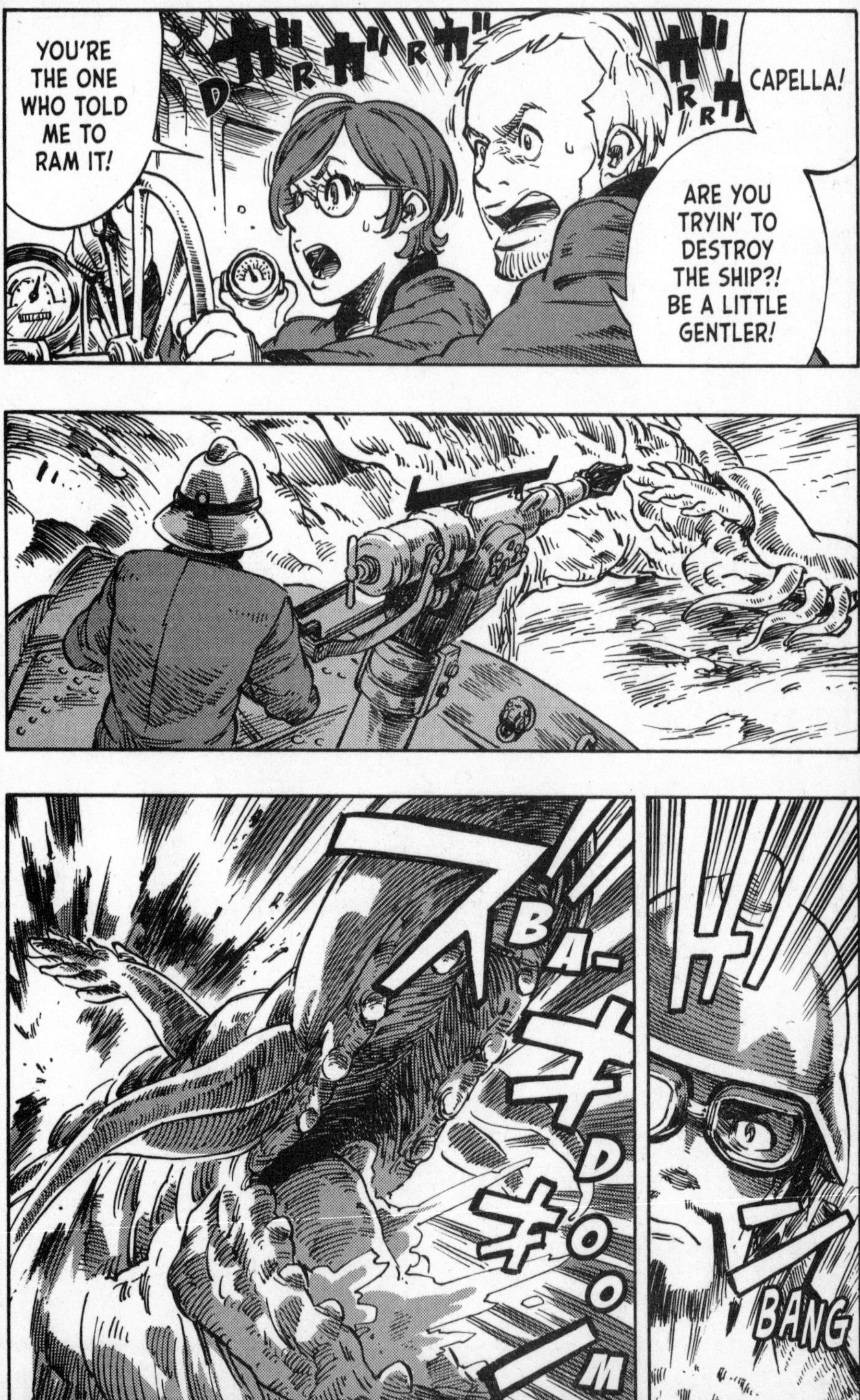
CAPELLA!
ARE YOU TRYIN' TO DESTROY THE SHIP?! BE A LITTLE GENTLER!
YOU'RE THE ONE WHO TOLD ME TO RAM IT!
BANG
BA-DOOOM

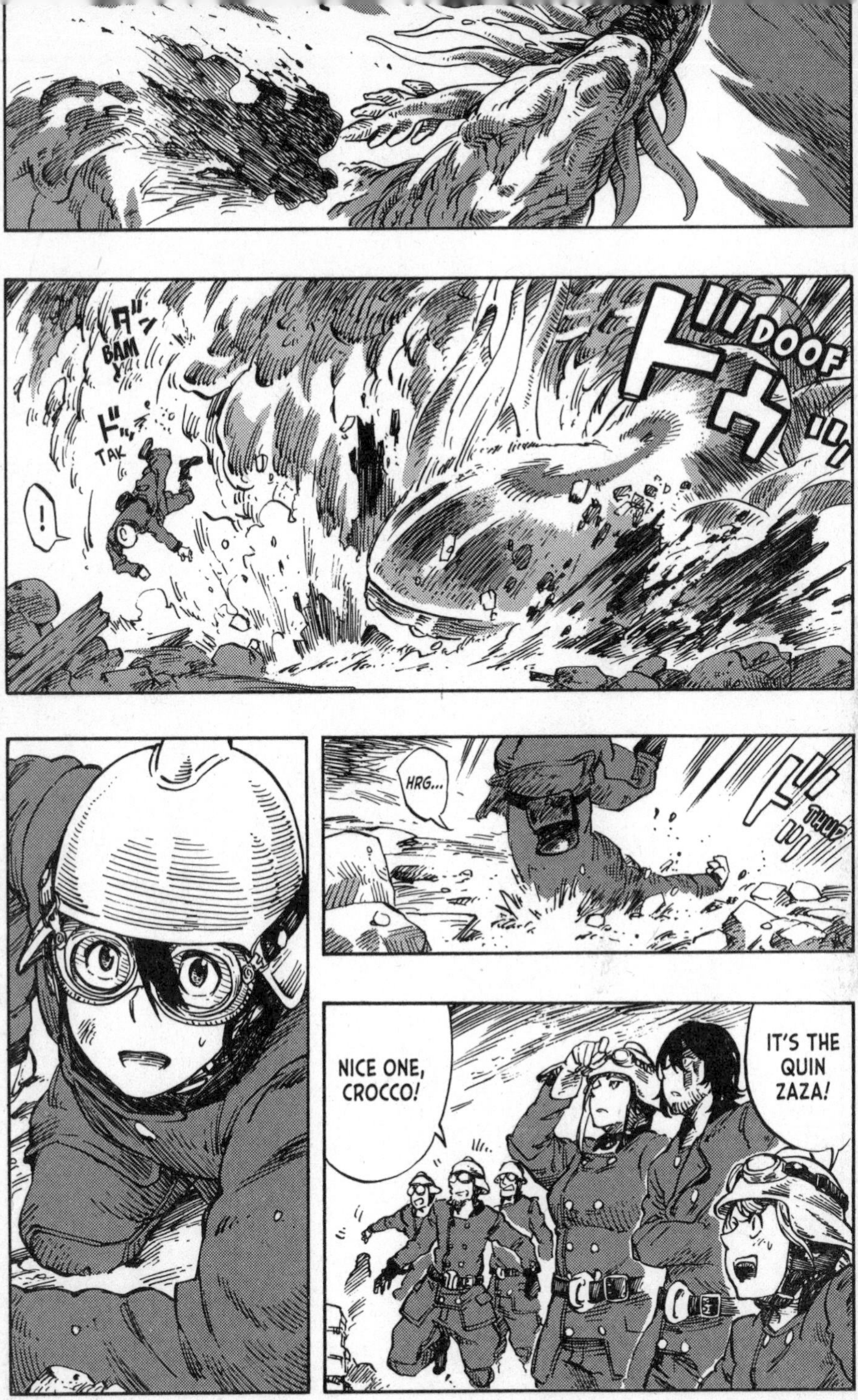
DOOF
BAM
TAK
!
HRG...
THUD
IT'S THE QUIN ZAZA!
NICE ONE, CROCCO!

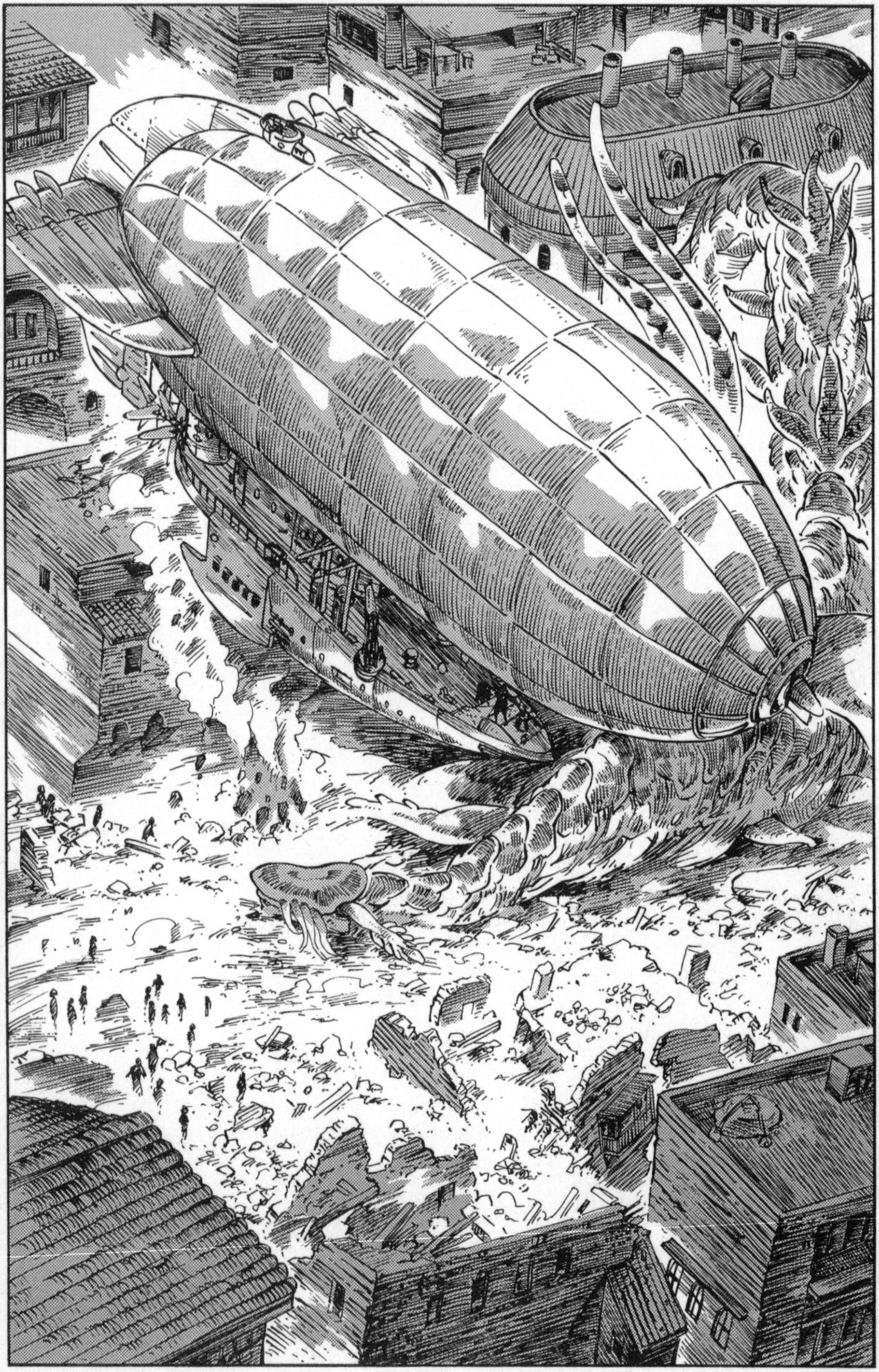

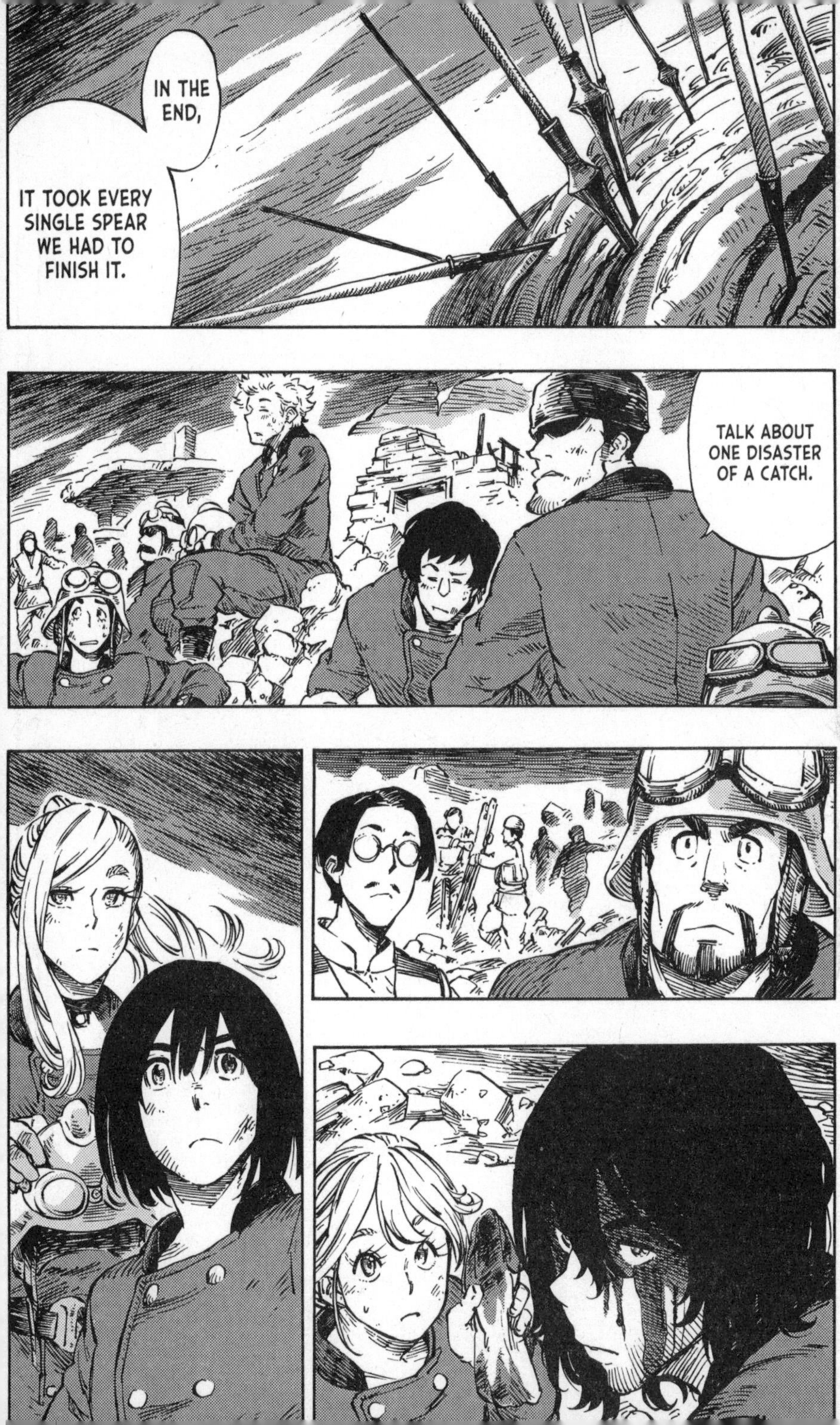
IN THE END,
IT TOOK EVERY SINGLE SPEAR WE HAD TO FINISH IT.
TALK ABOUT ONE DISASTER OF A CATCH.

Flight 10 Soup Kitchen Goulash & Dragon Cutlet

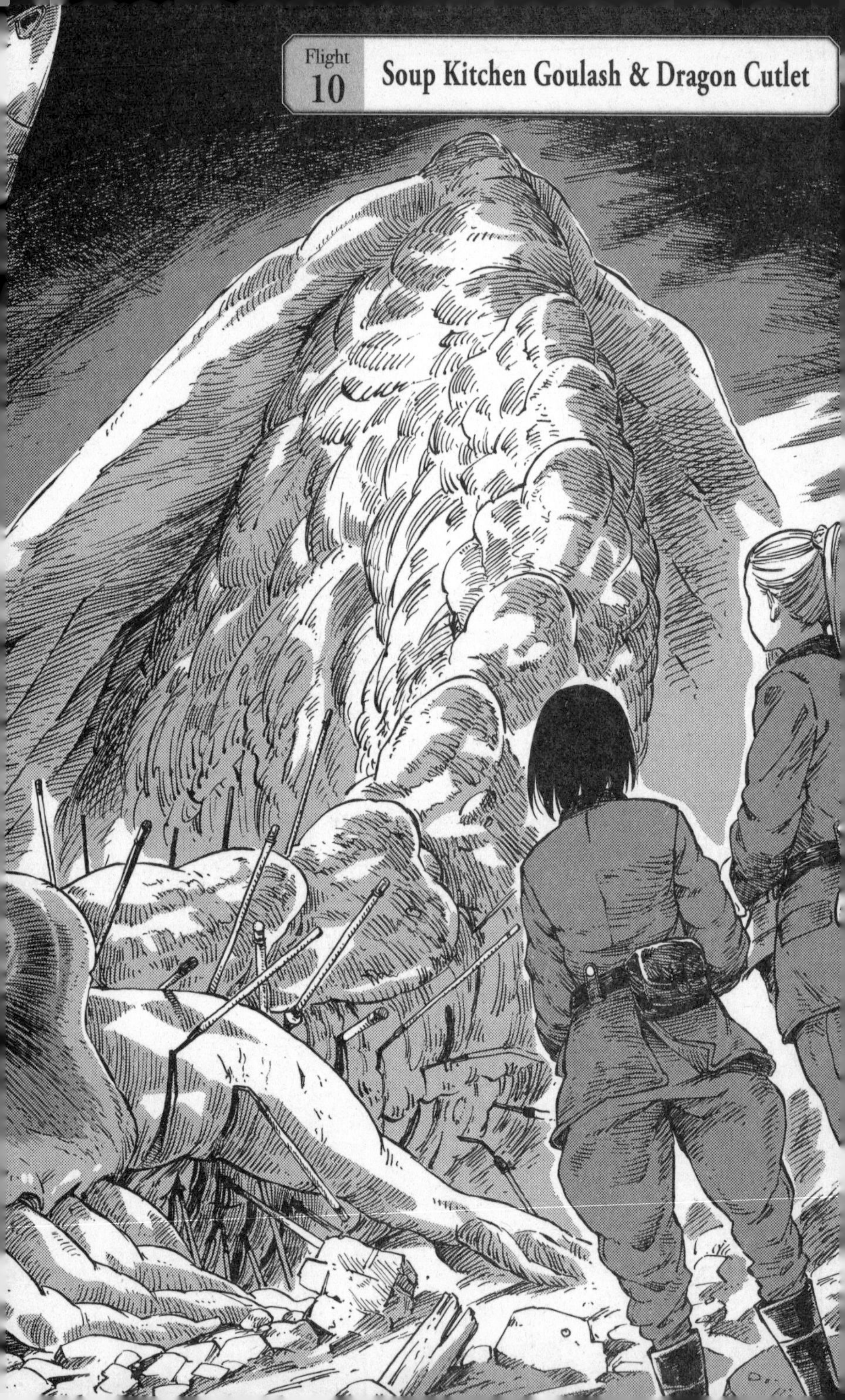

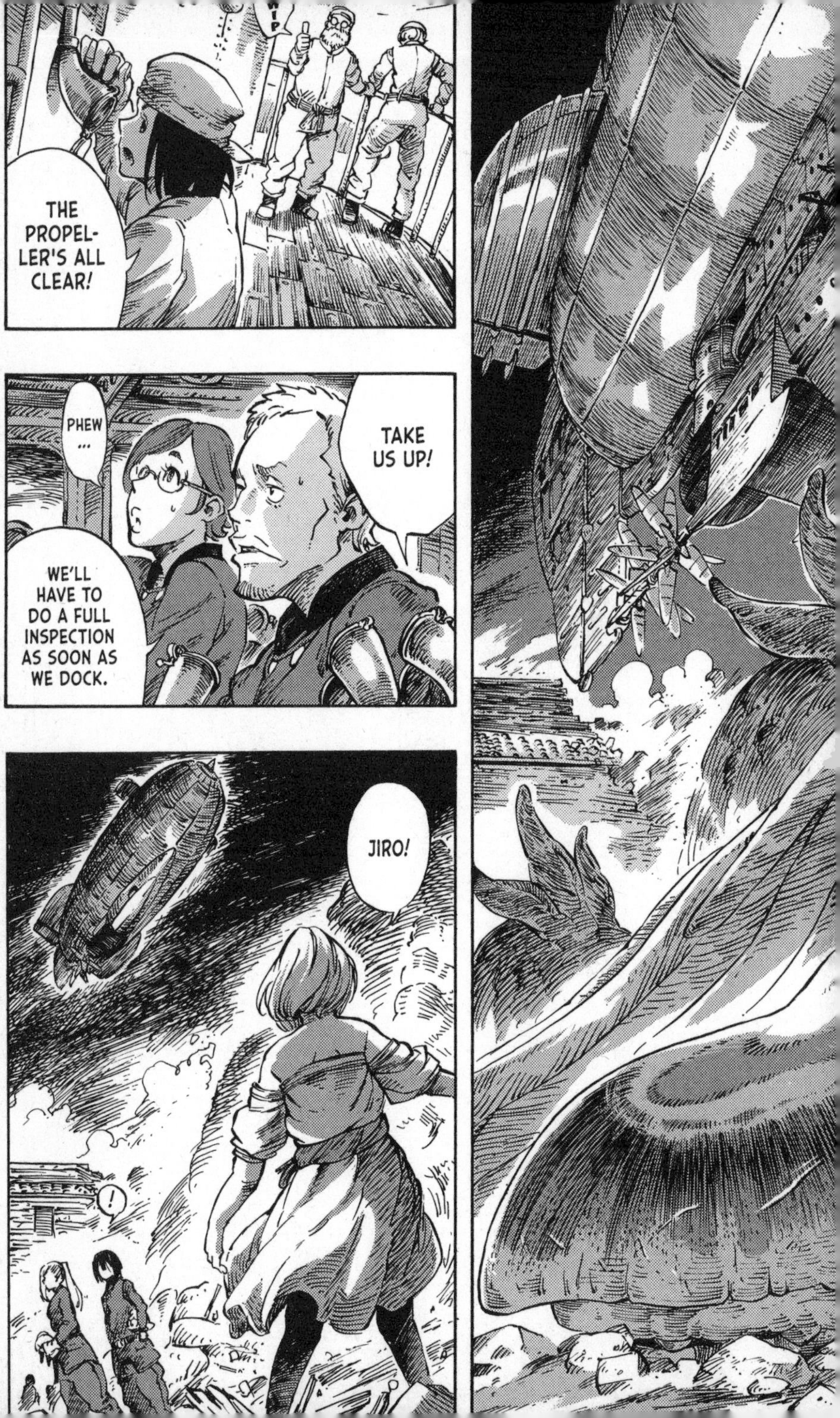
THE PROPELLER'S ALL CLEAR!
TAKE US UP!
PHEW ...
WE'LL HAVE TO DO A FULL INSPECTION AS SOON AS WE DOCK.
JIRO!
!

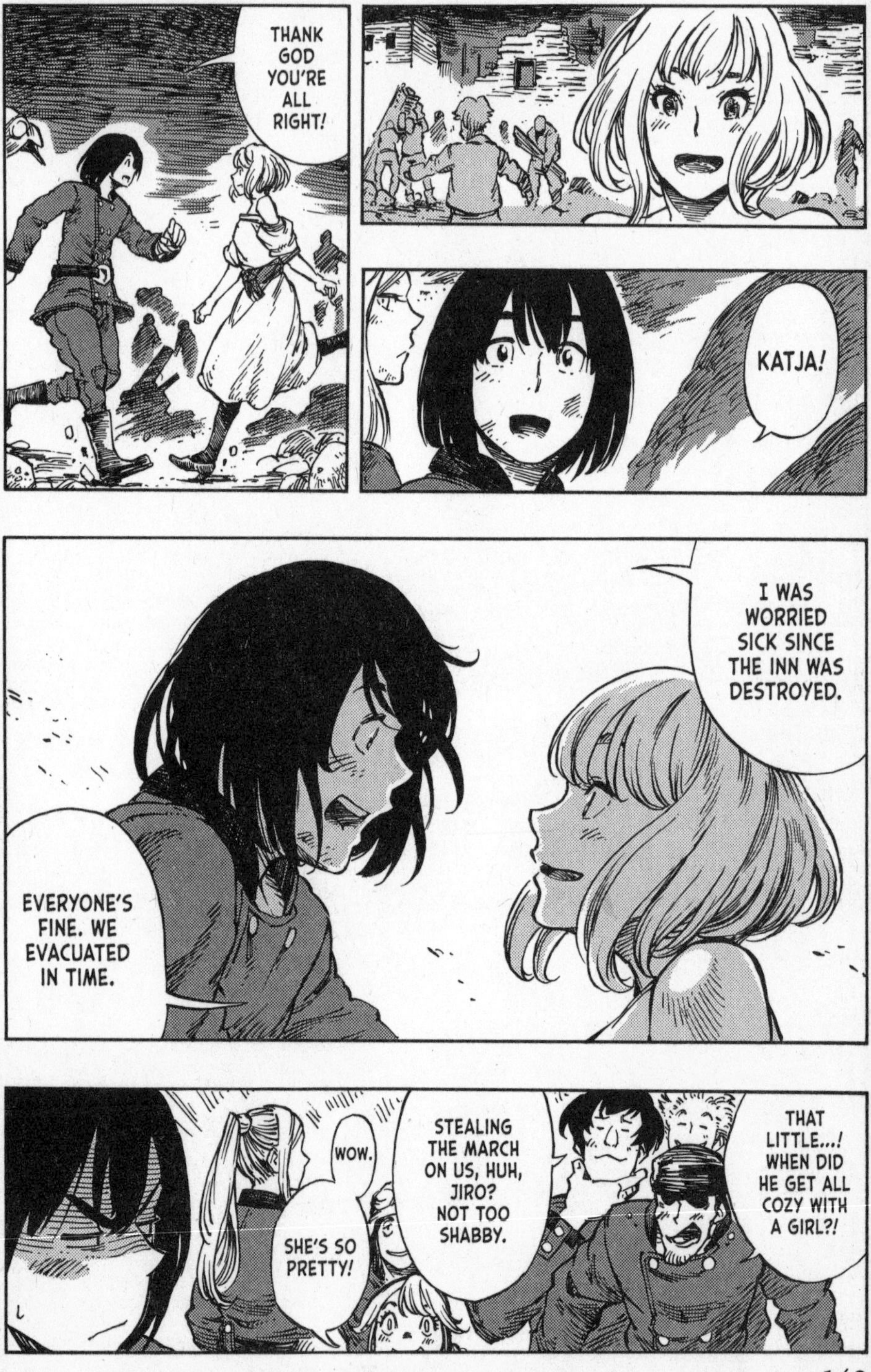
KATJA!
THANK GOD YOU'RE ALL RIGHT!
I WAS WORRIED SICK SINCE THE INN WAS DESTROYED.
EVERYONE'S FINE. WE EVACUATED IN TIME.
THAT LITTLE...! WHEN DID HE GET ALL COZY WITH A GIRL?!
STEALING THE MARCH ON US, HUH, JIRO? NOT TOO SHABBY.
WOW.
SHE'S SO PRETTY!

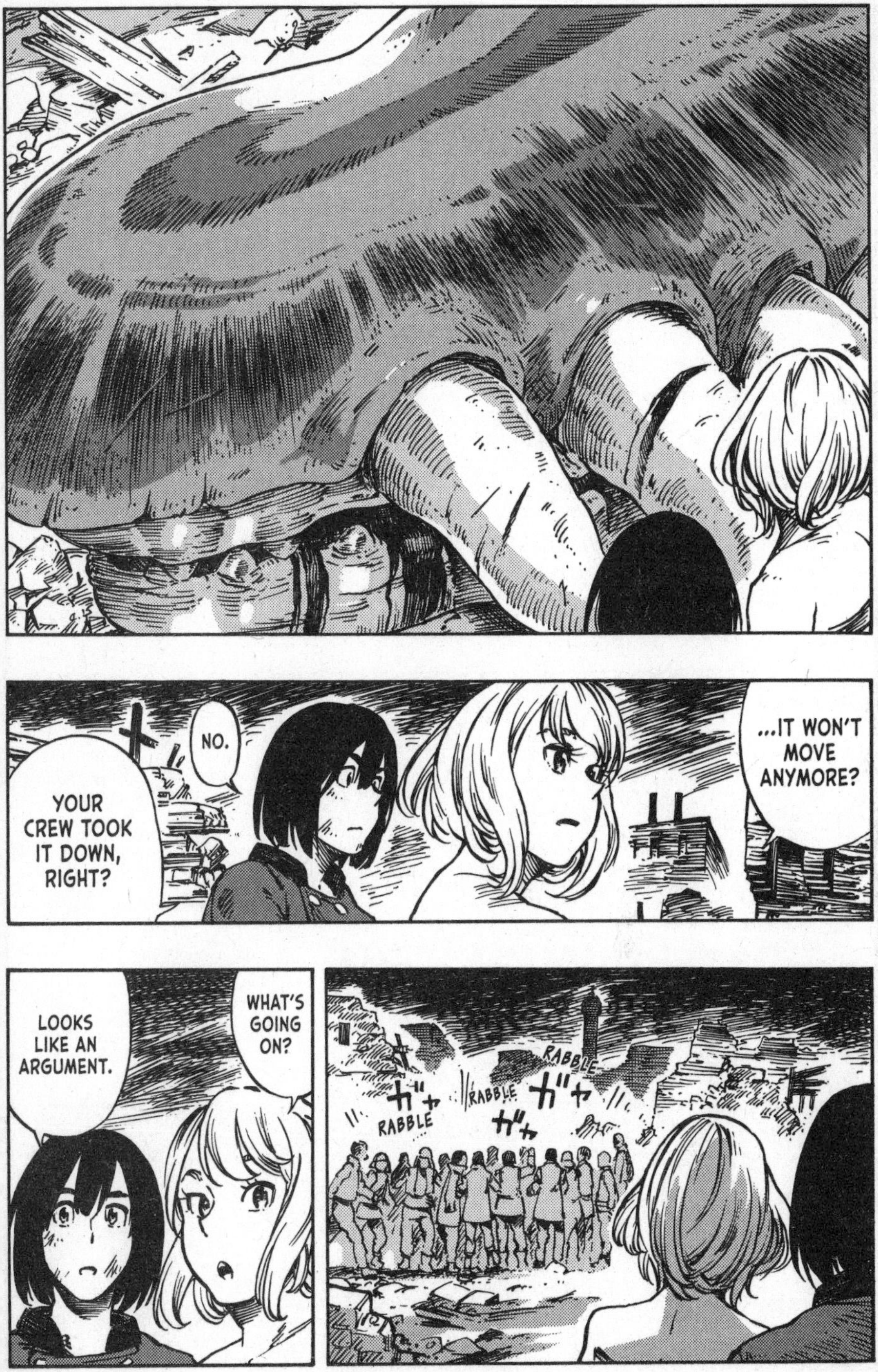
...IT WON'T MOVE ANYMORE?
NO.
YOUR CREW TOOK IT DOWN, RIGHT?
RABBLE
ガャ
RABBLE
ガャ
RABBLE
ガャ
WHAT'S GOING ON?
LOOKS LIKE AN ARGUMENT.

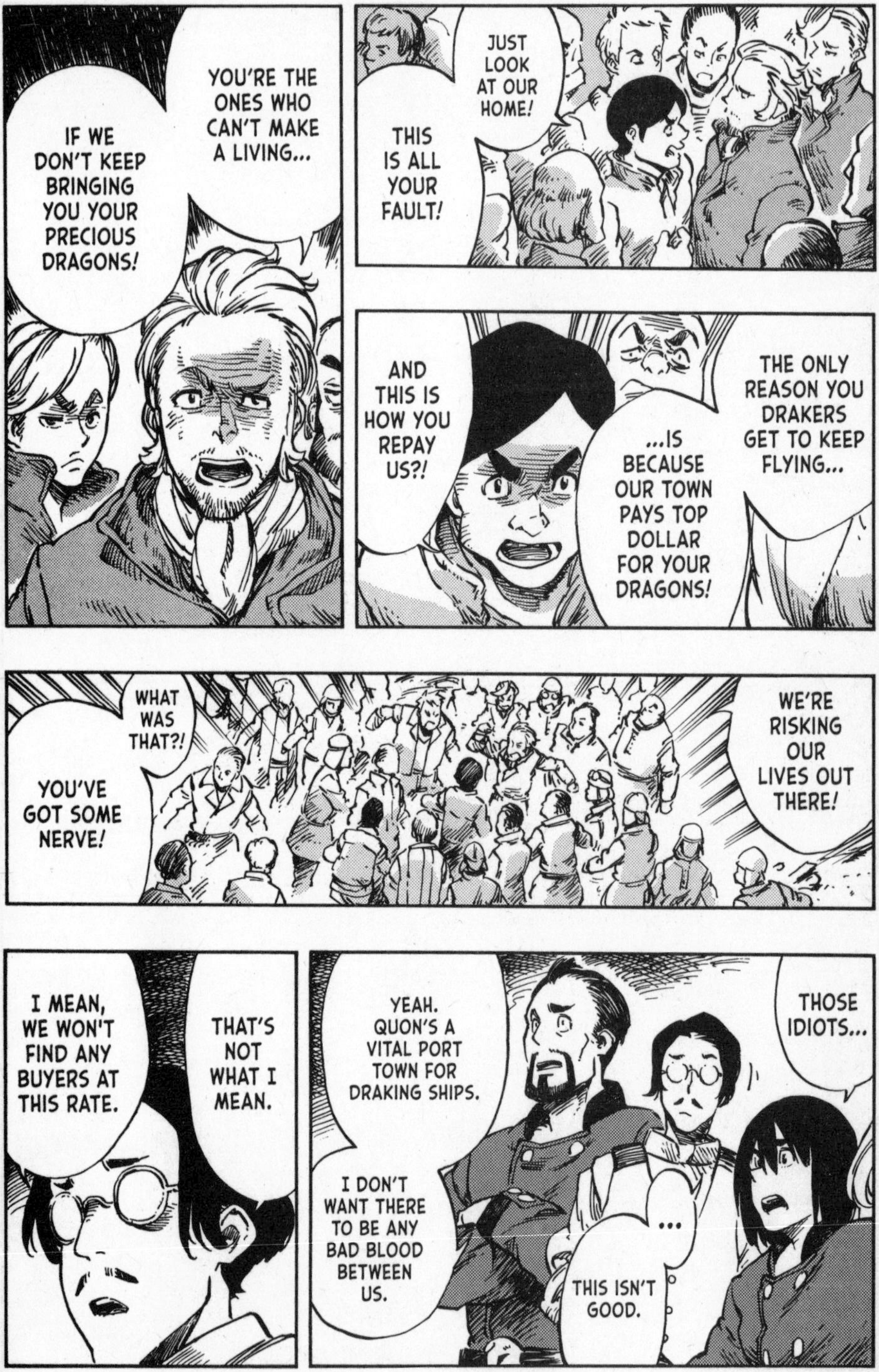
JUST LOOK AT OUR HOME!
THIS IS ALL YOUR FAULT!
THE ONLY REASON YOU DRAKERS GET TO KEEP FLYING...
...IS BECAUSE OUR TOWN PAYS TOP DOLLAR FOR YOUR DRAGONS!
AND THIS IS HOW YOU REPAY US?!
YOU'RE THE ONES WHO CAN'T MAKE A LIVING...
IF WE DON'T KEEP BRINGING YOU YOUR PRECIOUS DRAGONS!
WE'RE RISKING OUR LIVES OUT THERE!
WHAT WAS THAT?!
YOU'VE GOT SOME NERVE!
THOSE IDIOTS...
YEAH. QUON'S A VITAL PORT TOWN FOR DRAKING SHIPS.
I DON'T WANT THERE TO BE ANY BAD BLOOD BETWEEN US.
...
THIS ISN'T GOOD.
THAT'S NOT WHAT I MEAN.
I MEAN, WE WON'T FIND ANY BUYERS AT THIS RATE.

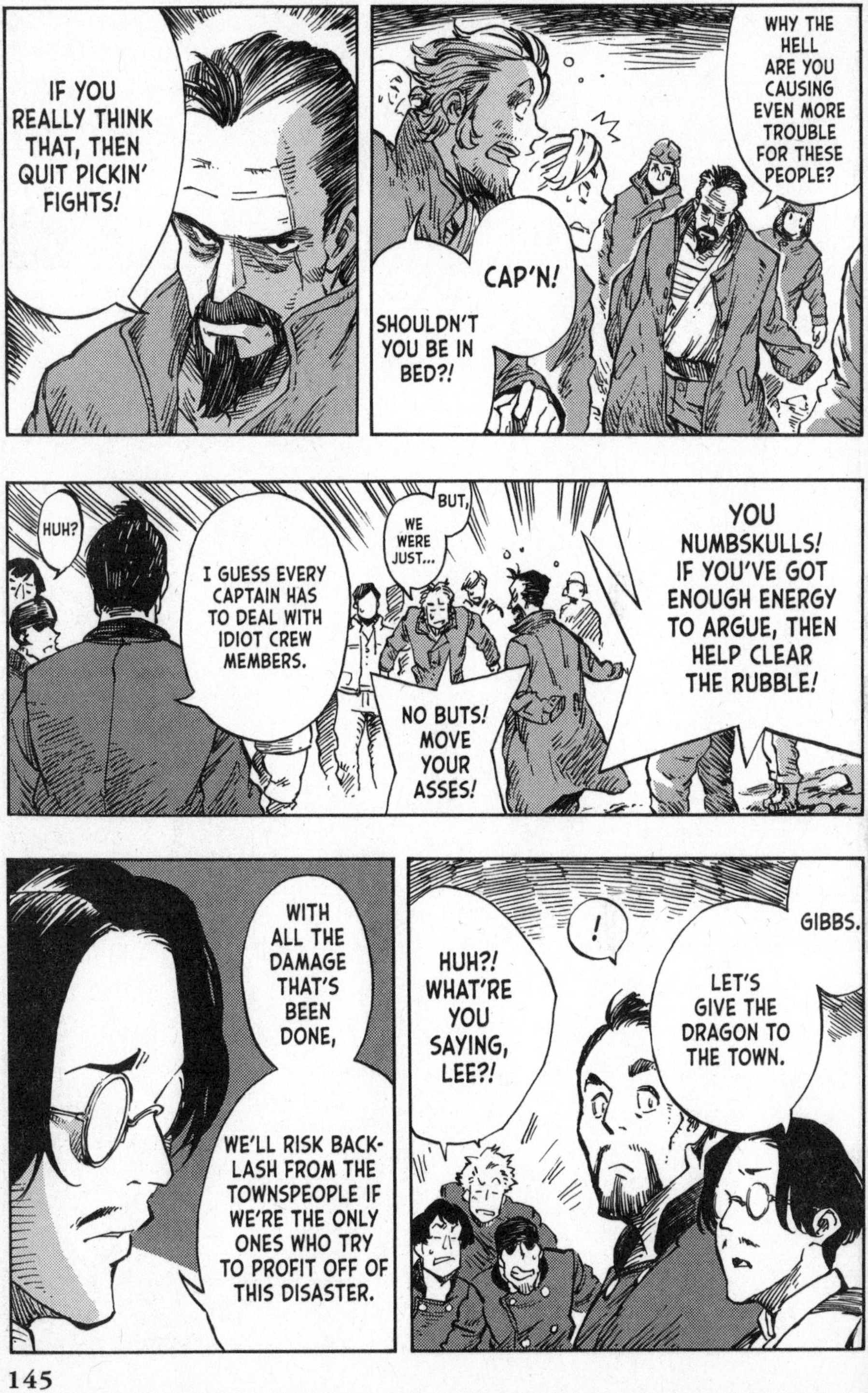
WHY THE HELL ARE YOU CAUSING EVEN MORE TROUBLE FOR THESE PEOPLE?
CAP'N!
SHOULDN'T YOU BE IN BED?!
IF YOU REALLY THINK THAT, THEN QUIT PICKIN' FIGHTS!
YOU NUMBSKULLS! IF YOU'VE GOT ENOUGH ENERGY TO ARGUE, THEN HELP CLEAR THE RUBBLE!
BUT,
WE WERE JUST...
NO BUTS! MOVE YOUR ASSES!
HUH?
I GUESS EVERY CAPTAIN HAS TO DEAL WITH IDIOT CREW MEMBERS.
GIBBS.
LET'S GIVE THE DRAGON TO THE TOWN.
!
HUH?! WHAT'RE YOU SAYING, LEE?!
WITH ALL THE DAMAGE THAT'S BEEN DONE,
WE'LL RISK BACK-LASH FROM THE TOWNSPEOPLE IF WE'RE THE ONLY ONES WHO TRY TO PROFIT OFF OF THIS DISASTER.

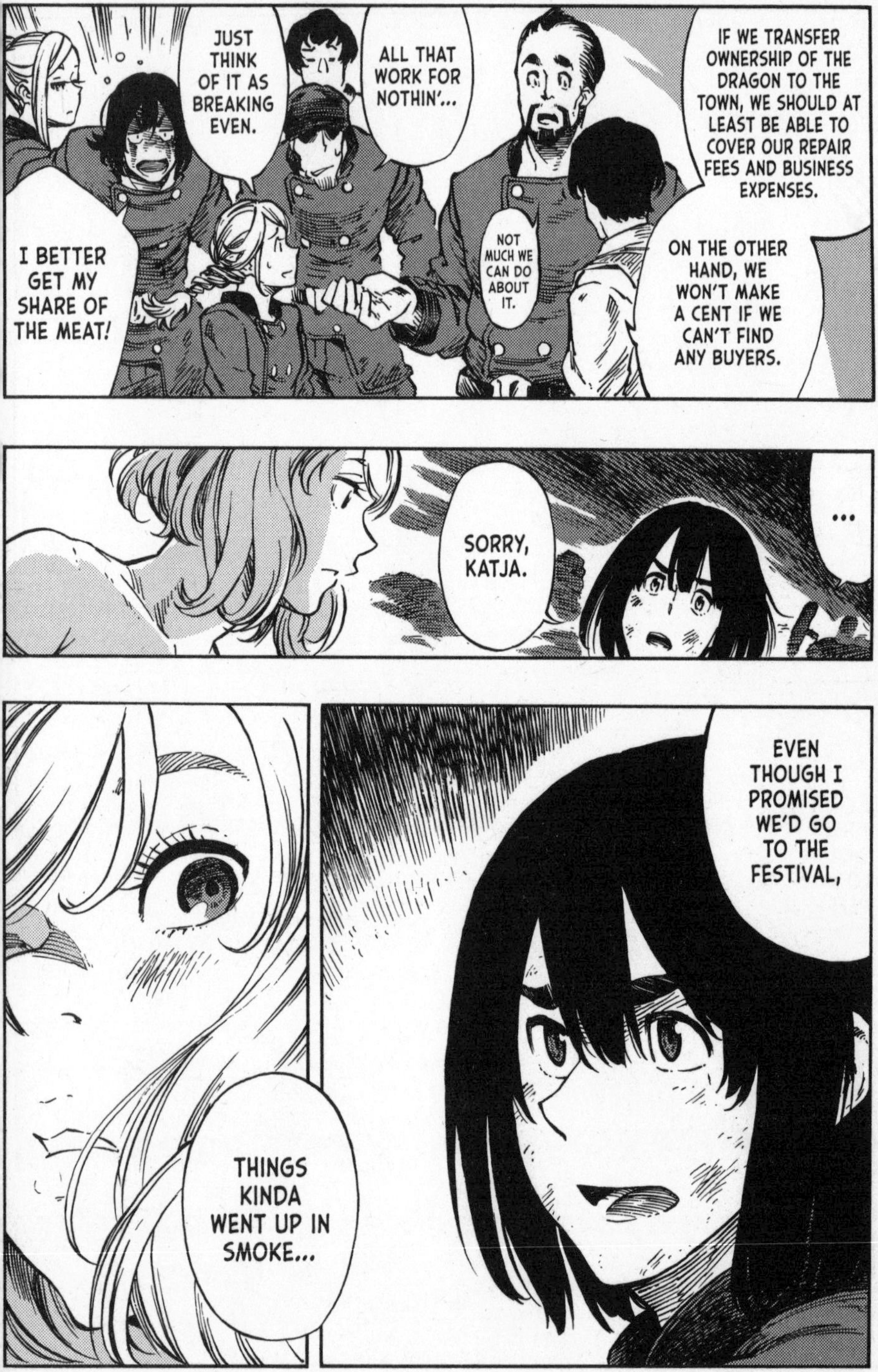
IF WE TRANSFER OWNERSHIP OF THE DRAGON TO THE TOWN, WE SHOULD AT LEAST BE ABLE TO COVER OUR REPAIR FEES AND BUSINESS EXPENSES.
ON THE OTHER HAND, WE WON'T MAKE A CENT IF WE CAN'T FIND ANY BUYERS.
NOT MUCH WE CAN DO ABOUT IT.
ALL THAT WORK FOR NOTHIN'...
JUST THINK OF IT AS BREAKING EVEN.
I BETTER GET MY SHARE OF THE MEAT!
...
SORRY, KATJA.
EVEN THOUGH I PROMISED WE'D GO TO THE FESTIVAL,
THINGS KINDA WENT UP IN SMOKE...

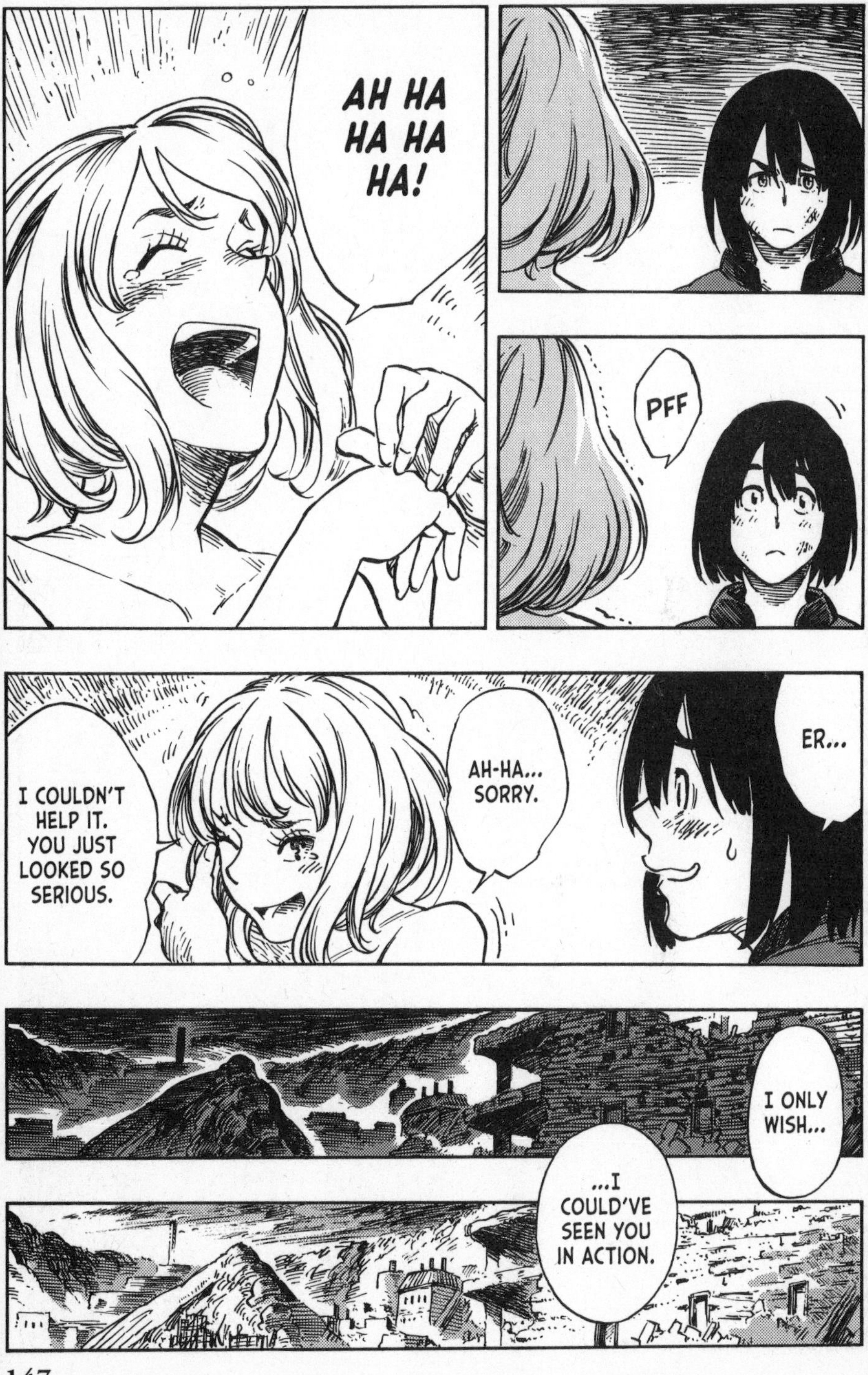
PFF
AH HA HA HA HA!
ER...
AH-HA... SORRY.
I COULDN'T HELP IT. YOU JUST LOOKED SO SERIOUS.
I ONLY WISH...
...I COULD'VE SEEN YOU IN ACTION.

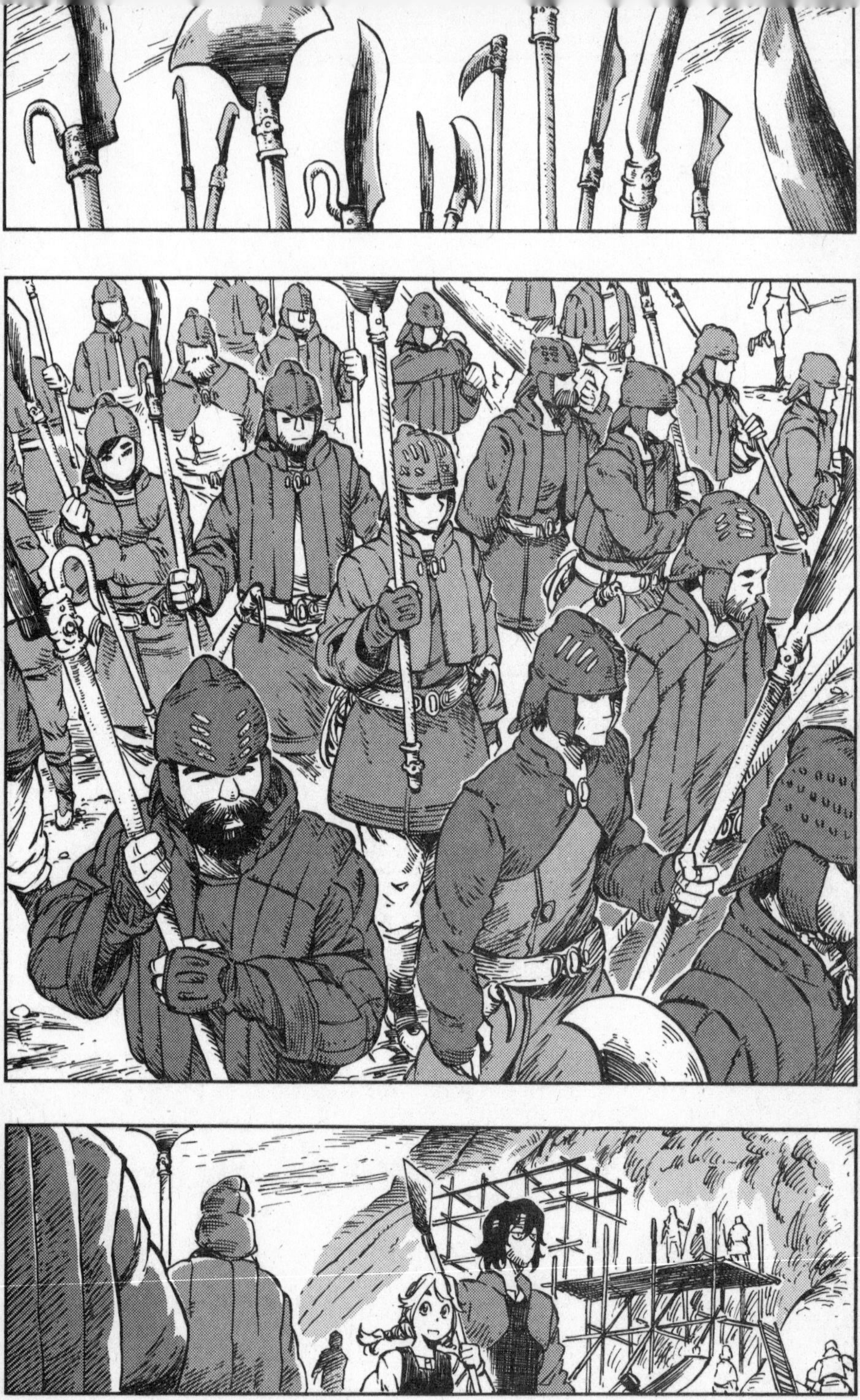

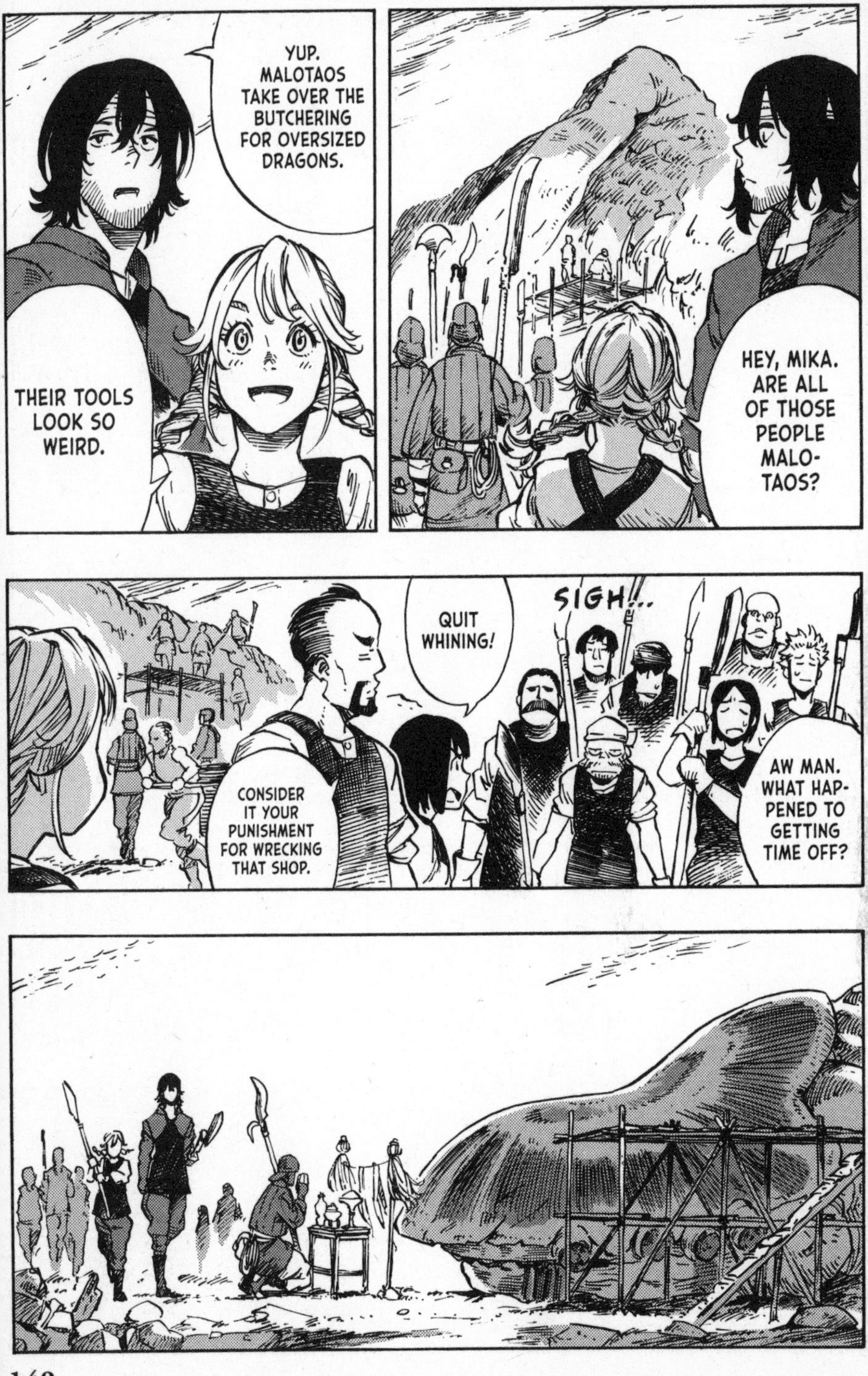
HEY, MIKA. ARE ALL OF THOSE PEOPLE MALO-TAOS?
YUP. MALOTAOS TAKE OVER THE BUTCHERING FOR OVERSIZED DRAGONS.
THEIR TOOLS LOOK SO WEIRD.
AW MAN. WHAT HAP-PENED TO GETTING TIME OFF?
SIGH...
QUIT WHINING!
CONSIDER IT YOUR PUNISHMENT FOR WRECKING THAT SHOP.

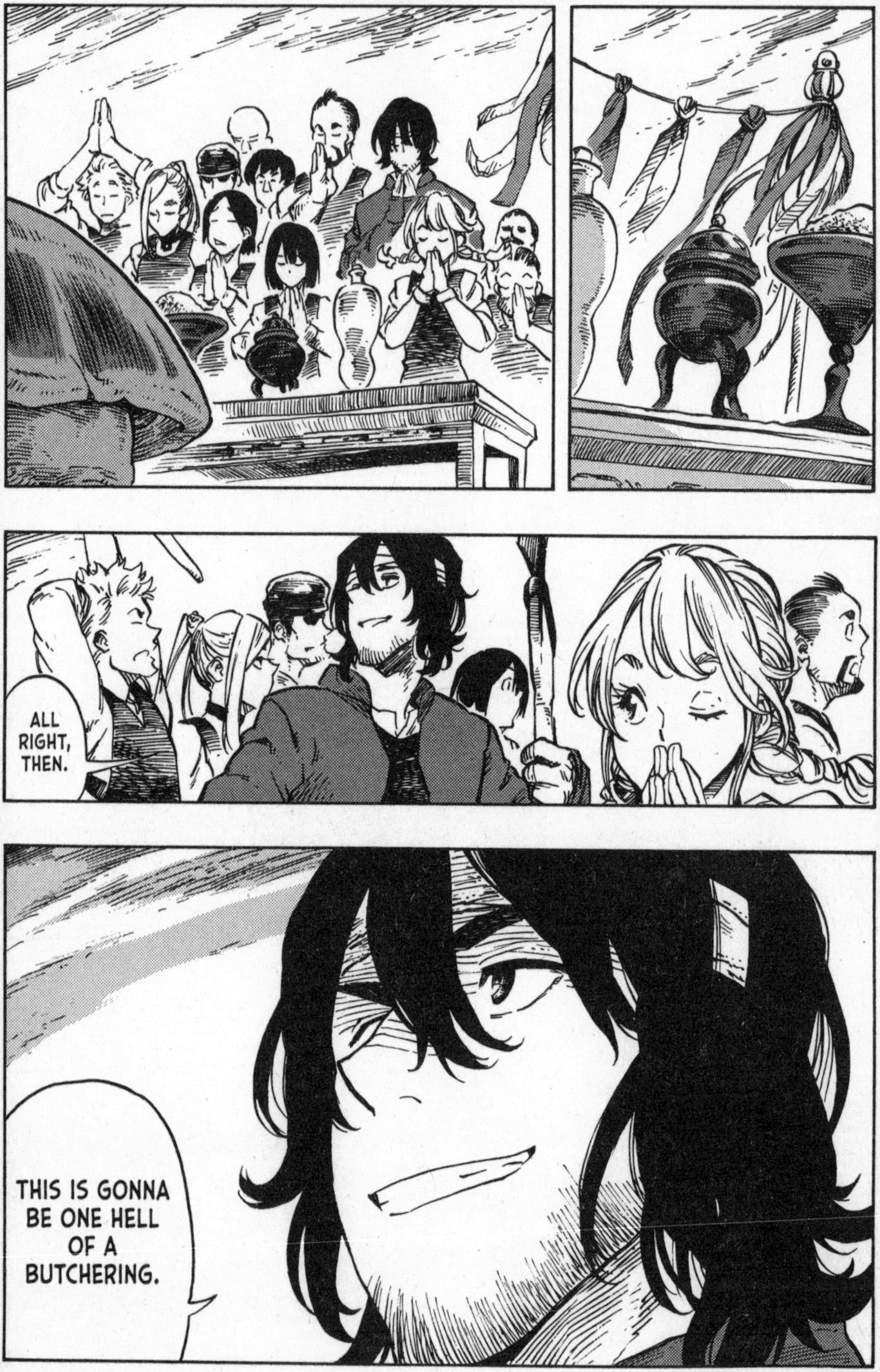
ALL RIGHT, THEN.
THIS IS GONNA BE ONE HELL OF A BUTCHERING.

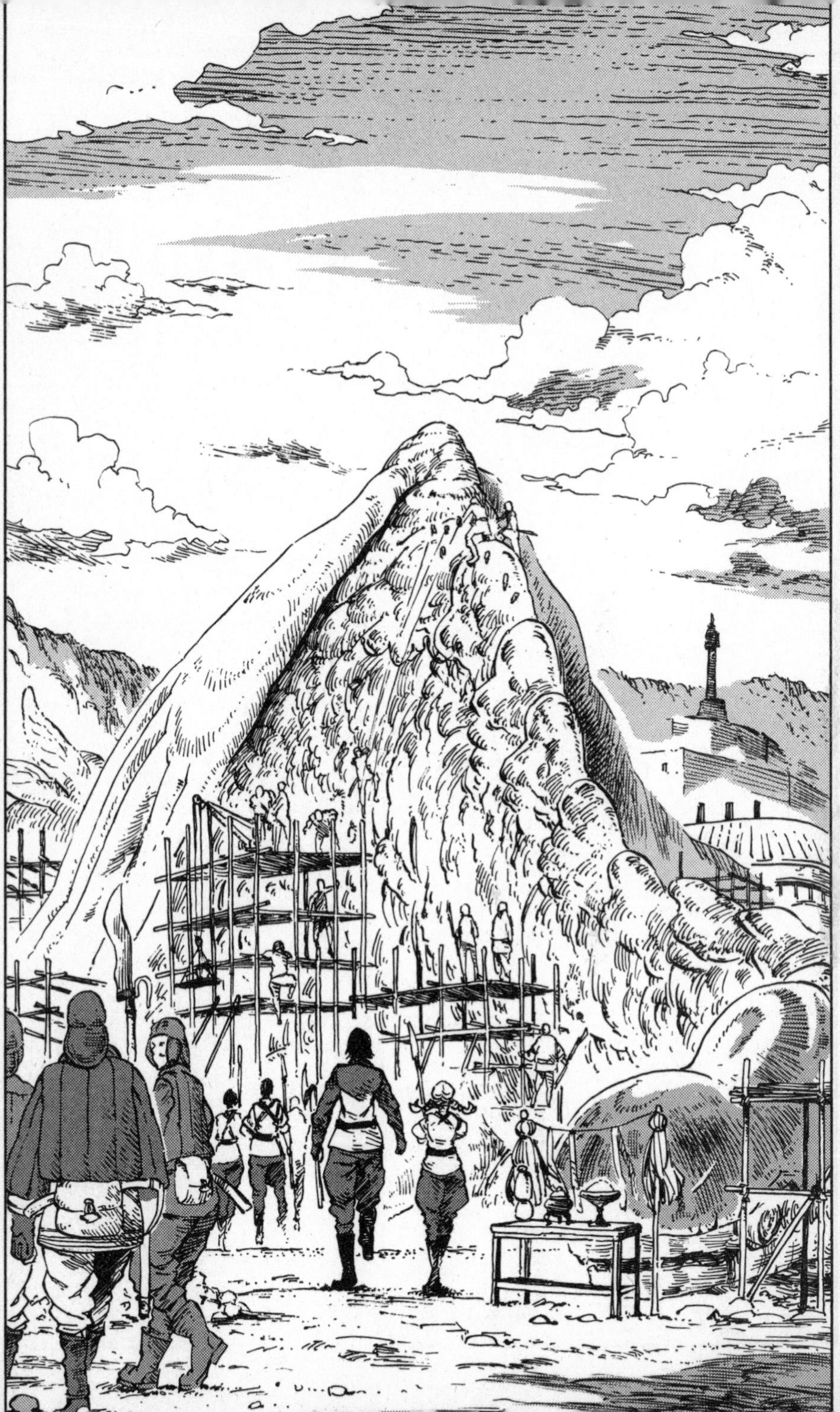

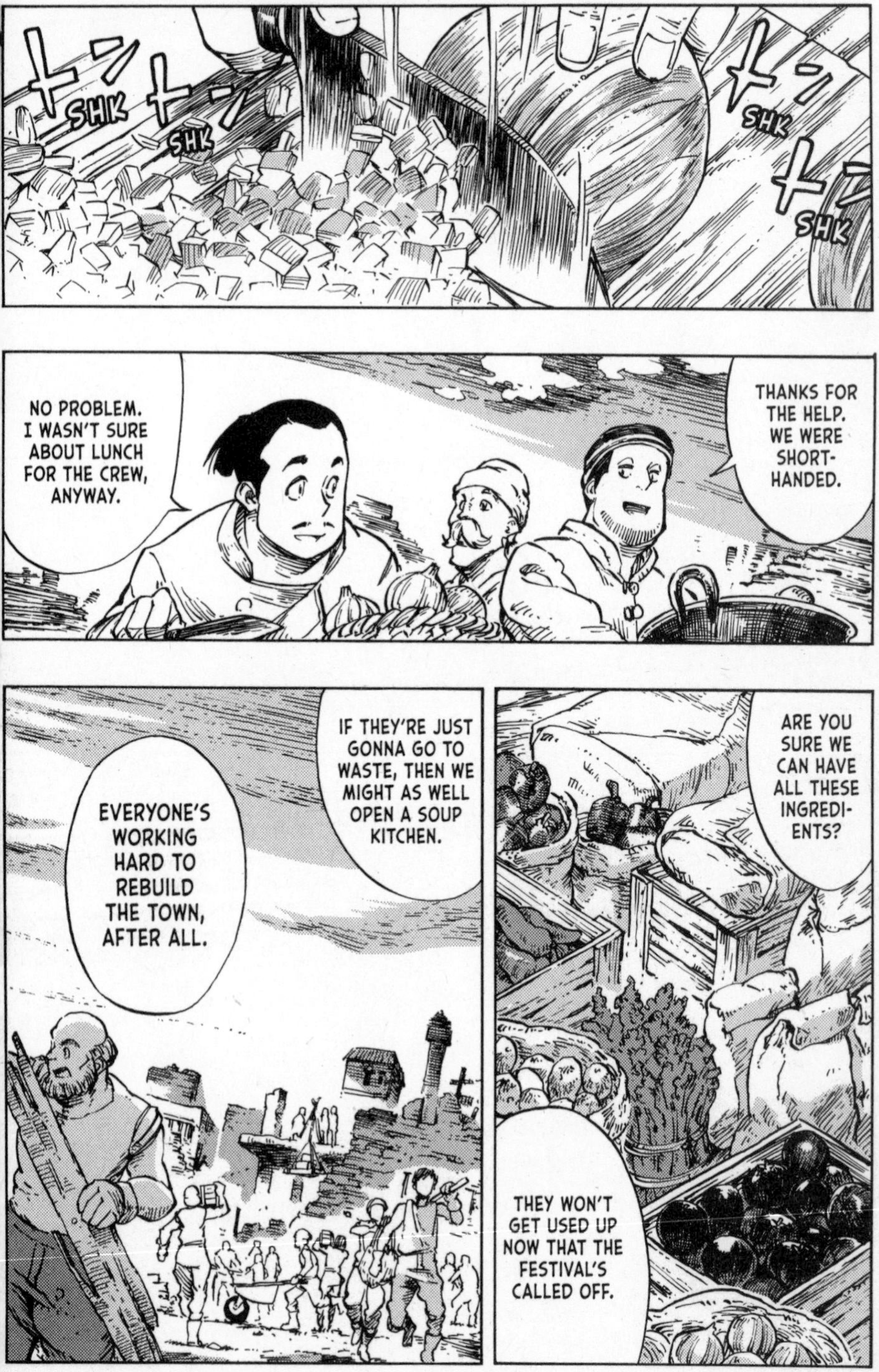
SHK
SHK
SHK
SHK
THANKS FOR THE HELP. WE WERE SHORT-HANDED.
NO PROBLEM. I WASN'T SURE ABOUT LUNCH FOR THE CREW, ANYWAY.
ARE YOU SURE WE CAN HAVE ALL THESE INGREDI-ENTS?
THEY WON'T GET USED UP NOW THAT THE FESTIVAL'S CALLED OFF.
IF THEY'RE JUST GONNA GO TO WASTE, THEN WE MIGHT AS WELL OPEN A SOUP KITCHEN.
EVERYONE'S WORKING HARD TO REBUILD THE TOWN, AFTER ALL.

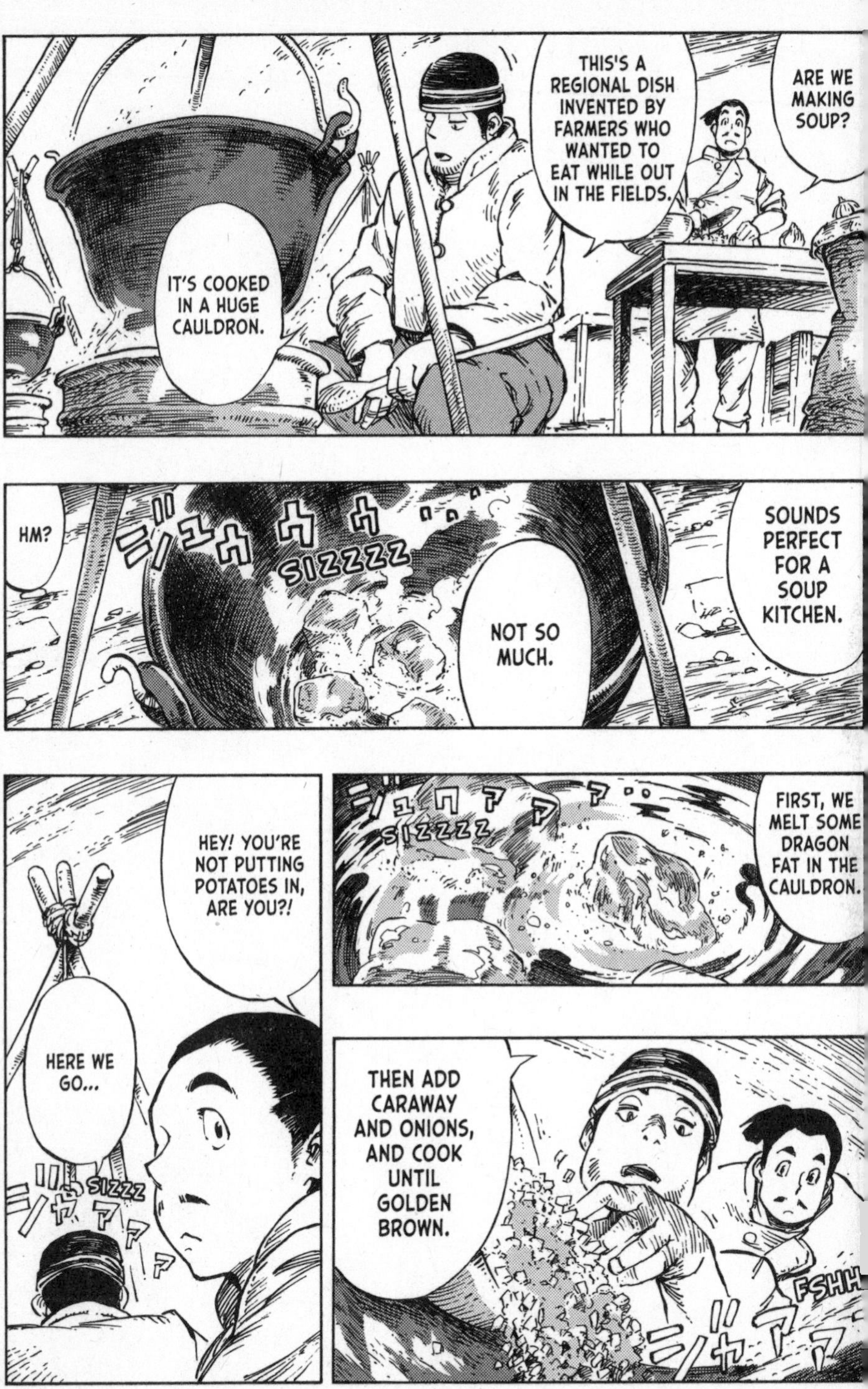
ARE WE MAKING SOUP?
THIS'S A REGIONAL DISH INVENTED BY FARMERS WHO WANTED TO EAT WHILE OUT IN THE FIELDS.
IT'S COOKED IN A HUGE CAULDRON.
SOUNDS PERFECT FOR A SOUP KITCHEN.
NOT SO MUCH.
SIZZZZ
HM?
FIRST, WE MELT SOME DRAGON FAT IN THE CAULDRON.
SIZZZZ
THEN ADD CARAWAY AND ONIONS, AND COOK UNTIL GOLDEN BROWN.
FSHH
HEY! YOU'RE NOT PUTTING POTATOES IN, ARE YOU?!
HERE WE GO...
SIZZZ

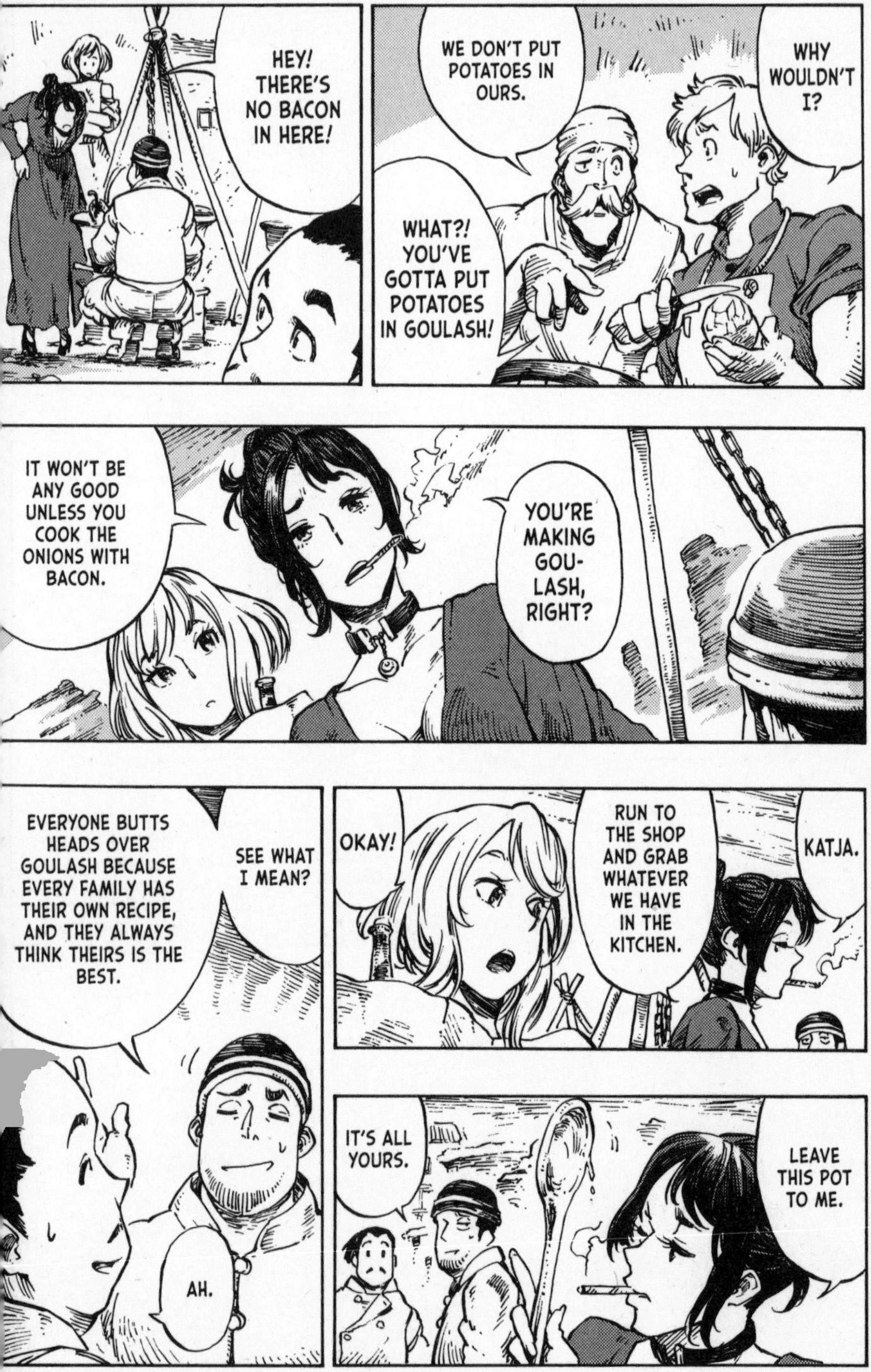
WHY WOULDN'T I?
WE DON'T PUT POTATOES IN OURS.
WHAT?! YOU'VE GOTTA PUT POTATOES IN GOULASH!
HEY! THERE'S NO BACON IN HERE!
YOU'RE MAKING GOU-LASH, RIGHT?
IT WON'T BE ANY GOOD UNLESS YOU COOK THE ONIONS WITH BACON.
KATJA.
RUN TO THE SHOP AND GRAB WHATEVER WE HAVE IN THE KITCHEN.
OKAY!
LEAVE THIS POT TO ME.
IT'S ALL YOURS.
SEE WHAT I MEAN?
EVERYONE BUTTS HEADS OVER GOULASH BECAUSE EVERY FAMILY HAS THEIR OWN RECIPE, AND THEY ALWAYS THINK THEIRS IS THE BEST.
AH.

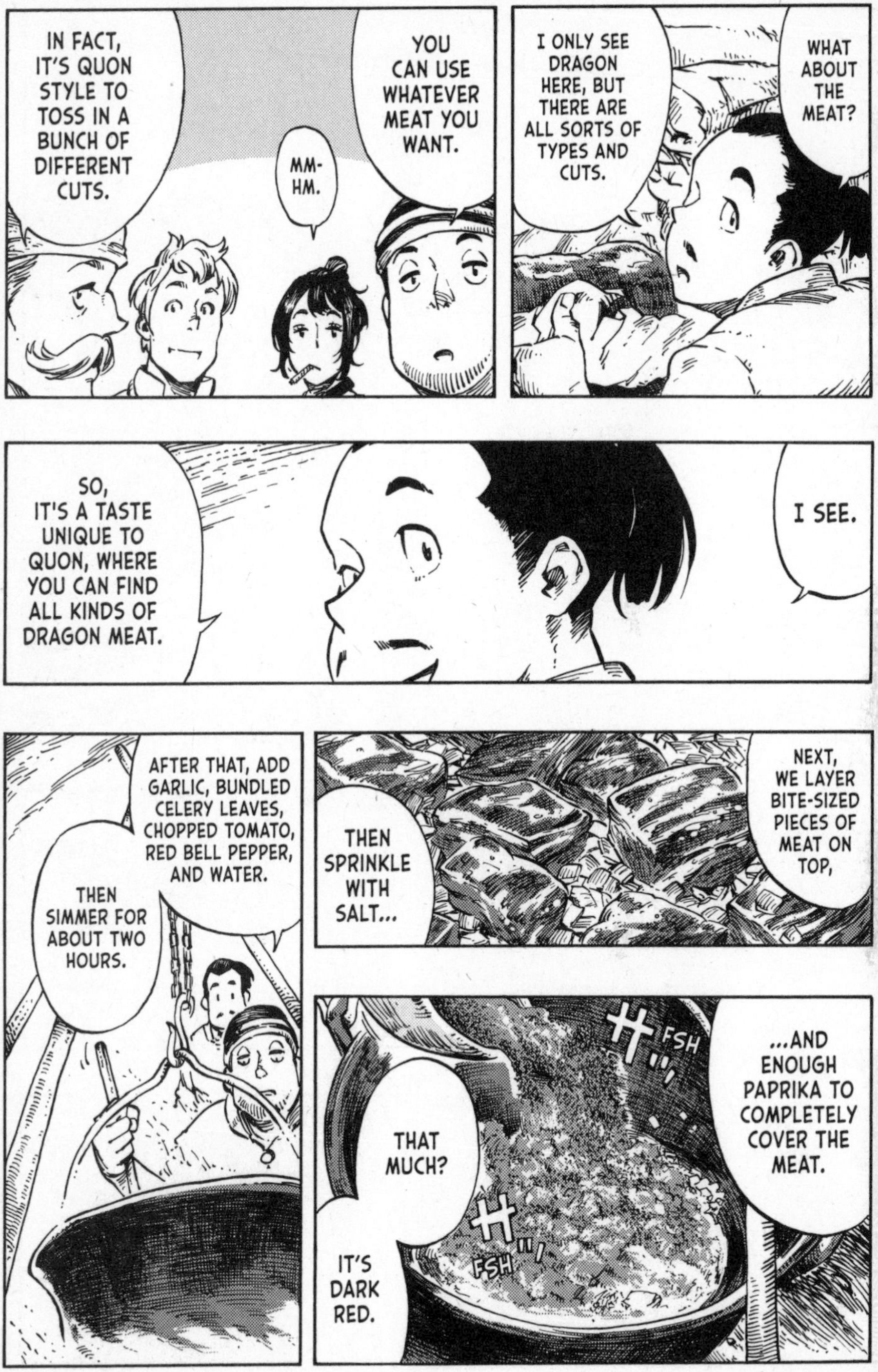
WHAT ABOUT THE MEAT?
I ONLY SEE DRAGON HERE, BUT THERE ARE ALL SORTS OF TYPES AND CUTS.
YOU CAN USE WHATEVER MEAT YOU WANT.
MM-HM.
IN FACT, IT'S QUON STYLE TO TOSS IN A BUNCH OF DIFFERENT CUTS.
I SEE.
SO, IT'S A TASTE UNIQUE TO QUON, WHERE YOU CAN FIND ALL KINDS OF DRAGON MEAT.
NEXT, WE LAYER BITE-SIZED PIECES OF MEAT ON TOP,
THEN SPRINKLE WITH SALT...
...AND ENOUGH PAPRIKA TO COMPLETELY COVER THE MEAT.
FSH
THAT MUCH?
FSH
IT'S DARK RED.
AFTER THAT, ADD GARLIC, BUNDLED CELERY LEAVES, CHOPPED TOMATO, RED BELL PEPPER, AND WATER.
THEN SIMMER FOR ABOUT TWO HOURS.

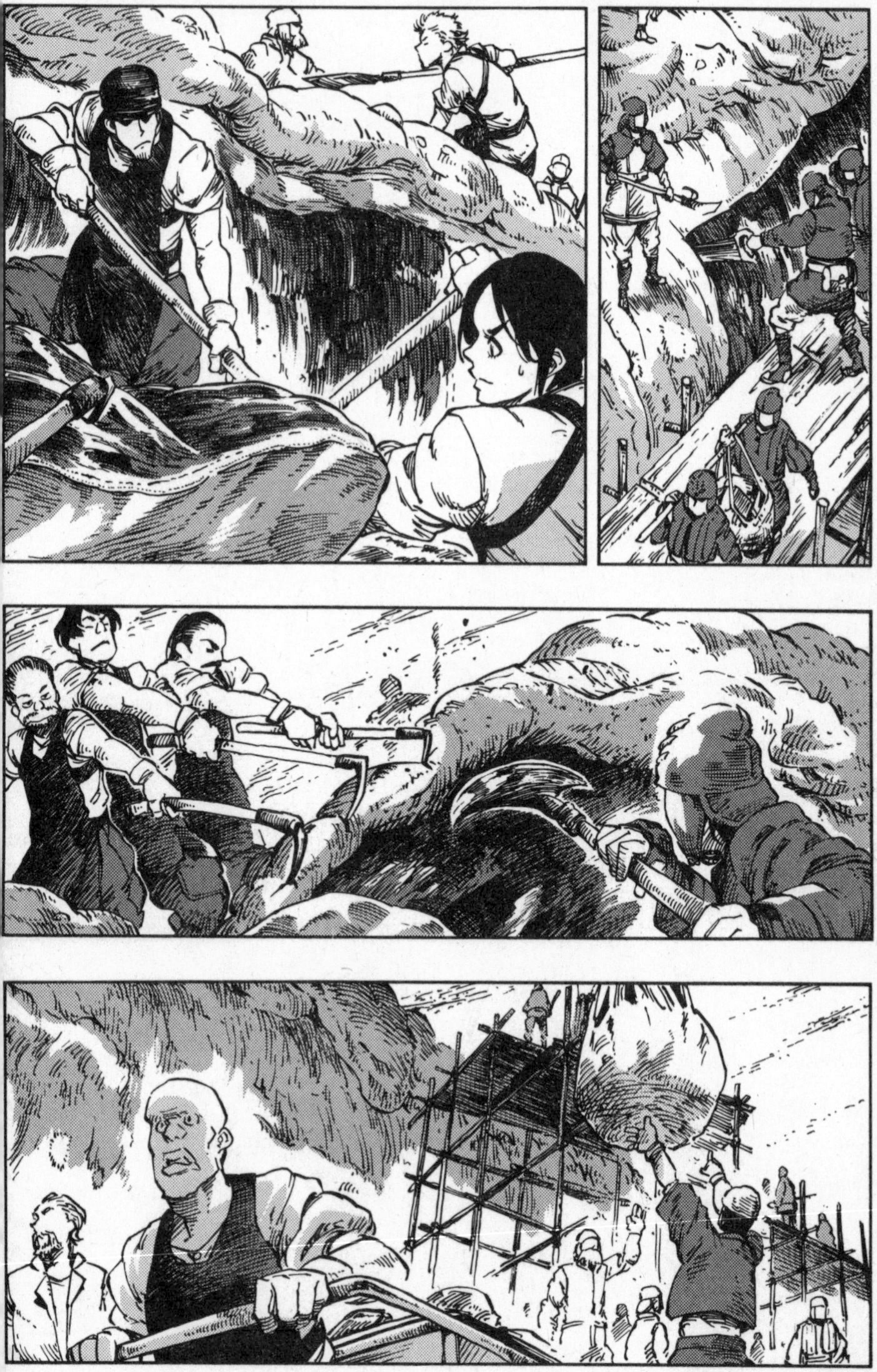

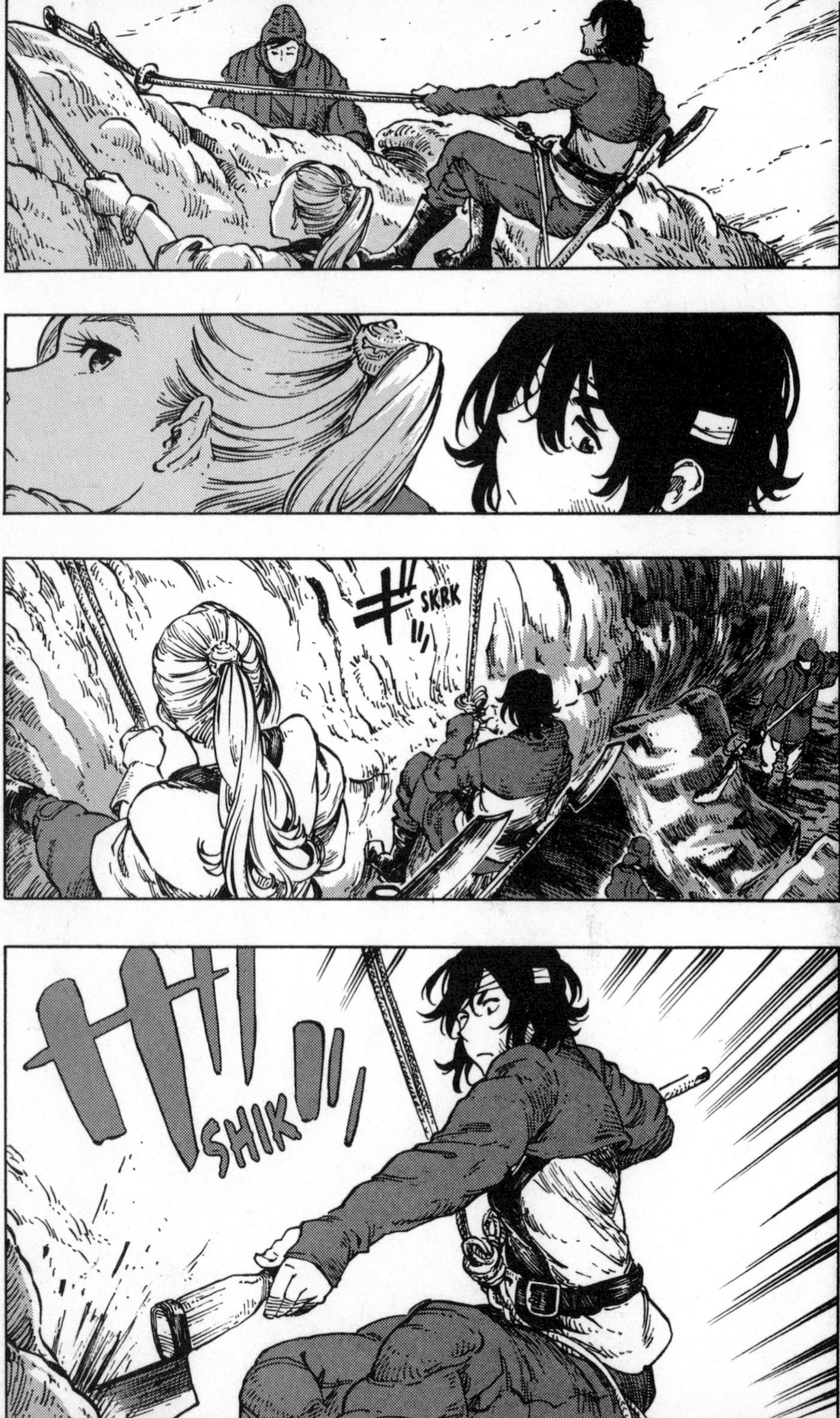
SKRK
SHIK

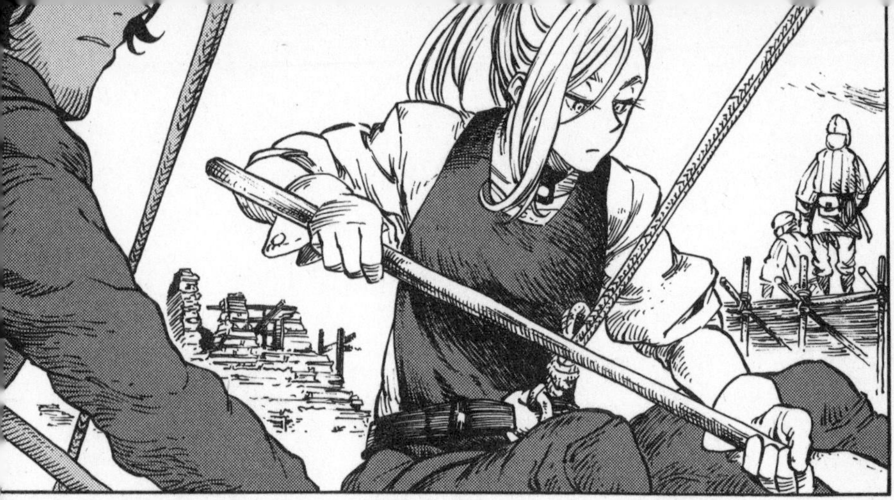
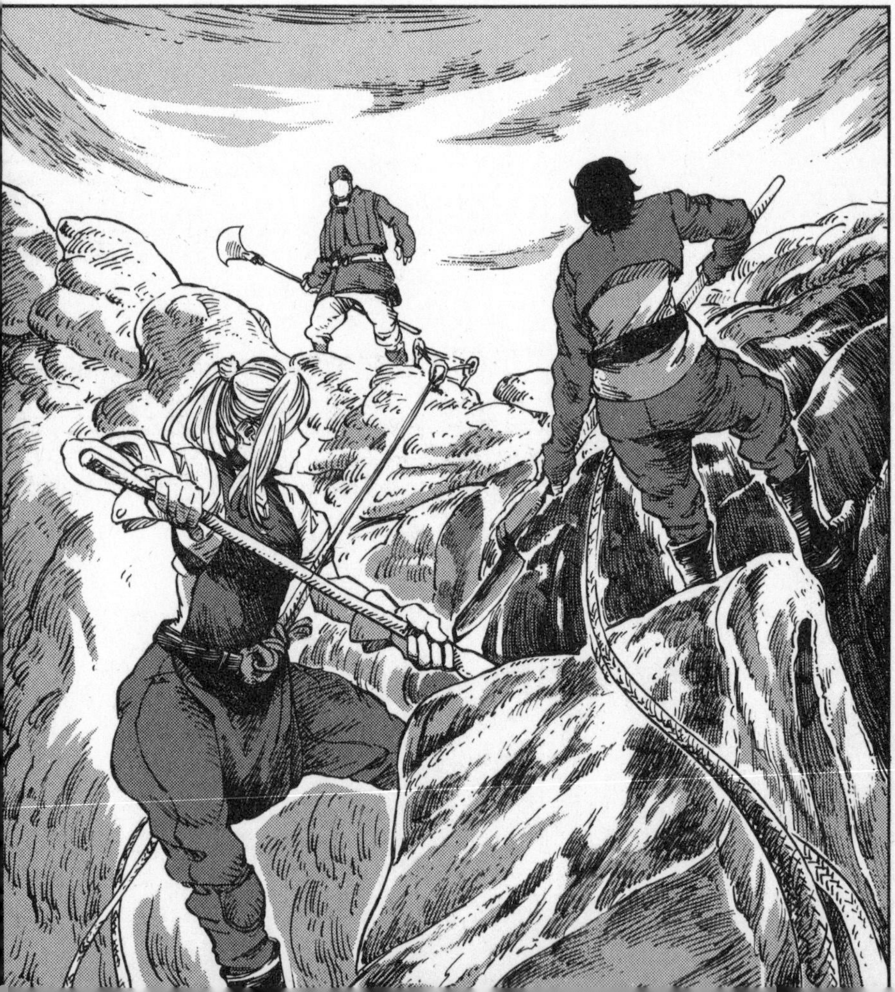

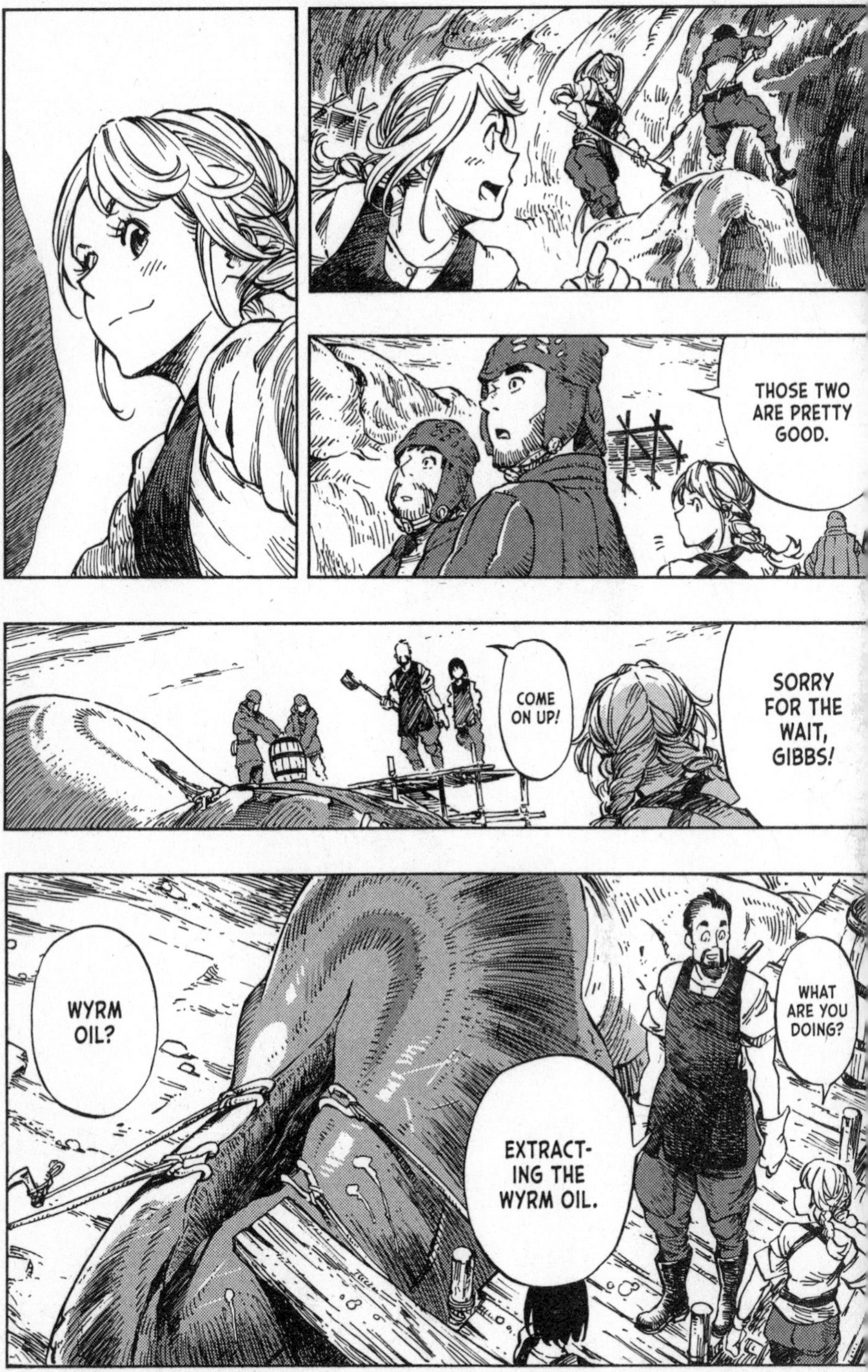
THOSE TWO ARE PRETTY GOOD.
SORRY FOR THE WAIT, GIBBS!
COME ON UP!
WHAT ARE YOU DOING?
EXTRACT-ING THE WYRM OIL.
WYRM OIL?

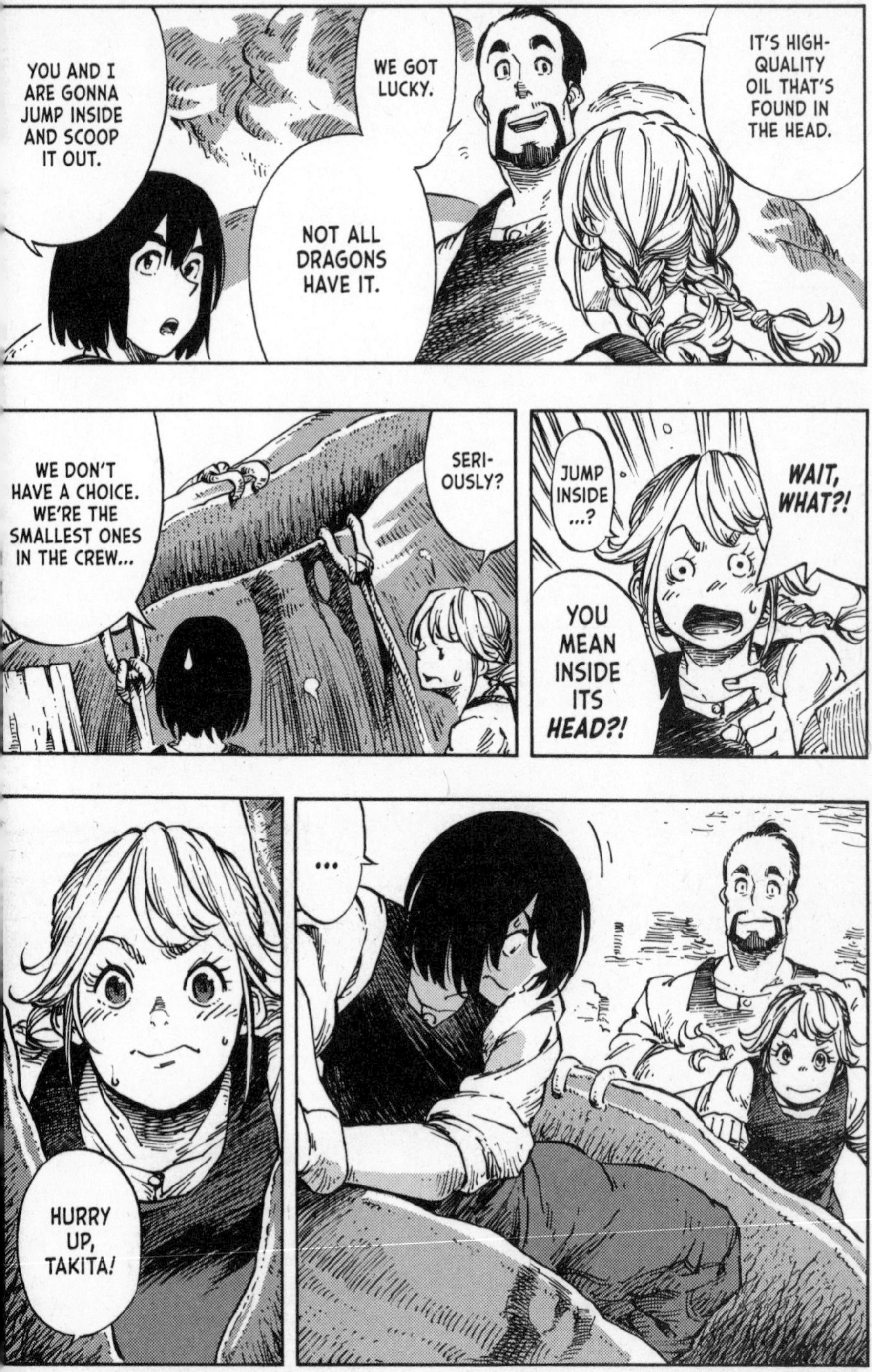
IT'S HIGH-QUALITY OIL THAT'S FOUND IN THE HEAD.
WE GOT LUCKY.
NOT ALL DRAGONS HAVE IT.
YOU AND I ARE GONNA JUMP INSIDE AND SCOOP IT OUT.
WAIT, WHAT?!
JUMP INSIDE ...?
YOU MEAN INSIDE ITS HEAD?!
SERI-OUSLY?
WE DON'T HAVE A CHOICE. WE'RE THE SMALLEST ONES IN THE CREW...
...
HURRY UP, TAKITA!

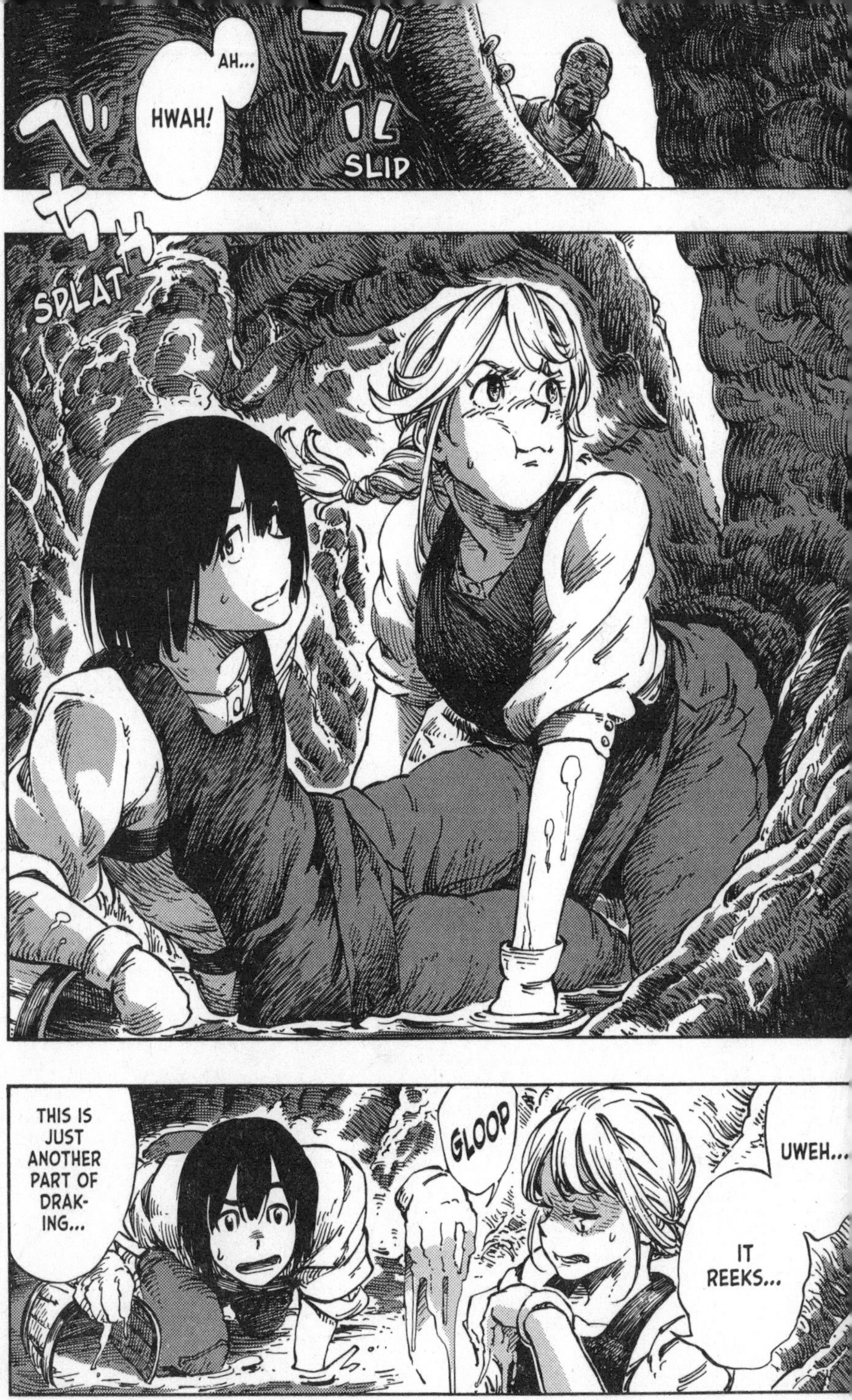
SLIP
AH... HWAH!
SPLAT
UWEH... IT REEKS...
GLOOP
THIS IS JUST ANOTHER PART OF DRAK-ING...

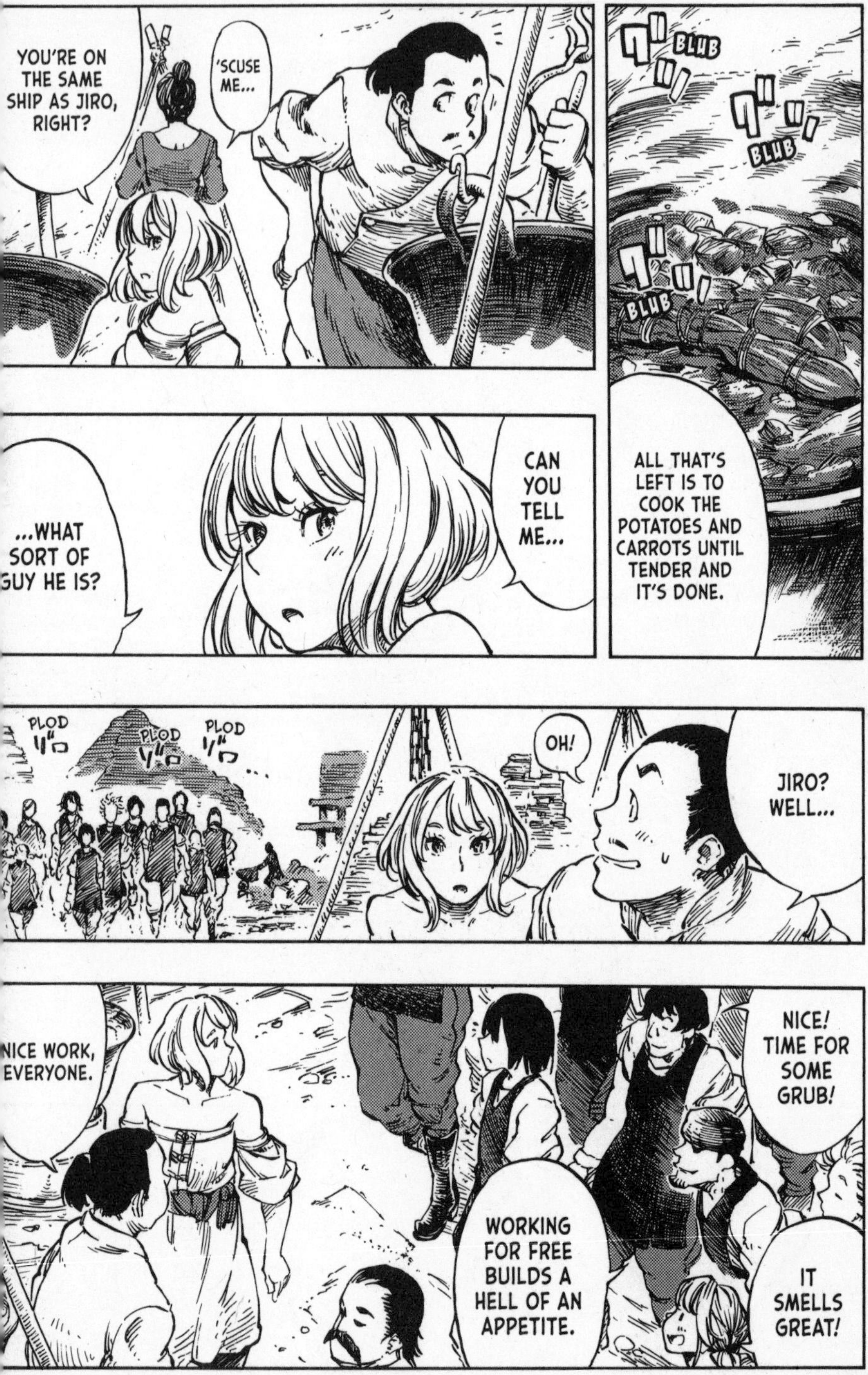
BLUB
BLUB
BLUB
ALL THAT'S LEFT IS TO COOK THE POTATOES AND CARROTS UNTIL TENDER AND IT'S DONE.
'SCUSE ME...
YOU'RE ON THE SAME SHIP AS JIRO, RIGHT?
CAN YOU TELL ME...
...WHAT SORT OF GUY HE IS?
JIRO? WELL...
OH!
PLOD
PLOD
PLOD
NICE! TIME FOR SOME GRUB!
IT SMELLS GREAT!
WORKING FOR FREE BUILDS A HELL OF AN APPETITE.
NICE WORK, EVERYONE.

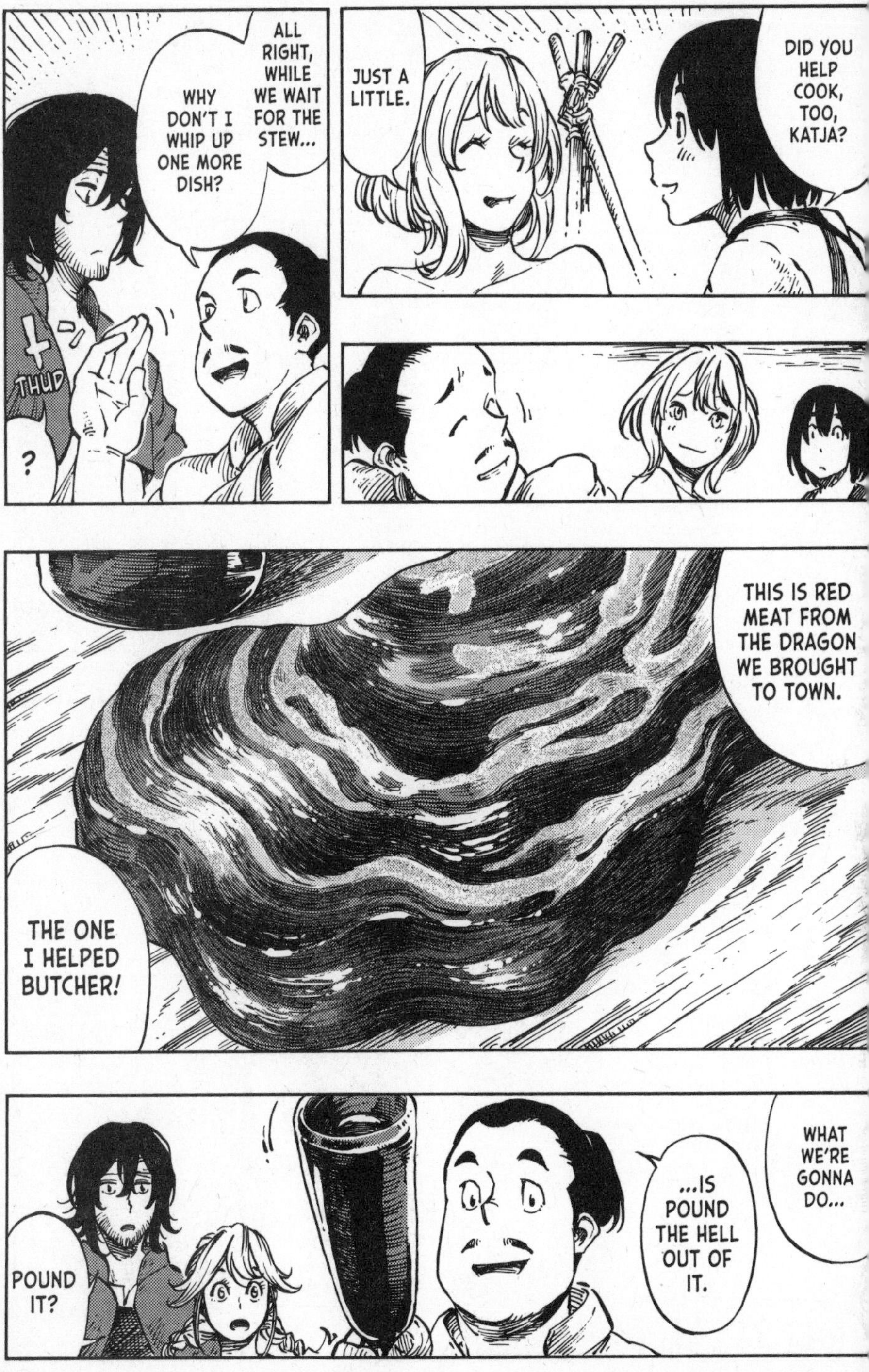
DID YOU HELP COOK, TOO, KATJA?
JUST A LITTLE.
ALL RIGHT, WHILE WE WAIT FOR THE STEW...
WHY DON'T I WHIP UP ONE MORE DISH?
THUD
?
THIS IS RED MEAT FROM THE DRAGON WE BROUGHT TO TOWN.
THE ONE I HELPED BUTCHER!
WHAT WE'RE GONNA DO...
...IS POUND THE HELL OUT OF IT.
POUND IT?

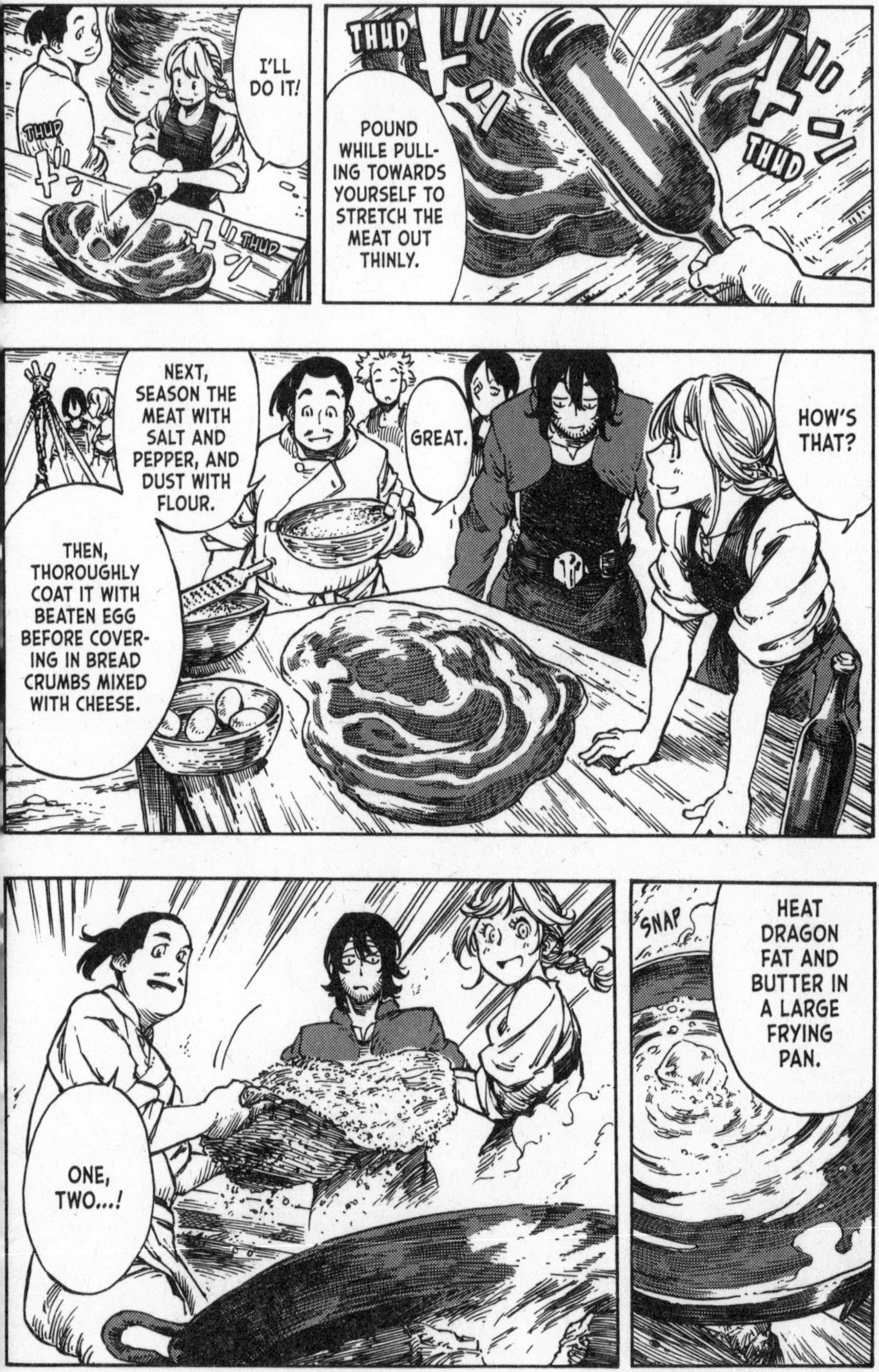
THUD
POUND WHILE PULLING TOWARDS YOURSELF TO STRETCH THE MEAT OUT THINLY.
THUD
I'LL DO IT!
THUD
THUD
HOW'S THAT?
GREAT.
NEXT, SEASON THE MEAT WITH SALT AND PEPPER, AND DUST WITH FLOUR.
THEN, THOROUGHLY COAT IT WITH BEATEN EGG BEFORE COVERING IN BREAD CRUMBS MIXED WITH CHEESE.
SNAP
HEAT DRAGON FAT AND BUTTER IN A LARGE FRYING PAN.
ONE, TWO...!

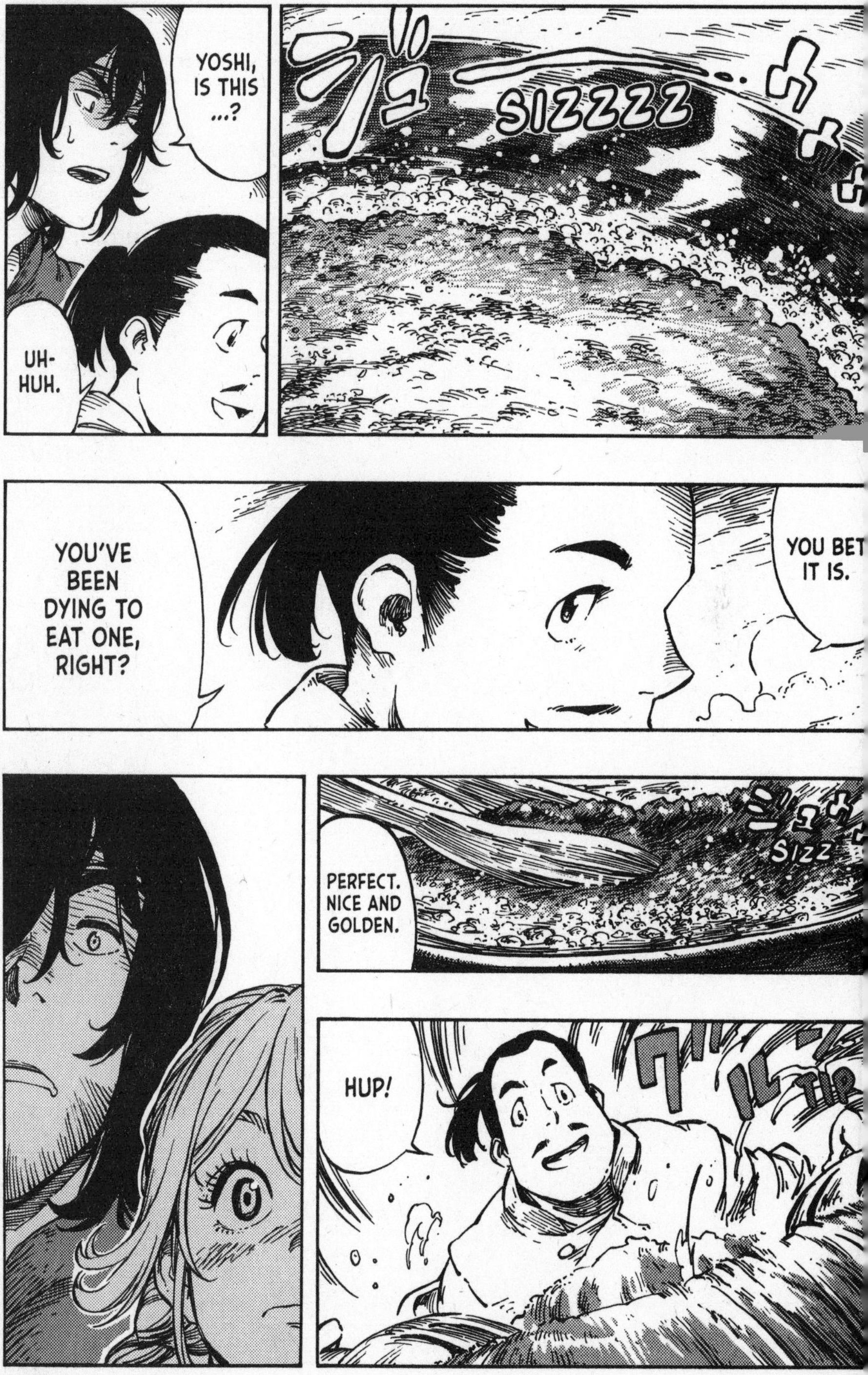
SIZZZZ
YOSHI, IS THIS ...?
UH-HUH.
YOU BET IT IS.
YOU'VE BEEN DYING TO EAT ONE, RIGHT?
SIZZ
PERFECT. NICE AND GOLDEN.
TIP
HUP!

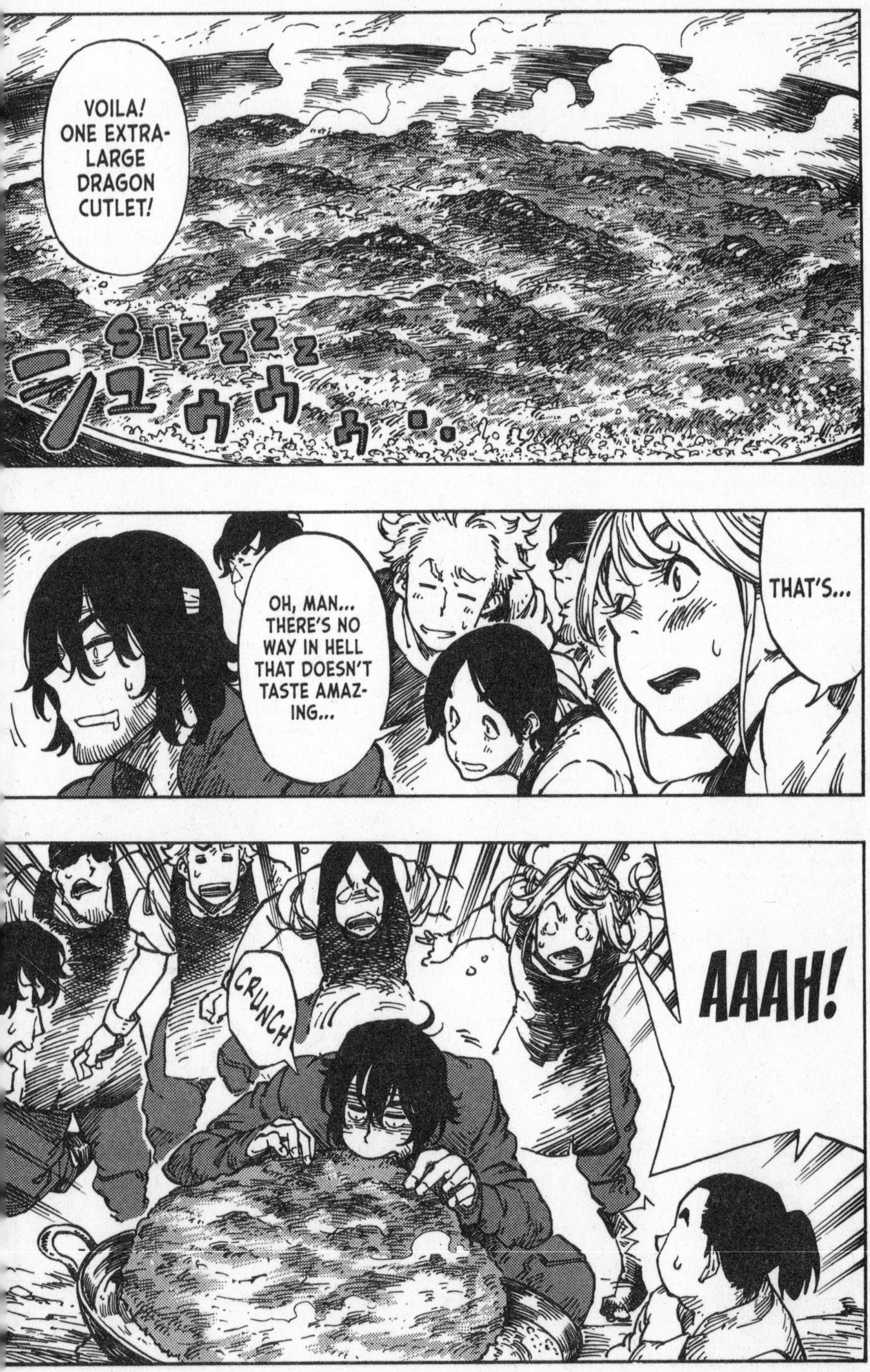
VOILA! ONE EXTRA-LARGE DRAGON CUTLET!
SIZZZZZ
シュウウゥ..
THAT'S...
OH, MAN... THERE'S NO WAY IN HELL THAT DOESN'T TASTE AMAZ-ING...
AAAH!
CRUNCH

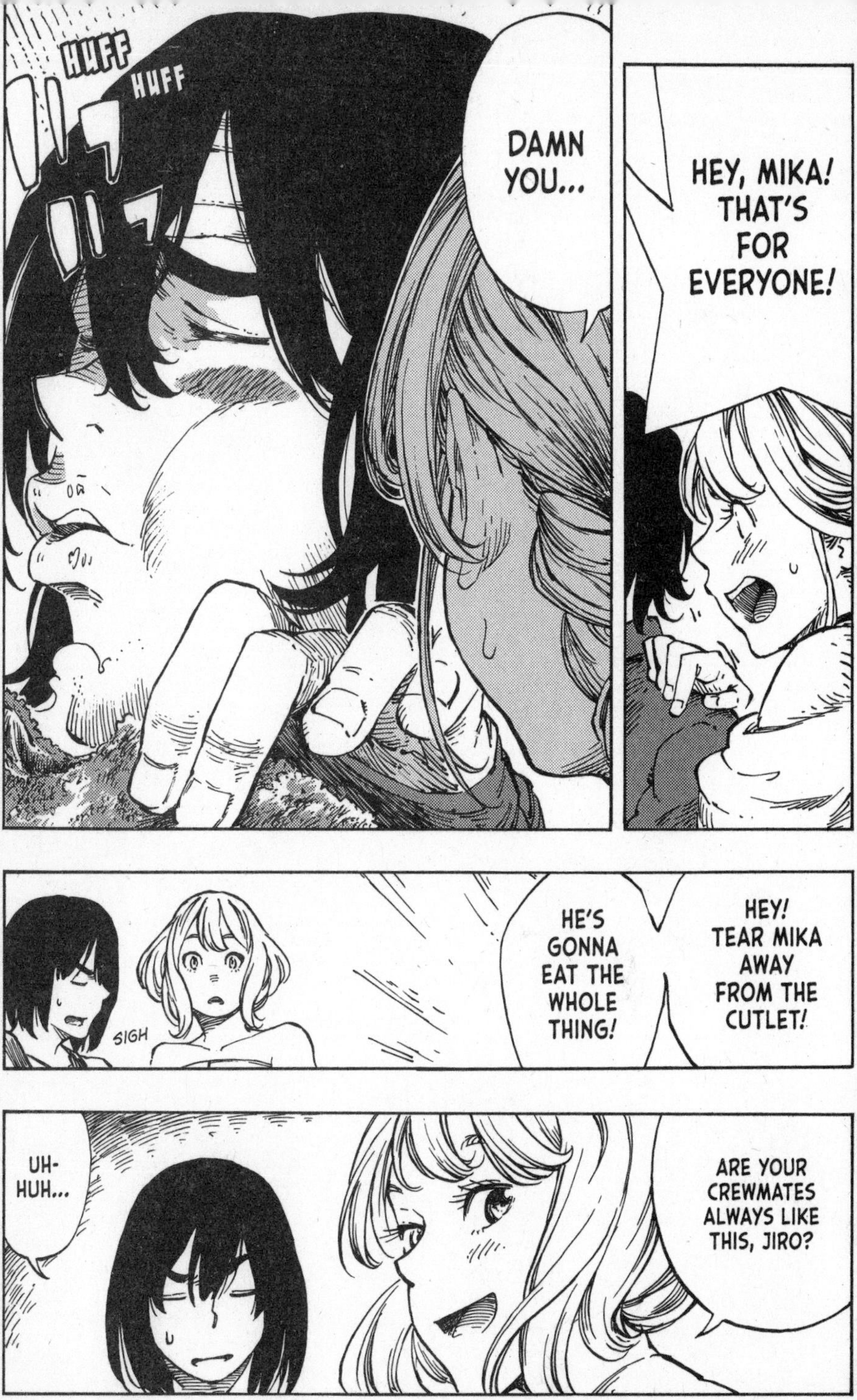
HEY, MIKA! THAT'S FOR EVERYONE!
DAMN YOU...
HUFF
HUFF
HEY! TEAR MIKA AWAY FROM THE CUTLET!
HE'S GONNA EAT THE WHOLE THING!
SIGH
ARE YOUR CREWMATES ALWAYS LIKE THIS, JIRO?
UH-HUH...

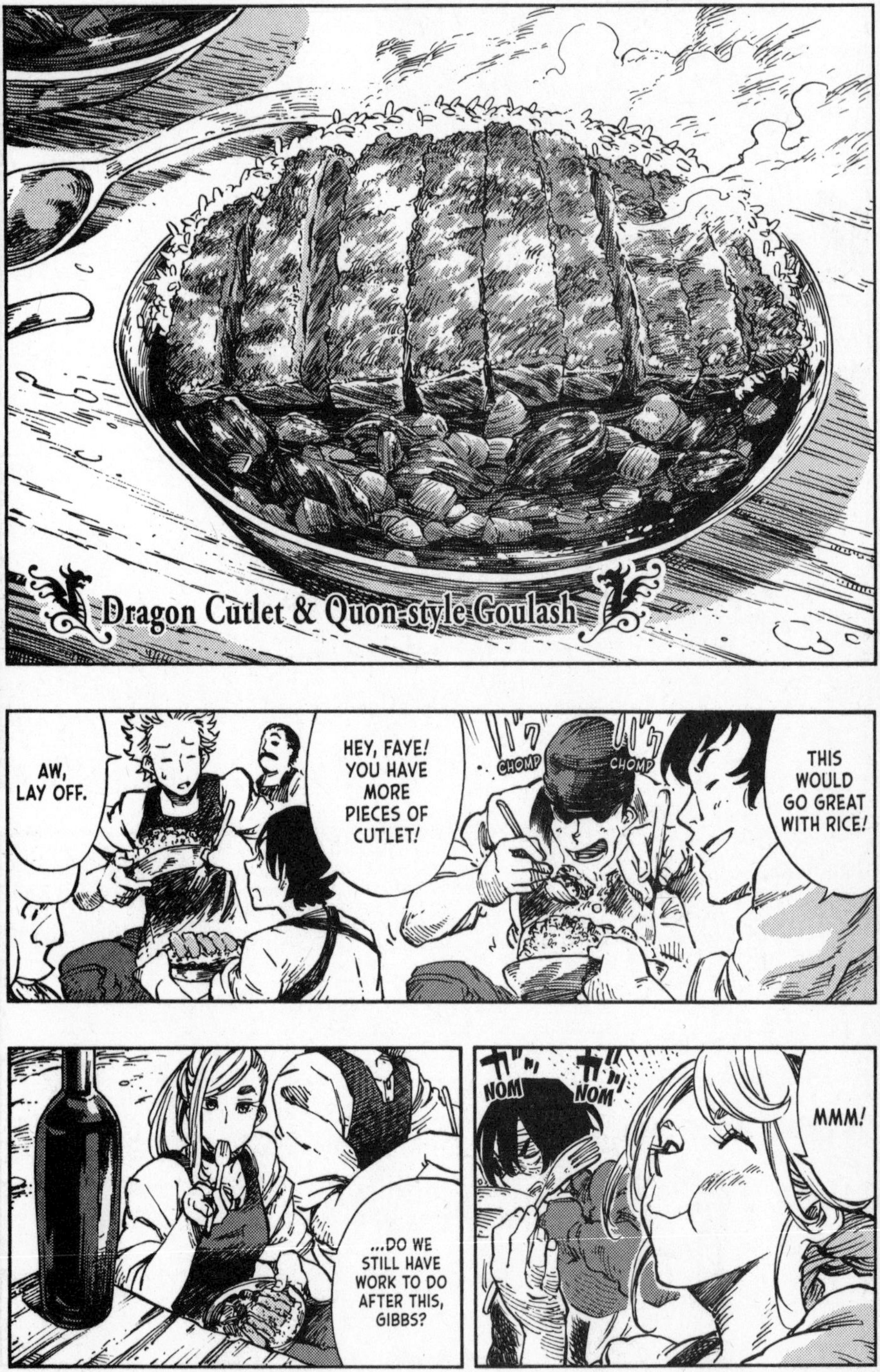
Dragon Cutlet & Quon-style Goulash
THIS WOULD GO GREAT WITH RICE!
CHOMP
CHOMP
HEY, FAYE! YOU HAVE MORE PIECES OF CUTLET!
AW, LAY OFF.
MMM!
NOM
NOM
...DO WE STILL HAVE WORK TO DO AFTER THIS, GIBBS?

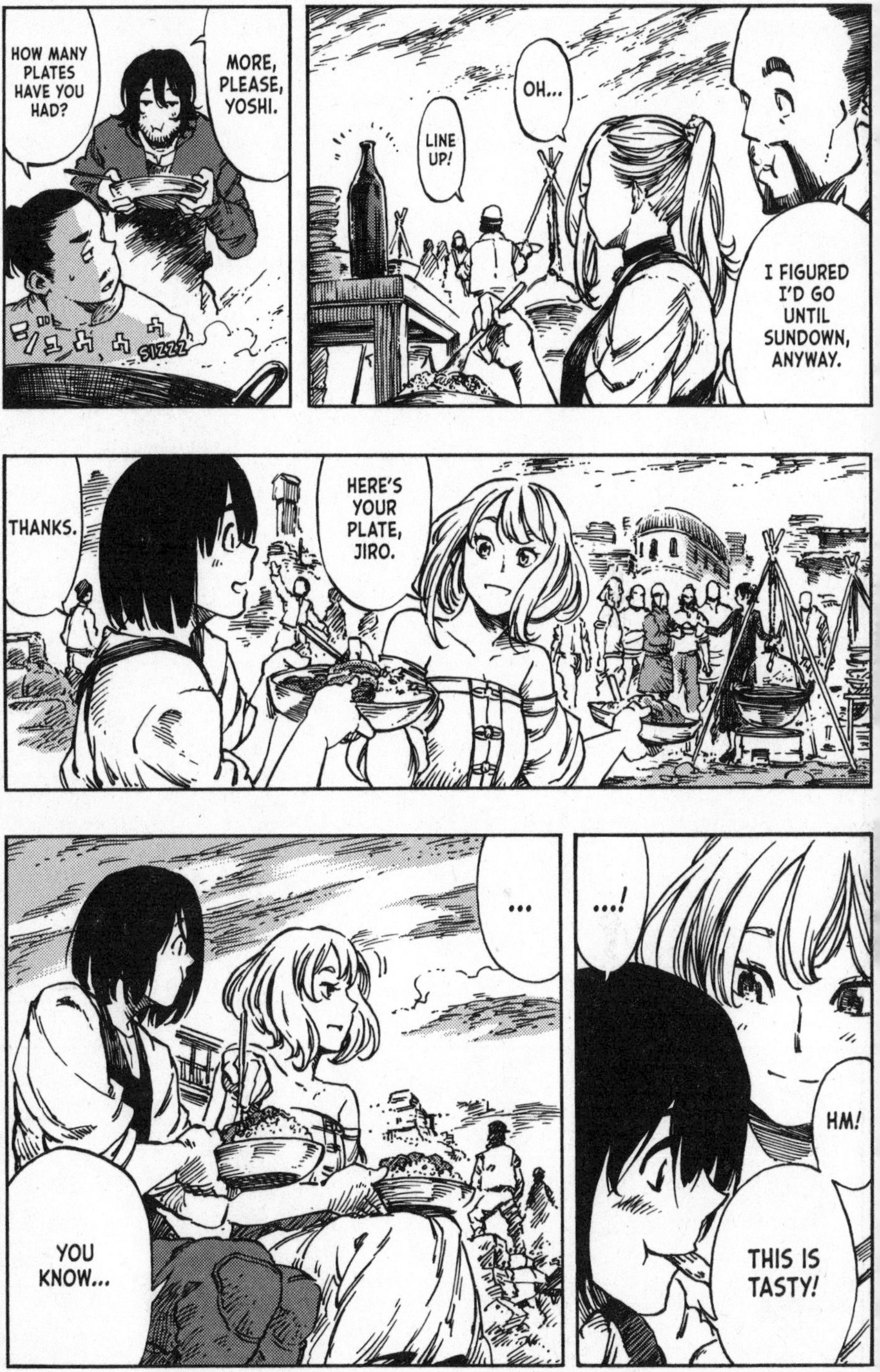
OH...
LINE UP!
I FIGURED I'D GO UNTIL SUNDOWN, ANYWAY.
MORE, PLEASE, YOSHI.
HOW MANY PLATES HAVE YOU HAD?
SIZZZ
HERE'S YOUR PLATE, JIRO.
THANKS.
...!
HM!
THIS IS TASTY!
...
YOU KNOW...

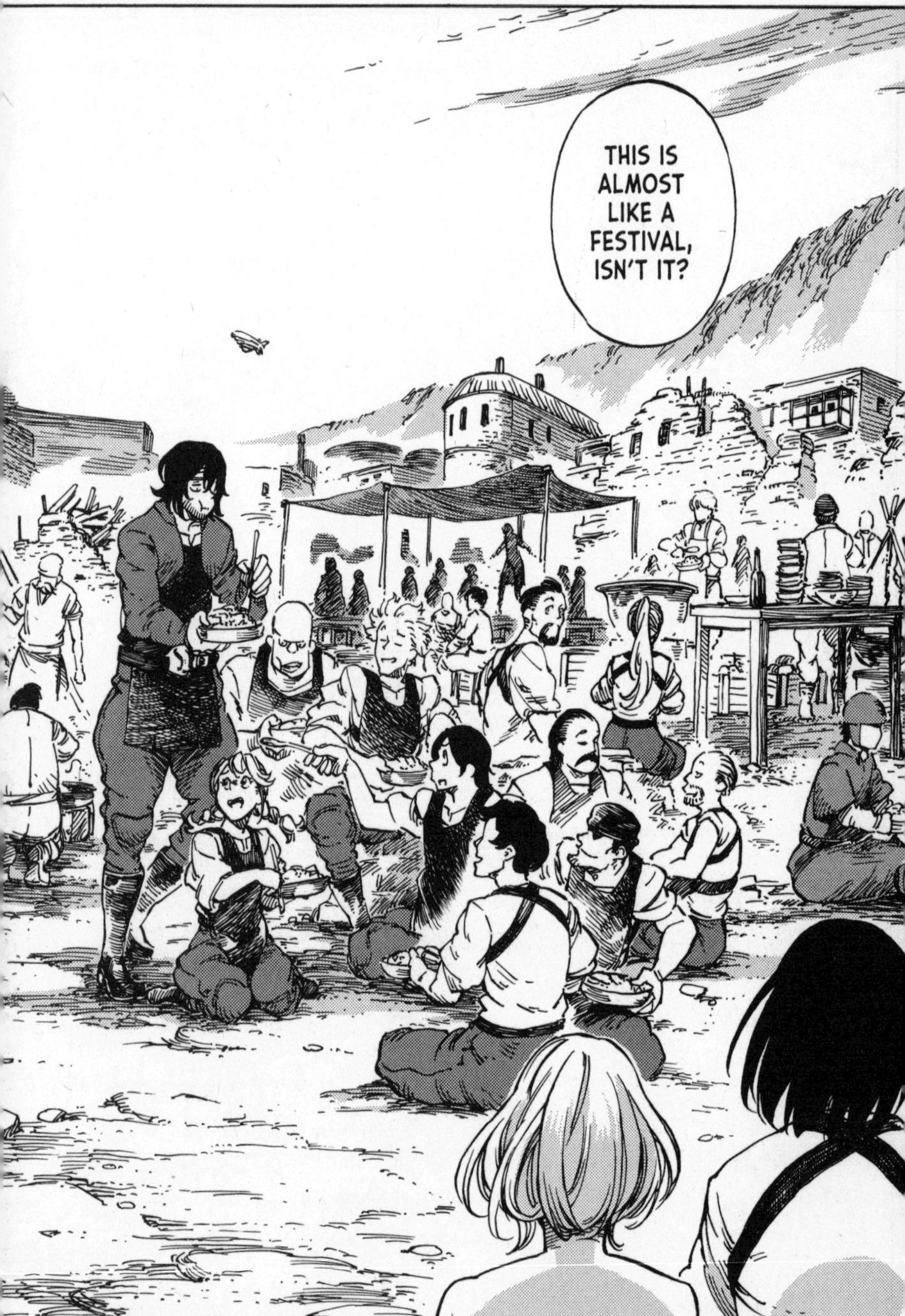
THIS IS ALMOST LIKE A FESTIVAL, ISN'T IT?

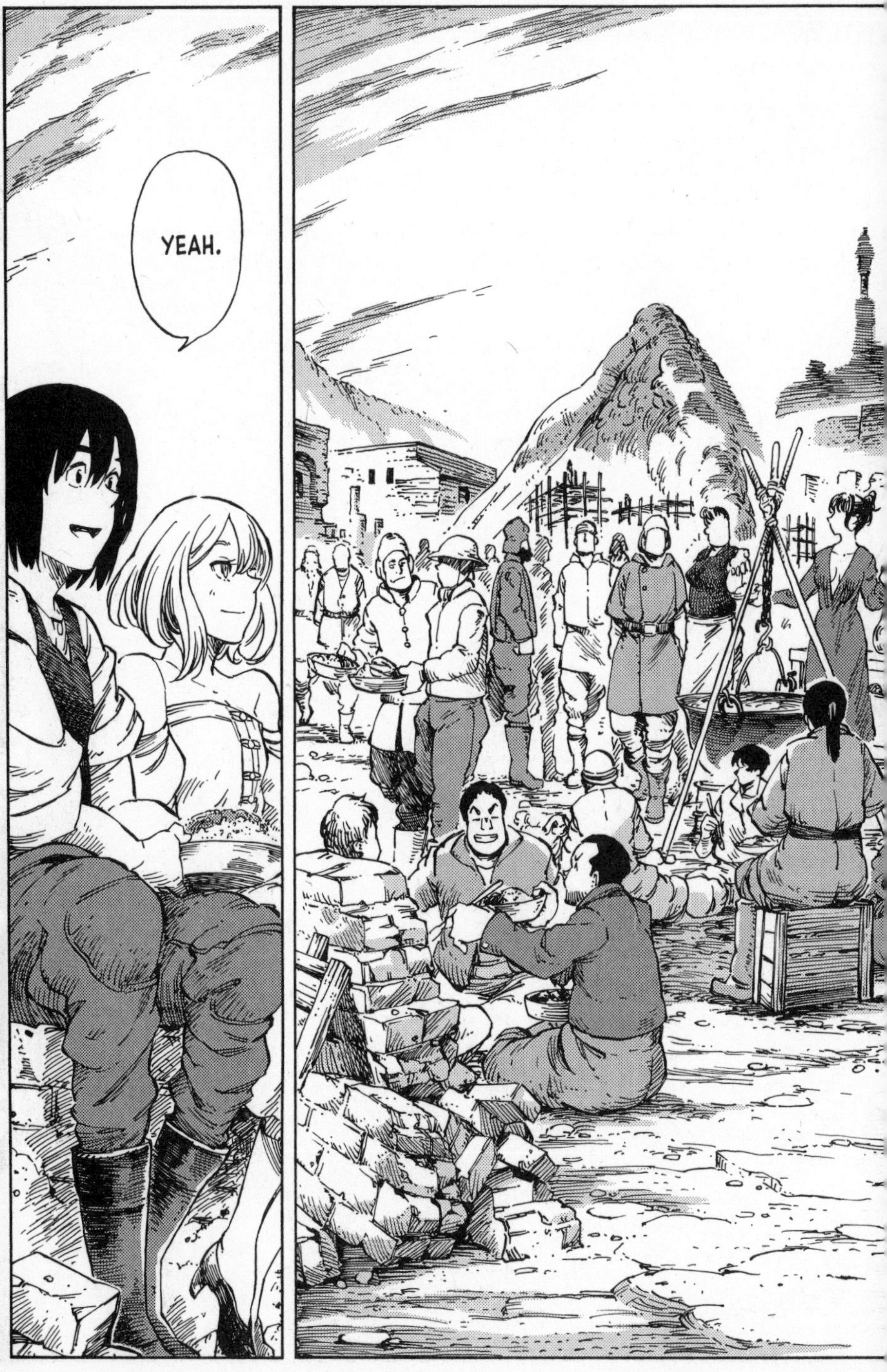
YEAH.

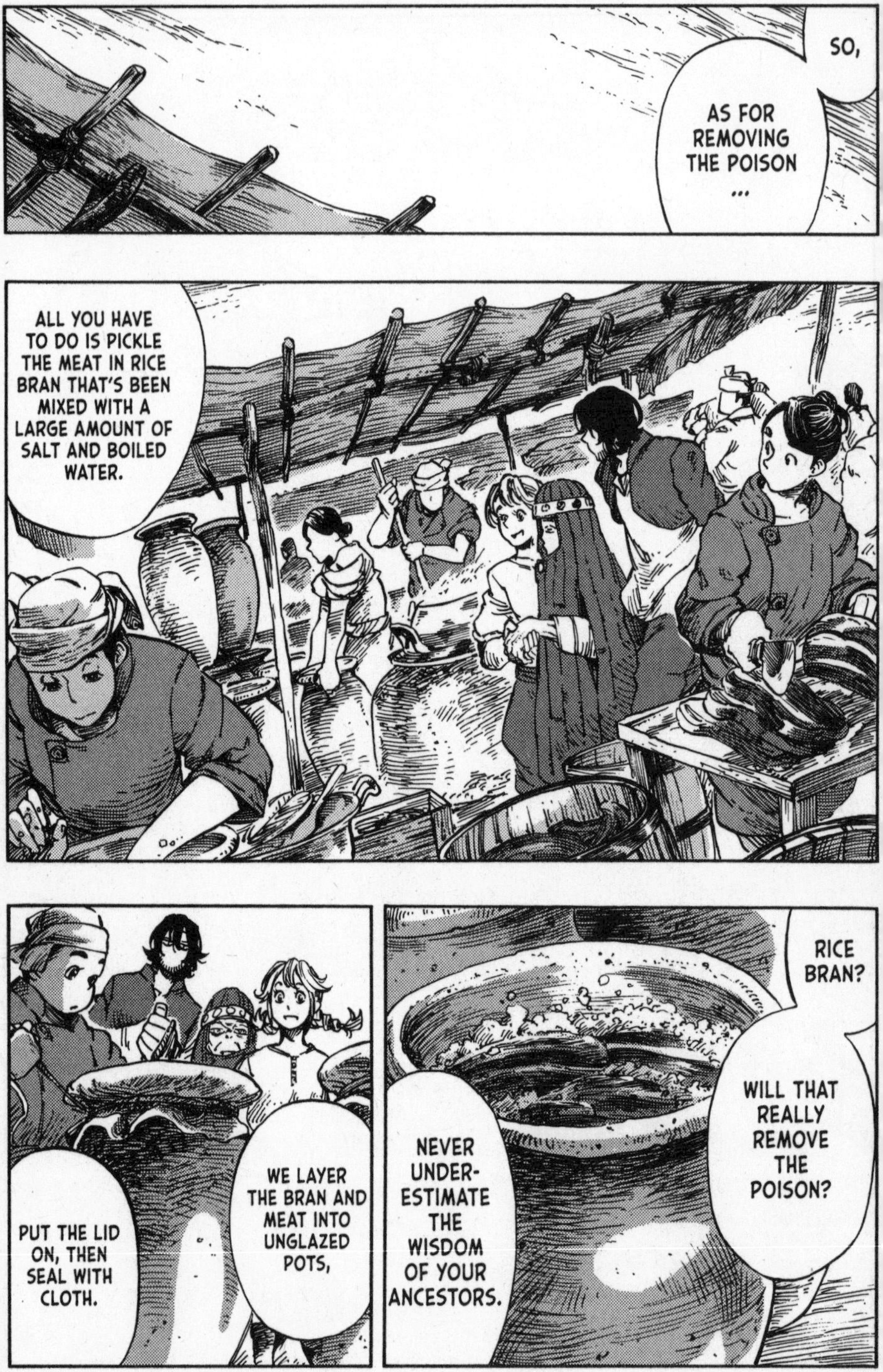
SO,
AS FOR REMOVING THE POISON ...
ALL YOU HAVE TO DO IS PICKLE THE MEAT IN RICE BRAN THAT'S BEEN MIXED WITH A LARGE AMOUNT OF SALT AND BOILED WATER.
RICE BRAN?
WILL THAT REALLY REMOVE THE POISON?
NEVER UNDER-ESTIMATE THE WISDOM OF YOUR ANCESTORS.
WE LAYER THE BRAN AND MEAT INTO UNGLAZED POTS,
PUT THE LID ON, THEN SEAL WITH CLOTH.

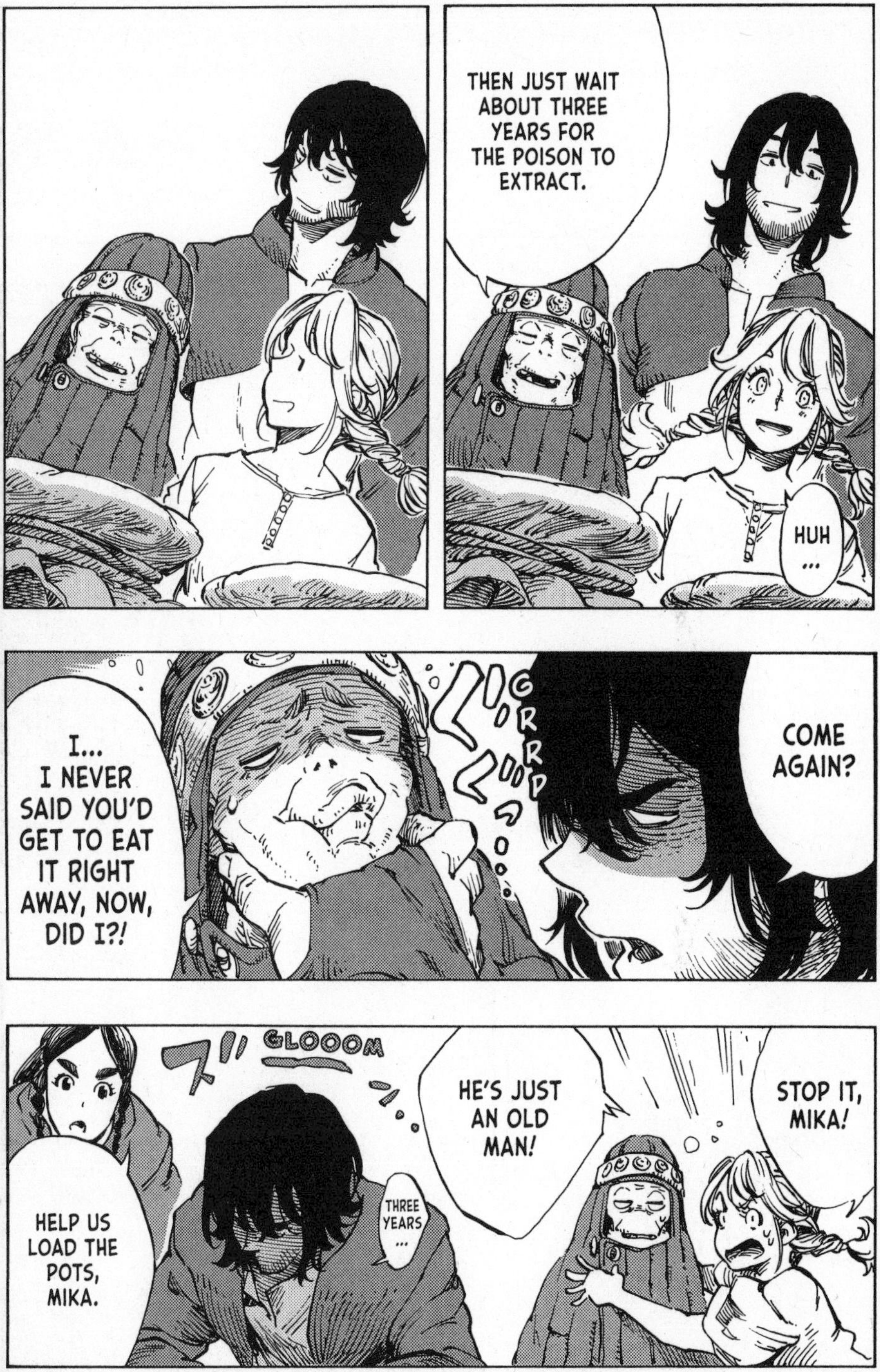
THEN JUST WAIT ABOUT THREE YEARS FOR THE POISON TO EXTRACT.
HUH ...
COME AGAIN?
GRRRP
I... I NEVER SAID YOU'D GET TO EAT IT RIGHT AWAY, NOW, DID I?!
STOP IT, MIKA!
HE'S JUST AN OLD MAN!
THREE YEARS ...
GLOOOM
HELP US LOAD THE POTS, MIKA.

Quon-Style Goulash

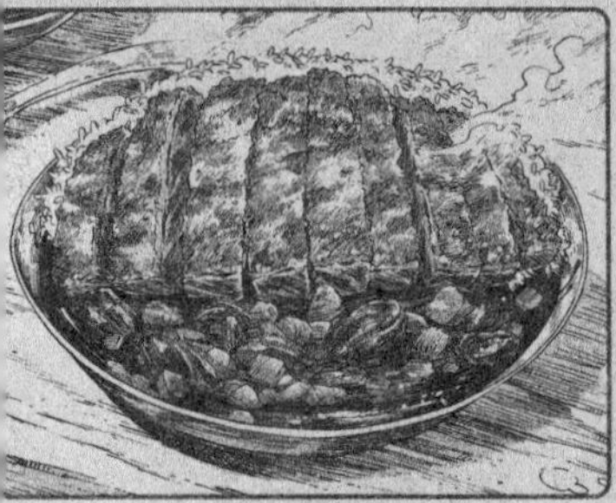

Ingredients (two servings)

- ✦ 200g dragon meat (at least two different cuts/varieties):
- ✦ 1 onion
- ✦ 50g dragon fat
- ✦ 1-2 tsp salt
- ✦ 1 clove garlic
- ✦ ½ tbsp caraway seed (or cumin)
- ✦ 2-3 tbsp paprika
- ✦ 1 bunch carrots
- ✦ 1 tomato
- ✦ 1 red bell pepper
- ✦ 1 stick worth of celery leaves
- ✦ 300g potatoes
- ✦ Bacon (if desired): 50 g

01
Cut meat into bite-sized pieces. Mince onion and garlic. Chop carrot, tomato, bell pepper, and potato into 1-cm pieces. Tie the celery leaves with a string.

02
Melt dragon fat in a cauldron or pot and cook onions until golden brown (along with bacon if using). Add caraway and garlic and lightly sauté.

03
Add dragon meat and season with 1-2 tsp salt. Sprinkle generously with paprika to coat, then close the lid.

04
Once the meat has cooked partway, add all vegetables excluding the potato and carrot, and add enough water to cover. Simmer for two hours (periodically add more water if too much evaporates).

05
Lastly, add potato and carrot to the pot and simmer until tender. Remove the celery leaves and it's done.

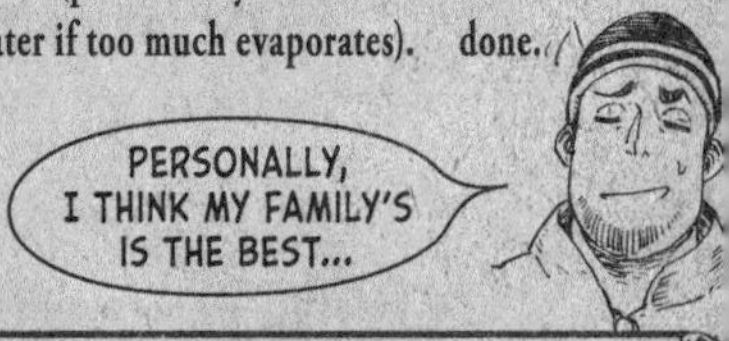
PERSONALLY, I THINK MY FAMILY'S IS THE BEST...

Dragon Cutlet

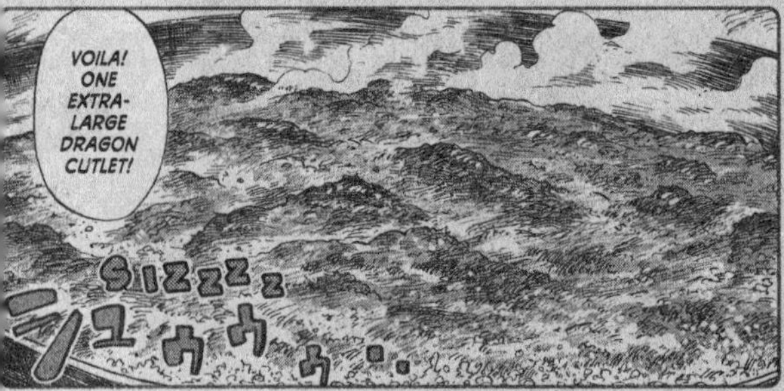
VOILA! ONE EXTRA-LARGE DRAGON CUTLET!
SIZZZZ

Ingredients (one serving)

- ✦ 200g red dragon meat
- ✦ 1 egg
- ✦ 1 cup bread crumbs
- ✦ 4 Tbsp finely grated cheese
- ✦ Dragon fat (or dragon cooking oil) as needed
- ✦ 15g butter
- ✦ Salt to taste
- ✦ Pepper to taste
- ✦ Flour as needed

01
Pound the meat while pulling towards yourself to thin and stretch it to desired size and thickness.

02
Season the meat with salt and pepper.

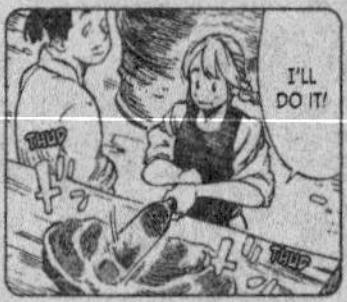
I'LL DO IT!
THUD
THUD

03
Add grated cheese to finely crushed bread crumbs and mix well. Dust dragon meat with flour, dip in beaten egg, then cover in bread crumb mixture to form breading. Lightly press down the exterior.

04
Melt enough dragon fat and butter in a frypan to fill about 5 mm up the side and heat. Fry the meat until golden brown on one side.

05
Flip and cook the other side, drain, and serve.

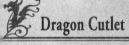

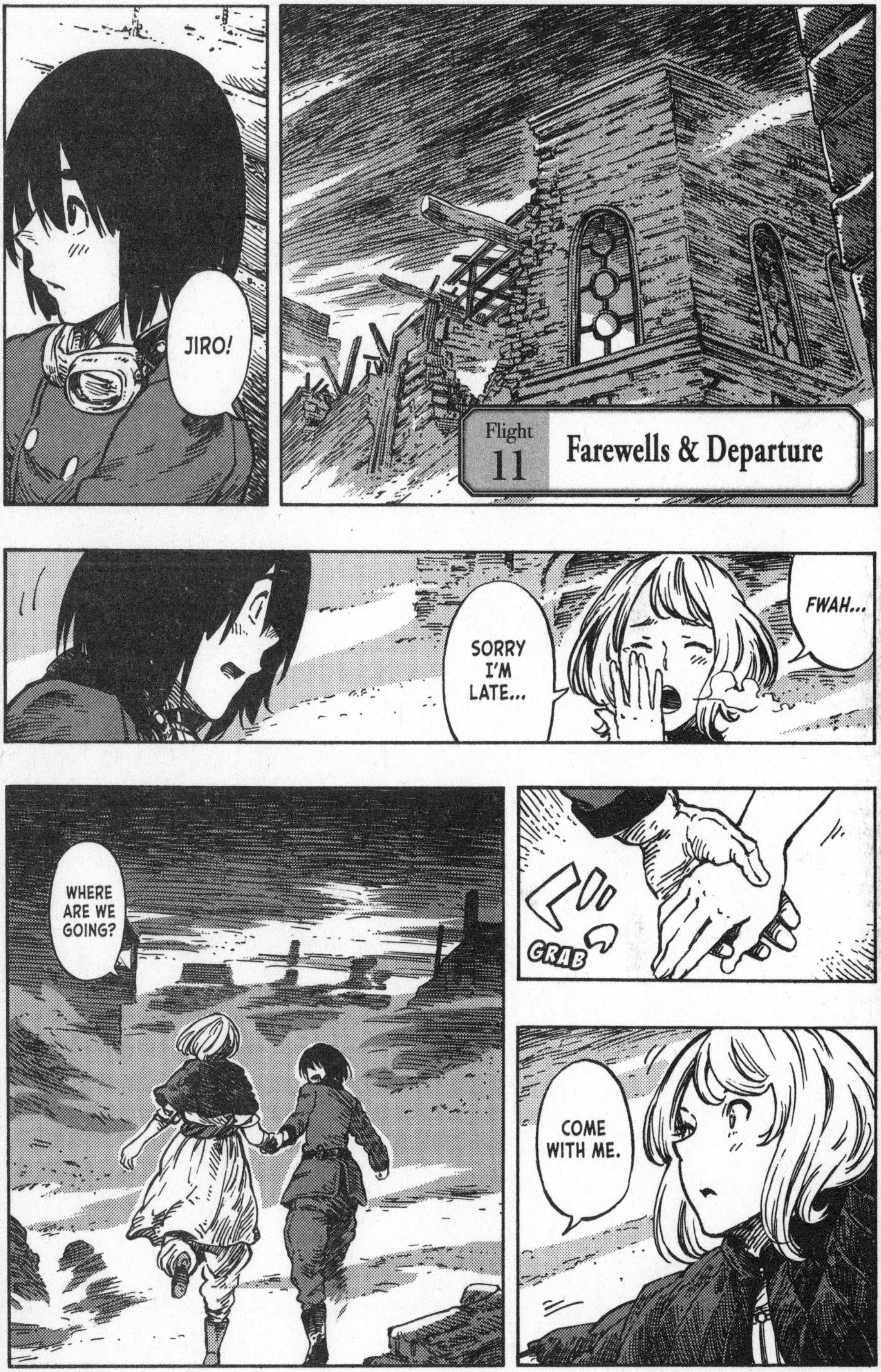
Flight 11
Farewells & Departure
JIRO!
FWAH...
SORRY I'M LATE...
GRAB
COME WITH ME.
WHERE ARE WE GOING?

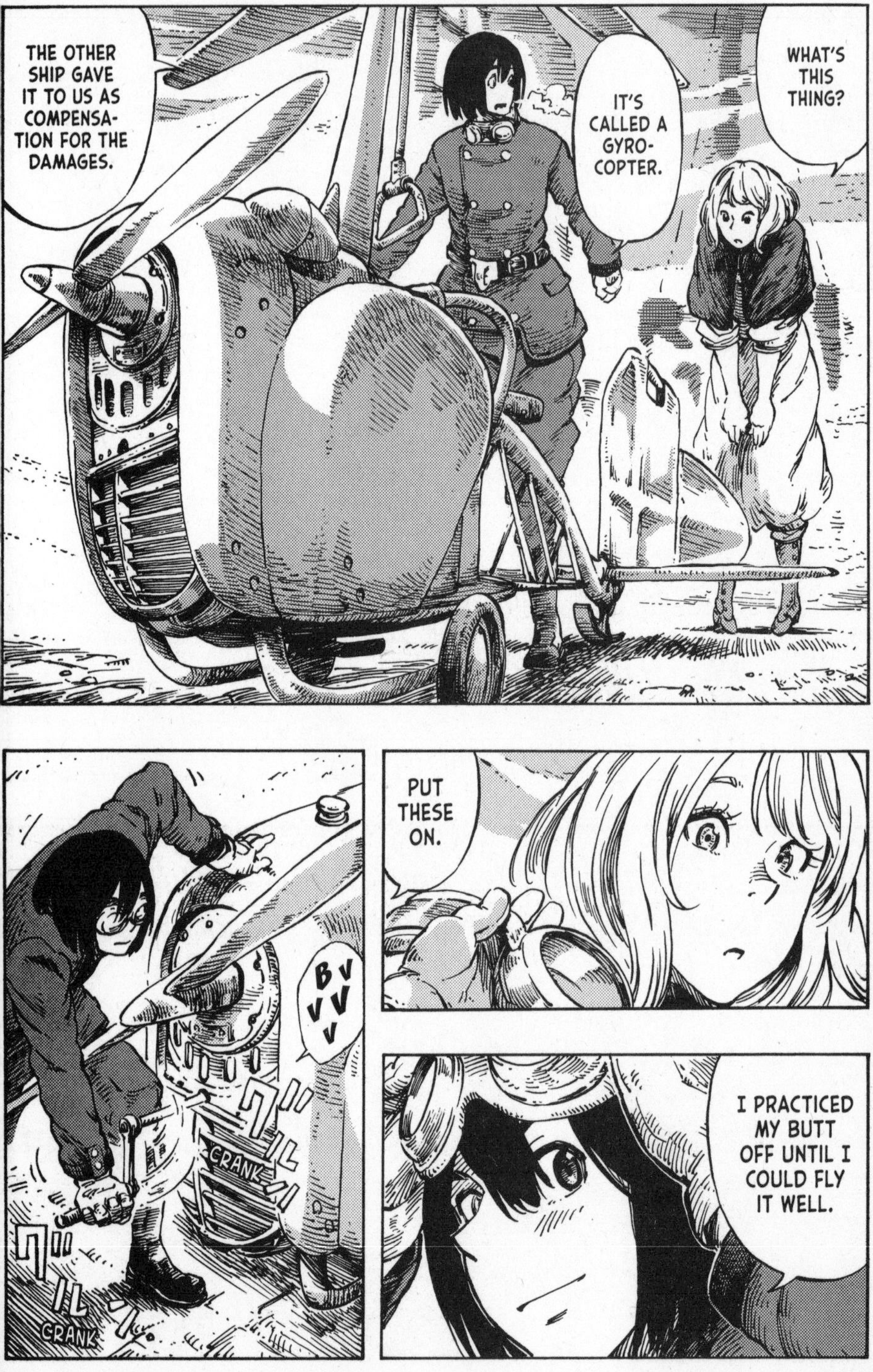
WHAT'S THIS THING?
IT'S CALLED A GYRO-COPTER.
THE OTHER SHIP GAVE IT TO US AS COMPENSA-TION FOR THE DAMAGES.
PUT THESE ON.
I PRACTICED MY BUTT OFF UNTIL I COULD FLY IT WELL.
BVVVV
CRANK
CRANK

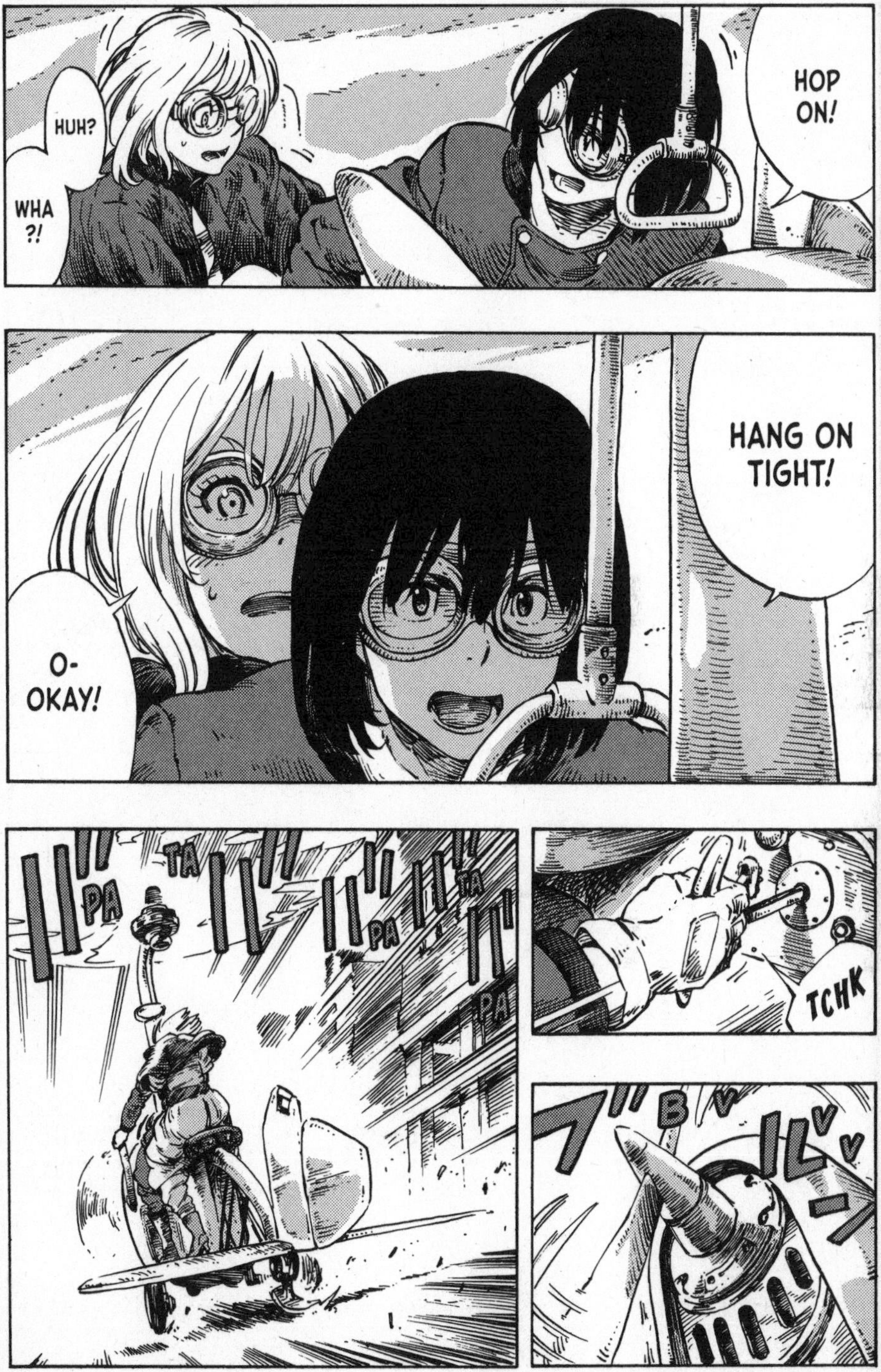
HOP ON!
HUH?
WHA ?!
HANG ON TIGHT!
O-OKAY!
TCHK
B v v v v
PA
TA
PA
TA
PA

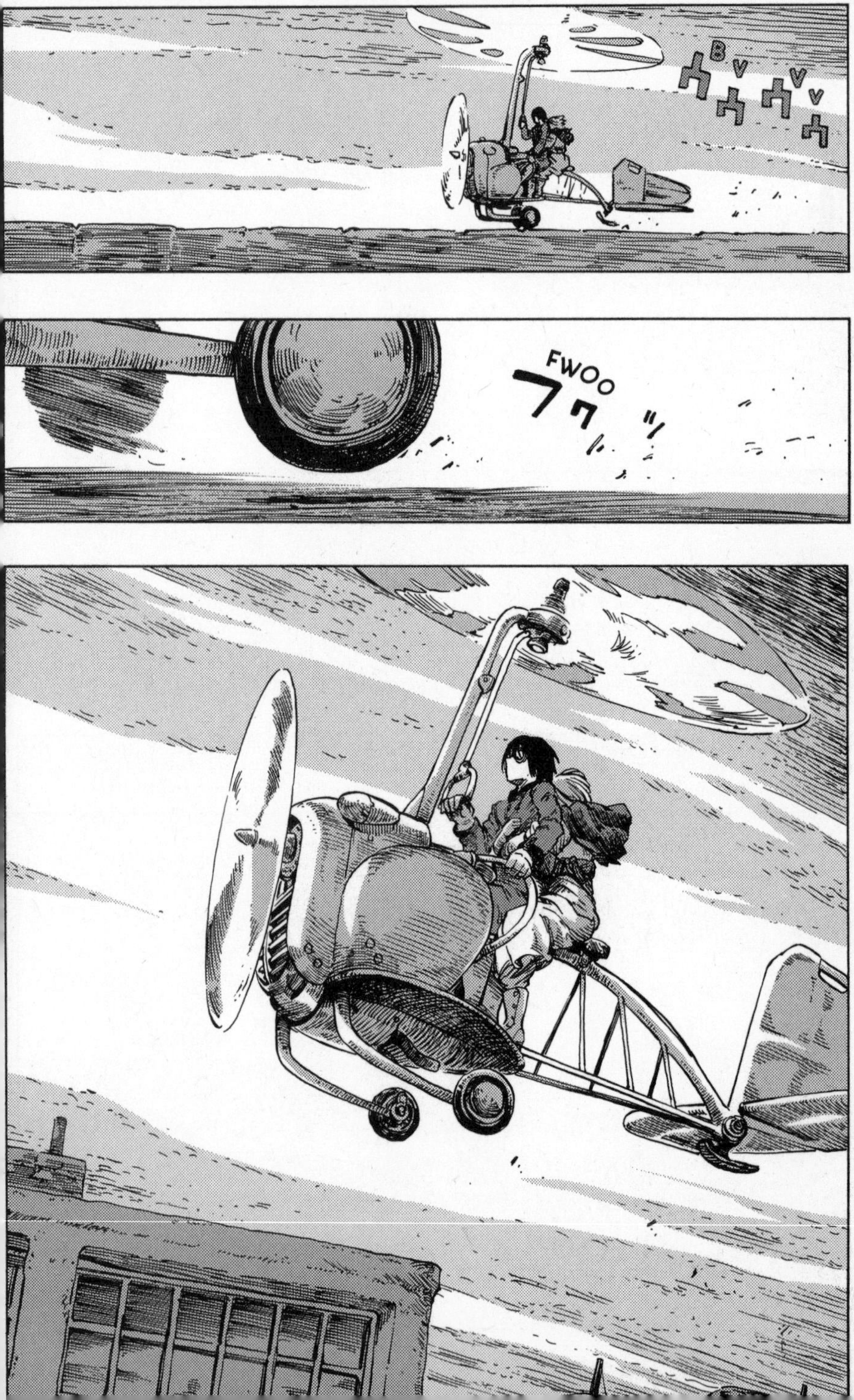
BVVVV
FWOO

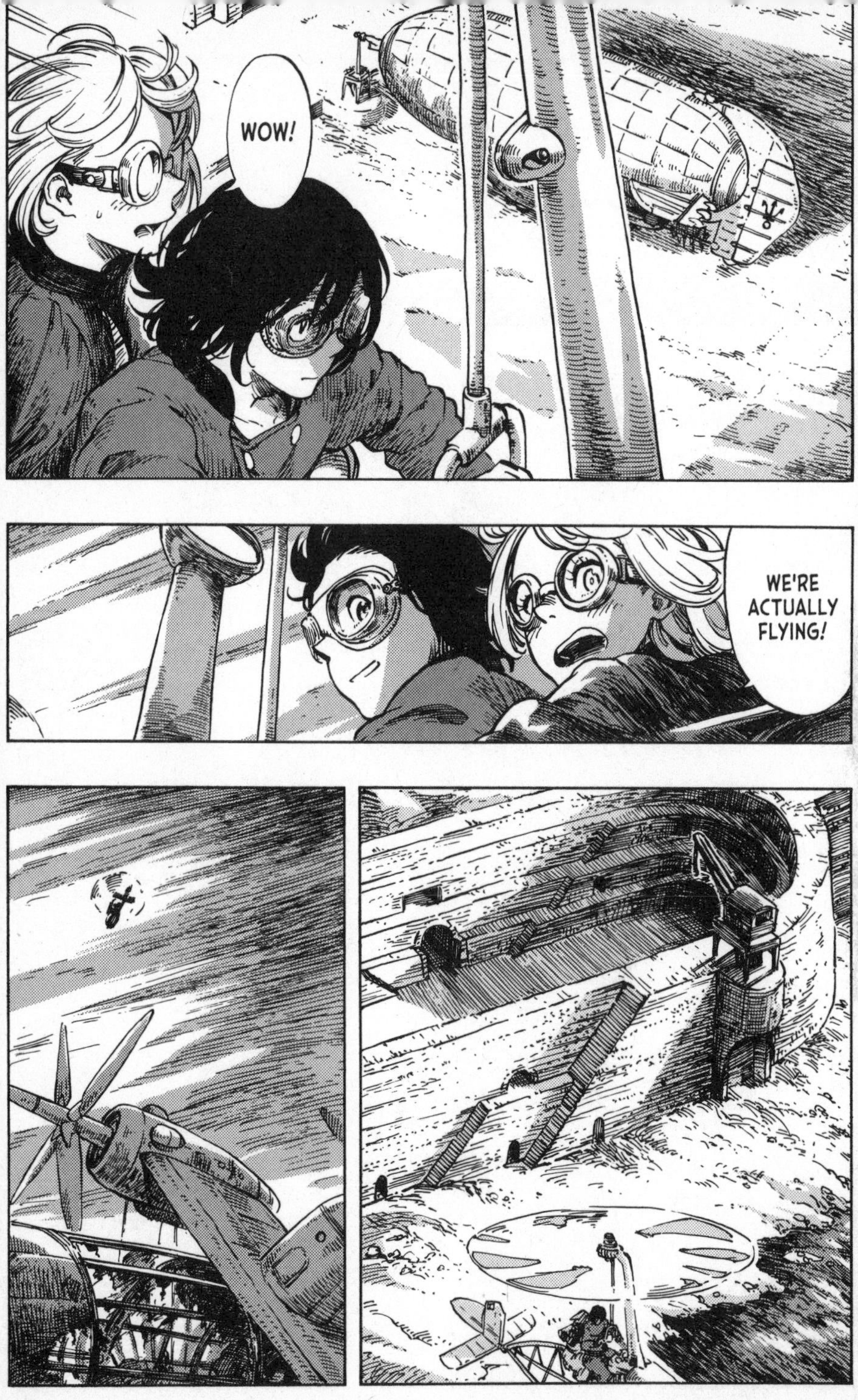
WOW!
WE'RE ACTUALLY FLYING!

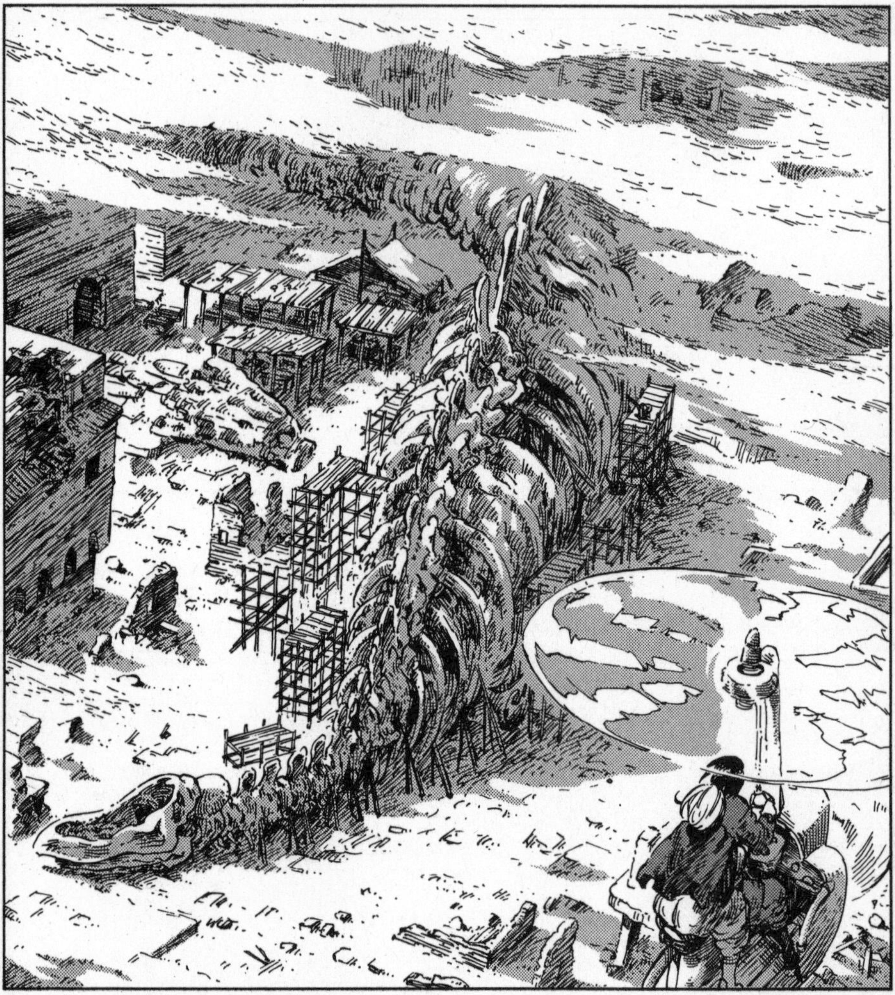

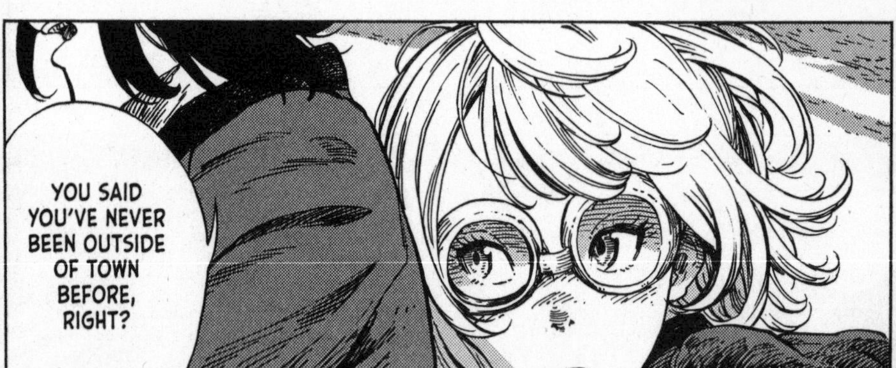
YOU SAID YOU'VE NEVER BEEN OUTSIDE OF TOWN BEFORE, RIGHT?

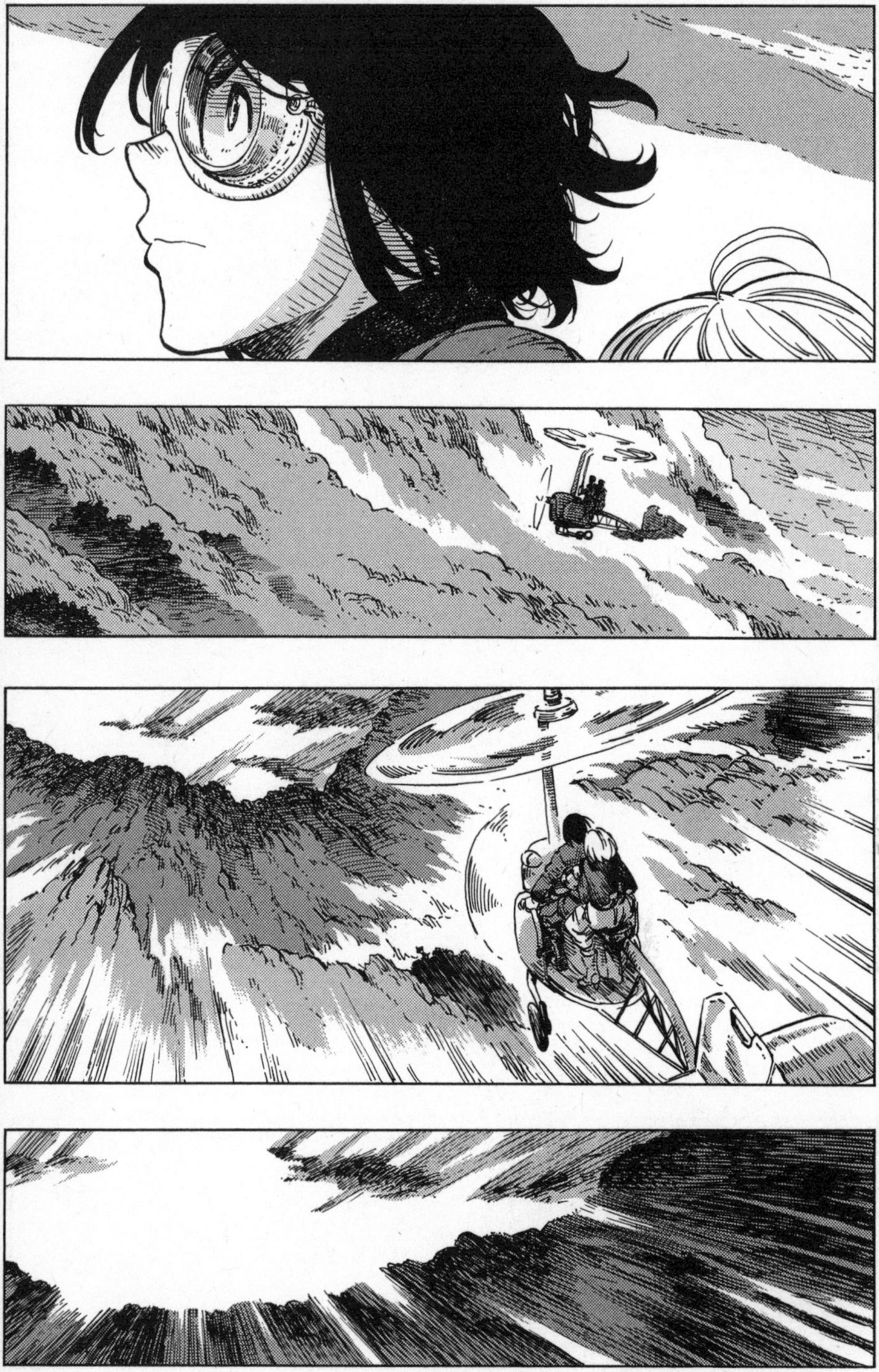

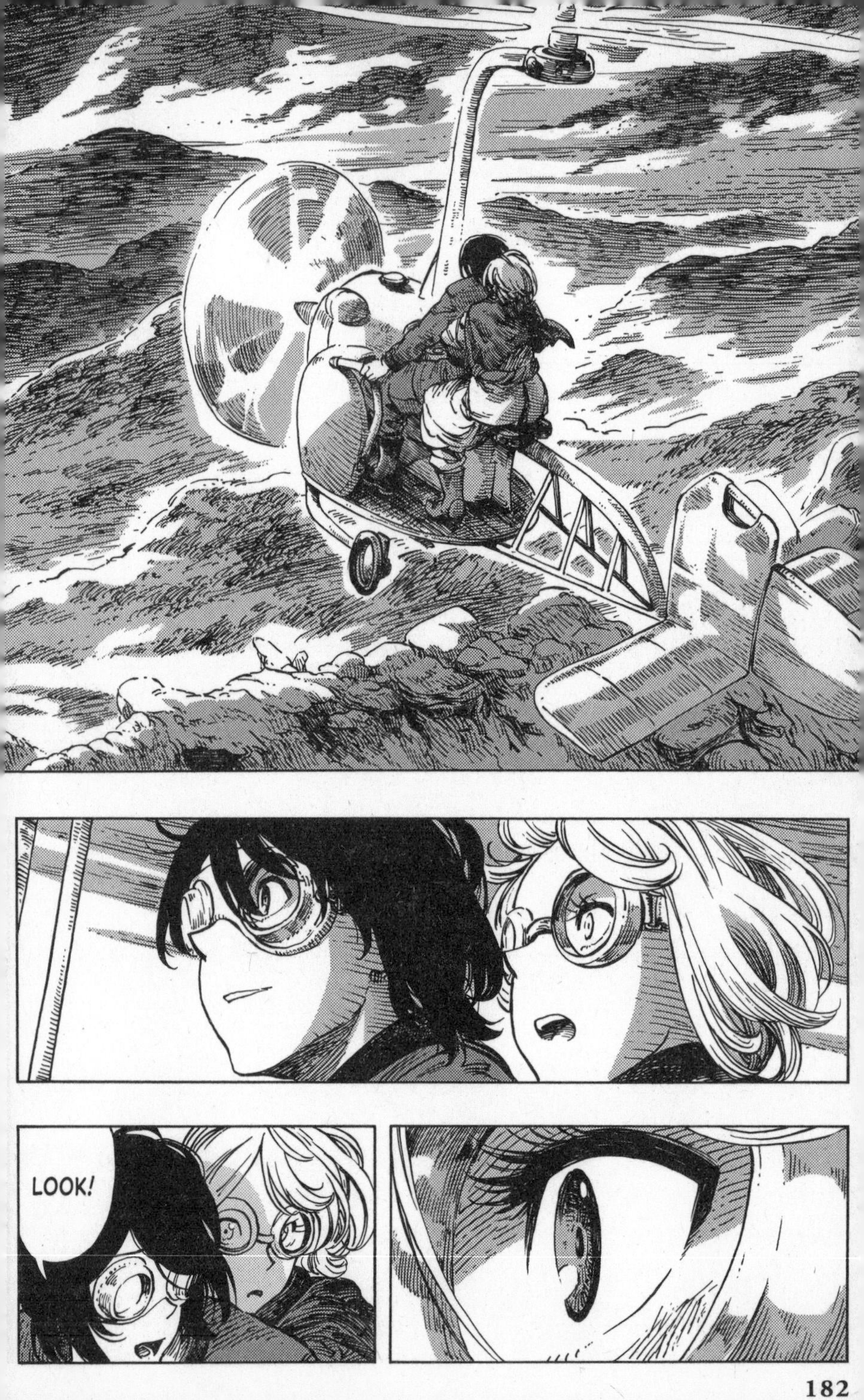
LOOK!

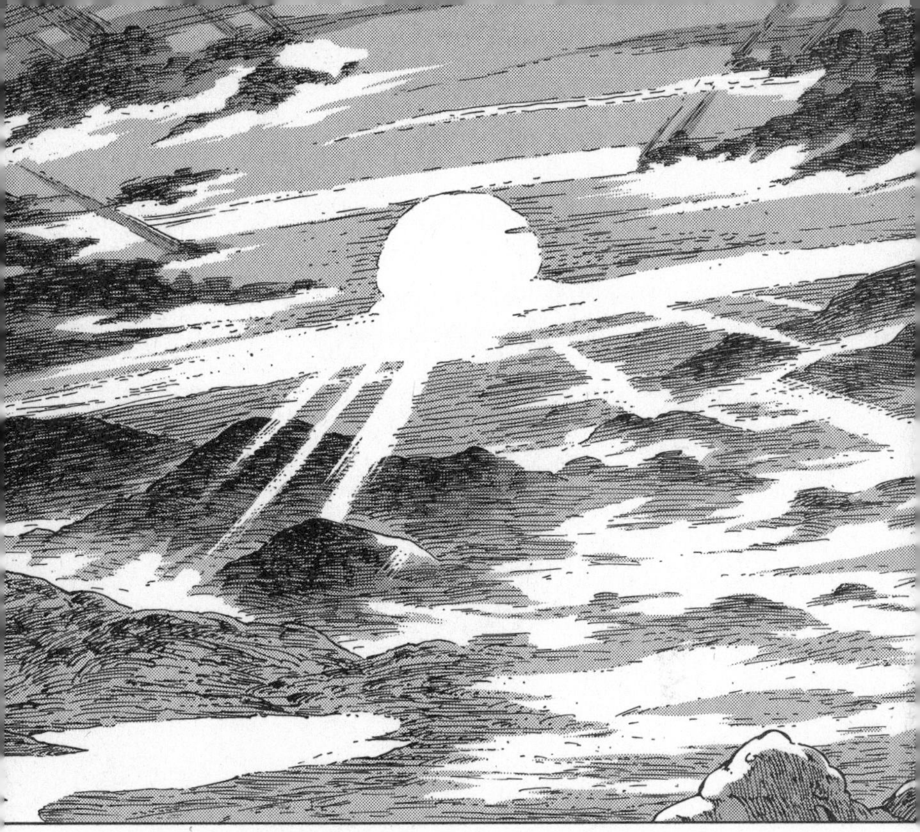

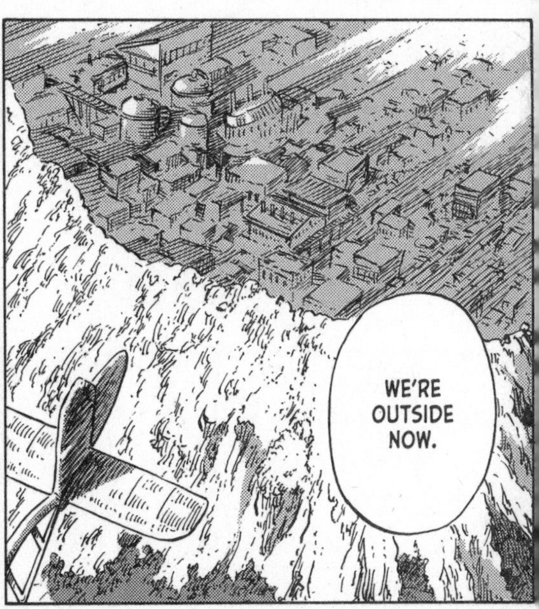
WE'RE OUTSIDE NOW.

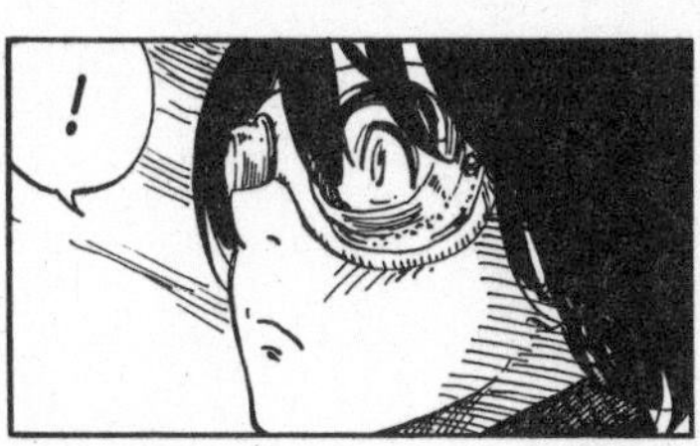
!

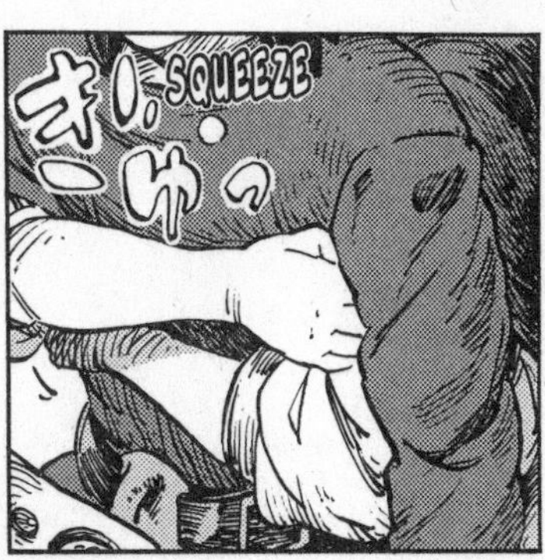
きゅっ
SQUEEZE

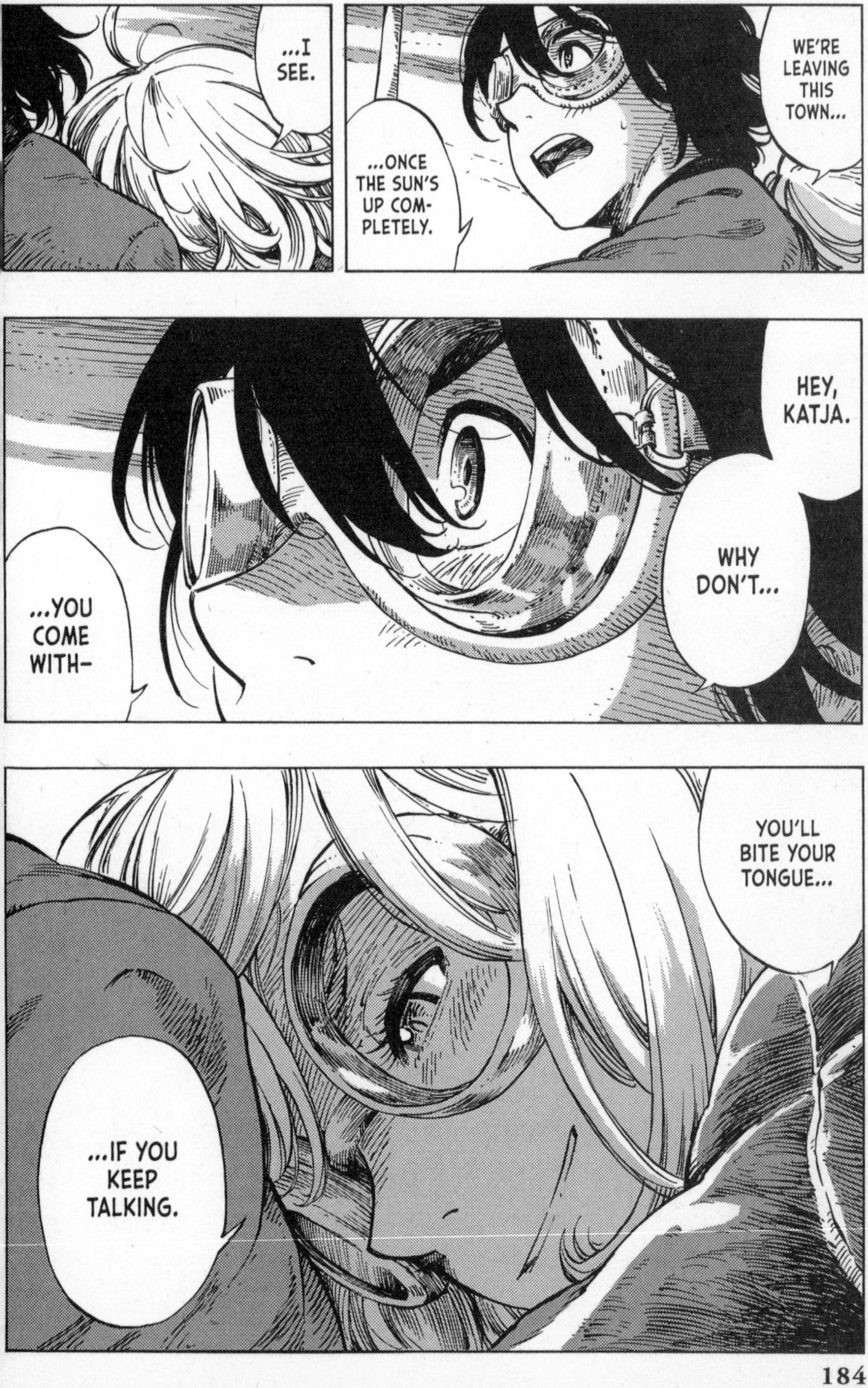
WE'RE LEAVING THIS TOWN...
...ONCE THE SUN'S UP COM-PLETELY.
...I SEE.
HEY, KATJA.
WHY DON'T...
...YOU COME WITH-
YOU'LL BITE YOUR TONGUE...
...IF YOU KEEP TALKING.

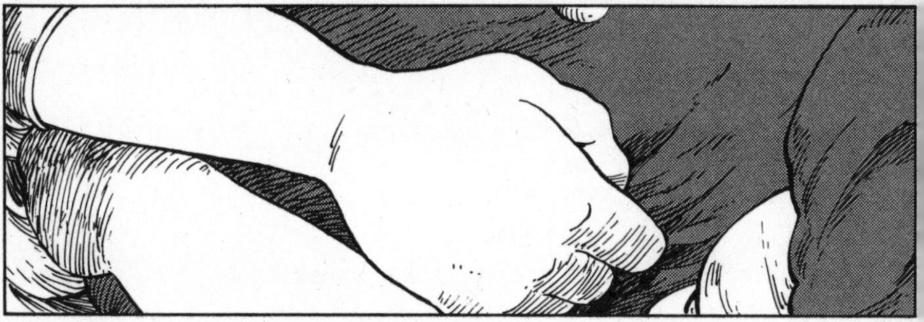

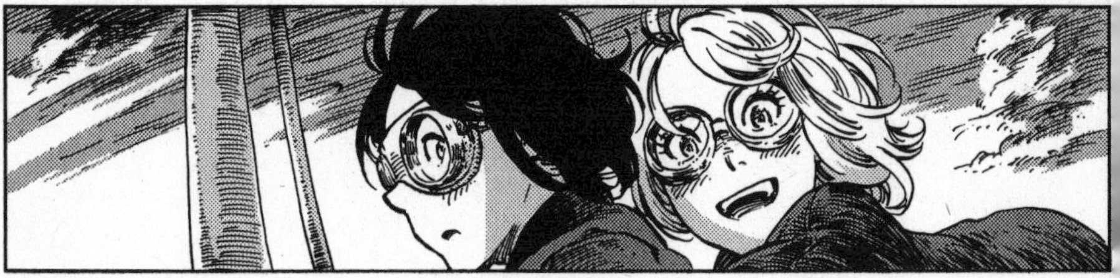

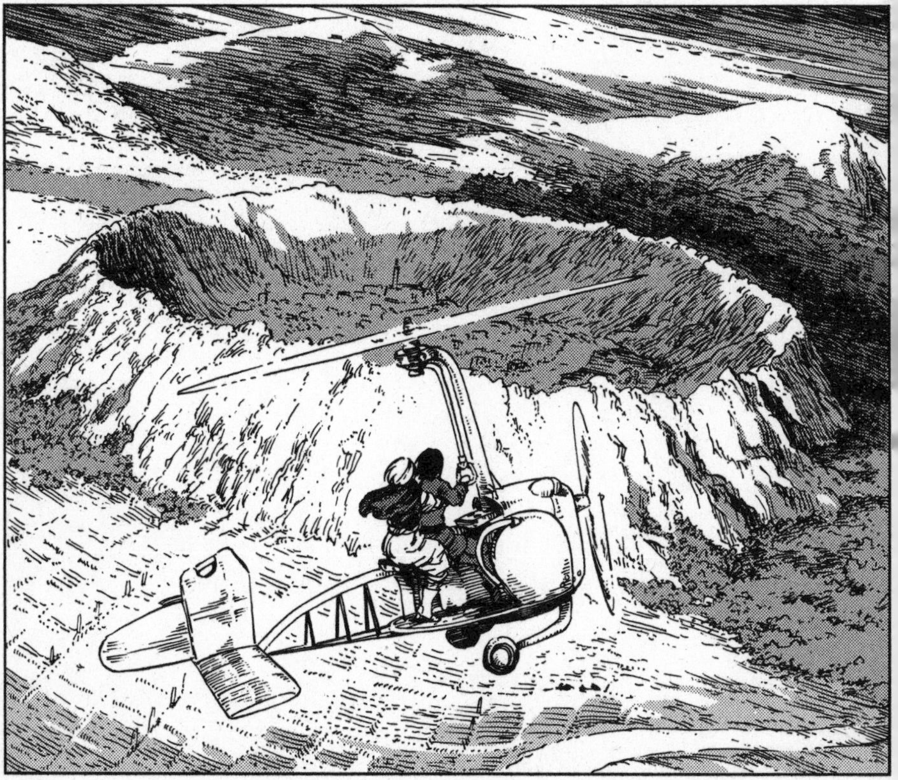

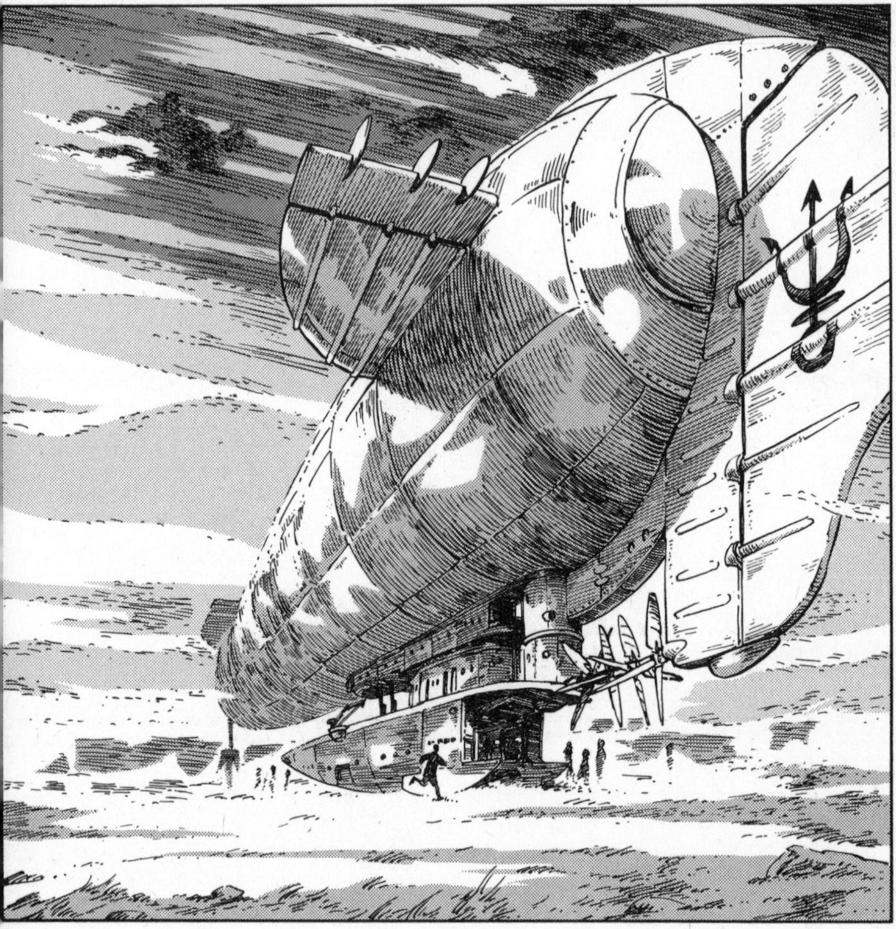

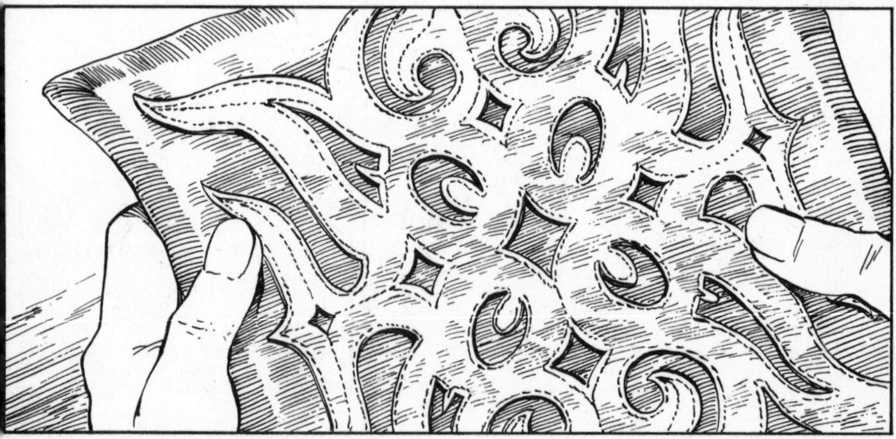

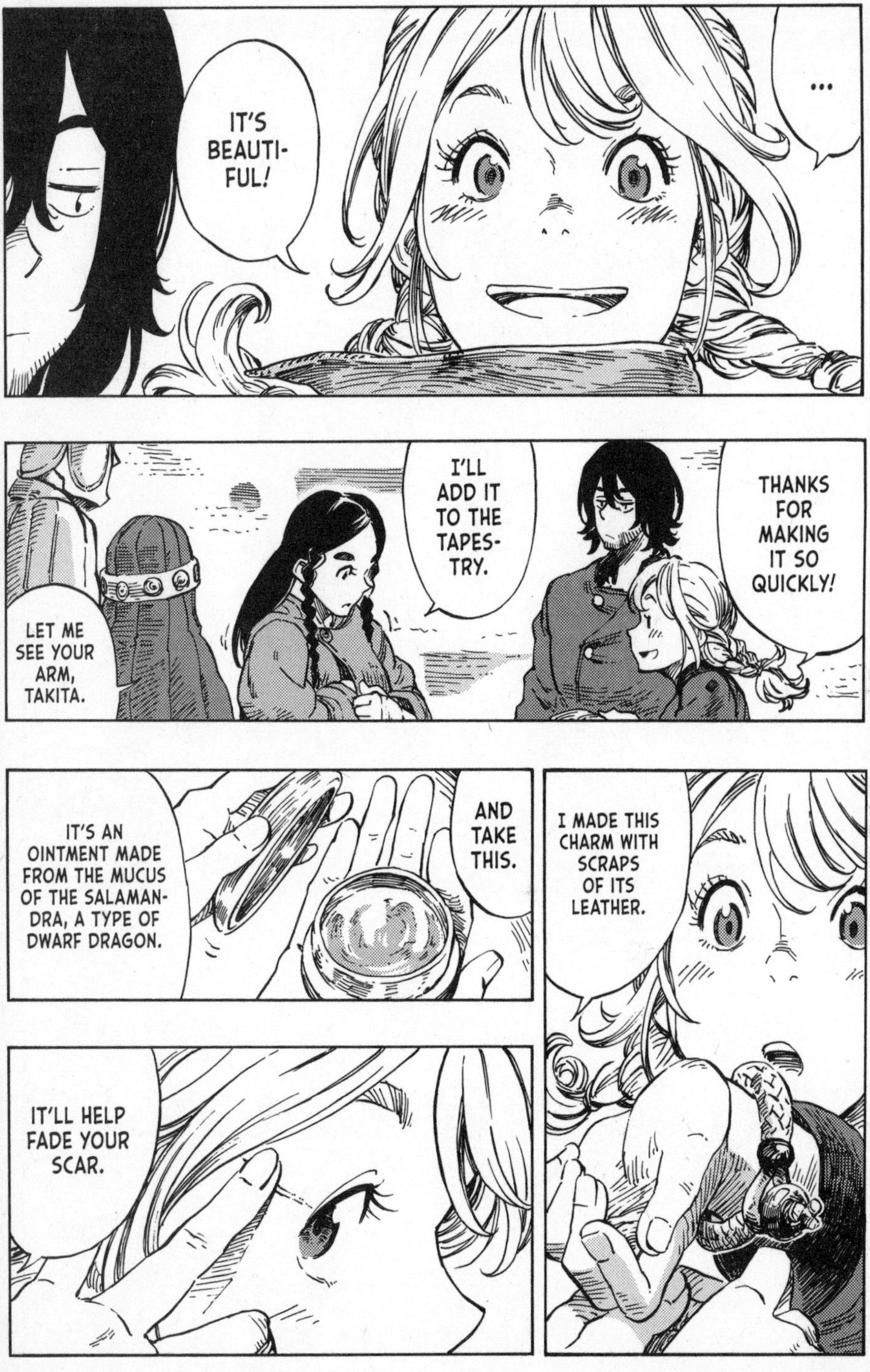
...
IT'S BEAUTIFUL!
THANKS FOR MAKING IT SO QUICKLY!
I'LL ADD IT TO THE TAPESTRY.
LET ME SEE YOUR ARM, TAKITA.
I MADE THIS CHARM WITH SCRAPS OF ITS LEATHER.
AND TAKE THIS.
IT'S AN OINTMENT MADE FROM THE MUCUS OF THE SALAMANDRA, A TYPE OF DWARF DRAGON.
IT'LL HELP FADE YOUR SCAR.

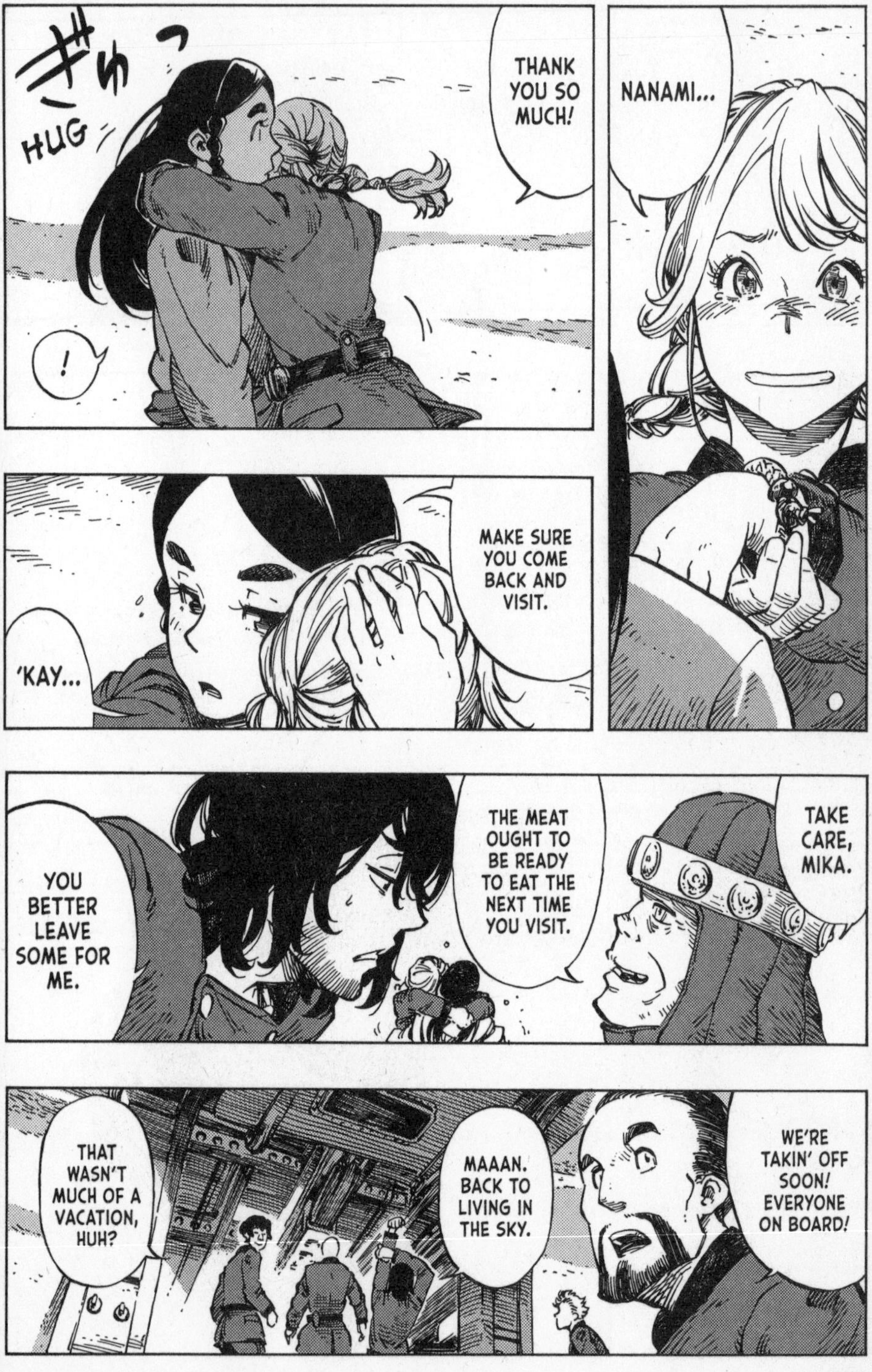
NANAMI...
THANK YOU SO MUCH!
ぎゅっ
HUG
!
MAKE SURE YOU COME BACK AND VISIT.
'KAY...
TAKE CARE, MIKA.
THE MEAT OUGHT TO BE READY TO EAT THE NEXT TIME YOU VISIT.
YOU BETTER LEAVE SOME FOR ME.
WE'RE TAKIN' OFF SOON! EVERYONE ON BOARD!
MAAAN. BACK TO LIVING IN THE SKY.
THAT WASN'T MUCH OF A VACATION, HUH?

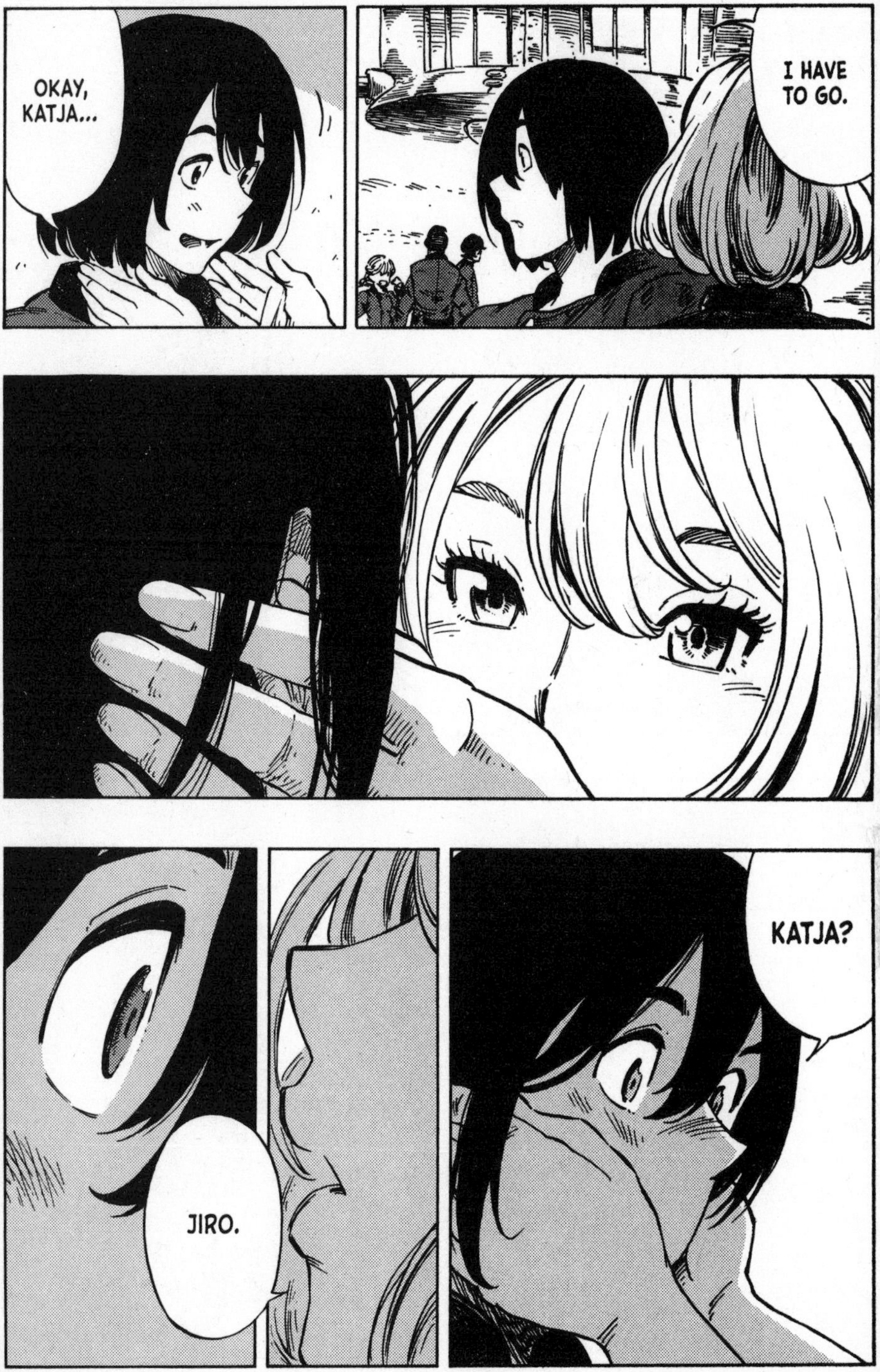
I HAVE TO GO.
OKAY, KATJA...
KATJA?
JIRO.

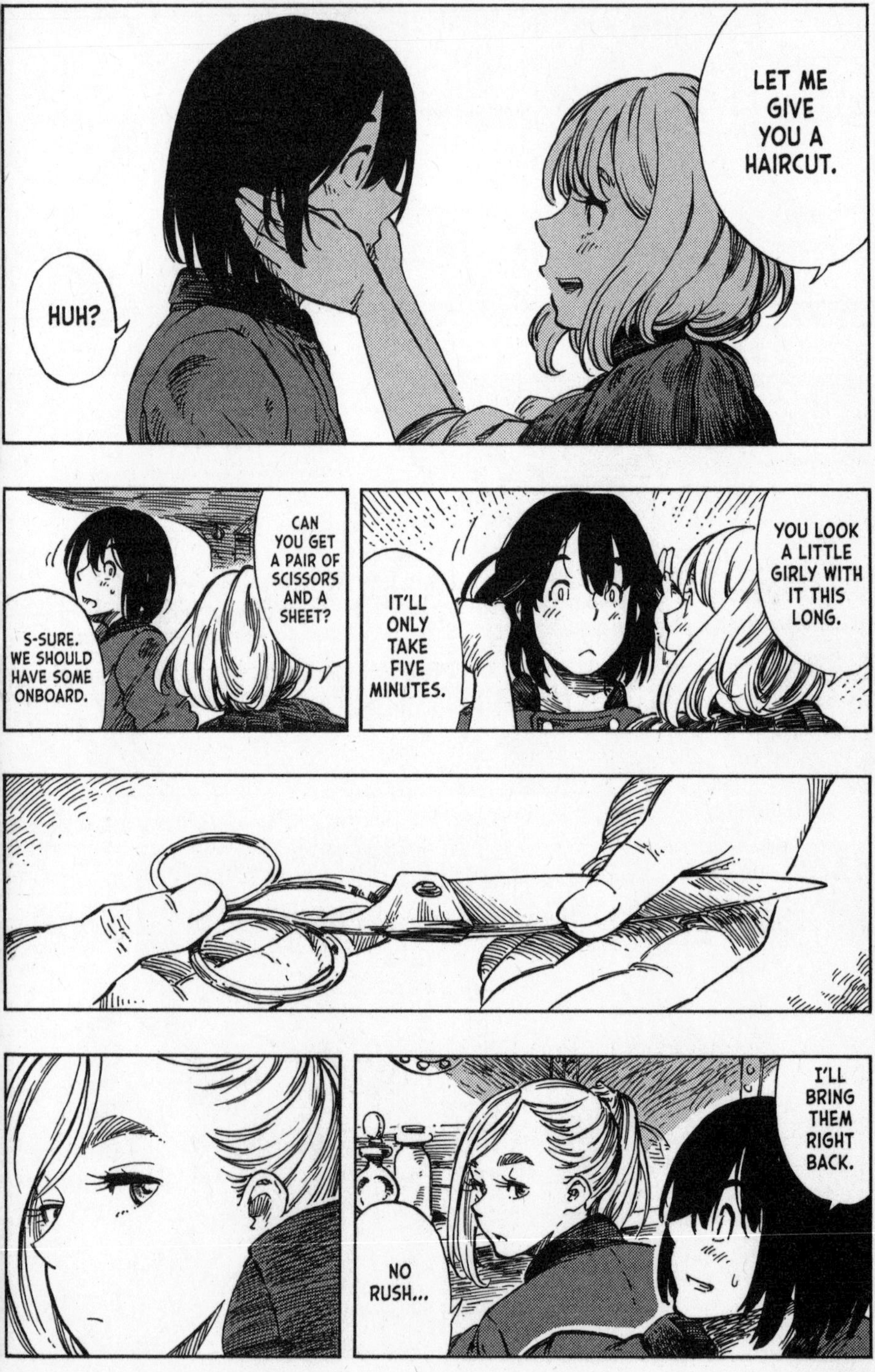
LET ME GIVE YOU A HAIRCUT.
HUH?
YOU LOOK A LITTLE GIRLY WITH IT THIS LONG.
IT'LL ONLY TAKE FIVE MINUTES.
CAN YOU GET A PAIR OF SCISSORS AND A SHEET?
S-SURE. WE SHOULD HAVE SOME ONBOARD.
I'LL BRING THEM RIGHT BACK.
NO RUSH...

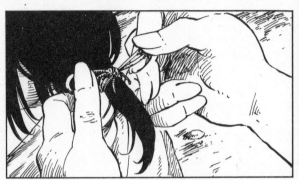

I'M REALLY GLAD I MET YOU.

TAKE CARE, OKAY?

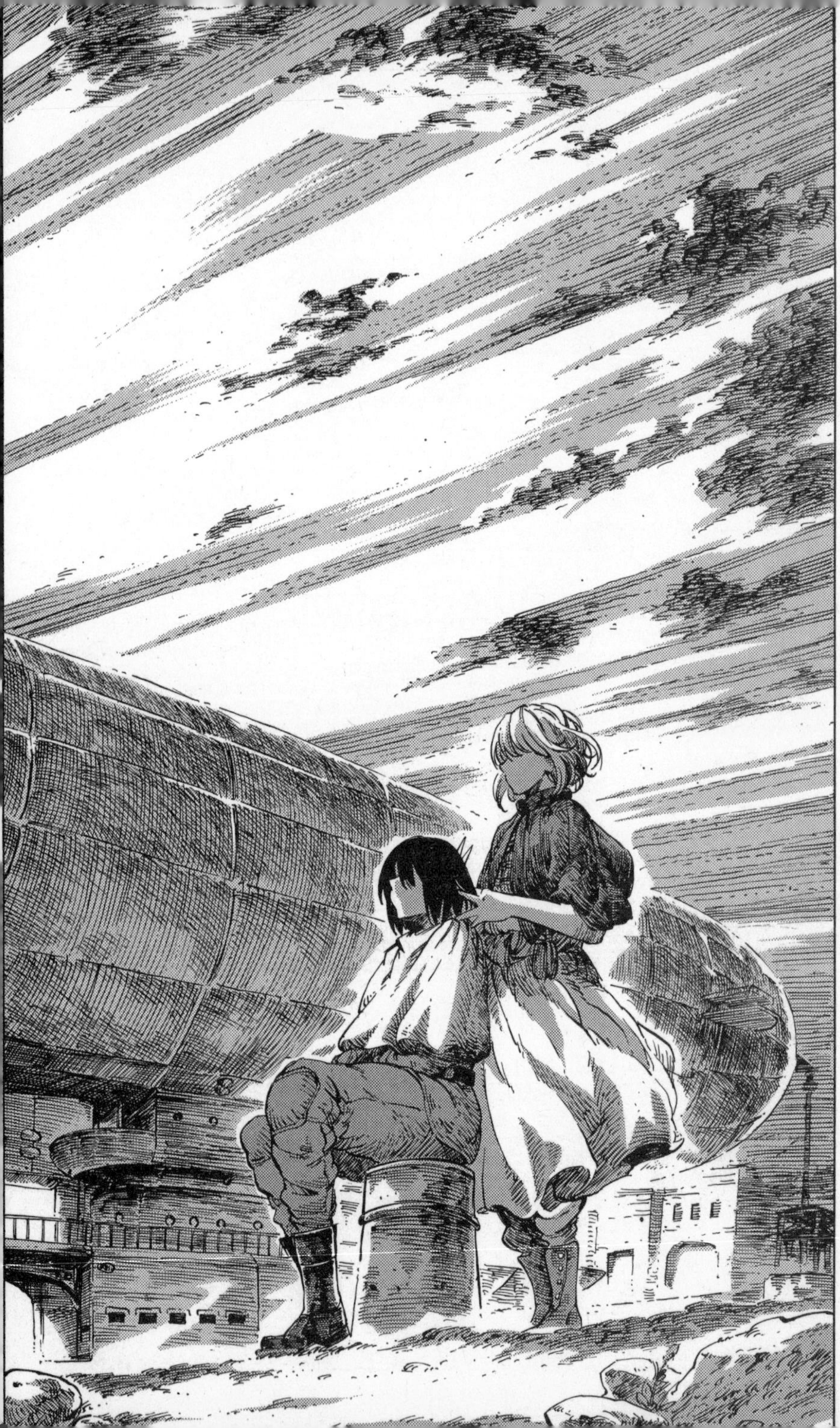

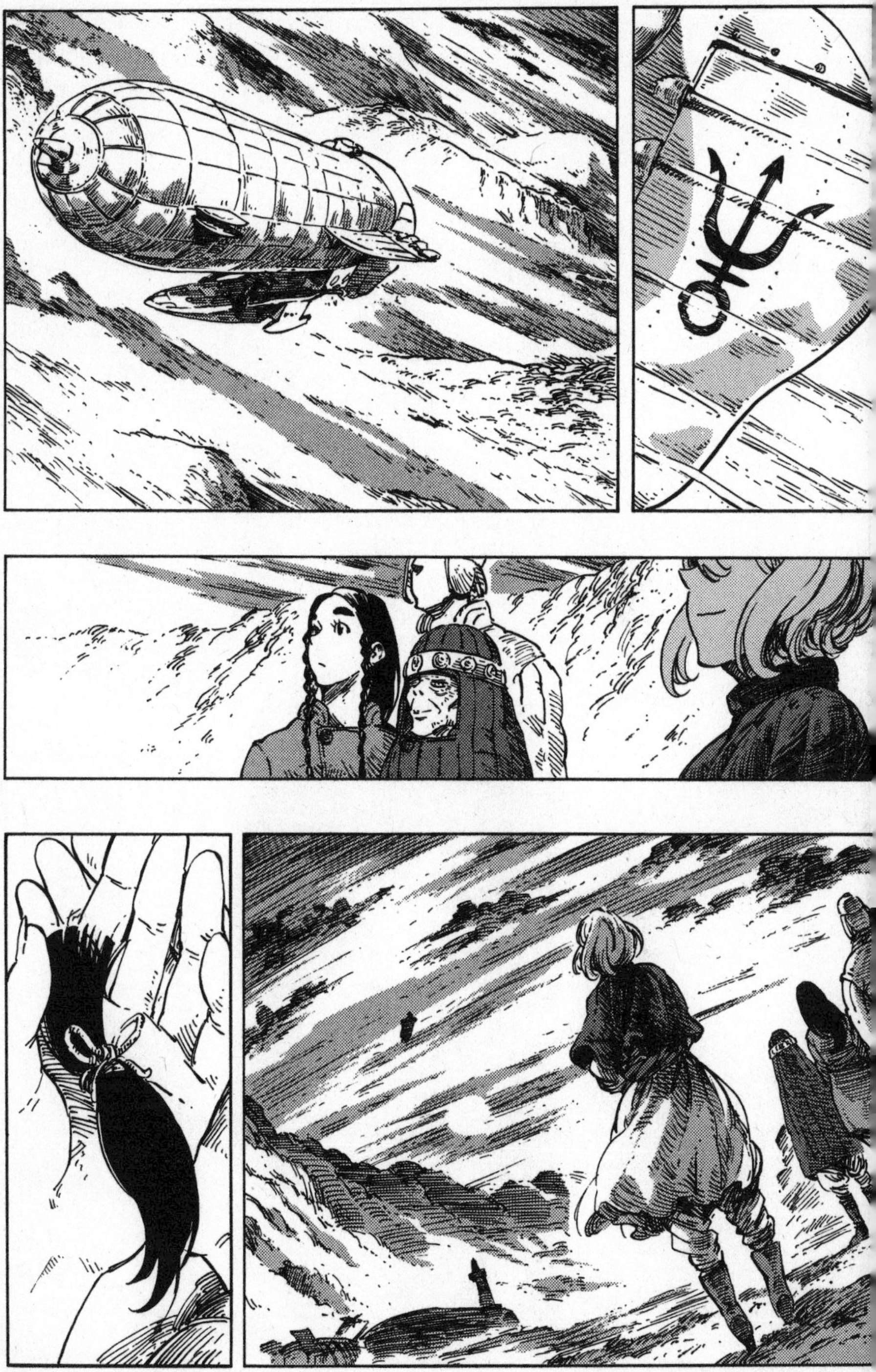

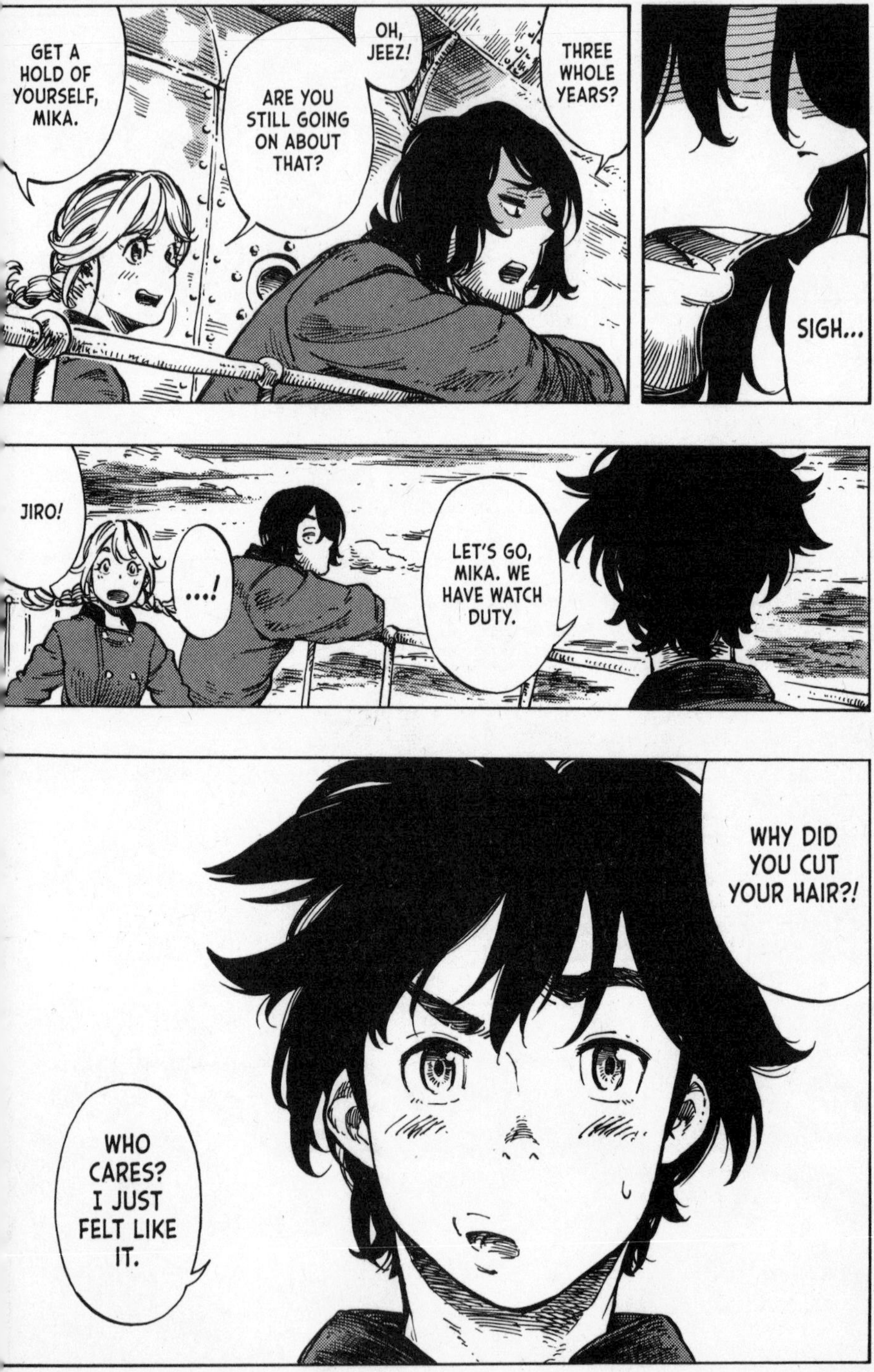
SIGH...
THREE WHOLE YEARS?
OH, JEEZ!
ARE YOU STILL GOING ON ABOUT THAT?
GET A HOLD OF YOURSELF, MIKA.
LET'S GO, MIKA. WE HAVE WATCH DUTY.
...!
JIRO!
WHY DID YOU CUT YOUR HAIR?!
WHO CARES? I JUST FELT LIKE IT.

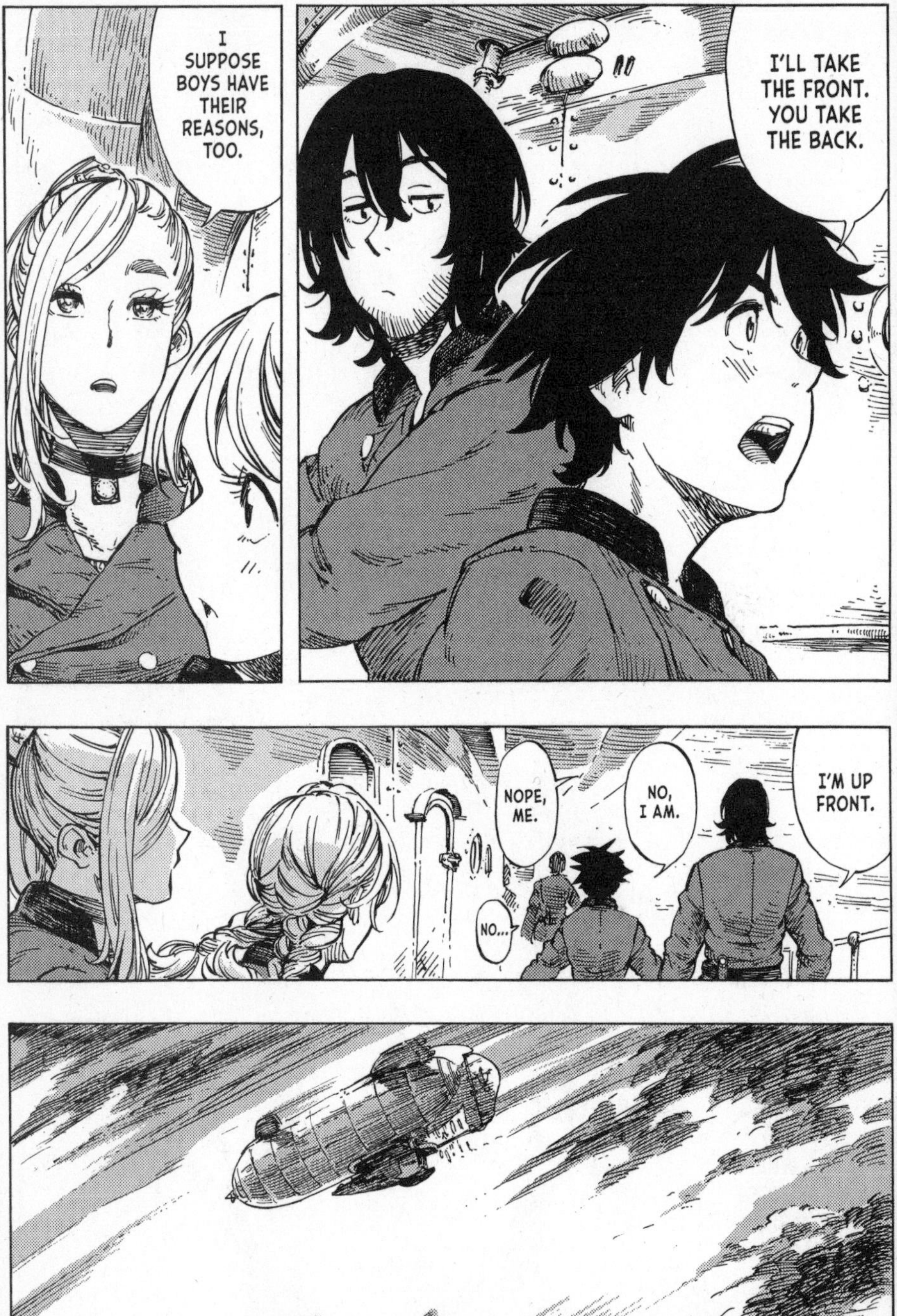
I'LL TAKE THE FRONT. YOU TAKE THE BACK.
I SUPPOSE BOYS HAVE THEIR REASONS, TOO.
I'M UP FRONT.
NO, I AM.
NOPE, ME.
NO...

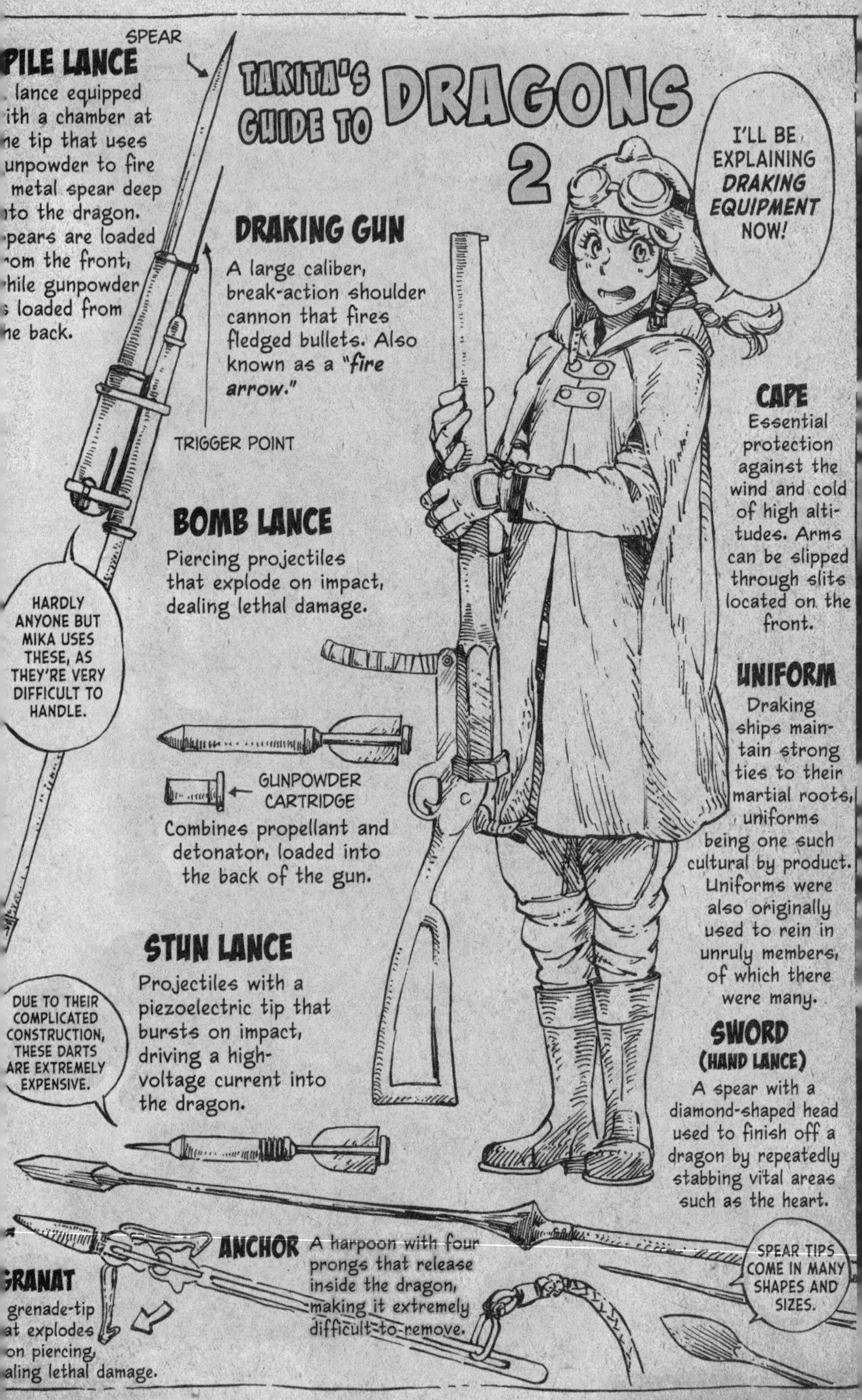
TAKITA'S GUIDE TO DRAGONS 2
I'LL BE EXPLAINING DRAKING EQUIPMENT NOW!
SPEAR
PILE LANCE
lance equipped ith a chamber at ne tip that uses unpowder to fire metal spear deep nto the dragon. pears are loaded rom the front, hile gunpowder loaded from ne back.
DRAKING GUN
A large caliber, break-action shoulder cannon that fires fledged bullets. Also known as a "fire arrow."
TRIGGER POINT
BOMB LANCE
Piercing projectiles that explode on impact, dealing lethal damage.
HARDLY ANYONE BUT MIKA USES THESE, AS THEY'RE VERY DIFFICULT TO HANDLE.
GUNPOWDER CARTRIDGE
Combines propellant and detonator, loaded into the back of the gun.
STUN LANCE
Projectiles with a piezoelectric tip that bursts on impact, driving a high-voltage current into the dragon.
DUE TO THEIR COMPLICATED CONSTRUCTION, THESE DARTS ARE EXTREMELY EXPENSIVE.
CAPE
Essential protection against the wind and cold of high altitudes. Arms can be slipped through slits located on the front.
UNIFORM
Draking ships maintain strong ties to their martial roots, uniforms being one such cultural by product. Uniforms were also originally used to rein in unruly members, of which there were many.
SWORD (HAND LANCE)
A spear with a diamond-shaped head used to finish off a dragon by repeatedly stabbing vital areas such as the heart.
ANCHOR
A harpoon with four prongs that release inside the dragon, making it extremely difficult to remove.
GRANAT
grenade-tip at explodes on piercing, aling lethal damage.
SPEAR TIPS COME IN MANY SHAPES AND SIZES.

DRIFTING DRAGONS

A Kodansha Comics Trade Paperback Original
Drifting Dragons copyright © 2017 Taku Kuwabara
English translation copyright © 2019 Taku Kuwabara

Published in the United States by Kodansha Comics, an imprint of Kodansha USA Publishing, LLC, New York.

Publication rights for this English edition arranged through Kodansha Ltd., Tokyo.

First published in Japan in 2017 by Kodansha Ltd., Tokyo as *Kuutei Doragonzu*, volume 2.

ISBN 978-1-63236-944-4

Printed in the United States of America.

www.kodanshacomics.com

9 8 7 6 5 4 3 2 1
Translation: Adam Hirsch
Lettering: Thea Willis
Editing: Paul Starr
Kodansha Comics edition cover design by Phil Balsman

Publisher: Kiichiro Sugawara
Managing editor: Maya Rosewood
Vice president of marketing & publicity: Naho Yamada

Director of publishing services: Ben Applegate
Associate director of operations: Stephen Pakula
Publishing services managing editor: Noelle Webster
Assistant production manager: Emi Lotto